CW00869275

Small Town Dreams

J F Cumming

Small Town Dreams is a novel based around true life events. The actions, thoughts, emotions and dialogue attributed to all characters are, however, based purely on the imagination of the author and are used fictitiously... (this especially applies to Abby and Laura swearing at Filbert Street).

First published 2016

Copyright © 2016 J F Cumming

The moral right of the author has been asserted.

All rights reserved.

Without limiting the rights under copyright reserved above, no part of this publication may be reproduced, stored in or introduced into a retrieval system, or transmitted, in any form or by any means (electronic, mechanical, photocopying, recording or otherwise), without the prior written permission of the copyright owner of this book.

ISBN-10: 1532718756
ISBN-13: 978-1532718755

For Alice and Emmeline

**Dedicated to those who cling to childhood dreams
or support their local football team**

ACKNOWLEDGMENTS

Thanks to all those that inspired this book; friends, family and the many generations who have served or supported the Wanderers; Ruth for support and infinite patience; The Charlatans and The Stone Roses for the imaginary soundtrack and keeping me company as I wrote; Bob, Pat, Tony, Nigel and Jimbo for kindly sharing stories; Charlie for York away; Brenda, Paula and Cameron for adding intelligence; Gareth for cover support; Paul for chairboys.co.uk; Cathy for sharing the ride.

1 - York

With face pressed against the ice cold glass my attention flitted between the snow-covered English landscape disappearing behind me and my breath steaming the window. The coach trundled endlessly up the motorway, hitting every bump for 200 miles between High Wycombe and York. It was January 4th 1986. I was 13 and feeling sick.

Why did I do this every time?

The coach had left my hometown at 8am that morning and was expected to take five hours to reach York. After a hearty breakfast, my mum had waved me off with sandwiches for the journey. With hindsight, I should have delayed lunch past the journey's first hour. The same could be said for the stash of sweets I'd secretly been building over the past fortnight, ever since being told I could go to the big match. But I hadn't, and here I was again, face pressed against the window trying to cool my skin, my self-prescribed cure for overeating and travel sickness.

"Don't be sick James, please don't be sick" became my silent mantra.

Over the next hour, as my blood-sugar levels returned to somewhere resembling normal, I eavesdropped on the conversations of fellow travellers on the supporters' coach. At the front, the older gents talked about teams of yesteryear, arguing the most trivial of details.

"It was definitely the Tuesday after we beat Slough... 'cos I was on backshift and missed the first half."

"No, no, no! It was a Wednesday... I had the afternoon off and went up downtown."

Towards the back of the coach the younger, more vociferous crowd sat, as if by magic finding can after can of beer hidden within their clothing and full of tall-stories from last night's adventures in town.

"So I told her I preferred her best mate" bragged Pisser. "She was fine about it..."

"She threw her drink in your face!" disputed Billy Connolly.

I sat silently, listening to their every word.

This younger crowd were still ten years my senior. I was fascinated by them, if not a little wary. They joked constantly, they knew some cracking swear words and, like me, they had the greed gene, although they had moved on from chocolate to alcohol.

I didn't know Pisser or Billy Connolly to speak to; I didn't even know their real names. I'd named one after a very slight resemblance to the Scottish comedian and the other for his tendency to urinate on the terraces, wherever he stood, seemingly oblivious to the fact that there were hundreds of people in very close proximity (and by 'very close' I mean within splash-back distance). One such occasion had been my first sighting of the motley pair some three years earlier when, luckily, I'd been stood to their side rather than downwind. Several people voiced their disgust to Pisser who just leaned back, smiled and closed his eyes, continuing the enjoyment of emptying his bladder. To a 10-year-old boy, this had been pretty impressive. I admired his confidence; he really didn't care what people thought. The icing on the cake was provided when Billy Connolly chimed in, telling the frowners, in no uncertain terms, to mind their own business before proceeding to zip Pissers pride-and-joy back into his jeans for him. Confusion took over for me at that stage, but still, Pisser and Billy had left a lasting impression. Now here they were, sitting behind me on the coach. All I could do was hope that neither needed the toilet before we reached our destination. I was pretty hopeful as we'd already stopped at a service station but, just in case, I kept checking the floor below my feet for any suspicious liquids flowing ominously forward from the back row.

Part of the fascination with Pisser's infamous 'Roobarb' gang was that I really wasn't like them. The mere thought of their antics made me blush with guilt. Only a couple of weeks before, my fear of doing anything remotely risqué had been given a timely reminder in the form of several sleepless nights.

I'd been at Loakes Park, the home of Wycombe Wanderers Football Club. While growing up, Loakes Park was my playground, my theatre, my absolute everything. I loved the place; its sweeping open terraces behind each goalmouth that seemed to go back forever - the Gasworks End and the Hospital End. One would always be packed and the other empty, depending on which goal Wycombe were attacking, with a mass migration around the pitch at half-time. These were the haunts of the more enthusiastic supporters (including those with an inclination for public urination and also the bizarre tendency to hurl sticks of rhubarb at player and spectator alike). Nestled between the terraces sat the Cowshed with its corrugated roof, stretching the length of the pitch, the position of choice for the older folk. The Cowshed was generally only heard when things weren't going well, generating more of a disgruntled rumbling as opposed to the encouragement heard from the terraces. The Cowshed would really come to life only when it rained, driving all but the drunk to seek shelter. Opposite was the glorious wooden grandstand, which sat proudly at the top of the ground. At this point, it might be worth explaining that Loakes Park's character was all the richer for being built on the side of a hill. There is nothing really 'high' about High Wycombe; its centre sits in a valley, but as the town grew it grew upwards, up onto the steep chalky Chiltern Hills. Loakes Park sat towards the foot of Tom Burt's Hill, but not quite at the foot; no, that would have been far too sensible. From the corner-flag between the Hospital End and the grandstand, diagonally down to the corner between the Cowshed and the Gasworks End, the pitch dropped 11-feet in height, so when sitting in the main stand you really were elevated to a grandstand view, looking down on all before you. This was a privilege that came at a premium, attracting a more refined clientele than the rest of the ground.

Like life in general, the ground had its pecking order; areas for the young, the old, the rich, the poor and the drunk. I was amongst the younger supporters and so my place was on the terrace. Not the back, the side or the middle; my place was down the front, the very front and the very centre, on 'The Wall'.

Directly behind both sets of goalposts were brick walls instead of the wooden advertising boards that surrounded the remainder of the pitch. These walls were the rite-of-passage for all young Wanderers fans. From the referee's first whistle we would spend the entire match jockeying for position, heaving ourselves up onto The Wall, dangling our legs behind the goal-nets until a blazer-empowered official would descend from the grandstand and march along the side-line and around the corner flag, steadily increasing in speed as he came downhill towards the goalmouth shouting breathlessly.

"Get off the wall... nobody's allowed to sit on the wall. You'll break your legs doing that... I'm warning yer... this is yer final warning."

By the time the 'Protector of The Wall' reached us, we would always be back behind it, angelically engrossed in the game and always avoiding eye contact. Message delivered, he would return on the uphill leg of his journey to the posh seats, muttering under his breath and generally being heckled by Pisser and his Roobarb gang. The second his back was turned, up onto the wall the young Wanderers fans would return. This would happen two or three times per game, followed by a stern tannoy message when the old chap had tired himself out. By the final 20 minutes he completely gave up and The Wall became the best seat in the house.

It had been during one such final 20 minute period that Wycombe scored a vital goal. Much to my delight, the visiting team's goalkeeper (who had been verbally jousting with the crowd throughout the match) had to suffer the humiliation of crawling into the back of the net to retrieve the ball, right in front of me. As he looked up, he was welcomed by the sight of a chubby kid flicking a two-fingered salute straight at him. This wonderful moment of sportsmanship was captured by the local newspaper's photographer. In the spark of a flashbulb my impulsive moment of joyous rebellion was stopped dead in its tracks. How was I going to explain my presence on the back page making obscene hand gestures and, even worse, doing it whilst sitting on the forbidden wall?

My life was over; I'd be banned forever, and if the Protector of The Wall didn't hunt me down first, the goalkeeper surely would. But why give a shit about them? My mum was going to kill me as soon as she saw the newspaper, anyway. I knew it; crime didn't pay and this was my comeuppance.

Upon the final whistle I found myself washed along in the tide of fellow Wycombians leaving the ground, all eager to get to wherever they were going, be it The Gate pub just minutes away down the alley past the gasworks or, behind that, the grim monument to 1960's cement-block architecture that was High Wycombe bus station. The station was a dark and gloomy place on even the brightest of days, but after the football on a drizzly December afternoon it was the most desolate place on earth.

Squeezing through the bottleneck at the exit gates the crowd dispersed, scurrying in all directions into the winter darkness. I skulked away slowly dragging my feet. I loved going to the football and never wanted it to end, but to add to the sadness of the week's highpoint being over, I now felt like a prisoner on death row awaiting the ultimate punishment. I was going to get my arse kicked so badly when my mum saw me in the paper. Oh the shame I was about to bring to my family. I felt sick to the pit of my stomach.

Down past the gasworks I walked through the dimly lit bus station to catch the number 326 bus, which would snake its way up and down the side of the valley through the housing estates before passing by my street, high on the outskirts of town. Head down, avoiding all eye contact past the Skins, Punks and Mods was always the best policy in the bus station and, as usual, I adopted the tactic, although from the corner of my eye I could see that Pisser and Billy had no such concerns and were happily regaling tales of the match to the fantastically plumed punks, while sharing a bag full of beers. I hurried past, just raising my glance in time to see the tail of the 326 queue disappear inside the bus and its doors slamming. Immediately, the engine began to rumble, belching out a filthy cloud of fumes to keep me company as the bus pulled away, its windows steamed up by the shoppers and football supporters staring back at me. There was no point trying to get the drivers attention. All Wycombe bus drivers had a gift for tunnel-vision which made fractionally late passengers invisible from view the very second the driver had decided he was off. I think they had to pass an exam on it before getting the job.

Decisions, decisions; should I wait 30 minutes for the next 326, or get the 303? The 303 was cheaper, but only took me half the way home, inconveniently dropping me at the start of 'ambush-alley' at the far end of the industrial estate. My mum told me someone had been murdered there and that I should never take that route in the dark. With hindsight, I either grew up in the roughest place on earth, or my mum was trying to instil a healthy fear of absolutely everything in me, as all the places I frequented appeared to have a history of vicious crime. The 326 and 303 bays were next to each other in the terminal, so the fates could decide which route I took home; next bus wins. Unfortunately, in the corner next to the 303 bay was The Kiosk. The Kiosk was the only ray of sunshine in the permanent twilight of the bus station, although I think it was the Kit-Kats that drew me towards it rather than the sensation of artificial daylight that beamed from its neon sign. Decision made, bus fare spent on one final bar of chocolate, the choice was now easy; I was walking home.

With Kit-Kat devoured and the walk back through the bus station safely manoeuvred, I found myself back outside the football ground. I stopped at the gates and peered in. Where, just an hour before the floodlights had illuminated the pitch as our stage, and its players as our heroes and villains, the terraces were now silent, the pitch empty, the players departed; the final curtain had been drawn for another week. Another game consigned to the history books, to be recalled years from now on coach trips by grumpy old men. Maybe someday I'd be one of those debating at the front of the bus. I took one last look at my spot on The Wall; that's where I was when Westy scored the goal, and that's where I was when the photographer took that bloody picture.

I trudged off home up the Everest-like Tom Burt's Hill in the drizzle, trying not to think about my moment of madness; thinking instead of far off exotic places, places that I could run away to, places to avoid the wrath of my mum. China, Easter Island, Australia, I'd seen them all on the telly and in books. Yes, that was it; I could just run away, brilliant. Hold on, what about school on Monday? And then there was my paper-round. The whole world was against me.

Some 45 minutes of daydreaming later, I was at the top of my garden path. My dad would want a minute-by-minute report on the game. Just the merest thought of the Wanderers win filled me with joy and eased my concerns. Yes, even my two fingered salute to that evil goalkeeper had been brilliant at the time, surely contributing to his team not finding an equalising goal. The crowd around me had certainly enjoyed it. At the football we were united as one, we were Wycombe Wanderers, the finest football team the world had ever seen. Be you 13 or 103, you were part of the tribe. It was just a pity that the tribe weren't going to be there to back me up when impending punishment came my way.

After several restless nights spent contemplating my fate, the local newspaper was published. I got to the newsagents earlier than normal that day to prepare for my delivery round. With gritted teeth and peering through squinted eyes I picked up a copy and flicked through the sports pages, working my way backwards through to the front page. With great relief I discovered that the sports editor had decided not to lead with a full-page photo of me making obscene gestures, opting instead for the less offensive image of my hero, Mark West, smashing home the winning goal. I was reprieved and able to sleep peacefully once more! I vowed that never again would I let my excitement get the better of me at the football, or at least to check that no cameras were pointed in my direction first. Now I could look forward to the next game, the big one; an epic trip to the other end of the country to face the professional players of York City in the FA Cup.

So there we all were; a chubby 13-year-old with more chocolate than was good for him, old men who had been doing this for 70 years, and the Roobarb gang, hell-bent on searching out good times regardless of the consequences. We had two things in common. We were all from a small town called High Wycombe, and we all supported the greatest football team in High Wycombe, if not the world, Wycombe Wanderers.

As conversations tired and the monotonous rhythm of the coach drew its incumbents into a lull, I again found my gaze drawn out across the frozen horizon, my thoughts drifting. Could this be the day? I was only 13 and today I was going to witness history. People had been watching the Wanderers for 100 years, ever since a group of lads from the local furniture factories formed the team sometime in the 1880's. The front-of-the-bus crew endlessly debated the year, some said 1884, others 1887. Either way, most looked old enough to have been in The Steam Engine pub when the inaugural meeting was held. Regardless, be it 99 or 102 years since Wycombe Wanderers were formed, it was a bloody long time ago. Nobody had ever seen them do what they would today, progress to the 4th Round of the world's most famous football tournament, The FA Cup. All we had to do was beat York City, in York. It didn't matter that York were a professional team, unlike the Wycombe players who all had real jobs. Sadly, these jobs were no longer in the dozens of local furniture factories that had been the foundation of our town; the workshops that had provided the living for those first Wanderers like Jim Ball and his cousin Ted, the Luker brothers, Bill and Thomas, and their captain Ted Webb. They were all chair makers; the original 'Chairboys' who gave the team its nickname. These players had passed into the annals of time, along with the furniture makers that had employed them. Wycombe was a town slowly losing its industry, its heritage and its very identity, just like so many other small towns across the country. I still had three years left at school and no idea what I was going to do when I left. What I did know was that, unlike generations before me, I wouldn't be getting the opportunity to enter the furniture trade. The fact that I'd already been banned from doing woodwork at school meant that this probably wasn't such a bad thing for me personally.

"You're a good lad James, but we think it's for the best if you switch to Home Economics, it's for your own safety... and everybody else's" my teachers had advised.

The world was moving on, leaving towns like mine behind, leaving skilled craftsmen behind too. At least we had football; at least we had our beloved Wycombe Wanderers. The town needed them now more than ever as, block by block, the other cornerstones upon which the town had been built were slowly but surely being eroded away.

Soon, I was there on the freezing terrace, down at the front just like at Loakes Park. But there was no wall for me to sit on; the imposing 10-foot high fence that stopped the crowds from going onto the pitch would see to that. This was York City; a proper football team; a Football League team. I was in awe of my surroundings and suddenly felt intimidated; I was a long way from home. I heard raised voices. It didn't take long to register that the people of Yorkshire, like those of Buckinghamshire, didn't take kindly to urination on the terraces either. I smiled at the sight of Pisser and his band of very merry men being escorted by policemen away from the York supporters and into the Wycombe enclosure. They were greeted by cheers; it was good to see their familiar faces, even though they didn't know me. The Roobarb's had benefited from Wycombe being seen as a little amateur team having 'a big day out'. One of the policemen even mocked "C'mon lads, the grounds segregated... bet yer never been t'big ground like this before, have yer?"

'Condescending git... you won't be laughing when the Wycombe boys win 5-0' I thought to myself.

I always think my team will win 5-0. We rarely have, and rarely do. We didn't win 5-0 that day either. We didn't win at all, although we should have, and we would have, if it hadn't been for a biased referee who disallowed three perfectly good Wycombe goals whilst allowing two dubious ones to stand for York. Why are referees only ever against you?

The travelling supporters, some tearful but all disgruntled, boarded the bus for the long journey home. For once there was consensus; indignation towards the referee who had cost our team a place in the 4th Round of the FA Cup; he'd denied us our place in history. To think, if those three goals had been allowed to stand, I would have been amongst the first Wycombe Wanderers supporters to see the team victoriously through the 3rd Round. Imagine that; the first after 100 years.

All conversation came to an abrupt halt with the reading of the football scores over the radio.

"Shush, it's the scores" hissed all corners of the bus.

As one, the coach fell silent in respect for the scores. Silent until the words... "York City 2... Wycombe Wanderers... 0."

This was met by a crescendo of jeers and expletives. I chuckled at the site of grown men of all ages heckling a radio, before joining in with the random shouting of swear words. It was just another reason for a boy to love going to the football. The noise levels calmed as the long journey home began. Soon most were asleep. I dreamt of next year, when we would surely get to the FA Cup 4th Round.

2 - Fifteen years later - Harrow Borough

Once again, I found my face pressed against the glass, attention flitting between my breath steaming the window and gazing across the rain soaked Chiltern Hills as the Wycombe-bound train escaped the urban sprawl of the capital. It was 2pm. This bloody hangover should have relented by now. The cold window was helping to numb the pain a little but, as had been proved far too regularly over the past 15 years, over-indulging really didn't make for a comfortable journey.

Thank god I'd managed to catch the fast train. I couldn't manage the additional 25 minutes of the slower train today, with its constant shuddering to a halt and jolting back up to speed at every one-horse town between London and High Wycombe. More importantly, the fast train might get me back to the Chair Metropolis with enough time to jump in a cab across town to Adams Park for the Wanderers game. Looking at my watch I knew it would be tight; if only we still played at Loakes Park in the town centre I could be off the train, through the High Street, past the gasworks and at the gates within five minutes.

But time moves on. Loakes Park was now but a wonderful memory. After 95 years as the home of Wycombe Wanderers, it was now underneath an extension to the hospital and fancy town centre flats. The sale proceeds had funded a new stadium on the outskirts of town, Adams Park; a ground that would see the club into the new century in style. It also provided the impetus and funds to catapult the team into the most successful period of its history, although a visit to the FA Cup 4th Round still proved elusive. In just four seasons, Wycombe had been victorious on three occasions at Wembley Stadium, the home of English football. Before this run of success, long suffering Wanderers supporters had waited 34 years since their only previous opportunity to see the team play at the national stadium and, even then, they hadn't tasted victory. It had been sad to see Wembley Stadium, now half demolished, as the train whistled out of London; just like Loakes Park before it, even the most famous stadium in the world couldn't hold back the forces of progress. Now, all that remained were its iconic twin towers, standing exposed amid a pile of rubble, soon to make way for a modern equivalent to play host to the hopes and dreams of future generations. I was lucky to be born at the right time to enjoy this golden era of success since the Wanderers had moved to Adams Park. The man the ground was named after, Mr Frank Adams (who had generously given

Loakes Park to the club as a gift for the people of the town), would no doubt have enjoyed the successes too, as would the thousands of Wycombians who had supported the team throughout the past century; the chair makers of the 1880's, escaping the drudgery of their workbench for a Saturday afternoon in the park; the soldiers of the Oxfordshire and Buckinghamshire Light Infantry in 1919, trying to find some semblance of normality upon returning from the Great War singing 'We are the old Bucks boys' on the terraces, just as they had in the trenches; and then their sons trying to do exactly the same a quarter of a century later in 1945. Indeed, being born in 1972 was a blessing in so many ways, far beyond being around to witness a football team's triumphs.

The Wycombe-bound train came to an abrupt halt, startling me from my thoughts with a jump.

"This station is Gerrards Cross" the tannoy announced.

My sudden resurrection appeared to have scared the wide-eyed girl sat across from me too. Wonderful; I'd been blissfully ignorant to the fact that I'd been sitting opposite Buckinghamshire's candidate for Miss World for the past 15 minutes whilst, for good measure, dribbling against the window. She looked awkward, I felt embarrassed. Luckily, I always managed to find a way to make a bad situation that little bit worse.

"I've got a girlfriend you know!" I blurted.

'I've got a girlfriend,' did I really just say that out loud? Oh crap.

"I'm sorry, what I meant was ... it's just ... erm, you know ... I startled you. I just meant that you're fine. Nothing to be worried about... I mean, I'm normal ... no really, I am... just a bit hungover."

They just kept coming; random words that made perfect sense in my head, but by the time they came out, the ramblings of a madman; not the calming reassurance I was trying to achieve. With hindsight, an apologetic smile and a quick return to drowsing and memories of Wycombe's footballing successes would have proved far less awkward. Mercifully, it wasn't long before the train made its next stop, Beaconsfield, where my beautiful travelling companion alighted, probably to head for the nearest police station. It wasn't a surprise that she got off there, despite my suave sophistication. People who looked like her generally got off the train at Gerrards Cross or Beaconsfield. Rich people lived in these small commuter towns. Rich people attracted beautiful well-dressed partners, and 'the beautiful people' generally breed beautiful well-dressed children; it's in their genes, and their designer jeans.

The next Miss World's vacated seat was soon taken by a Dad with his young son and daughter; both appeared very excited about going to the football. I listened as Dad told the kids about the FA Cup, and how this was just the first round, but that if Wycombe won and then won the next round too, then they might get a chance to play Liverpool or Manchester United. The childrens' eyes widened with excitement at the thought, as did those of the man with the hangover sat opposite them.

The little girl said, "Daddy, Wycombe will win today, won't they?"

I wanted to blurt out "Yes! Yes, little girl, they will! And they might even go on and win the FA Cup this year; it doesn't matter if there are seventy better teams than us. Yes! It really could happen! Believe little girl, believe!" but with my last outburst not having gone so well, I decided to sit back and watch the outskirts of my hometown come into view instead.

Self-inflicted headaches and cringe-worthy embarrassments aside, this was going to be a great day. Wycombe Wanderers could always save my day, and today was FA Cup day. Surely this would be the year when we made it to the 4th Round? Yes, I'd been disappointed before (okay, I'd been disappointed every year since the age of four), but after 113 years of waiting, this might be the year. As the train pulled into High Wycombe the excitement swelled inside me, the same excitement I'd always felt on a Saturday as the match approached. Today it felt even greater than normal; the children on the train knew it, their father knew it, and I knew it too. Beaconsfield's Miss World didn't, but that was her loss. Today the possibilities were endless. League position didn't matter, past form didn't matter. All that mattered was today. Added to that I was skiving for the afternoon from a revision course for exams I was to sit a week later; yes, this was living on the edge!

Skiving? Playing truant? Absent without leave? I'm not sure these terms can actually be applied to a 28-year-old trainee accountant who had paid decent money to be locked in a classroom for six days solid, being subjected to mind-numbing levels of boredom in the process. It was a form of torture to someone with a limited attention span, someone like me. I'd stayed focused on my studies for five whole days, but the warning signs for day six had been there since I'd agreed to meet up with Scotty and Sanj for a few Friday night drinks. They were two of my dearest friends, and had been since our first day at school 23 years before. Both were now living and pursuing highly successful careers in London, but with everyone having increasingly busy lives our chances to catch up were becoming less frequent. The Christmas Eve High Street blitz back home would always be on our social calendars (in my case on a post-it note, for Scott a Filofax entry, and for Sanj, several gentle reminders from his PA), but gone were the days when we had walked to and from school together for 11 years, day in, day out. After a week in study hell, I was looking forward to a quick beer with the boys. Unfortunately, when we get together, the 5-year-old mentality that never truly leaves any man takes over, and last night had ended up all too predictably, with far too many beers, and me unconscious on Scotty's sofa.

Now let's be clear; nobody wants to be an accountant, not really, and certainly not initially. I wanted to play centre-forward for Wycombe Wanderers and, barring that, my back up plan had been to have adventures travelling the world. Unsurprisingly, neither Plan A nor B had come to fruition upon leaving school. Plans C, D, E and F hadn't panned out too favourably over the years either. When I'd first walked into the night school classroom clutching my old school calculator some five years before, I'd been 20 exams away from qualifying and now, with just five left and maybe another year or so of studying ahead of me, there was some light at the end of the tunnel. I wasn't a million miles away from becoming a fully-qualified accountant. Well, that was the optimistic take on things. It would have been equally realistic to suggest I was at least a million miles away from qualifying, based on the fact that I was up there with, or rather more accurately, down there with, the least mathematically-minded candidates studying for the mother-of-all mathematics exams. I'd managed to blag my way through this far, but there was more chance of Wycombe Wanderers winning the FA Cup than of me passing the exam in a week's time. The fact that I was crap with numbers hadn't been factored into the equation when I'd decided to try accountancy as my Plan G. I hadn't factored anything into an equation, ever. And therein lay my problem; I didn't understand equations at all. So, after a Saturday morning wasted typing rude words into my calculator instead of attempting the indecipherable conundrums, my mind had been made up. 'Sod this… I'm going to the football.' At the age of 28, and for the first time in my life, I was skipping class.

Books closed, train travelled, taxi ridden, I arrived at Adams Park at 3.01pm on Saturday 18th November, 2000. One minute into Wycombe's latest FA Cup adventure. I raced through the gates of Adams Park like an excited child; I really should have grown out of this by now, but I hadn't, and I didn't want to. Through the turnstile I bounded up the steps towards the upper-tier of the Woodlands Stand. I stumbled, just like always. I couldn't resist taking my eye off of the stairs to get that first glimpse of the pitch that the stairway offered, before disappearing into the concourse within the belly of the stadium. I'd graduated from the walls behind the Loakes Park goalmouths, now watching from the side of the pitch elevated far beyond the heights that the Loakes Park grandstand could ever have offered. Through the concourse I continued, listening for clues from the crowd sat above me before taking the final three steps out into full view of the pitch; I was home. I stood mesmerised by the view of my adored Wycombe Wanderers out on the pitch. I smiled as childhood memories, teenage memories, adult memories, all collided into a joyous rush of adrenaline.

The first of several chips soon flew into the side of my head, bursting my bubble.

"Sit down!"

"Get out of the way, you bloody idiot!"

I looked round to see the Roobarbs all leaning forward, shouting and straining to see past me as I blocked their view of the Wanderers, who were about to take a corner at the far end of the ground. I was home, and had been greeted accordingly.

"Alright boy, thought you weren't coming today... ain't you supposed to be doing some college course or something?" greeted Smudger. "Don't know why you bothered anyway... this is shit" he continued, before breaking off from our embryonic conversation to launch a tirade at the unfortunate Wanderer who'd just delivered the poorly struck corner straight into the welcoming arms of Harrow Borough's goalkeeper.

"They've only played two minutes Smudge, give 'em a chance!"

I looked down the line of seats to see a dozen of my friends, some transfixed on the game, others laughing and joking. I was looking for a spare seat further into our block; Smudger always had a seat spare beside him (and generally in front and behind him too). He liked to get into the action, and could easily become frustrated. That's one of the attractions of going to the football; it's great for letting off steam. Sitting next to Smudger came with a government health warning; during the game, probably sooner rather than later, he would inadvertently elbow you in the head or send you flying with a forearm smash as he exploded from his seat to offer his own form of encouragement. A gentle giant without an aggressive bone in his body, but likely to leave you requiring medical attention all the same.

"Come on... shift up... he's nearly taken me out already" I pleaded, shuffling along the line of seats, greeting each person in turn.

"In 'ere Jamesyboy, get in here lad."

"Cheers Buz... here we go again, you 'up for the cup' then?"

"Course I am, this is the FA Cup! This is what it's all about! This is the year boy! ... C'mon!!!!!" roared Buz happily.

Buz was our self-appointed leader, 'The General', although admittedly the General of a rag-tag army of reprobates of all ages, whom he more often than not led down blind alleys; into awful pubs; to missed train connections; and invariably, the wrong place at the wrong time. To the outsider, we probably didn't look to have much in common, but through a shared love of a football team, this motley crew had, somewhere along the line, grown from being casual Saturday acquaintances to being as close as any family.

"Out the way Jamesyboy, I need a piss... shouldn't have downed that last pint!" said Buz, as he hauled himself up and edged along the row, standing on a dozen feet as he left a trail of destruction in his wake, hugging, chatting and generally causing a commotion the entire way.

A minute later the crowd erupted as Wycombe's Jamie Bates smashed the ball into the Harrow Borough net. We leapt from our seats as one; man, woman and child; even the hard to please Smudger; hugging stranger and friend alike in celebration of a ball being kicked into an eight-yard-wide by eight-foot-high net, as if it were the most important occurrence in the world. As the euphoria subsided, we settled back into our seats, only to rise again seconds later to taunt The General as Buz rushed back into view, eager to confirm that the crescendo of noise that had disturbed his call of nature was, indeed, due to a Wanderers goal.

"Every time... they do it every time!" he protested, taking the mock applause of the surrounding crowd. "Seriously, every bloody time" he muttered, finally bundling back into his seat beside me. He consoled himself by taking full credit for the goal... "Yep, pretty certain we wouldn't have scored if I hadn't gone for a leak" he summed up, using the logic only possessed by football fans. I smiled, recalling my childhood memories of

Buz, on the terraces at Loakes Park. He hadn't always been so bothered about using a toilet when he needed to 'go'.

I'd raised this point on several occasions in the past but he was having none of it. "It's true Buz... we even called you Pisser, and Roger was 'Billy Connolly'... because... well, he looked like Billy Connolly." The closest he ever came to an admission of guilt was a begrudging "Well, Roger always was a hairy sod."

Although both protested their innocence, they couldn't dispute that there was a semblance of truth in my recollections for several reasons; on account of me being the most sensible member of the Roobarbs (not a huge feat on my part); the undisputable fact that they had drunk a lot 'back in the day' (a skill never lost); and finally, the most damning evidence of all, whenever the topic was discussed, my accusations were always backed up by numerous other witnesses, not necessarily people who were even part of our conversation, just other supporters who happened to be within earshot; victims of Buz's infamous al fresco splash-back from years gone by. The increasing weight of evidence as more witnesses came forward always proved a source of hilarity for all, and equally a hefty dose of embarrassment for the legends who were Pisser and Billy. I like to think that these kangaroo courts, held in the bar after games, helped provide closure for Pisser's innocent victims. I made a mental note to convene such a court sitting again after the game, as the FA Cup seemed to stir up memories of old, and there were sure to be some old-timers in the bar today; fans who had turned up to experience 'the magic of the cup' once again, who would gladly point an accusing finger in the direction of Buz and Roger.

Buz managed to sit relatively still for the next half an hour before deciding to beat the queue at the bar for a half-time beer. No sooner had he re-trodden on everyone's feet and disappeared from view when Wycombe scored again, providing all the ammunition necessary to tease the poor guy throughout the break. All thanks to Buz, Wycombe were 2-0 up and as good as in the hat for Round 2. This made the half-time beer taste all the sweeter.

With a third goal in the second half (which, sadly, Buz had managed to witness), the Wanderers were indeed safely through. Everyone prayed for an easy opponent when the balls were drawn for the 2nd Round. In the meantime, we had a victory to celebrate. Eventually, after finding Buz guilty-as-charged in what must have been his hundredth retrial, we reluctantly stumbled out of the Adams Park bar and into the cold November night; always the first at the bar, always the last to leave.

We waited in the car park for the two youngest members of our hardened crew of football hooligans to get picked up... by their mum. Bob always brought his two little girls to the games and, just as I'd found when I was young, the football was just a small part of the overall attraction. Whereas I used to go home exhausted after my adventures on The Wall and from collecting conkers behind the Gasworks End at Loakes Park, Laura and Abby would sleep well tonight, having stood with their dad on the Adams Park terrace for two hours, before leading the charge of dozens of children on endless laps around the bar as the adults discussed the game over a beer.

The 15 minute walk through the deserted industrial estate to the closest pub always served as a respite from the high-octane banter of the day. We'd meander past the factories and office buildings, breaking into smaller groups as various conversations began. I was with Smudger who, following the final whistle, had transformed back into his gentle giant incarnation from a contender for the heavyweight championship of the world.

"Any jobs going in there mate?" he asked, shifting his glance towards the large building at the end of the estate where I worked.

"I don't know Smudge. I could find out for you... you know we don't make chairs though, right?" I replied, smiling at him.

"Yeah, time to try something else mate... I'm sick of it. It's all I've done since I was 15... nearly 20 years. Anyway, they're knocking Ercol down and moving out into the sticks."

"Moving? Out of Wycombe? How can they?"

"They say we'll keep our jobs, but they aren't spending millions on a modern factory for no reason, are they?"

"Oh, shit, sorry to hear that mate... yes, absolutely... I'll see if there's anything going. I'll ask on Monday, first thing."

I tried to sound positive, but Smudger was right, 'state-of-the-art investment' really meant 'streamlined operations'; 'process efficiencies'; 'reduced overheads'; 'increased shareholder value'. Call it what you want, it would eventually mean people losing their jobs. I'd seen this scenario played out over and over in case-studies at night school. Only this time it was real, and this was my friend and the oldest furniture company left in town; with over 450 employees, it was also the biggest.

"At least it's only 20 minutes on the train. You might still have a job. That's better than when Gommes packed up" I irritatingly added, trying to be optimistic by comparing Smudger's plight to the 700 jobs that were lost when the other of the 'big two' furniture firms which dominated the town, Gommes, decided to cash in on their prime town centre land, moving production of its world-famous G-Plan furniture completely out of the area.

Smudge shrugged his shoulders. "You did the right thing Jamesy... going to college and all that. I can't use computers... I wouldn't know what to do in an office. I just thought Gommes and Ercol would be there forever."

Smudge wasn't alone; the entire town had thought that too. My mum, aunt and both uncles had worked for either Ercol or Gommes, if not both. Many school holidays were spent sneaking quietly around my Nan's house while my Grandad slept, before accompanying him down the hill to Gommes for the start of his night shift. I guess my woodwork teacher had done me a favour after all when he banned me from the school carpentry classes.

Leaving the industrial estate behind us we embraced the warmth of the first pub on the route back into town. Smudger forgot about his woes, I stopped worrying about equations, and my football family talked, laughed, drank, sang and danced into the early hours. As a small boy, my football-bubble popped with the referee's final whistle, but The Roobarb's met early and stayed out late, regardless of result. Our motto... 'win or lose, support the Blues... win or lose, get on the booze', summed us up. A shared love of Wycombe Wanderers had brought us together. A further common love of having a good time had bonded us further, and despite our weekday guises as factory workers, teachers, painters, drivers, company directors, social workers, carpenters, postmen, plasterers, gasmen, roofers, gardeners and would-be accountants, when the weekend came, we proved on a weekly basis that little boys and girls who go to the football don't really ever grow up.

As the evening wore on everyone took a turn to model Tony's 'lucky' FA Cup hat which, as tradition demanded, always reappeared for the 1st Round before normally being consigned back to the wardrobe for another year. The Stone Roses booming from the jukebox provided my cue to don it whilst doing my best Reni impression, safe in the knowledge that the hat would be making at least one more appearance this season.

3 - If at first you don't succeed...

I walked down the hill with a spring in my step that Monday morning. The Wycombe boys had won; we'd had a brilliant night celebrating; even my Sunday morning football team had won. Yes, the weekend had proved successful and, following a week of intense revision classes, I was looking forward to catching up with my friends at work. By lunchtime I'd know who Wycombe were playing in the 2nd Round, too. As I passed through the gates I looked up the street in the direction of Adams Park, remembering my Saturday night chat with Smudger. I'd check with Human Resources for any vacancies as soon as I sat down.

The accounts office was on the top floor, a sprawling open-plan affair that was home to over fifty bean-counters. I spent 15 minutes en route to my desk chatting about the weekend's football and comparing notes on how the revision was going with other junior accountants.

"Good weekend? Classes go okay? Who did Wycombe get in the next Round? Bet you're gutted you missed the game though?" said a smiling Gibbo from the Treasury department, hitting me with a barrage of questions.

"Hiya Gibbo… yep, the course was tough, but worth doing. I thought the draw wasn't until lunchtime today? And yes, I hate missing a game, but you know… needs must and all that." I replied guiltily, concealing my Saturday afternoon truancy. I could feel my cheeks begin to flush.

Saturday night must have been a really good one; how had none of us realised the draw for the next round had already been made? First task of the day would be to see who we'd drawn, hopefully another home tie against non-league opposition. Smudger wouldn't mind being demoted to second on my to-do list for that.

Sinking into my seat, I looked out across the factory rooftops to the far side of the estate. There it was; Adams Park, looking back at me. Thoughts of Smudger's predicament suddenly made me feel very grateful for my own situation. I had a decent job, a desk with a view, my girlfriend's flat was only a five minute walk up the street and, despite the upcoming exam which was hanging over me, I was content. I finally had a plan that seemed to be working out. Admittedly, it wasn't my original plan or my back up plan, or the series of disasters that had followed that. But, after a bumpy ride not dissimilar to my coach trip to York 15 years prior, I finally had a plan that was working out.

Plan A - Wycombe Wanderers footballing legend

If I'd spent less time following the Wanderers around the country, and instead dedicated my Saturdays to practicing on the park across from my house, I might have achieved my initial chosen career path. Sadly, it became apparent that this wasn't likely to happen with the realisation that I wasn't even the best player in my school team, let alone the best in the town. Alas, I was always destined to be 'Clubman of the Year' and never 'Players' Player' at the end of season disco.

Plan A... file under 'A for Ability lacking'.

Plan B - International Adventurer

Travelling the world, experiencing different cultures, exploring different landscapes - yes, this appealed to me. I was never overly sure what this would actually involve doing though; possibly piracy? Joining the army? Becoming a drug mule? All of these might involve getting shot. To be honest, I'd held on to Plan A for longer than I'll ever admit, so hadn't really thought through the practicalities. Exploring the world would require finances, of which I had none. It might also require some practical skills which, again, were sadly lacking.

Plan B ... consigned to the file 'B for Back in the real world'.

Plan C - Wycombe Wanderers back-of-house legend

If I couldn't serve my beloved Wanderers on the pitch, why couldn't I do it off it? When I left school, I stumbled onto a college course, mainly to buy myself more time to figure out what I could do next. At school I wasn't great at anything in particular but, flicking through the college brochures, there was a course in Leisure Management. My selection process wasn't sophisticated.

'Leisure? I could study that... it must be about sport. It's in the college down town too, so I don't even need to get the bus to Amersham.'

Amersham Art College was my only other option, but I figured nobody was going to give me a job at the end of it just because I was good at drawing. Amersham would also mean getting up an hour earlier each day. A quick shout down the stairs to my parents, and the decision was made...

"Mum! Dad! I'm ticking the box for this course; I think it's a bit like Business Studies... but less boring, alright?"

The course did, indeed, look at the off-field side of sports and entertainment. I had my third plan; study hard to obtain the tools needed to make me a useful employee of Wycombe Wanderers Football Club.

Five years of study later, I sat in the boardroom at Adams Park being interviewed for the job vacancy of my dreams; working in the club's Commercial Department. The chairman sat across the table from me, beside him the commercial manager. In my hastily purchased suit I handled all the questions they could muster, answering them sensibly like a recent graduate should, answering them passionately like only a true fan could. I was down to the final two candidates from over a hundred and I'd nailed the interview. Yes, I was prone to blurt out the most stupid of things at the most inopportune of times, but I'd really nailed it. I couldn't have done any more. I was going to become a Wycombe Wanderer, a non-playing Wycombe Wanderer admittedly, but the next best thing and, for me, all I wanted to be. As the chairman walked me out to the car park after the interview he'd asked if I'd driven there. I smiled and said "No, I walked down, I live very close." I told him that I could drive, but didn't have my own car yet. My part-time supermarket wages barely covered my entrance fees to games so, no, a car would have to wait until I'd got a full-time job. With a confident handshake I turned and practically floated down the street, not quite believing that everything had come together so well, just as I'd planned it.

A few days later I sat at the foot of the stairs, trembling with excitement as I struggled to open the letter. I was 21-years-old and playing football in the lowest tier of the Wycombe pub league but, despite this, allowed myself a moment to pretend that this was a letter from the team manager offering me a trial. I needed to be careful so as not to rip the letter; I would want to keep it as a reminder of the day I got my job at Wycombe Wanderers. Maybe I'd frame it and hang it up in my office in years to come when I was the chairman. At first I just gazed at the headed paper, in awe of the clubs logo proudly looking back, then to the bottom, just to confirm this was indeed from the chairman and not the manager, then finally, to the content of the letter itself.

"'Firstly, we would like to thank you for...' yeah-yeah-yeah, no problem", I muttered to myself, whilst scanning further down the page.

"Unfortunately..."

Unfortunately.

Unfortunately?

First there was just a dull ache in the pit of my stomach, soon followed by a feeling of nausea. I struggled to breathe. My mouth was suddenly devoid of moisture. My hands shook as I read and re-read the letter. I waited to wake up from the nightmare.

Tears; where were the tears? I'd never been the toughest of kids growing up, and was prone to having a blub whenever it felt necessary. I'd been dropped from my football team for the Cup Final when I was 12, after playing in every game during the season until contracting tonsillitis the week of the Semi-Final. On the day of the Final, the manager thought it best not to mention that he was keeping the same team from the previous week. No, he didn't mention it until me and all my teammates were in the changing room, practically climbing the walls with excitement. When he announced the line-up I was heartbroken and wept in front of all my friends. My crying continued through the warm up, the first half, the half-time team-talk and most of the second half, before I pulled myself together for the photos as we posed with the trophy. Years later, any girlfriends getting the obligatory 'parents embarrassing their son' photo session were told I'd had terrible hay fever that day, hence the red eyes. This set an early precedent. Following scuffles with mates, I'd generally cry regardless of who'd won or lost. Then, when we'd grown out of fighting and discovered girls, if they got the girl instead of me, I'd rub salt in my wounds again, with a good cry. It goes without saying that I cried in front of hundreds of people when Wycombe Wanderers got themselves relegated in 1986 when, inexplicably, Graham Pearce managed to score a spectacular own goal from the halfway line. It was late on in a game that had been devoid of incident. We only needed a draw. The opposition were just days away from a Cup Final at Wembley and had not made a single tackle; their sole aim to avoid injury before the biggest game of their careers. It was evident, even to a daydreaming youngster on The Wall like me, that this game was impossible to lose, until we lost it. Just four months earlier I had been full of dreams on a bus to York for the biggest FA Cup game of my life and, now, the season had ended in complete disaster. I cried all the way home. The following season my friends and I thought it would be fun to run across the pitch at Loakes Park at the end of a game. I slipped, covering myself from head to toe in mud from the hallowed turf, with a white line of penalty-box paint running neatly down the full length of my body for good measure. At least on that occasion the mud and paint covered the tracks of my tears from the thousand laughing witnesses.

But there were no tears today. This just hurt too much. This was the one I'd waited for, the one I'd waited five years for to be exact. Getting rejected by the prettiest girl on the dance floor was one thing; but by the football club I'd grown up with? No, it was too much. My heart was broken, my Plan C in tatters. Yes, there were other football clubs I could work for, but the few vacancies that eventually arose didn't even muster another interview. My heart wasn't in it. Would working for just any football team be as much fun? Not for me.

Plan C ... forever archived under 'C for Crushingly cruel'.

Plan D – the Supermarket safety net

I'd worked in the supermarket since leaving school. All the student employees worked all day on Saturday, plus one evening during the week. All the students bar one. I'd been quite insistent at my interview that I was unavailable on Saturdays and Tuesday evenings due to 'prior commitments', but that I could work all the other evenings. I didn't explain that my prior commitments related to watching football, rather than study or voluntary work or anything else of note but, then again, the HR lady never asked.

I tried to avoid the checkouts like the plague. I was crap with numbers and the thought of having to count out change filled me with dread. Fortunately, my choice of shifts meant I usually had a good shot at getting the best job in the building each night, or rather the best job out of it; trolley pusher extraordinaire. This meant being released into the fresh air and getting exercise or, at least, out in the fume-filled car park instead of being confined to a checkout listening to the relentless 'beep-beep-beep-beep' of every item as it was scanned. Left to my own devices by the managers, I was free to roam the multi-storey car park and to chat to the girls on the cigarette kiosk. It was, indeed, the best job going, despite involving walking around in full view of the public whilst wearing brown flares and an orange clip-on tie that risked a tracheotomy every time I sneezed. For the student boys, we all knew that this was the plum job, and for the student girls it was just a forbidden fruit, with pushing trolleys not deemed as 'suitable work for young ladies'. Unfortunately, not all customers viewed the position with the same high regard. One Friday night, in the middle of a fearsome thunderstorm, I was pushing a row of trolleys to the store. I was soaked to the bone, freezing cold and being pestered by customers awaiting a trolley. I braved electrocution and weaved the trolleys through the car park noticing a mother screaming at her little boy. As I walked by, the woman looked up at me and pointed.

"Do you see him? If you don't buck your ideas up, you'll end up just like that idiot!"

Charming; it hurt even more that the tearful blighter looked genuinely horrified at the thought. It was a low moment, admittedly. But, deep down I knew I was only 18 and about to begin a Degree course; I had the world at my feet, or at least a chance at getting a job with Wycombe Wanderers once I'd graduated. I also knew it was only an hour until I got paid, an hour until me and the checkout girls would be hitting the bar across the road. Surely one of them would fall in love with me eventually?

College taught me a lot, but so did the supermarket. Pushing trolleys provided a perfect platform to observe life's ups and downs. There was the Friday girl who always popped in after the gym to buy bread pudding. She started seeing the quiet Thursday guy with the glasses, the one who always took his trolley back to the bay. Two regular faces that always looked lonely until becoming the Wednesday couple; she would put the bags in the boot of their car, always taking her bread pudding back to the passenger seat, while he returned their trolley. Then, one night, she just got in the car without her bread pudding and slammed the door, leaving him to load the bags before abandoning the trolley. He went back to Thursday nights and she sourced her bread pudding elsewhere. I guess happy endings are never guaranteed.

The supermarket work had served its purpose. It had helped me pay my way through college and allowed me to follow the Wanderers around the country, but it had always been a temporary thing; a 'temporary thing' which had lasted for six years. My years of service, combined with a freshly completed Degree, now seemed to be providing me with a Plan D.

Wycombe Wanderers didn't want me, maybe it was time to grow up; time to knuckle down and get a proper job. If I was going to have to work weekends, so be it. 'The Chairboys had their chance' I told myself, although deep down, there was no escaping it had been my loss, rather than theirs. The store manager pulled some strings to get me added to the next Graduate Training selection process, and assured me that it would be a formality... "Just be yourself."

I spent the next few months working full-time, garnering as much experience as I could from the store management team before heading to a hotel for the three day assessment. I had one foot in the door already and simply couldn't fail.

Now, which was more embarrassing? Was it walking back into the store, to inform all the lovely old ladies on the checkouts that I wouldn't be coming back as a manager after all, or was it having to tell my family that I hadn't got the job at Wycombe Wanderers, despite my completely misguided optimism following 'that' interview? The Wanderers still won easily but this was another huge blow. Even my 'can't fail' option had failed. I had no idea where Plan E was going to come from.

Plan D; stored in the fruit and veg aisle under 'D for Depressing'.

Plan E – Sales

More through desperation than good judgement, I next convinced myself that sitting with a telephone directory, cold-calling companies to sell them corporate hospitality at sporting events, was a good idea. The key problem was that I had no selling skills. Nobody knows if they're a natural-born-salesman until they try, and here I was trying. It soon became apparent that I wasn't a salesman. I'd lasted six years at the supermarket; my sales career lasted six days.

File Plan E under 'E for Embarrassing error'.

Plan F – Temping

Having left the supermarket with high aspirations for my sales career in London, I didn't even have my trolley pushing job to fall back on anymore.

And so I entered the wonderful world of temping, which proved to be full of revelations.

I soon found that I didn't have a future as a receptionist, especially with companies that had tongue-twisters for names; I wasn't cut out for labouring; gardening played havoc with my hay fever; and although being quite good fun, being a drivers mate wasn't going to pay that well. I even managed to get three weeks working in a furniture factory, which I loved. Wow, maybe the furniture trade was in my blood after all? I had high hopes of getting kept on but then, out of the blue, the factory closed down overnight, like so many before it. It was back to the temping agency for me, along with the 200 'real' furniture workers who lost their livelihoods that day too. The following week, when I'd found myself celebrating my 23rd birthday with a nightshift assignment in solitary confinement, pulling blisteringly hot plastic moulds from a machine repeatedly for ten hours, I decided that I really needed another plan, and fast.

The next day, I marched into the temping agency and said, "I need to learn computers, can you teach me?"

'I need to learn computers'. A telling statement that spoke volumes about just how little I knew about computers or the world they operated in.

Sally, the girl in the agency, raised an eyebrow, but thankfully took pity on me. By good fortune, we had started our part-time jobs at the supermarket on the same day. This bond had led to many a Friday night in the pub spending our wages and dancing. There was also 'that' incident in the car park behind the pub one night when we'd kissed; a kiss that had started full of teenage promise, but ended abruptly as the cigarette-kiosk-girl vomited. It hadn't been the reaction I'd hoped for. My Adidas trainers were ruined, along with any thoughts of romance. Stood in a pool of vomit, I held her hair back whilst she coughed up the remains of her stomach, then we reverted back to being 'just friends'; never to discuss that evening again.

"Look, this isn't some sort of IT college, but if you want to sit in that room in the corner, we have some self-learning classes that Head Office sent for our staff development. You could take a look if you want... they're pretty basic, but it's a start. Try this one first, it's for Excel."

"Excel? Nice one, I'd like to excel" I replied unconvincingly, with what was becoming an all too familiar blank expression on my face; the same one that greeted the initial instructions I received from most of my temporary employers. I was starting to wonder if I was completely unemployable.

"Yes… spreadsheets… it's what they use in accountancy" Sally politely added, trying to give me a clue.

I spent the day working through the two hour 'how to use Excel' course and returned the following morning with the best intentions of discovering the delights of something called 'Word'. I hadn't had time to recall how to turn the computer on before an irate driver came barging into the office shouting at Sally. She escaped to my cramped cubicle looking flustered.

"Someone's not turned up for work, leaving this guy in the lurch… would you fill in… just for today? He needs a driver's mate."

"Sure… I could do with the money anyway."

"Thanks James, you're a life-saver. Come back in tomorrow for the computer training if you like… I'll help you."

After my day spent reading the newspaper and listening to the lorry driver's awful singing, I headed back to the agency office bright and early to have another attempt at mastering the art of Word. As I turned the corner I bumped into Sally who was fumbling around in her bag for the office key, alongside another girl.

"James! Sally said you'd been around this week… long time no see!" said the girl, giving me a hug before I'd managed to see who she was.

"Vonnie? Bloody hell! How are you?" I replied, finally recognising Vonnie 'from Fruit and Veg'. Vonnie was quite possibly the most beautiful girl ever to have worked in a supermarket.

"I'm good, really good. I'd love to chat but I've got to get to the hospital, I'm late. It's nice to see you though. Sally said you saved her yesterday… thanks!" she continued before turning to Sally… "See you tonight Sal."

And with that the whirlwind that was 'Vonnie from Fruit and Veg' turned and dashed across the road towards the hospital. Sally finally unlocked the door. I followed her up the stairs to the office, where she thanked me again for taking the delivery job, before handing me a piece of paper.

"This is yours if you want it … a new job came in yesterday afternoon. It's a small company, mainly warehouse work, but with the possibility of helping the accountant out for a couple of hours a day… I told them you were an Excel expert" she explained, before giving an 'I won't say if you don't' smile.

"Oh, and another thing... I'm really sorry about, well, you know... your trainers that night."

"No, please, it was fine... I'm sorry I made you sick. To be fair, that was further than I generally got with girls back then."

Another awkward silence followed. We looked at each other again briefly, sharing a knowing nod that said 'Okay, we've acknowledged it, now let's never discuss it again... ever.'

At that point I should have disappeared into the Computer Room to start confusing myself with how to load the 'Teach Yourself Word' floppy disc but, as ever, I continued the agony.

"It was nice to see Vonnie again; she's still bloody gorgeous, isn't she!"

"Erm, yes... she is" replied Sally, looking surprised to see me still loitering by her desk.

"Are you two good friends?" I continued.

"Yes, actually we live together" said Sally, while simultaneously logging on to her computer, firing up the coffee machine and rearranging the piles of paper on her desk.

"Flat-sharing, that's cool. Is she okay?"

"Is she okay?" Sally looked up from her desk, now looking confused.

"She said she was going to the hospital... sorry, it's really none of my business" I stepped back having reached that familiar point of having said too much.

"Oh... no, she works there now. She's a Junior Doctor."

"A doctor? Wow! When she said she was going to the hospital and was late... I thought she meant she was pregnant!" I blurted, before continuing, "I'm glad I didn't say anything. That would have been bloody awkward wouldn't it? Seriously though, I'm always putting my foot in it. I just say things out loud without thinking sometimes."

"Really?" Sally looked increasingly uncomfortable. "So, I'm guessing that you don't know about me and Vonnie then?" she added, looking up from her desk, now giving me her full attention.

"Know what?"

"Vonnie is my partner."

"But you're a girl… oh. Oh shit. I'm sorry, I didn't know. You know what I mean, I'm not sorry for you… I'm very happy for you; I just mean I'm sorry that I said she was gorgeous… and pregnant. Not that she looks pregnant. I didn't mean she was fat; she isn't… she's got an amazing figure. Oh shit. I'm sorry."

"Stop!" Sally raised her palm towards me. "James… It's okay, really."

For a moment we both enjoyed the sound of silence.

"Okay. Thank you, I'm really sorry for being such a gobby twat, but I'm very happy for you both, you make a great couple."

I managed a whole sentence without causing further damage.

"Thank you" replied Sally, sounding as relieved as me.

"Just one more thing…" I gingerly muttered.

"What?" replied Sally; the short lived relief visibly drained from her face as she looked up.

"Was it because of that kiss?"

"Erm, no… I just hadn't worked it out back then" answered Sally.

"That's good to know" I countered, sounding relieved.

I wasn't enjoying this conversation and neither was Sally. By now we both looked exhausted, as if we'd just completed an utter bastard of a day at work, even though it was only 8am.

"Having said that though… you were the last boy I ever kissed" she added, with a mischievous grin taking over her face.

"I guess I deserved that" I conceded, to which Sally took a bow in acknowledgement.

With that, I walked over to the computer booth.

"Sally… I think I'll just re-do the Excel session again today; I'll leave the Word one. I want to make a good go of the new job tomorrow… I don't think I can face coming in here and seeing you again… it's too stressful!"

"Sounds like a plan" she agreed without hesitation.

The next day, Plan G began.

Plan G – Accountancy

The job was great, allowing me to fund monthly additions to my Adidas trainer collection and to keep my weekends free for the Wanderers. Although I spent most of the day in the warehouse, I got to spend a little time helping the accountant, honing my less than basic Excel skills and, after a few months, I enrolled on a night school class so that I might understand some of the technical terms he used.

After Plans A, B, C, D, E and F had seen me fall flat on my face, I'd somehow stumbled on Plan G, accountancy. I'd been crap at everything else, so decided to give it a go. G-Plan was Wycombe's past, but an unlikely Plan G looked like being my future.

Over the next five years, Plan G had continued to flourish. I'd moved on from the agency job and now I got to sit in this nice comfy chair, in this nice warm corporate office, with this wonderful view of Adams Park.

As I reminisced, a colleague popped his head around my office cubicle. He was holding a piece of paper. He looked serious.

"James, have you seen this?"

"Seen what?" I inquired innocently. I'd been so busy daydreaming that I'd yet to turn my computer on.

"There's a meeting… downstairs… in ten minutes. It's compulsory. We've been bought out!"

4 - This is the one

The staff canteen was packed; row after row of chairs had hastily been arranged and every seat was taken. More people stood at the back, others crouched in the aisles; I'd no idea that so many people worked here.

"... I didn't see this coming. I've just walked into it this morning, just like you."

"... To recap, all production will continue on site for the short-term, with shared-service resources transferring to our new parent company's European Head Office."

"... We will be reaching out to you shortly regarding consultation periods, severance arrangements and exit strategies."

The Head of Human Resources waited for questions, looking visibly shaken himself; the room fell silent. I could see people crying and, although I wasn't grasping the full magnitude of what was happening, it didn't sound good. I was sitting next to the Receptionist. I'd never seen her without a smile during my two years with the company but, today, her face was ashen. In a barely audible voice, unrecognisable from the one that vibrantly greeted every visitor, she tearfully spoke...

"I've worked here since I left school... 40 years... what am I going to do?"

I wanted to blurt out "What! You've worked here for 40 years? Seriously, how old are you? Did you leave school when you were 5-years-old? You look amazing considering!" but I thought better of it, and so replied with no more than a sympathetic smile.

Now didn't feel like the best time to enquire about Smudger's job prospects either.

There wasn't much accounting done on the 3rd floor that morning. I spent my time drifting around, listening to various viewpoints and trying to garner an opinion of my own. I loved working in this corporate environment. I'd ended up here more by luck that judgement, and whilst I only had a short walk each morning, some of my colleagues willingly commuted for hours. This was a good place to work, and it attracted top professionals. Being around them had inspired me to keep pursuing my exams and to become a 'proper' accountant. I'd only planned on doing a few low level exams initially. I'd just wanted to understand some of the technical jargon, but I'd grown and so had my ambitions. I'd come a long way from marching into Sally Cinnamon's office demanding 'to learn computers'.

The rationale driving the takeover started to become clear. We had a blockbuster drug about to hit the market; a drug to safeguard jobs and bring the company untold riches. Well, that had been the plan. Basically, the big boys liked the look of our new football more than their own and had taken it away. To add insult to injury, they weren't even going to let us play anymore.

Everybody was dealing with the bombshell in their own way, regardless of age or seniority. Some office juniors were already on their phones to recruitment agencies and updating their CVs, while some senior managers were sat at their desks holding head in hands. My response was in line with my initial reaction to most things; I was just a bit confused. It slowly started to sink in that I didn't have a choice about whether I was staying or going. I was going; I was going in six weeks' time. I was going back to the jobless masses, again. As I watched my friends arranging interviews, I wondered if Sally was still working at the local agency. When I got back to my desk I found that she was; she had already left a message to say that she'd heard the news. I was to call her back as soon as possible to discuss 'several exciting opportunities'. In a daze I decided to take a stroll up to my girlfriend's flat instead. I needed to find out who Wycombe had drawn in the FA Cup, and also to escape the atmosphere in the office.

Millwall?

Millwall away?

Millwall at The Den?

The day couldn't get any worse. Of all of the teams in the draw, Millwall were the highest ranked; top of our league whilst we were sat mid-table.

I walked back to work; the spring that had been in my step earlier had definitely sprung. I took a few deep breaths and tried to figure out how I felt. I wasn't angry like some, and after the initial shock I wasn't in a state of panic. I was pleasantly surprised by my lack of worry. The past few years had improved my stock with regards to being employable. Plan G had really been working out and I now had some tangible skills to offer potential employers. It felt good to think that, instead of scouring the vacancy pages of the local newspaper and narrowing down the search by eliminating the

99% of jobs I knew I couldn't do, I would be able to call Sally and say "I'm looking to do this... and I want to earn that." But most of all, I was impressed by the fact that I hadn't reverted to type and cried in public. Maybe I was growing up at last; just that bit later than everyone else.

I was taking the news better than some, but I was disappointed; it didn't seem fair. This was just a chess game to some corporate high-flyers. My colleagues and I were the pawns, unceremoniously being knocked from the board. It didn't seem to matter if you worked for a hometown furniture factory or a global pharmaceutical giant, you were still just a pawn in someone else's game. Unfortunately, most of these pawns had mortgages to pay and families to feed. I kept coming back to the same conclusion - it didn't seem fair.

The HR department had been very busy while the rest of us had been digesting the morning's news. When I returned to my desk I was handed a letter by my boss.

"That's your settlement package" he advised. "Take a look and we'll catch up later... are you okay?"

I nodded and smiled. I was okay, although the fact that some of my colleagues had already arranged job interviews was making me think I was being slightly slow on the uptake. I reassured myself that having arranged an interview for the next day, less than four hours after being told you were being made redundant, was slightly on the eager side; although I really should think about returning that call from Sally. I still didn't like picking up the phone though, following my six day telesales career, so that could wait. Seeing how much redundancy I was going to get was of greater importance right now, so I opened the envelope.

I stared at the page for a while. My mind went into overdrive. This just couldn't be right. Three month's pay plus notice period, even though I only had to work half of my three month notice - plus holiday entitlement?

I read it again.

'That's seven months' pay... I've only worked here a couple of years; at best they'll give me a month a year, surely?'

The letter looked too good to be true.

'Crap, this must be a mistake. I'll have to tell my boss. But what if I don't? No, someone would find out. But if we're all getting sacked, who'd be left to find out? Someone would... someone from the new owners; they'd do an audit... they'd find out... they'd scour the world and hunt me down.'

I tried to calm myself. I'd just been given an erroneous letter, that's all... no big deal. Having barely survived a torturous week as a teen waiting for the fallout from my 'caught on camera, flicking the two-fingered salute' incident at Loakes Park, I certainly wasn't about to defraud my employer.

"Phil, can I have a word?"

Phil was probably the coolest Finance Director possible; we shared a love of the Manchester music scene and football. He just didn't fit the stereotype of someone befitting his position. Even when he'd interviewed me he'd been wearing scruffy jeans and a T-shirt. He had sat alongside a smartly dressed young lady from HR and after just 15 minutes asked her to 'complete the rest of the stuff'. He got up and shook my hand saying he was heading away for the weekend. I'd assumed his casual attire was due to his trip, but that was just his style. During the interview he'd found out that I liked The Stone Roses and The Charlatans, I supported Wycombe Wanderers, and that I played football for the pub team that the company sponsored. If I'd realised he was leaving so soon I would have also tried to mention some of my work experience. As the door closed behind him the straight-laced HR girl looked up from her notepad, giving me a very serious look; then threw her pen at me from across the table.

"You don't even recognise me do you!" she laughed.

"Erm, what?"

"I had the misfortune to watch you play football on Sunday before kicking your arse at pool in the pub. You don't even remember me... I'm sorry, but there is no way we're employing you!"

My jaw dropped, it was my friend's new girlfriend. She'd been dealt the dubious honour of being 'brought to football' for the previous couple of weekends, which in our circles meant 'it was serious'.

"Becky! You look different like that..." I said, waving a pointed finger in her general direction.

"Like what?" she replied, sounding concerned.

"...Like a grown-up! In that power-suit and make-up... oh Becky, I'm so sorry."

33

I cupped my increasingly crimson face in my hands.

"You did good James... Phil liked you, he gave me the signal."

"The signal?"

"I can't divulge any more" she stated with mock sternness.

As we got up to leave, Becky continued...

"Oh, James, just one more thing; play well this Sunday... Alan is unbearable if you lot lose. We're going to the cinema after your game... I could do without his sulks all afternoon."

As she escorted me through the building back to the reception desk Becky put her 'work-face' back on and, in a very business-like manner, thanked me for attending and said that I would hear from her 'in due course'. The following Saturday I was in bed by 10pm, and sober. This was the first time I'd tried this pre-match ritual since the age of 17. I like to think that my vastly improved performance not only won us the game that Sunday, but got me the job too.

The next two years had flown by, and today, Becky was the busiest person in the building.

I hovered outside my boss's office.

"Yes James, what's the problem mate... is it the package?"

"I think this is wrong Phil."

I pushed the letter across the desk towards him.

"It looks right to me... you've been here for two years haven't you? What were you expecting?"

"Not that much!" I yelped, failing miserably to conceal a smile.

He laughed, looking relieved, and then asked what I was going to do next, but I wasn't really listening; I was in shock. I'd never had money. My parents had never let me go without, but we didn't have much. I'd never understood how some students could afford cars and 'went travelling' during the summer, while I pushed shopping trolleys just to cover the cost of my Wanderers season-ticket. I returned to my desk, once more in a daze, trying to make sense of it all.

An hour later, when one of my colleagues came over to inform me of the three job interviews he'd set up, I was still staring at my letter.

"Not bad for a day's work... tax-free too!"

"Tax free?"

I wondered how everyone else knew so much, yet I knew so little.

"Yep, we don't earn enough for it to get taxed... great eh?" he said, slapping me on the back, before heading off to tell more folk about his interviews.

Whilst daydreaming through my teens and into adulthood I'd always clung to the thought that one day something good would happen; something out of the ordinary; something that would let me do the things I'd always wanted to do and see the things I'd always wanted to see; dreams of visiting China or Easter Island. One day I'd win the Premium Bonds or the Pools, maybe Spot-The-Ball. Then, when the National Lottery started, I rushed home from the pub early after football and sat in front of the television for the first ever draw. It was with utter disbelief that none of my six numbers came up. Something had to happen. It wasn't worth contemplating that I'd trundle through life without a lucky break. Deep down, despite my stuttering start to adult life, I knew I wasn't stupid, but also that I wasn't going to finance those childhood dreams on my modest wage. As I sat back looking across to Adams Park it dawned on me; this was it, this was my 'something good' finally happening.

"Are you just staring at your football ground again? Oh to have a room with a view" came a familiar voice from behind me.

"Don't I know you from somewhere? Your face looks vaguely familiar... hmm, I just can't place it."

I ducked as Becky's pen flew across the room towards me again; my friendly HR representative had surfaced from her basement office for a few minutes.

"How's your day?" I asked.

"I've had better" she said. "So, what are you going to do? Have you told Cathy yet?"

"No, I'll see her after work. But you know what... I'm thinking about just taking off, going to see a bit of the world. I thought I'd missed my chance... what with having a proper job at last."

There, I'd said it out loud. And it sounded bloody fantastic.

"Good for you. I wish I could do that. I've just bought a flat, so I'll need to get another job, pronto. I thought you and Cathy were looking too?" Becky said, before noticing a gaggle of people loitering nearby, all wanting to speak to her.

"We are... well, we were. Anyway, your audience awaits. See you later Becky."

I left work early that day and waited for Cathy outside her office. She looked surprised as she saw me.

"Leave the car parked here tonight... we're off to get drunk. I've got something I need to talk to you about."

5 - Into the Lions' Den

"So... what do you think?" I asked, sinking the remains of my second pint.

Cathy sat bouncing in her chair, clapping excitedly and knocking four glasses and an ashtray flying in the process.

"How soon can I hand my notice in?"

My girlfriend wasn't one to hide her feelings, and her reaction suggested she was okay with me not taking the sensible options of looking for a new job immediately, or focussing on completing my exams, or putting my redundancy windfall into the deposit for a house.

"Where are you taking me then?"

Cathy loved to travel and have a good time; she wasn't overly enamoured with her job and she had no concept of money. With hindsight, she would have agreed to the plan even without the redundancy. She was in complete disbelief about the day's chain of events, events that had conspired to find us sitting in a pub on a Monday night creating a world map on the table out of beer mats.

"Stop!" she said suddenly, as I returned with more drinks and beer mats.

Crap. What had she thought of that could scupper our increasingly drunken plans?

"You do realise you're going to miss half of the football season, right?"

She knew I hadn't thought about that at all. It was a high risk strategy to bring the football-factor up, but I knew that this really was the once in a lifetime chance I'd yearned for.

"Well?" she added after a long pause.

"Well... we've drawn Millwall away in the FA Cup... so we're as good as out of that for another year. No, let's go for it."

My response was met by further hysterical squeals and bouncing, followed by more smashing of glass.

I returned to the office the next morning feeling slightly the worse for wear. It looked like I hadn't been the only person to have hit the bottle. I was conscious that, although I'd been celebrating a golden opportunity, most were commiserating the loss of the income that fed, clothed and sheltered their families. The atmosphere wasn't nice; we were all going through the motions in the knowledge that our efforts were no longer wanted or required. It was dispiriting but also sad. These people, who spent their working lives together, would soon be going their separate ways. I was glad to make it through the day, before taking the next week off to prepare for the dreaded maths exam.

I knew it was going to be difficult, but with my employment status about to change significantly it would be helpful to have this exam successfully completed and on my CV upon return from my travels. Yes, I was finally getting a chance to resurrect my Plan B, but it was only going to be a temporary once-around-the-world detour from Plan G. This exam would prove to be a real bottleneck if I failed. It had to be completed before I could sit the final set of four papers, which were more strategic in nature and far more achievable for someone who thought like me. That's not to suggest I was a strategic guru by any means; more that I was just truly awful at the pure maths paper. I would need a miracle to pass it, but with the redundancy package, I'd already had one of those this week!

A week later, I came out of my self-imposed exam exile, just in time for the Wanderers' next league game, at home to Bournemouth. The exam had proved to be as painful as expected, whilst at work, we plodded on towards our leaving dates. December had arrived, and I was ready for a fix of my football team and a Saturday with my friends. I broke the news about my work closing down, and about my plans to travel the world. Everyone was shocked, but excited. If I was happy, they were happy. Smudger was a bit annoyed that I hadn't managed to get him a job, but seemed to be appeased by the fact that I had lost mine in the process.

Following my announcement, I waited for the inevitable question. Not "where are you going first?" or "how long will you be away?" It was Smudger who bit first.

"Who's getting your season ticket then?" he asked, to cheers from all.

And so the day began, full of early festive cheer and high hopes for the game. Bournemouth soon put paid to that by thrashing Wycombe 3-0 but, as ever, the result would not deter us from having a celebratory drink that evening. I would need to savour these moments, as there would only be a few more before I headed for distant lands. On the pitch it didn't bode well for next weekend's trip to South London; Millwall in the FA Cup.

A combination of Christmas shopping, a booze cruise, 'work do' hangovers and overtime opportunities conspired to find me travelling solo to South Bermondsey. This felt very strange as in all the years I'd been travelling around the country with Buz and the Roobarbs, we'd always had at least a car load wanting to travel and, generally, a dozen or so. When the team had entered the unparalleled period of success under the stewardship of Martin O'Neill, we couldn't find buses big enough. Be it in 'White Lightning' - Pat's long-lost Capri, Lee or Oggy's paint-filled vans, Silver's delivery truck, Ian's train deals or Buz's work's minibus (which he hired for a suspiciously high volume of 'family weddings'), we always got to our destination just as the bar was opening, regardless of whether we were travelling to Carlisle near the Scottish border, or just across the county border to Slough. As the train rumbled on, I realised that I'd soon be getting used to travelling without them. I would leave England in mid-January, just as soon as the Christmas holiday-season flight prices dropped. I hadn't been to many places in the world; in fact I hadn't been to that many places at all unless it involved attending a Wycombe Wanderers away game. But I was sure that if I could manage travelling around the country with my rapscallion friends, then Cathy and I could manage the rest of the world without too much fuss.

My first trip with the Roobarbs had been to an FA Cup game at Kettering nine years before. An old school friend, Craig, was travelling to the game on a coach organised by a work colleague. They had a couple of spare seats and, as we had yet to work out our own travel plans, my mate Jason and I said we'd tag along. We waited in the railway station car park that Saturday morning, armed with refreshments from the off-licence, and watched as a brand new mini-coach pulled up. As we got in Craig shouted, beckoning us to the back of the bus. We started edging along the central aisle, offering mumbled greetings to the bus full of strangers as we passed, until one of them got up and stood in our path.

"Welcome aboard gentlemen, and welcome to Busby Travel... we'll be travelling at an altitude of about two-feet for this FA Cup special to Kettering... please make yourself familiar with the fridge down there at the front, and the bog at the back. Now, where's my cash?"

He sat down as we handed over our fare, grinning as he counted our money.

"Right, that's my beer money sorted... drive on!"

As soon as he cleared the aisle we scuttled swiftly to our seats at the rear of the bus, directly opposite the toilet; no wonder they were the only two seats left. As we sat down I looked at Jason and he looked at me before simultaneously and silently mouthing the words "that was Pisser!" to each other.

Jason and I were as-thick-as-thieves and travelled everywhere together to watch the football. If we weren't on a coach we were risking life and limb, hanging precariously over the tail-lift on his dad's delivery van. He had been with me that fateful day when we'd first been exposed (quite literally) to Pisser and his antics, and so the panic in my eyes was mirrored by his. We both turned and glared at Craig who just looked bemused.

"What's wrong? This is class... tables with lamps, a bog... it's even got a fridge!"

Craig had a point; this did appear a classy way to travel. Had Pisser mellowed with age? I was 19 and it had been six years since the legend of Pisser had been created. Maybe he'd grown up; I certainly had. Well, I'd got taller.

As the coach roared into life a chorus of beer cans opening in unison set the tone for the remainder of the day. This was brilliant; these were the 'big boys' from my coach trip to York all those years ago. Now I was with them, part of the gang. Pisser, who was actually called Buz, proved to be wonderful company; as did everyone on the bus. But, as the beers flowed there appeared to be no sign of anyone mellowing with age. The initial concern on our faces had soon disappeared, replaced with laughter and smiles that remained for the entire journey. The only concerned face remaining was that of the driver, as it transpired that we were only on the fancy new coach because his old one, which was normally reserved for football bookings, had broken down en route to picking us up. He cursed its ill-timed demise, and the rabble partying in his rear-view mirror.

It turned out to be my turn to leave a lasting impression on Buz that day. The exuberance of youth, and the impossible task of drinking with these hardened professionals, had seen me receive a polite warning from the Kettering police (who advised that my singing could do with less swearing), followed by a less than polite second and final warning. At this stage, ensuring that I learnt from some of his past mistakes, Buz took me under his wing and I avoided further incident. Friendships were formed that day. Watching the Wanderers would never be the same again.

Despite quickly becoming a fully-fledged member of the Roobarb's escapades, I was the junior member. The fact that I was a student only cemented this.

"James? Oh, you mean 'Student' James?" became a familiar term, when booking travel arrangements.

Being a student didn't get me any discount, and being the youngest of the squad definitely didn't get me any preferential treatment. A couple of months after the Kettering trip, I found myself standing with the usual hungover suspects outside a pub at 8am. As usual, we were all looking down the street for a first glimpse of Buz, keen to see what mode of transport he had sourced for the day's adventure. We were heading up to Northwich Victoria to watch the Blues playing at the oldest football ground in the world, The Drill Field. Buz, as normal, was late. Eventually, we saw a people-carrier come screeching around the corner at speed, with Buz (who conveniently couldn't drive), hanging out of the car's sunroof waving his arms in the air in a strange dance. He and our designated driver for the day had come straight from a nightclub.

"We haven't come straight from the club... we had to go and get the hire-car first" corrected Pat, our soon-to-be-asleep chauffeur. This wasn't the most auspicious start.

As Pat curled up on the back seat, a new volunteer to drive was found. The rest of us started to pile into the three rows of seats.

"Buz... what car did you ask for?" I asked.

"The seven-seater."

"Buz... how many of us are there?"

"Me... you... Pat, Nicko and Smudge... Roger, Beany, Mike and Flipper."

He pointed to each person in turn through the car window. "Why?"

I didn't have time to answer before he received a torrent of abuse from everyone except for Pat, who was by now asleep (and wouldn't be waking up until we'd arrived in Northwich).

Ever the optimist, Buz was confident that we could squeeze eight into the seven seats, plus "the student in the boot."

41

"You're the one who cocked up, why do I have to go in the boot?" I protested.

"You're the youngest."

"I'm the tallest" I countered.

"It's not that far, you'll be alright."

"It's nearly 200 miles you twat! You go in the boot!" I protested again, despite realising that I was fighting a losing battle. By now everyone else had managed to secure a seat and, while we'd been debating, Buz had been inching his way backwards and now had his hand firmly on the door handle, leaving me as the last man standing.

"Look, there's a hatch. We can still pass beer through" he said giggling, slamming the door firmly shut behind him.

"Great, just bloody great."

I climbed into the car's boot and assumed the foetal position, before offering my last comments for the next three hours...

"Will one of you tossers at least come and shut me in... if it's not too much trouble?"

I survived the journey, listening to muffled conversations and music through the six-inch-wide hatch, which afforded a small window to the outside world from the darkness in the boot. To be fair, I was fed a constant supply of beer and even got my turn on the cassette player eventually, although I could hardly hear anything above the noise of the car. As ever, we arrived far too early and the pubs were yet to open. The rest of the guys stood looking impatiently at their watches outside the pub that Buz had insisted we visit. He always managed to find a pub that had a fine selection of 'real ales', which generally meant my lager-drinking tastes would be sneered at by a snobby landlord, and that the pub would have no jukebox or, at best, a shite one. Buz banged on the door to remind anyone inside that it was nearing 11am and opening time. I needed to stretch my legs after the cramped journey and so took a stroll into town. Before long I stumbled across Omega Records, which was owned by the manager of The Charlatans who, along with The Stone Roses, do battle in my head on a daily basis for the position of greatest band in the world. It was a pretty standard record shop but with a side room dedicated to The Charlatans. To me it was an Aladdin's Cave and to its owner I was a pay-day.

An hour later I made my way back to the pub laden with signed posters, rare records and even rarer videos. I was ecstatic about my shopping spree; it had made my 'kidnapped hostage' style journey worthwhile. The rest of the Roobarbs were by now comfortable in the pub and were happy to inspect my newly acquired stash of musical rarities. It had been football that brought us all together but, invariably, if you find a passionate football fan you'll find a passionate music fan too; they just go hand in hand. I'd been introduced to Ska, Punk and Northern Soul by the boys, whilst I brought the Manchester baggy-scene into the mix. Unfortunately, on this occasion my passion for music and The Charlatans had got the better of me. I'd spent all my money, but I didn't care; I was happy to wait out the remainder of the day in the car, looking at my new prized possessions. But my friends weren't having any of that, and bought me drinks and paid my way into the game too. I was, however, made to travel in the boot again for the journey home; a journey that was even more uncomfortable than the trip up. Along with my Charlatans stash I now also had to share the boot with a pickaxe that Mike had 'borrowed' from The Drill Field, his rationale being that "if this is the oldest football ground in the world, then this pickaxe must be the oldest pickaxe in the world too... I'm having it."

There were so many memories from away days with my friends that it seemed decidedly flat to be sitting on the train alone. Under normal circumstances I might have decided to give the Millwall match a miss, but my Wanderers games were now running out fast. Just three weeks earlier life had been trundling along quite mundanely, but now I was about to be handed the opportunity of a lifetime in the form of a severance cheque. I took out my fixture-list to see how many games I had left. It wasn't many. What I really needed was a victory today against Millwall followed by the impossible dream of a glamour-tie against Manchester United or Liverpool in the 3rd Round, preferably at Old Trafford or Anfield. Yes, that would provide the perfect send-off before my travels. All we needed to do was beat top-of-the-table Millwall and play about ten times better than we had against Bournemouth last week.

The train pulled in and I followed the crowds flowing towards The Den, the infamous home of Millwall. I'd been several times before with my mates, but today proved that the saying, 'safety in numbers' doesn't always apply. Millwall supporters had a fearsome reputation, while it was fair to say that fans of Wycombe Wanderers were at the opposite end of the spectrum. If the more extreme element of Millwall's support could be described as a pack of rabid Pit Bulls, Wycombe's faithful were more akin to a dopey Labrador looking for a chocolate drop and a cuddle. In fairness, none of my trips to Millwall had ever resulted in trouble, although we generally marched from the station to the ground quickly, with mouths firmly closed. If we'd ever achieved a decent result we would return to the station at an even greater pace, for fear of annoying the locals. But today, on my own, I appeared to be invisible and was happy to remain so.

Millwall started the game with a confidence befitting their position at the top of the league table. Their vociferous support provided a true lion's roar that reverberated around The Den, pushing the home team forward relentlessly. Time and time again Wycombe were saved by the heroic efforts of goalkeeper Martin Taylor.

Taylor had been a Wanderer for three seasons and was, by far, the best goalkeeper I'd seen representing them. His career had nearly been cut short when, whilst plying his trade for Derby County at a much higher level, he suffered a horrific injury breaking his leg in several places. It was an injury that meant he wouldn't play again for two years, effectively depriving him of his opportunity to make it at the very top level of the game. The injury had been so bad that it left him with a permanent limp. Week after week he made saves that I thought impossible, bringing the crowd to their feet in adoration. Normally, it would take no less than a goal to muster such a response from Wycombe's often docile crowd; for a goalkeeper to provoke such a reaction was unheard of.

As ever, Martin was a hero at The Den and had earned his slice of luck when, late into the second half, the Millwall forwards twice found a way to get the ball past him, only to see it rebound from the goalposts. Wycombe had fought tirelessly and, despite the constant pressure, had managed to deny the elusive winning goal that would have knocked the Chairboys out of the FA Cup for another year. As the referee blew the final whistle the Wycombe fans acclaimed the battling performance, relieved to have seen the team survive to fight another day. I was the most excited of all; the draw would mean a replay, an additional game for me to savour before heading abroad.

At work the following day, Phil was soon at my desk to inform me that he'd booked the company executive box at Adams Park for the replay. The box was directly beneath the seats that my friends and I frequented. Most weeks I would peer down over the balcony to see if there was anyone I knew within the hospitality party, in the hope that I might sneak in after the game for a free beer or two. Generally, there wasn't anyone I recognised, apart from Dave from Payroll. He managed to get himself an invite each and every week, regardless of who was being entertained or doing the entertaining. Dave always smuggled me out a beer at half-time and after the game. The box was normally used by the sales team for entertaining customers but, on the odd occasion that it wasn't being used, I'd invite myself in just to check if the fridge needed emptying of bottles. The finance department didn't have much need for entertaining clients but, as we were all leaving soon anyway, Phil had acted quickly to commandeer the box for his team with the twelve tickets going on a first-come, first-served basis. In truth, there weren't too many 'true-blues' in the office, so he made sure that both the ever-present Dave and I were on the list before publicising the event to the rest of the department.

The day of the replay was a week before Christmas and just three days before the site closed for good. The previous couple of weeks had been surreal and, after the initial shock of the announcement, everyone had started to focus on the future. Despite everyone being in the office as usual, the days were spent updating CV's, looking for new jobs, taking training courses to brush up on skills, and generally appreciating each other's company while we still could. I'd enjoyed working in a big company; there were lots of people my age, also studying for exams and with similar aspirations. The fact that I could see colleagues applying themselves and, as a result, getting on in life, was a real motivation. After so many disappointments and false starts, my Plan G really looked like a viable option for the longer term, even if I was planning to put it on hold for the next six months. Whilst everyone busied away, I worked hard too, mainly on planning potential routes around the world and working out budgets to see how long we could afford to stay away. A constant stream of people appeared at my desk, offering recommendations of places to visit, and also to tell me how they wished they could 'just bugger off' too. But because of children, partners, mortgages, elderly parents and a host of other good reasons, the remainder of the workforce, apart from me, seemed to be doing the sensible thing. One of my mates in the office, Russy, advised that I set up a Hotmail account so that I could keep everyone updated on my adventures, and also for networking when I returned and had to start looking for a job.

Networking? I started to panic. Was I being a bit stupid? Would I be able to get another job when I returned after six months with no more than a sun tan? I'd not exactly had a spectacular start to my working life following college. Would things really be that different next time around? I quickly set about updating my own CV using the best bits of everyone else's. Neatly summarised onto a single piece of paper I thought I looked quite employable. Five years of practical experience, with two decent employers and some relevant accountancy exams. It looked infinitely better than my old CV; a list of temporary jobs, along with the fact that 'I liked football and socialising'.

Panic over, it was time to file the CV away and send a test Hotmail all the way across the office to Russy, before heading up the road to the football. It was already dark and the floodlights were on, illuminating the rooftops across the estate. Any pre-match nerves I had were drowned in the executive box. We threw ourselves an impromptu early leaving party with everyone enjoying the food and drink in great quantities, happy in the knowledge that the company's new owners would eventually be picking up the bill. Dave and I led the way and, despite the rest of the group not being Wanderers supporters, they all adopted the team for the night, even Matt and Russy who were Oxford fans and, therefore, local rivals. Our section of the hospitality tier appeared more vocal than the average corporate party. We weren't there to broker business deals or network with potential suppliers; we were there to eat, drink, and cheer the Blues into the 3rd Round of the FA Cup.

As the players warmed up I took great pleasure in parading around beneath my Roobarb friends, who were sat up in our normal seats. I taunted them with my free beers and food before sneaking a tray of sandwiches up to them in the 'cheap' seats. Nobody in the box minded, as we'd purposely ordered more food than was humanly possible for us to eat. I soon wished that I hadn't bothered, as the remnants of prawn sandwiches repeatedly rained down on me throughout lulls in the game.

Despite becoming honorary Wycombe fans for the evening, my colleagues were still accountants at heart. This was proved when the resident bookmaker came through to take bets on the game and most of them put their cash on Millwall to win. It was understandable, even if a blatant act of treachery. Millwall could easily have won the original tie the previous Sunday, and they were still top of our league. Dave and I both tried to prove a point by betting on our team, even if deep down we didn't expect to see our money again. After the initial game, Millwall's manager claimed that only their muddy pitch had stopped his team from winning and that Wycombe wouldn't be so lucky in the replay. But, as the evening progressed, Wycombe put up a wonderful performance and it was they who took advantage of the pristine Adams Park pitch, attacking their opposition in the same vein as Millwall had done the week before. The players believed they could win the game, and the crowd responded to their efforts. As expectation levels began to rise, so did the volume around the ground which, much to the relief of the clientele in the other executive boxes, drowned out the encouragement that Dave and I had been giving since kick-off. Twenty minutes into the game Wycombe made the pressure they'd been exerting pay; Millwall conceded a free-kick directly in front of our seats. With advice from both me and Dave ringing in his ears the Blues midfield warrior, Steve Brown, drilled the ball into the penalty area where it was flicked on by Paul McCarthy directly into the path of the on-rushing centre-forward, Andy Rammell, who rose above the defenders to head the ball down into the corner of the Millwall net. Dave and I leapt from our seats almost as high as Rammell, followed by our friends. I looked around to see the delighted celebrations up in the stand behind us, and also those who had foolishly sat next to Smudger assuming the crash position as he swung his arms with wild abandon.

"There's a long way to go yet lads" Gibbo helpfully leaned over to remind us, but Dave and I were too busy celebrating to care.

Millwall weren't to be beaten easily though. Immediately, they were stung into action by Wycombe's goal, and by the reaction of their travelling supporters who demanded a quick response. They soon had that response. Within five minutes the Wycombe faithful were sat back in their seats as Millwall scored an equaliser.

"Told you" quipped Gibbo, once again providing his unwanted insight on proceedings. "You scored too early... 3-1 to Millwall; you just watch."

Gibbo sat back, using his fingers and all his Treasury know-how to calculate how much he would win from his wager on a Millwall victory.

Much to my relief, Wycombe didn't buckle to any onslaught and carried on playing as they had in the first 20 minutes. Again, the momentum gradually built as the game drew towards the end of the first half. Wycombe won a corner and the crowd roared its encouragement. Dave and I stood, leaning over the barrier to get as close to the action as possible, as if preparing to head the ball into the net ourselves. The corner sailed over without any apparent danger to the Millwall goal, but was then headed back into the congested penalty-box. All eyes in the stadium followed the ball as it first bounced into the grass before looping up into the dark sky, illuminated by the floodlights, towards the imposing frame of Paul McCarthy. His eyes were fixed on the ball too. But, unlike the crowd, the referee, or the other 21 players on the pitch, all of whom appeared to be frozen in time, he twisted towards the ball. Acrobatically, he threw his legs up over his body allowing him to hook the ball over his head and catapulting it into the top corner of the Millwall net. Adams Park exploded into wild celebration at the sight of such a spectacular goal, a goal that had restored Wycombe's lead and completely changed the half-time team talks of both managers. Wycombe just needed to hold on for another 45 minutes to achieve a famous victory, while Millwall had to somehow raise themselves again to get back on terms with the home side who had turned the tables on them from the first game. Vitally, Wycombe had managed to convert their superior play into a lead, which had been Millwall's only failing at The Den.

The second half saw both teams fighting desperately to stay in the competition, with one side attacking and then the other; Millwall determined to get back on level-terms, with Wycombe looking to score a decisive third by exposing the gaps in the visitors defence as they increasingly committed players forward. Both teams came close to achieving their respective objectives and, with only seconds remaining, Millwall raced forward again. The ball was crossed to their dangerous attacker Neil Harris, who headed the ball towards the Wycombe goal. Martin Taylor was beaten but, as in the last minute of the first game, the ball hit the post and bounced away to safety.

The battle was won. Victory belonged to Wycombe Wanderers. Gibbo had lost his money and been made to eat his words. Dave and I hugged triumphantly before heading back into the warmth of the hospitality suite to toast the victory long into the night. And to wait for the bookmaker who would soon be bringing us our winnings!

We had made it into the 3rd Round once more and the winner of tonight's game had already been awarded another home tie, this time against Division One side Grimsby. It wasn't to be the Manchester United or Liverpool tie I'd hoped for, but it would still present an even tougher task than beating Millwall. For now though, that didn't matter; while the others savoured the free drinks, Dave and I could also dream of just one more victory, a victory that would send us into the unknown realms of the FA Cup 4th Round.

6 - Last one out turns off the lights

Friday was strange. I went to work, as normal. I chatted, as normal. I went to the canteen, as normal. I replied to emails, as normal. I gazed across towards Adams Park, as normal. Then, at 3pm, people starting turning off their computers and saying goodbye. Not 'See you on Monday, have a nice weekend' goodbyes, but proper 'Bye then, it's been nice knowing you' goodbyes.

I felt a mix of emotions; panic, rejection, anger, sadness, excitement, disbelief. This was really happening. After all the talk during the previous six weeks, the time had come to down tools and leave. Just leave and never come back. I joined in with the surreal making of small talk, hugging and wishing everyone all the best, whilst concentrating on not contributing to the tears. I was sad to be leaving, but even sadder for those who desperately didn't want to. As I walked out through the gates for the final time, I felt as I had on the day my first girlfriend had dumped me. I'd worked hard for the company, but now they didn't want me anymore, and so that was that, I had no say in the matter. Just like when I was 19 and the girl told me she didn't want to see me anymore. That was another occasion when I'd shown enough confidence in my masculinity to cry like a baby in public; for the entire 50 mile bus ride back to Wycombe. My dad was waiting to pick me up, parked outside the turnstiles of the recently vacated Loakes Park. As I dejectedly walked up the alleyway from the bus station past the gasworks the ground looked sad and lonely, not too dissimilar from me. Nineteen and the owner of a broken heart; I hadn't known anyone or anything that could make me feel this bad, apart from Wycombe Wanderers getting relegated. It had taken 18 years to find a girl remotely interested in me, and I was certain it would take as long to find another. My dad, a proud Aberdonian of few words, was true to form.

"Listen, there isn't anything I can say to make you feel better... just try to avoid women who smoke or get bad PMT."

He handed me four cans of lager, then gave me a hug.

"These might help too."

I took my dad's advice regarding alcohol, cracking open the first can before he'd started the engine. With regards to avoiding women who got bad PMT, I didn't even know what PMT was and I wasn't about to ask him. It was all I could do to focus on breathing; complicating things would have just invoked another flood of tears. As for the pearl of wisdom about avoiding girls who smoked, I didn't envisage a queue of girls forming to offer a shoulder to cry on, be they smokers or not, so decided to discount that advice too. Besides, it was summer and long lazy days in the beer gardens of the High Street beckoned; and all pubs stank of cigarettes anyway.

They say that time is a great healer and, as the summer wore on, it became apparent that being 19 years old, single and broken-hearted were all attractive traits to girls. I also discovered that a derelict town centre football ground could provide a unique setting for impromptu 'after closing time' parties and moonlit heart-to-heart's that lasted until the sun rose over the Hospital End terrace. Just when I thought that the cherished Loakes Park of my childhood was gone forever, it invited me back in; gifting a summer of love before sending me on my way into adulthood at Adams Park.

Those beers from my dad, along with his hug, had started my healing process back then. So it seemed only fitting to try the same remedy again nine years later, only this time after being jilted by my employers. The Friday night beers would help, and the bank transfer a week later should seal the deal. The weekend provided a distraction from my unemployment. The Wanderers kicked off the Christmas festivities on Saturday, beating Swansea 2-1 in the league. The game was followed by the Roobarb Christmas 'office' party in the pub, which lasted into the early hours. The excesses of Friday and Saturday should have been followed by a Sunday of recovery, but Sunday was Christmas Eve and I didn't do Christmas Eves quietly.

Scott and Sanj would both be back from London, and David, Jason, Mario, Danny, Jamie, Willsy and Smasher would be out too. Even Alan, who had inadvertently helped me to get the job I'd just lost by dating Becky from HR, would be making his annual visit to the High Street, which really wasn't his style. These were my oldest friends, and this would be our last gathering before my adventures. As tradition dictated, we would hold court in the pubs of town from opening time until closing. Other friends would come and go, taking a break from their last minute shopping; often old school pals we'd gone a year without seeing, safe in the knowledge that, come Christmas Eve, we would be there again, and so would they. It was a test of endurance and there would inevitably be casualties, but it was a tradition that needed to be upheld. That is, upheld for as long as we could hold ourselves up. Christmas Day mornings would often prove challenging, but these Christmas Eves with friends were worth it.

We always started by catching up on news about friends and family, our jobs, bands we'd seen and football; then alcohol would invariably lead us down the most random of paths. But, on this occasion, there was an added topic.

"The plan is to fly to Thailand and stay for a couple of months, then a month over in Hong Kong and China... down to Australia for about six weeks... over to Easter Island to see the big stone heads, then Chile and finally New York before heading home to find a job."

A thoughtful pause followed.

"You bastard" replied Scotty.

"You complete bastard" added Mario.

"Are you going to get work anywhere?" asked Jamie.

"Nope, work would only spoil it... besides, I'm crap at most things, remember?"

We drank and talked until the sun went down, then danced and drank more until the early hours of Christmas morning before heading home to be welcomed by the buckets that our parents, girlfriends and sisters had strategically placed by our beds as early Christmas presents; a reminder of many a Christmas Past.

7 - Grimsby

Christmas with my family and New Year with Cathy's soon passed. The gifts of sun cream and diarrhoea tablets were gratefully received, but the present I was really waiting for arrived on New Year's Eve; my redundancy. It was all there; everything that Phil had confirmed as being correct. By my standards, I was rich, rich beyond my wildest dreams. There was only one thing to do; start spending.

As soon as the holiday season was over we headed into London to finally cement the plans I'd been sketching in my office notepad for the past six weeks. Sitting in the travel centre, waiting to speak with an agent, I gazed at the giant map of the world covering the walls and ceiling.

"It's really big isn't it?" I declared, thinking out loud.

Cathy looked confused... "What, this office?"

"No, the planet... this map makes it look massive. I hadn't really thought about it before."

Cathy had that familiar look in her eye, where she wasn't sure if I was trying to be funny or if I really was that stupid. We had been together just three days short of seven years, yet she still hadn't quite worked me out.

On what proved to be a fateful day, also three days short of seven years ago, Norwich City had knocked Wycombe out of the FA Cup 3rd Round, thus, making 1994 just another year when my dreams had been dashed. I didn't know at the time that the long haired Norwich supporter who ran onto the pitch before falling flat on his face following Norwich's second goal had been to visit his sister-in-law before the game. I didn't know that his sister-in-law was a girl from Norwich who was studying in High Wycombe. I didn't know that his sister-in-law was 'that' girl with the cool hair who I'd been admiring from afar for the past year, and generally boring my mates about on a daily basis. I didn't know that his sister-in-law was going out that evening to The Roundabout which, by coincidence, was the same pub where I was meeting Jason and David. I didn't know that, due to drowning my FA Cup sorrows, I would be arriving late, so late in fact that David would get drunk before my arrival; so drunk that he'd think it a good idea to tell the pitch-invader's sister-in-law that I was crazy about her. But he did, and now here we were seven years later sitting together in a travel agency, about to seriously broaden our horizons.

Two hours later and a couple of thousand pounds poorer, we meandered back through the streets of central London to Marylebone Station. The next train to Wycombe was the slow train, but we didn't care; we didn't need to be anywhere in a rush. My next pressing engagement was at Adams Park 24 hours later for the cup-tie against Grimsby, then a return to London next week to collect visas for visiting China. A few days after that, on Wednesday 17th January, we needed to be at Heathrow to board a flight to Thailand.

We sat in the carriage comparing the bumps on our arms from the painful vaccinations we'd received at the travel centre. To add insult to injury, we'd paid a small fortune for the privilege. A city worker lowered his Financial Times beneath his nose for just long enough to send us a withering scowl, before raising it again to distance himself from the two obvious junkies sitting opposite. Even if we had been junkies, at least we were only taking up one seat each on what was becoming an increasingly congested commuter train, unlike Mr Financial Times who, with the aid of his briefcase, raincoat and fully opened newspaper was taking up the majority of the four seat section we were sharing.

"So Cathy, tell me... what are you looking forward to most over the next six months, when we'll be travelling the world?" I asked in an intentionally loud voice, whilst gesturing towards Mr Financial Times.

Cathy's eyes lit up.

"Well James, that's a great question. I think I will mostly enjoy not having to sit on commuter trains opposite arrogant, obnoxious pricks who think they are better than us" she replied with a sugary sweet smile.

Shit, I thought she'd just say 'Australia or Thailand'.

The knuckles of fat fingers visibly whitened as their grip on the newspaper tightened. I instantly regretted the little game I'd initiated, and also the pints of cider I'd bought Cathy in the pub around the corner from the station. Oh well, it wasn't the first time I'd been sitting on this train recently in an awkward situation. All we needed now was the Beaconsfield-bound Miss World to join us and, to be fair, she would probably be the only person in London with a figure capable of squeezing onto the edge of the seat remaining next to Mr Financial Times. If she did get on, she would also get to see that I hadn't been lying about having a girlfriend.

The next day, as ever, Buz left his seat just before half-time and missed seeing a goal. Unfortunately, this time he missed Grimsby taking the lead. Beating Millwall had been a great achievement, but Grimsby were proving an even tougher challenge. They were plying their trade in the division above, which meant bigger budgets, better players and higher expectations. The first half had proved this and, although Wycombe were holding their own against the visitors, Grimsby seemed assured in all that they did. When they scored it didn't come as a surprise. My friends filed out towards the bar for a half-time beer but I remained in my seat looking around the ground, trying to etch the images into my memory. It was only January but this was my last game of the season; it looked like being Wycombe's last FA Cup game too.

As winter threw a veil over Adams Park for the second half, Wycombe toiled but to no avail. With just 15 minutes remaining, Martin Taylor launched the ball high into the gloomy sky from deep inside Wycombe territory. Paul McCarthy had been given licence to abandon his defensive post in a final throw of the dice by the Blues' manager, Lawrie Sanchez, to try and force an equaliser, and it was McCarthy who rose highest to connect with the ball as it came back to earth following Taylor's huge punt upfield. In an instant, the ball fell into the path of Andy Rammell who had a clear sight of the Grimsby goal in front of him. Rammell was a clinical finisher, having earned his living for the past decade by converting chances like this into goals. There wasn't another player in the team who I would rather the chance fall to. The ball sat up perfectly in front of him, Rammell pulled back his right leg as if cocking the trigger of a gun, ready to fire. This was Wycombe's chance. Inexplicably, as he thrust his trusty right boot towards the ball, he mistimed his shot terribly, sending his foot flying past the ball and missing it completely. The momentum of the Wycombe forward and desperately tracking Grimsby defenders continued to send them towards the visiting team's goalmouth and the ball bounced up, embarrassingly hitting Rammell on the back of his leg, stopping it in its tracks behind them. The ball fell to Wycombe's Matt Brady, who had the presence of mind to delicately slide it to his left towards the on-rushing Paul McCarthy, who was in a far better position to shoot. Within a flash, Rammell's blushes were spared and the Chairboys' players and supporters alike were sent into ecstatic raptures. McCarthy had once again smashed the ball into the top corner of the opposition's net; just as he had so spectacularly against Millwall. The Blues were back in the game and, in the dying minutes, almost stole victory outright when young Andy Baird powered a brave header goalwards, only to see his effort spectacularly thwarted by the flying goalkeeper's outstretched hand, thus earning Grimsby a replay back at their own stadium ten days later.

Having been unable to make home advantage count, the chances of beating Grimsby away were slim. That concern was for another day though, and the Wanderers and Grimsby supporters alike rose to salute the efforts of the players as they left the stage, before themselves departing the scene for the long journey north to Grimsby, or for the home fans, the short journey to the bar under the stand. I peered down to the executive box below which had been so full of life for the Millwall replay. The lights were out; it was empty and not even Dave was there. I wondered if he'd managed to blag a seat in one of the other boxes, but I couldn't see him. As at half time, I was finding it hard to leave. Within minutes the 10,000 capacity stadium had an audience of just one. I wasn't crying, but my view became increasingly blurred as the hint of a tear welled in my eyes. I sat for ten minutes more before heading to the bar to join my friends.

"Replay's on Tuesday 16th, you in Jamesyboy?" asked Tony, still proudly wearing his lucky FA Cup hat.

"I... I don't know. I'm flying out the next day... what if we get drunk and I get arrested? Cathy would kill me... and I'll have wasted all that airfare."

"Don't be daft! What could possibly go wrong?" said Buz.

His remark prompted several eyebrows to be raised.

A moment of contemplation followed as everyone, including Buz, considered the numerous things that could go wrong and, indeed, the many occasions on previous escapades when they had in fact done so. A general consensus was reached that it would probably be for the best if I didn't risk going to Grimsby. With that debate concluded we headed into town and got on with the serious business of the evening; drinking and deep, meaningful discussions...

'Whose turn is it to feed the jukebox?'

'Who will we get in the 4th Round if we beat Grimsby?'

'Whose round is it at the bar?'

'Which players would make the Wanderers 'all-time greats' team?'

'Why does Smudger drink twice as quickly as everyone else?'

And hypothetically, following a mis-keyed jukebox entry from Smudger...

'Which Spice Girl would you go for?'

Hoots of derision flew towards Smudger as Joy Division's 'Love Will Tear Us Apart' ended, seamlessly flowing into 'Wannabe' by The Spice Girls.

"That was supposed to be 'I Wanna Be Adored', not 'Wannabe'!" protested Smudger.

A deluge of beer mats rained down on him from all corners of our local, The Rose and Crown.

"Ginger... no, Sporty, she likes football" reasoned Smudger breathlessly, as he slumped himself down next to me for a rest, having danced his way through the first nine of ten songs that his two pound contribution had coerced from the jukebox.

"Baby, it's got to be Baby" declared Ian.

"Scary, I see her in Waitrose over in Marlow on Sundays... she's lovely" chose Beany, who'd arrived straight from work to spend his Saturday overtime earnings.

This drew everyone's attention.

"Hold on..." replied Ian, "You shop in Tesco's down town... and in the 'Value' section at that!"

"Yeah, you're too tight to go to Waitrose!" chimed in Sharon, before her sister Jackie tried to come to Beany's defence.

"Leave him alone you lot, he might go over to Waitrose... I love a walk by the river in Marlow on a Sunday morning."

"Yeah, I can see it now" mocked Tony, "Beany and Scary Spice... walking romantically hand in hand by the Thames, him with a carrier bag full of value-pack cider in his other hand... with the paparazzi following!"

"Waitrose don't do a value-pack" said Beany, unfazed and bizarrely confident that the rest of Tony's vision had a reasonable chance of becoming reality.

"Sporty... good working-class northern lass" added Buz.

"All of them! I've got enough love to go around!" bragged Pat, as he got up and started dancing to the remainder of the song.

"Baby" stated Lee, generating nods of approval from both Ian and Bob.

"Yep, Baby all the way for me too" said Little-Wanker... "and I'll tell you why... it's because she's blonde... just like my Julie!" he added triumphantly, safe in the knowledge that he'd contributed to the debate wisely in what could have been a tricky situation, considering his girlfriend was sitting beside him listening intently.

"Ah, thanks Darren" replied Julie, giving Little-Wanker a hug.

"You little wanker!" scolded Teddy.

As usual, Teddy admonished his son using the wonderful nickname that had stuck since the day he'd been introduced to our stunned group some years before. Teddy was well known for his colourful use of the English language and, despite being in his sixties, time hadn't dampened his fine choice of words. Upon arriving in the pub for pre-match drinks, Teddy hauled his trademark Farrah trousers up around his ample waist before greeting everyone.

"Gents, this is my boy... Little-Wanker. We call him that because he's a right little wanker. Oi, Wanker... I'm going for ciggies, you get the beers in." And so that was that.

"Is Little-Wanker really called Darren?" I whispered to Smudge.

"I dunno... never heard anyone call him Darren until now though; maybe he's just told Julie his name's Darren?"

"Posh has got lovely hair" I shouted, refocusing on the debate, before scanning the table for any further nominations. "Roger? What do you think?"

Roger took a sip of his Real Ale, before sitting back and thinking deeply.

"I think..." he said thoughtfully, before pausing and drawing in everyone's attention. "I think... that in my considered opinion... most importantly... it's Smudger's round, and that you lot are a bunch of idiots. I haven't got a bloody clue who any of the Spice Girls are!"

It was an outburst that brought cheers from most, but jeers from Smudger who protested that it wasn't his shout at the bar before stomping off to start ordering anyway.

"Diet coke please, Smudge" I shouted over towards the bar.

"Me too Smudge" added Lee.

"Piss off! What do you really want?" grunted Smudger, gesturing towards the barmaid to ignore our requests.

"Seriously, we're 'up London' tonight... so I'm taking it easy" I replied.

"Northern Soul do" explained Lee. "I'm driving."

"I'm not driving...I'm just a lightweight" I quickly added, pre-empting Smudger.

"Who's going then?" Smudger asked.

"Me, Jamesy and Ian... heading up in my van about midnight."

"Where is it? Midnight? What sort of music is it?"

Smudger was perturbed that there were plans afoot that he wasn't privy to.

"It's at the 100-Club in Oxford Street... starts at one in the morning, goes on until nine. It's Northern Soul... so no Spice Girls" answered Lee.

"Can I come?"

"Yep, but the bar shuts at 2 o'clock... there's no drink after that."

Lee awaited the inevitable response.

"No drink? Sod that! I'm staying in Wycombe. I'll be wrecked by midnight anyway. Ian... do you want a nice soft drink too?"

"No... lager... pint of!" replied Ian without hesitation, allowing Smudger the opportunity to shake his head disapprovingly towards me.

An hour later we left Smudger gently cradling his kebab at the back of the taxi queue and made our way to Lee's van.

"You're roughing it in the back James... it'll be good practice for your travels" declared Ian, smartly claiming the passenger seat. I didn't protest; an hour crashed out on the dust sheets now might be a godsend the following morning. It couldn't be any less useful than my other token gesture of preparation for our night on the dance floor; abstaining from the last two rounds in the pub, having started drinking at lunchtime.

My plan to snooze lasted no longer than it took Lee to start the van's engine, firing up its stereo in the process which blasted out the coolest Jamaican Ska and obscure soul music. Lee could play records for 24 hours straight without me hearing a bad tune, although I'd barely recognise a song. What I lacked in knowledge, I made up for in enthusiasm. A few years earlier, Lee and Ian had invited me to London for my first Northern Soul all-nighter. This wasn't like the indie-disco back in Wycombe. The music, the fashion and the dancing just blew me away. Upon arrival, Lee and Ian disappeared straight to the bar, buying as many beers as would fit onto the small table in the corner that they'd sent me to claim. It proved to be enough beer to last until the next morning; Lee and Ian were indeed seasoned veterans of the all-nighter. In my excitement, I headed straight to the dance floor and started bouncing in time with the music. My Happy Mondays-inspired moves worked for me regardless of whether I was dancing to Indie, Hip Hop, Techno, or, as on this occasion, Northern Soul. Watching head-spins, backflips, and fast-foot shuffles being performed all around me, I realised I might need to raise my game. As the first song came to an end the already packed dance floor stood and applauded as the needle left the vinyl; I'd never seen anything like it. As the night wore on and the temperature rose, talcum powder was liberally sprinkled across the floor making it feel like an ice rink, but allowing the sweating masses to effortlessly glide to and fro in hypnotic unison with the music. Eight hours of dancing and applauding later, I was hooked.

Over the next couple of years these midnight pilgrimages become frequent, and yet I still failed spectacularly to recognise a familiar tune month after month. It had become a regular ritual between songs for my friends to glance across the floor to check for any sign of recognition on my face. On our previous trip I'd achieved a personal best of three songs. Not a great return from eight hours, but I was delighted all the same. This night was no different. I'd once again danced until morning to amazing tunes that I didn't know, all except for the last song which traditionally signalled the end of the night and so, as Lee always reminded me... "That doesn't count!"

We left the club to find central London already bathed in sunlight and preparing to greet its influx of Sunday shoppers. The January chill which met us back up at street level attacked our sweat-drenched clothes, sending us racing to the sanctuary of a café, where mugs of steaming drinks and plates of toast would help to bring us back into the real world.

Three strong cuppas later and with windows wide open, Lee pointed his van west on the road that would take us all the way home. I lay exhausted on the dust sheets, happy to drift off to the sounds on the stereo while Lee somehow concentrated on staying awake. But Ian, who had barely spoken during the eight hour marathon, was now full of beans; there would be no sleeping for him.

"What I don't understand is... why are you taking a bird?"

I looked up from my drowsy slumber; I could see Lee taking a deep pull on his cigarette and looking out of the window, as if to say... "He's not talking to me."

"I went travelling when I left the Army. It was brilliant. Spain. Morocco. Turkey. India. Thailand. Vietnam. Nepal. Australia. Everywhere... there was shagging non-stop... shagging without fail."

Ian's second outburst had managed to grab Lee's attention, prompting a nod of interest. I didn't get time to reply before he continued. Now that Ian had warmed up, there was no stopping him.

"You see... these girls... they're away from home, they're savouring a new found freedom. It's a bit like Fresher's Week down at the college... just better. They're free of the shackles of what people think back home... they go a bit crazy; best of all, they get really horny. They don't care about today, because tomorrow means another town... another country. They love the freedom, but they're a bit intimidated by it too... they need reassurance... and that's where you come in."

I caught Lee's glance in the mirror. His eye's, like mine, were screaming "what on earth is he talking about?"

Ian continued, oblivious to whether or not either of us was listening, although, by now we were - intently, and waiting for the next pearl of wisdom.

"The whole game's completely different when you're travelling... it's not like down town when you have to chat the birds up first."

"I've never really been one for chatting up girls" I tried to interrupt, but to no avail.

"No, they come to you. They're a long way from home... they see you and feel safe because you're a traveller too... instantly you've got something in common... and boom... before you know it... you're at it."

Lee finally deemed it necessary to speak.

"That's bollocks!"

"Lee, have you been travelling like me?" said Ian calmly.

"No, but I don't believe every girl turns into a nympho the second she gets a passport!"

"Well they do... I know, I've seen it... and so will you Jamesyboy, just as soon as you've been dumped by your girlfriend... believe me, she'll be no different, she won't want to miss out."

I was too tired to argue and drifted in and out of consciousness as Ian continued to blether. Before long I felt the van come to a halt.

"Home-sweet-home 'shagger'!" Lee shouted, announcing our arrival at my folk's house.

"You look after yourself mate... send some postcards back to the workers so we can see what you're getting up to."

"Cheers Lee, I'll try. I'll probably be too busy shagging though!"

"You'll see boy... you'll see!" said Ian, not rising to our mockery as I ambled down the path in search of my bed.

8 - What's the radio saying?

"Well, you won't fit all of that into there" said my Dad, pointing out the blatantly obvious.

The travel bag I'd bought didn't look quite so big now that it was sitting on the floor of my bedroom surrounded by clothes, trainers and guide books. The whole day had been spent making neat piles on the bed before purposefully placing them into their designated spot in my bag, then removing them, screwing them up and ramming them into half of the space. It was 7pm and I'd had enough of packing; I was no further forward now than when I'd started.

"Do you really need six pairs of trainers?" queried Dad.

"Yes, two pairs of Gazelles for when it's sunny... one for Thailand, then another for Australia; white Stan Smiths for if it rains; black Stan's for if it's muddy; grey Stan's for smart, plus the Campus for travelling and wearing indoors" I replied.

"What's in the carrier bag?"

"Underwear."

"It's massive! How many pairs have you got?"

"Twenty."

My dad laughed; I was becoming increasingly annoyed.

"Ten pants... ten pairs of socks?"

"Erm, no... twenty of each, I'm not off to Spain for a week you know."

My dad turned and left the room, coming back a minute later with my mum and Cathy.

Cathy had spent a summer working in a beach bar in Thailand before we'd met, and it would be fair to say that she'd often regretted ever coming back. This experience, therefore, made her the authority in the room on packing; based on the fact that my parents had never been abroad and I'd only been on a college field trip to Malta.

"I told him a backpack holds more" remarked Cathy.

The three of them stood with arms crossed looking down at the clothes explosion on the floor.

"How can he be a backpacker without a backpack?" my mum added.

"I said that to him in the shop! But did he listen?" Cathy replied.

"I doubt it; he's never listened to me, and I'm his mother."

"No, I want the one with wheels and a handle" mimicked Cathy.

"He'll look like an air hostess!" giggled my dad.

"Erm, I'm sat right here you know... right in front of you!" I interrupted, as the hen meeting risked getting out of hand. This focused attention back to the problem of my unpacked bag.

"Don't mess with my trainers!" I pleaded, whilst being manhandled down the stairs by my dad.

"Best to just leave them to it son, it will keep your mum busy instead of worrying about you both... anyway, the game's about to start."

He opened two bottles of beer, while I tuned into the local radio station, 11-70, which was broadcasting a commentary of the replay with Grimsby.

My dad wasn't so bothered about football these days, but standing there in the kitchen reminded me of late nights huddled around the radio when I was 11. Back then, his hometown team, Aberdeen, won the European Cup Winners Cup, beating Bayern Munich and Real Madrid in the process. It hadn't been until the Semi-Final that the national stations had become interested in Aberdeen's exploits, and so we had to try and find the Radio Scotland broadcasts for earlier rounds by delicately nudging the frequency dial until we could pick up the faintest of receptions. Even with the volume turned up to full blast, it sounded like the broadcast was coming from another planet, rather than from just 500 miles to the north. It dawned on me that, rather than being overly interested in Wycombe getting to the 4th Round, he just wanted to spend as much time with me as possible before I left him with just my mum and sister, and no male company for six months.

On the rare occasion that I missed an away game, listening to 11-70 commentaries was the only alternative, as around the country there would always be bigger games for the national stations to focus on. The local station didn't have the resources to invest in the best equipment or professional broadcasters, and so it was left to enthusiastic amateurs to bring the game alive for the listening millions; or in the case of 11-70, the listening dozens. There was a skill to listening to these broadcasts, as the commentator would often get so wrapped up in the game that he'd forget the radio audience wasn't actually sitting next to him in the ground. It was common to hear cries of 'Did you see that?' leaving the listener pleading to be given a clue as to what had happened.

Two years before, I'd been studying hard for more accountancy exams when Wycombe travelled to play Manchester City. City were true giants of the English game but had found themselves relegated to their lowest ever level, just as Wycombe were venturing to their highest. For one season only the two would be paired together in the same division. I sat in my bedroom with my dad listening to Wycombe claiming a famous victory that day and in the excitement of the moment Alan Hutchinson, the Wycombe commentator, had lost all sense of professionalism. As the final whistle blew he cheered and celebrated along with the other 1,000 Wycombe fans in the crowd; as nearly 30,000 Mancunian's angrily left the ground having seen their team humiliated. Unfortunately for Hutch, he was sitting in the press seats surrounded by Manchester City supporters, some distance from the celebrating Wycombe fans housed in a distant corner of the stadium. Their improbable victory had given the Wanderers a slight chance of avoiding relegation, while in the process dealing Manchester City's promotion ambitions a serious setback. His jubilation was not appreciated by the locals and several started to climb into the press box to confront him. Again, the excitable commentator appeared to believe that his radio audience were actually there beside him in his moment of need.

"They don't like it! The City fans do not like it that the Wycombe boys have beaten them!"

Both my dad and I were excitedly jumping around in my bedroom, punching the air in ecstatic disbelief at the result, as Hutch continued to report from Maine Road.

"Hold on... they're coming for us."

His voice quivered.

"Don't worry... I think we'll be alright... oh no, no... they are still coming..."

After taking on an increasingly concerned tone his sentence trailed off, then silence. Next came the greatest moment of broadcasting I have ever been privileged to hear.

"Take one more step sir and you'll get my boot in your face!" roared the commentator.

We stood in my room; paralysed by the dramatic turn of events. Instinctively, I raised my fists, ready to defend us against any attackers that might jump out of my portable radio. Again, silence momentarily took over the airwaves, and then a whispering Hutch returned.

"It's okay. Don't worry everyone; I think we're going to be alright... they're going."

I dropped my defences as Hutch continued, growing in confidence and volume with every word.

"Yep, I think we're safe... they're going... but they do not like the fact that the mighty Wycombe Wanderers have just come to Maine Road and beaten Manchester City. I'll say it one more time... Manchester City, one... Wycombe Wanderers, TWO! And with that, I'll hand you back over to the studio."

Cathy entered the kitchen.

"I've left you one pair of Gazelles, your Campus and the black Stan's, now get packed."

And with that the men were banished back up to my bedroom with the portable radio to listen to the Grimsby match. In the middle of the floor lay one empty bag, sitting beside a worryingly diminished pile of clothes.

"Oh that was close! What a save" shouted Hutch.

"Who's attacking? Who made the save?" asked my dad.

"Grimsby attacking... Taylor saving" I replied.

"How on earth do you know that?"

"Listen to the crowd's reaction... there's only 200 Blues fans, but over 3,000 for Grimsby. If Hutch shouts and there's a lot of crowd noise, then that means it's Grimsby on top... if we can only hear Hutch, then it means it's going Wycombe's way. There was lots of excitement in the crowd just then, so it must have been Grimsby attacking."

"Right... can't you just tell by the excitement in his voice?"

"No, he's always excited, regardless of who's got the ball. Have you got that? You aren't going to have me here to help for the rest of the season."

"Aye... and you won't be going anywhere unless you get this bloody bag packed!"

"I know, but it's difficult. It's going to be boiling in Thailand, anything from scorching to freezing in China, Autumn in Australia, sub-tropical on Easter Island... whatever that means... snowy in Chile, and hot in New York."

I received zero sympathy and even less advice.

"Luckily, I've got this bad boy!" I cheered, proudly holding up the quartered Oxford and Cambridge Blue Wanderers shirt I'd bought on an extended lunch break from work, just prior to leaving.

"Long sleeved... so good for the cold, but lightweight and silky material too, so good for the heat. I'll show the world that I'm from Wycombe and proud!"

"Will you just shut up and bloody pack! Listen, it's a free kick... I think it's to Wycombe."

It was a Wycombe free kick and the Blues had started the game strongly. Following Martin Taylor's early save they'd more than held their own against the home team. Martin Lee placed the ball out on the right flank, deep inside Grimsby territory, before whipping a cross into the packed six yard box. As the ball flew towards the Grimsby goal an outstretched Wycombe leg managed the merest of touches, steering it beyond the stranded goalkeeper and into the net.

"Goal!" shouted Hutch.

There was near silence from the crowd, apart from a distant cheer from the small Wycombe contingent, signalling that the Blues had taken the lead. Once again, Paul McCarthy, supposedly in the team to stop goals at the other end of the pitch, had managed to score.

"Get in! Come on Wycombe... just try and hold them out now" I yelled at the radio.

Within a minute, Hutch was screaming again.

"Simmo! Yes! It's two now!" he shouted in shocked delight, as the cultured Wycombe midfielder, Michael Simpson, let fly with a thundering shot from just outside the penalty area. The strike zipped across the greasy surface before crashing into the bottom of the Grimsby net.

The sound of the dismayed Grimsby fans voicing their disapproval echoed around my room. I didn't know whether to laugh or cry; Wycombe had suddenly taken a two goal lead and were within touching distance of their first ever FA Cup 3rd Round victory. This couldn't be happening; not now, I wasn't there; this just wasn't fair. I fell to my knees in disbelief; I was going to miss the 4th Round.

The 4th Round draw had already been made and either Wycombe or Grimsby would play host to Wolverhampton Wanderers. Wolves were a massive club with a long and successful history. They would bring a huge away following; a tie against Wolves would be amazing. I reminded myself not to get too carried away. Yes, we were 2-0 up but there was still a long time to go. Ah yes, of course; we'd committed the cardinal sin of scoring too early; it wasn't even half-time. I'd had my heart broken by these boys in blue on too many occasions to remember. Grimsby just needed a goal, then nerves would set in, the crowd would get behind them and the tide would inevitably turn against us. This game had '3-2 to Grimsby' written all over it. I tried to focus on packing; the pressure of the game was becoming too much. Just as Hutch stated how important it was for the Wanderers to hold onto their two goal cushion until half-time, Grimsby scored. And, by the time Hutch had stopped castigating himself for cursing the team, the players were back in the changing rooms receiving the pep talks that their managers could only hope would see them to victory 45 minutes later.

Lawrie Sanchez's half-time words certainly had the desired effect, and Wycombe immediately set about attacking their opponents, wrestling back the game's momentum that had seemingly been snatched from them prior to the break. This was the closest Wycombe had ever been to the 4th Round, and the players seemed inspired by this potential date with destiny rather than burdened by it. Grimsby, meanwhile, appeared increasingly rattled at the thought of becoming the victims in a giant-killing. Having assumed that their hardest task would be avoiding defeat at Adams Park, surely back on their home soil victory was all but assured? Wycombe were turning the tables on their opponents. Whereas at Adams Park the Division 1 team had looked the stronger for long periods, it was now the turn of the Division 2 boys to dominate.

With the Blues continuing to see the majority of possession, time was slowly running out for Grimsby, who were tiring as they desperately chased around the pitch trying to regain control of the game. But if they couldn't get the ball, they couldn't score the all-important next goal. An equaliser would surely break Wycombe's spirit, but a third Wycombe goal would provide an almost unassailable lead. Entering the final 20 minutes, Wycombe gained a corner. Once again, the dangerous left foot of the diminutive Martin Lee swung the ball over at pace. As had been the case all night, when the Blues defender Mark Rodgers attacked the ball he jumped higher and more purposefully than the two Grimsby defenders who trailed in his wake. He powered the ball into the net before becoming submerged under a mass of bodies, players and supporters coming together to celebrate one of the most significant goals in the club's 114-year history.

The game was not yet won, but Grimsby were broken. With heroic performances all over the pitch, and each player continually winning every mini-battle in the form of the next tackle, header or pass, the Wanderers of Wycombe held out to earn a famous victory. And, for the players on the pitch that night, a place in the history books of the club forever. They were the first Wanderers ever to progress to the FA Cup 4th Round.

The Blues were heading into the unknown. And so was I.

9 - Bangkok-bound

I wasn't happy. It was stiflingly hot inside the plane and we'd already been sitting on the runway for over an hour whilst, ironically, it was being de-iced. London was in the grips of winter. The big Australian sitting next to me was still wearing his down jacket, despite the heat, having fallen asleep within minutes of boarding. His arms and legs had already invaded my airspace; he was due his first gentle nudge in the ribs. If that didn't have the desired effect, it would be followed by a firmer warning from my elbow, delivered in the style that Wanderers hard-man Jason Cousins might despatch a troublesome opponent. "Jason wouldn't put up with this shit" I grumbled.

As I contemplated my next move and also what Cousins would do in the same situation, his beaming face once again flashed across the small TV screen in front of me, celebrating Mark Rodgers winning goal from Grimsby the night before. I'd now spent 90 minutes watching the news-loop repeatedly; Wycombe had just knocked Grimsby out of the FA Cup for the twentieth time!

"I can't believe I'm going to miss the Wolves game."

"Will you give it a bloody rest? We're on our way to Thailand! We're going around the world... get excited!" replied Cathy.

"Well, he's doing my frickin' head in, taking up all the space. When I need the loo I'll have to get you and the couple beside you to move. These are crap seats... why couldn't we get the window or aisle? I thought all seats were either window or aisle... this planes way too big. It's too hot... I want to cool my head against the window."

Cathy rolled her eyes and then put her headphones on; another 14 hours of my moaning loomed.

This wasn't a good start. I was freaking out before we'd even taken off.

I wasn't just upset about the football or the cramped seats. I was nervous; scared; sad about the emotional goodbyes at the gate, I also wished I hadn't eaten the burger in the airport bar, as my stomach was already churning. I yearned to be outside gasping the cold air, but even a cold window to lean my head against wasn't an option on this journey. With hindsight, the three pints of lager just before boarding hadn't been the brightest of ideas either; that had been Big Bri's fault.

I'd been trying to calm my nerves in my parents' frost-bound garden earlier that afternoon, when I heard the toot of Brian's Land Rover.

"Big Bri's here! Come on, everyone out, we don't want to be late!" shouted my dad, who had never been late for anything in his life.

I took in one last lungful of the freezing High Wycombe air before heading through the house that had been my safe haven since the age of two.

"Looks like you're in the back with the bags Jamesyboy... haven't you got a backpack then?" chortled Brian.

Cathy had claimed the back seat along with my mum and sister, while my dad was up front with his best mate Big Bri.

'Bloody hell, this is Northwich Victoria away all over again' I thought to myself as I rearranged our bags to make some room.

Brian had travelled south from Aberdeen with my dad over 30 years before when they were just kids searching for adventure and excitement; instead they found High Wycombe. How my dad had ever made the decision to move 500 miles from home was beyond me, as he could never be accused of being the adventurous type.

A brilliant father? Yes.

A natural adventurer? No.

There was no way my dad would entertain driving the short distance to Heathrow Airport, he 'didn't do' motorways; hence Brian saving the day. Thirty years 'down south' hadn't dampened their Aberdonian values though. Brian and dad had insisted on a farewell pint or two at the airport and, while there, we thought it wise to get some familiar English food too. It would be some time before we would get that opportunity again; a 'last supper' would also delay our tearful farewells.

"Did you go to Grimsby last night? You must be gutted about missing the 4th Round!" asked Brian as we sipped on our pints, leaning back into his chair with a hearty laugh at my expense. Brian loved football and knew it would be a big deal for me to miss the next round.

"You won't need me to get you a Cup Final ticket this year then... where will you be for that... Australia? Outer Mongolia?" he continued, with reference to the time he'd managed to get me and Jason tickets to see an actual FA Cup Final back when I was 16.

He'd sourced tickets in the Liverpool end for the game against Wimbledon at Wembley. I went to two FA Cup games that season. First I witnessed Wycombe falling at the very first hurdle by losing 2-0 to local rivals Aylesbury United in the 1st qualifying round in September, a humiliating experience watched by 1,500. I didn't expect that eight months and 12 rounds later I would be standing surrounded by over 98,000 supporters watching Liverpool, the most successful English football club in history. That day had been forever etched into football folklore as the day that 'the Crazy Gang beat the Culture Club', with Wimbledon producing one of the greatest ever shocks in sport, beating Liverpool 1-0. The goalscorer that day was Lawrie Sanchez. Thirteen years later, Sanchez now found himself earning a living as the manager of lowly Wycombe Wanderers; the club's excitement at reaching the 4th Round didn't really compare to his own personal achievement in the FA Cup.

Even though they had lost that day, watching the superstars of Liverpool had been an amazing experience, a million miles removed from watching my Wycombe Wanderers. At the end of the game, those Liverpool supporters who stood beside me were full of the same pain that I'd felt months earlier as I skulked away from Aylesbury United, tearful, as thoughts of Cup glory evaporated for another year. The vast army of Liverpool supporters may have followed footballing royalty, but that hadn't made them immune from the same pain of defeat as the rest of us. No matter where you're from, or the colour of the scarf around your neck, football fans are the same the world over.

Just 11 months later, 96 of those Liverpool fans went to support their team again in the following season's FA Cup Semi-Final. They never made it home. Life offers no guarantees, and when opportunity beckons you have to grab it before it's gone. My opportunity had come. It was my time to grab it. Having put some perspective on my lot, I tried to relax. I was sure that if I had an aisle seat I wouldn't be regretting the beers, and would probably be happily looking forward to another. As for the churning stomach, it was probably just nerves rather than the burger. As I reminisced and thought a thousand thoughts, Wycombe's celebrating players suddenly disappeared from the TV screen, to be replaced by an airline safety video. I felt Cathy's fingers tighten around mine and the plane began to accelerate down the runway.

10 - Bangkok

Fourteen hours from London, the Australian finally awoke as the plane touched down. Whilst I hadn't managed a minute's sleep he'd enjoyed at least 15 hours; most of it while dribbling onto my shoulder. Despite this, the adrenalin was pumping as we exited the plane. Just being able to stretch my legs again raised my spirits. This was it; Plan B, an international adventurer at last!

Luggage reclaimed, we headed for the exit, looking for the bus our travel book advised would take us cheaply into Bangkok. Leaving behind the comfort of the airport's air-conditioning, we were attacked by the oppressive mid-afternoon heat. I'd never felt anything like it.

"What the...? Let's go back inside" I said, only half-jokingly.

Cathy spotted the budget bus and marched off in its direction, pulling my bag along behind her.

"I'll carry your backpack then shall I?"

Once on the bus we got our first taste of how life was going to be a little bit different in Thailand. As it departed we hit speeds far beyond those that the 326 in Wycombe had ever achieved; even on the downhill journey into town. I tried to process what I was seeing.

'This is insanely fast... but the vehicles we're swerving past are still made of metal, just like the ones in England, and those concrete central-reservations look pretty solid too.'

I concluded there was a good chance that we weren't going to make it to the city but comforted myself with the fact that, if we did, it was going to be an exciting ride. I sat with my knees raised against the seat in front, with knuckles white upon the handrail, trying to remember if we'd taken out medical insurance. A few hundred yards ahead I could see a blur of brake lights. Mercifully, the bus screeched to a halt, albeit with its occupants all sitting a foot closer to the windscreen. We were shaken, but alive. I looked around the bus and, seeing my look of concern mirrored on the other passengers faces, felt slightly better that 'it wasn't just me'.

"Cathy, when we fly out of here, we're getting a taxi, okay? I know I said we were on a tight budget, but no more budget buses."

I spoke calmly, but with an air of '...and that's not negotiable' in my tone. Cathy didn't argue.

Our attention was soon drawn back to the driver, slamming his hand on the dashboard and cursing. I don't speak Thai, but in any language I know when someone is swearing. He stood up and got off the bus, again shouting towards the general direction of the traffic jam in front of us; a jam that appeared to snake for several miles towards Bangkok.

"What's he doing, can you see?" asked Cathy.

I stretched towards the window, straining to see.

"Erm, it looks like he's taking a leak up against his bus."

'Buz would approve', I thought to myself. The driver soon hopped back onto the bus and, while chuckling to himself, shouted back towards his passengers. The locals didn't appear to take much notice, and the newly arrived tourists just stared back at him blankly. Just when we thought things couldn't get any stranger, he pulled the cushion from his seat and lay down in the aisle, tucking the cushion under his head.

"He's asleep!" I whispered to Cathy after a couple of minutes.

"He's probably just meditating" she replied.

"But he's snoring!"

I giggled, deciding that laughter was better than crying; we were stationary at least and so out of immediate danger. Thankfully, when he awoke some ten minutes later he seemed slightly less manic, content to just follow the slowly moving traffic as it worked its way into the bustling Koh San Road backpacker district.

"Koh San Road! You, you and you! Get off bus!" shouted the driver, whilst pointing at me, Cathy and another startled-rabbit of a guy who I recognised from our flight.

"I guess this is our stop then" I mumbled.

"Hi, I'm Mark" said the third person to have been unceremoniously dumped by the roadside. The bus pulled away, kicking up a cloud of dust in our faces. "Do you know where you're staying yet?"

"No, we've got a shortlist from our book though... just going to see which looks best. Do you want to walk with us?" I said casually, but secretly grateful of the reinforcements.

I had it all planned out in my head. We would cruise past all the hostels to see which we liked the best, then get them to knock down the price; nobody would turn away business in the middle of January. As we walked past one 'No Vacancy' sign after another, I started to get concerned.

"What shall we do now? That's all the places on my list full, plus the dodgy-looking ones too."

Mark tried to look calm, despite the realisation that he'd hitched his wagon to a couple equally as clueless; a classic case of the blind leading the blind.

"Look, there're people leaving with backpacks up there; let's try that place."

Cathy broke into a brisk march as she spoke. Both Mark and I dithered, frantically fingering through our travel guides, trying to find a review for the hostel that Cathy was by now entering.

"Anything in your book?" asked Mark.

"Nothing at all... it looks pretty old though."

Juggling books and bags, we followed.

"Come on, we've got a room!" exclaimed Cathy triumphantly, as we caught up. "Quickly though, it's the last one."

Mark stopped dead in his tracks, his shoulders slumped. After an awkward silence I wanted to say... "Well, nice to meet you then Mark, have a great trip"; but my mouth blurted out... "What about Mark? We can't leave him on his own."

Despite having only known him for 30 minutes, the three of us had been thrown together into the sea of chaos that was downtown Bangkok; it seemed the most logical thing in the world to share the only lifeboat floating by, in the form of a fleapit hostel room.

"It's okay... it's just for one night," the three of us chorused upon entering the room. It was undeniably a complete shit-hole. Dark, smelly, hot, noisy and dirty; it scored the full five stars. On the plus side, with four single beds, we at least had somewhere to rest our weary heads. I guess if we'd entered the room to find just one bed, our initial reactions would have been even worse.

It quickly became apparent that the less time we spent in our room, the better. We ventured back out into the sultry heat of the Bangkok evening, feeling slightly less conspicuous without our luggage in tow. We soon found a bar and grabbed a table that looked out onto the hustle and bustle of the city. Mark and Cathy ordered some food, but for the first time in my life I wasn't hungry, and hadn't been since that burger at Heathrow which now seemed like an age ago. I felt as though I'd landed on a different planet, let alone in a different country. Back home, at 10pm on a Thursday in January, the streets would be deserted, but in Bangkok things appeared to be just getting going. People jumped from the back of still-moving scooters wherever they could find a prominent spot to set up a makeshift stall on the pavement, before unfurling mats full of trinkets or snacks to sell. Everything about the city was different; the smell, the heat, the sounds, the packs of wild dogs that roamed, the volume of people, the craziness on the roads; even the apparent lack of street vending regulations which were keeping us entertained as the traders jostled for space.

"Do you want a bit of mine?"

Cathy looked concerned; she'd never seen me go for so long without food.

"No thanks, I'm fine... just not hungry."

"He didn't eat on the plane either" Cathy said to Mark, sounding like a concerned mother.

"Really? The food was good on the plane... I thought the flight was great, did you?" replied Mark innocently. Cathy rolled her eyes at the inevitable rant that she knew was to follow.

"It was too hot, we had shit seats, and the prick next to me didn't move the entire flight, blocking my path to the toilets and taking up all the space between our seats. No... I didn't enjoy the flight."

"Yeah, I was in the row behind you... but across the aisle. I thought the bloke in the jacket was dead! I mean, I'd been to the loo twice before we even took off... and had watched a whole movie... but he just slept the whole time, in that huge coat too... mental!" recalled Mark, much to my annoyance. "Was your telly not working properly James?"

"It was okay, why do you say that?"

"Well, whilst they were de-icing the plane, whenever I got up to go to the loo or stretch my legs, you were just staring at the sports news... over and over again; I thought it must be stuck."

"Nope, that's what I wanted to watch... the mighty Wycombe Wanderers knocking Grimsby out of the FA Cup."

"Oh, right. Cool. I'm not really into football that much."

Mark's attention returned to his food.

"So Mark, where are you from?"

Cathy tactfully interjected, keen to avoid our temporary companion saying anything else that could darken my mood further, leaving me free to enjoy my sulk in peace.

After they'd finished eating, we sat back quietly sipping ice-cold beers and trying our best to absorb everything that was going on around us. This new life I'd signed up to was going to take some getting used to; I'd left my comfort zone some 6,000 miles to the west. As the night drew on, and with the steady flow of beers taking effect, we started to relax a little, although our pale skin, clean clothes and 'that' look around the jaw line that suggested we'd enjoyed the recent festive season to the full still made it painfully obvious that we were the new kids in town.

The Koh San Road was a magnet for travellers, and seemed to be the place that everyone passed through en route to somewhere else. Mark was heading north into the jungle, before flying on to Australia where he was going to work for a year, whilst Cathy and I were heading south to the beaches of Phuket. Where all the lean, tanned, relaxed and happily-haggard looking folk had been, was anyone's guess, but they looked a damn sight more comfortable in their surroundings than we did. As we sat 'people watching' I felt hugely inadequate in comparison; that was, until Cathy pointed out a well-travelled guy walking past with a backpack.

"Did you see what he's done James? Look at his feet."

"No... no way! How could anyone do that? That's outrageous!" I replied, having seen the customised Adidas trainers that he had callously hacked into a makeshift pair of sandals.

"I could do that with your Gazelles if you like."

"Over my dead body! I'll wear my trainers as Adi Dassler intended… and I won't be wearing any bloody flip-flops either."

I had already become a true Englishman abroad.

The cocktail of 36 hours without sleep, the city's assault on our senses and an evening of beer began to take its toll; we settled the bill and, reluctantly, staggered the short distance back to our salubrious abode to spend our first night in Thailand.

As I lay there I couldn't decide what was making my head spin the most; was it the beer or watching the flies whizzing around above my head? I finally fell asleep as the noise of the city began to quieten at about 5am, only to wake again to the sound of a crate of empty bottles getting tipped into a skip two hours later. My body was crying out for more sleep, yet my brain was in overdrive. I hoped that dawn would bring with it a less stressful day. Try as I might, I couldn't get back to sleep, eventually deciding to freshen up instead. I made my way through a dimly lit hallway to find the bathrooms. I wondered how bad the conditions must be in the Thai prisons I'd heard about on the news back home, when there would occasionally be a report about drug smugglers who get caught abroad, then plead to get sent home to a British jail to escape the squalid conditions. When I'd heard about such places, this hostel was exactly what I'd imagined; yet here I was, paying for the honour. The heat in the hostel was already unbearable, despite the day having hardly begun, so I was only wearing a pair of shorts as I tiptoed through; the thought of having to don a t-shirt being worse than that of my untanned belly being displayed. 'Those prisons must be really bad' I thought to myself, before making a mental note to ensure that nobody slipped any dodgy packages into our bags. Upon finding the bathroom, I pushed open door after door in the vain hope of finding a cubicle with a western style seat, but my search proved fruitless. We were planning on being in Thailand and China for three months so I would need to master the art of the Asian 'hole-in-the-floor' style loo eventually; but I decided to delay the inevitable a while longer, instead opting for a shower.

I heard a girl gasp. Within seconds, the wooden slatted door of a shower cubicle burst open and a young woman stormed past me, wearing nothing but a small towel.

"Merde! C'est putain de froid!" she yelled with an angry frown on her face, before storming off.

'Shit, I'm in the ladies... I'm in the wrong bathroom!' A wave of panic hit me. I assumed she'd said something along the lines of '...you pervert... my boyfriend will kill you'. I'd recognised some swearing, and French, but my language skills didn't go much further than that. Before I'd had a chance to escape, a second door crashed open. Another girl bundled out, only this one hadn't even grabbed her towel in her haste. I stood rooted to the spot with a look of utter shock on my face, only matched by the look of horror on hers. She scrambled frantically to cover whatever she could with just her crossed arms and legs. I'd stumbled into a scene from a 'Carry On' film. All that was required now was for Cathy to walk in, waving a rolling pin in my direction.

"I'm so sorry!" I managed to plead.

Still unable to move, I squeezed my eyes so tightly shut that they risked exploding through the back of my head.

"It's okay, I've got a girlfriend!"

Shit; that line hadn't gone down well when I'd used it on the train with Miss Beaconsfield. At least on that occasion I only had the British Transport Police to fear. Now I was going to end up in a Thai prison, pleading my innocence next to the drug mules and begging for leniency on the evening news back home. I could just imagine my parents choking over their dinner when my ugly mug popped up on the television.

'Next... a pitiful story from Thailand; a British man, 28, has been given a life sentence in a notorious Bangkok prison, having been found guilty of sneaking into the women's showers at a hostel and ogling at girls. One, a young French woman, sent her boyfriend to give him a well-deserved kicking, before handing the pervert over to the Thai police. Hanging's too good for him we say... leave the scoundrel to rot and throw away the key... and now, here's Bill with the weather forecast.'

"Okay, you can open your eyes now Romeo."

The husky American voice came from the general direction of where the girl had been stood just before I'd plunged myself into darkness. I did as instructed, but only partially, squinting to offer the smallest semblance of protection if the figure was in fact an incredibly annoyed Frenchman about to defend his girlfriend's honour.

"Dude... my names Hayley, not Medusa, open your eyes."

This was promising. Hayley was definitely a girl's name, and that voice didn't sound like it came from a French assassin holidaying in Thailand. I opened my eyes. There stood Hayley, now sporting a towel.

"I... I'm James, pleased to meet you."

I held out my arm to shake hands; Hayley lent forward to reciprocate, only for her newly recovered towel to slip. We both stepped back, formal introductions were out.

"I didn't see anything good... I mean I didn't see anything at all... sorry... I didn't mean you didn't look good..."

Once more my eyes were firmly closed; unfortunately, I couldn't say the same for my mouth.

"Listen, I'm really sorry. I only flew in yesterday and I'm all over the bloody place, I didn't realise this was the ladies bathrooms... honestly I didn't."

"It's not the ladies... it's a free for all. Welcome to Thailand!" giggled Hayley, who by now seemed to be revelling in my obvious discomfort. "Seriously though, are you going to open your eyes?"

Hayley was brunette and had the deepest tan I'd ever seen. Unlike me, she now seemed completely comfortable as we stood facing each other in the shower room. She proceeded to tell me that she was jealous, as she was at the end of her month long trip and heading back to college in America.

"Your tan is amazing!" I mistakenly said out loud, in a far too admiring manner.

"Why thank you kind sir" she replied, beaming a perfect All-American smile, before leaning towards me, "And guess what... no tan lines."

"Well, I know that, don't I!" I blurted, once again, thinking out loud.

"I thought you had your eyes closed? Oh man... your accent is just adorable."

I started to blush.

"What's that?" she enquired, pointing towards the Wycombe Wanderers shorts I was wearing.

Immediately I covered my crotch with both hands, practically collapsing with embarrassment.

Hayley rolled her eyes, "Oh please... you saw me naked... I'm pretty sure I know what 'that' is... I mean what's that on your shorts?"

I was mortified. This level of humiliation surely couldn't be survived. As my face turned crimson, I waited for internal combustion to put me out of my misery. Unfortunately, nothing appeared to be happening and Hayley was waiting for an answer.

"It's a swan... it's the badge of a football team... the team from my town back home."

"You mean soccer? I play soccer at NYU."

"You mean football. It's football... not soccer. Your football is really American Football; soccer is proper football."

Despite my awkward situation, I wasn't keeping quiet on that issue.

"What's your 'soccer' team called?" said Hayley, sure as hell not about to apologise to a stranger who'd just gawped at her naked body.

"Wycombe Wanderers 'Football' Club."

"Who? I like European soccer... Real Madrid, Barcelona, Liverpool, Manchester United... but I've never heard of The Wycombe Wonders!"

"It's 'Wanderers', not 'Wonders'." Again, I felt compelled to correct her. "We never play those teams... they live in a different world. Liverpool players earn a hundred times what the Wycombe boys get... Wycombe are a bit crap to be honest."

"Really?"

There was a pause. It sounded as if Hayley had concluded this line of questioning. She took a step forwards, leaving little but the width of her towel between us, and then spoke again, but this time whispering directly into my ear.

"You know... I leave for the airport in an hour. I'll never see you again, and yet here we are... alone... together... you and your soccer shorts... me and my little towel..."

As she spoke, she gently ran her finger down the length of my arm.

Suddenly, getting beaten up by the French boyfriend or being arrested by the Thai police seemed like viable alternatives to Cathy finding me in the showers with this gorgeous girl. The innocent 'Carry On' scene was turning into the introduction to a 1970's porn film.

"Wow, Hayley... like I said... I... I've got a girlfriend; a real one. But thank you, thank you so very much, but I really... really can't. Honest. You're bloody gorgeous, it's been lovely meeting you, really lovely... but I think I should just take a shower now... on my own. You have a safe journey home."

"Okay Mr James from England... no worries" she said with a sigh, while shrugging her perfectly formed shoulders.

I smiled and shrugged my less than perfect shoulders in return. Whilst concentrating on not saying anything else that could get me into further trouble, I edged back from her and into the shower cubicle that she'd so spectacularly appeared from just moments before. I quickly locked it behind me and collapsed in a heap on the floor.

"There's no hot water you know... that French bitch used it all up" advised Hayley.

"That's fine... a cold shower is just what I need."

Never had a truer sentence been uttered.

"Okay. Don't say I didn't warn you. You have a great holiday James."

I listened to Hayley's footsteps trailing off down the hallway. For a couple of minutes I remained sitting on the cool tiles clutching my knees to my chest. I was fairly certain I was having a heart attack, but tried to calm myself by taking deep, slow breathes. As I sat there, I slowly regained some semblance of composure before pulling the chord to start my much needed shower.

Any good that the deep breathing had done in reducing my pounding heartbeat was soon destroyed as the ice-cold water plunged onto my head; my body contorted, instinctively trying to evade any further body parts coming into contact with it. Before I knew it, I'd fallen through the door and was sitting naked on the floor, swearing profusely. The girls' reactions now made perfect sense. I scrambled on my knees back into the shower. I slammed the door behind me and leaned up against it; the smashed lock was now somewhere out in the middle of the room. What on earth was happening? I'd barely slept for 48 hours; I'd gone over a day without eating; I was in a country that was completely alien to anything I'd ever experienced. And after seven years of complete faithfulness to my girlfriend, in the space of two minutes I'd practically been seduced by one naked girl and seen almost as much of another, before finding myself, also naked, on the floor of a public bathroom. I wanted to go home. Had Ian been right all along? Maybe it hadn't been the sleep deprivation talking after the 100-Club. I would have to email Lee and confirm it; something really did happen to girls when they went travelling. I hadn't even lasted one day before they had started throwing themselves at me. A sober girl; a really pretty sober girl too! Maybe I shouldn't email him. Lee would tell the others and they'd all be out here like a shot.

On my return, Cathy asked how the showers were.

"No hot water" I replied.

Avoiding all eye contact, I busied myself packing the few items that I'd risked taking out of my bag the night before.

"Showers were fine when I went in earlier" chimed in Mark, "...I feel like a different person now. Sorry if I used up all the hot water."

I thought about sharing my shower room experiences but still wasn't entirely sure what had happened myself, so decided against it; instead I just looked mildly unimpressed at Mark's rejuvenated cheeriness.

"Right then... breakfast downstairs and then Thailand! I'll pay... a thank you for letting me share with you two last night."

Mark ordered what looked like half of the menu, and Cathy also appeared ravenous following the previous day's travels and first night tensions. They both seemed full of excitement, whereas I felt like having one of my public crying sessions before getting a flight back to London. I still wasn't hungry but thought I'd better order something as we had another day of travel ahead. Mark had booked onto a minibus heading north to Chang Mai, whilst Cathy and I were hoping to get an overnight bus down to Phuket. Flying would only take about an hour but would be too expensive, and so the bus was our best option. Our guidebook had recommended a VIP bus which, although considerably more expensive than the regular bus service, offered a high level of comfort; and was also 'less likely to get hijacked'. As I read this fact to Mark, I seriously wondered again what on earth we were doing here.

Before long our food arrived. Maybe due to the powers of tomato ketchup, my taste buds kicked back into action. As we ate, Mark talked us through a map of where he was going and what he planned to do; then Hayley walked past with her bags.

"Hey James, you have a great trip... maybe I'll see you around someday? Look me up when you get to New York, y'hear?"

Hayley handed me a scrap of paper with a scribbled address on it. The big 'X' at the foot of the note didn't look like it was part of her Zip Code. Maybe her surname was Xavier; yep, that's what I'd tell Cathy when the inquisition began. Cathy and Mark both looked at Hayley, but I could feel Cathy's gaze turn towards me. Mark continued to stare at Hayley, who wasn't wearing much more now than she had been in the bathroom.

"Yes, I'll do that ... we, I mean we... we'll do that" I stammered.

I waited for Hayley to move on, but she didn't.

"Hayley, this is my girlfriend Cathy, and this is Mark."

Cathy smiled at Hayley, before looking back in my direction again. Mark continued to stare at Hayley.

"Hi Cathy, pleased to meet you... you're one lucky lady!"

Hayley smiled while shaking Cathy's hand. My heart beat even faster as I recalled the result of our earlier attempted handshake.

"How do you two know each other?"

Cathy's question was a fair one; we'd spent less than ten minutes apart since leaving London. I sat there looking for the right words, but they weren't springing to mind very quickly.

"We met in the shower" said Hayley.

These definitely weren't the 'right words' I'd been looking for.

"Oh" replied Cathy, her gaze towards me intensifying.

Mark continued to admire Hayley.

84

"Not 'in' the shower! God no! You know what I mean; in the shower area; we had 'a moment'. He was quite the English gentleman!"

Hayley giggled, seemingly oblivious to the fact that she was messing with a woman on the verge of tearing her beautiful face apart.

"A moment?" repeated Cathy. She laughed politely.

Who would she kill first; me or Hayley? Both at the same time maybe? I couldn't decide. I felt a strange sense of calm, driven by the knowledge that I would soon be getting put out of my misery.

"Yes, a brief encounter" replied Hayley with a twinkle in her eye, before turning towards Mark. "Are you okay?"

Mark's unwavering stare was proving slightly unnerving.

"Mark! Stop gawping!" snapped Cathy.

Mark and I both sat with our heads bowed. Thoughts flew frantically around in my mind... 'Why couldn't she have stumbled out of the shower in front of Mark instead? Look at him, he's besotted... he'd scrap his plans and fly back to the States with her if she told him to. But no, it had to be me; now she's pissed off because I spurned her advances... if she can't have me, then nobody can. Cathy hates me too... I didn't even do anything... I'm the victim here! I said no... I should be getting an award for 'Boyfriend of the Year'!'

"Yes, we had a moment... a moment when Hayley here used up the last of the bloody hot water... just before I got into my shower."

I didn't even blink as I replied. I was an innocent man, with nothing to hide, fighting for his life.

"I had a hot shower too" added Mark, who was again looking adoringly into Hayley's eyes.

The conviction of my explanation, combined with the randomness of Mark's contribution, seemed to diffuse the situation. And the day was completely saved by a taxi pulling up outside the hostel to take Hayley to the airport, much to my relief, and Mark's dismay. She'd propositioned me within minutes and bewitched Mark within seconds; I was sure her flight back to New York would be eventful.

It was 10am on our first full day abroad, and I'd already had more drama than I could take. We waved goodbye to Mark soon after Hayley left as he clambered into an old minibus for the arduous journey to Chang Mai. I wouldn't have been confident in that minibus surviving the three mile journey from pub to Adams Park back home, let alone the ten hour road trip that Mark had signed up for. But he was on his own now, and we had our own transport to arrange. We hailed a taxi for the 20 minute journey across town to the bus terminal, where we bought tickets for the VIP bus leaving for Phuket that evening. The terminal made even Wycombe's equivalent seem like a wonderful place to spend an afternoon, and so with tickets secured and six hours to kill, we decided to take the short cab ride back to the more tourist-friendly Koh San Road.

I'm not sure if it was due to the fact that neither the French girl's boyfriend or my own girlfriend, or any of the numerous dodgy characters that skulked in the shadows of the bus terminal, had killed me that morning, but I felt a lot more confident when we arrived back on Koh San Road. We dumped our bags back at the hostel so were free to explore the area in a relaxed manner, trawling through the market stalls which were mainly selling fake Liverpool and Manchester United football shirts, along with suspiciously cheap designer handbags and watches. Having eaten nothing but a plain omelette over the past 24 hours, I decided to give the many food stalls that appeared to specialise in stir fried insects a wide berth. We found another street bar and sat, like only English folk could, in the midday sun sipping lemonade and people watching, as even the packs of street dogs retreated to any patch of shade they could find. Two sought refuge under our table. As I sat back and tried to ignore them, Cathy decided that both they and she could do with a sandwich, which soon led to another dozen strays joining our party, until the bar's owner pulled out a very well used broom handle. At the first sight of the stick the dogs disappeared without as much as a thank you for the sandwich. We soon followed suit; my dog-loving girlfriend hadn't appreciated the broom handle wielding intervention either. We strolled around again lackadaisically in the stifling heat which by now, I had realised, was more bearable if you moved at a third of your normal pace. The fact that I had nowhere particular to be or anything of importance to do for the next six months made this all the easier to embrace. To find some shade we paid a first visit to an internet cafe to see if the Hotmail account that Russy and I had set up and tested across the distance of two office desks actually worked for real. I really wasn't a 'techie' kind of person and wouldn't have thought to create an email account. But, like a true accountant, Russy had pointed out that I would save loads of time and money by not having to write dozens of postcards individually, and then paying to post them. Instead, a quick email update every now and again, sent to as many people as I wanted, would suffice; genius. Okay, blatantly obvious to most, but genius to me. This genius was borne out by the mass of people using the internet cafes, and the high number of cafes too. This internet thing might just catch on.

Accompanying the test confirmation email from Russy, I found a barrage of emails from ex-work colleagues, friends, family and some of the football crew, who were all helpfully reminding me that the Wanderers were entering into the unchartered waters of the FA Cup 4th Round. I suddenly realised that I'd entered a parallel universe, with the real world of work, rain and football carrying on as normal in the emails sent from home, whilst here was I, in the heat, beating off naked girls and flea-bitten dogs in Thailand. After composing an email to everyone back at home we headed towards the hostel to pick up our bags. For the first time, as we ambled along the Koh San Road, I actually felt more excited than anxious. In about 24 hours' time we'd be dropping our bags and not having to pick them up again for a couple of months, as we made our home on the beach beside the Andaman Sea. This was a good feeling. As we approached the hostel I felt a strange rumbling in my stomach. This feeling wasn't so good. Despite the heat, I ditched the newly adopted 'Asian dawdle', hastening my step with each stride.

"What's the rush?"

Cathy was struggling to keep up with me.

"I need the loo... like now."

I abandoned her at the door of the hostel and disappeared into the gloom towards the bathroom. I don't think there was any public nudity on display as I crashed into the first available cubicle, but I was too focused on the task at hand to care anyway. I also lost all inhibitions about using an Asian style toilet fairly rapidly too; this was no time for messing about. When you've got to go, you've just got to go; and that's exactly what I did, and continued to do for the next 30 minutes. On the plus side, I'd mastered the art of how to use the Asian loo in a classic 'sink or swim' fashion.

"James... are you in here?" whispered Cathy from the doorway to the bathroom.

"Yes."

"Are you ok?"

"No."

My 30 minute toilet break should have made that fact abundantly obvious.

"Have you got a dodgy stomach?"

"You could say that."

I cursed the burger I'd eaten back at Heathrow, the Thai heat and the lack of sleep over the past two nights; even the nervous breakdown invoked by Hayley in this very room; all surely contributing factors to the predicament I found myself in.

"I'll get you the Imodium your mum packed... we need to get going soon."

With my legs in danger of seizing up as I attempted the world record for 'longest ever squat', I took one of the tablets that Cathy slid under the door, and then another for luck. I hoped they would settle my stomach for, at least, our second journey of the day to the Bus Terminal, if not the overnight bus ride that was to follow.

The traffic was noticeably busier as we made our way through the centre of Bangkok, but we had left ourselves a good hour to make the journey that had taken no more than 20 minutes in either direction earlier in the day. My mind was focused on my dodgy stomach and I didn't take much notice of the different route the taxi was taking, until Cathy pointed out that we had been driving for 40 minutes yet still hadn't arrived. A minute later, we breathed a shared sigh of relief as our driver pulled over and pointed to the metre to let us know how much we owed him. As I started to count out the fare Cathy looked concerned.

"Hold on... this isn't the right place."

She frantically pointed to a map in the guide book and looked for a Thai translation for 'bus terminal'. The driver looked bewildered and kept pointing across the street to a row of trains. It soon became evident that our driver's grasp of English was as non-existent as our Thai language skills.

"No! That train! That train! Choo-Choo! Choo-Choo! We... wan... Southern Bus Terminal... bus! No train... bus!"

I panicked; for some reason beginning to speak with a Thai accent in the vein hope that it might resonate with our clearly confused driver.

"Bus! The wheels on the bus go round and round; round and round, round and round; the wheels on the bus go round and round, all day long! Bus... no train... bus!"

I was now singing with a Thai accent too.

I sang a nursery rhyme; Cathy held her head in her hands, swearing repeatedly; and the taxi driver started to cry. We had no idea where we were, other than it was a train station, and that somewhere else in Bangkok our bus was due to leave in 15 minutes time. I proceeded to have my second nervous breakdown of the day, while the taxi driver called over a passer-by for advice. Miraculously, he recognised our map and gave the driver animated directions. Immediately, the taxi screeched back into life with an about-turn back in the direction from which we had come. Finally, we started to recognise some landmarks from our earlier journey, although time was rapidly ebbing away before the 5.30pm departure time. We jumped out of the taxi at exactly 5.30pm, only to realise that the station was huge, and we had no idea where we needed to be. Our hearts sank, but we spotted a smartly dressed official and rushed over to him, frantically shouting.

"Phuket bus... we on 5.30 VIP bus!"

"You are very late sir, follow me please."

His pronunciation was perfect; I continued using my Thai accent. He took my wheelie bag from Cathy and briskly marched off towards the buses. Cathy and I followed, our hopes raised that we might still have a chance of making the bus but also bitterly upset that, at best, we would be the last two people getting on and would surely be separated for the overnight journey, sitting next to strangers. I was annoyed with myself and concerned for Cathy.

"That must be it!" shouted Cathy.

The man carrying my bag almost got himself killed by a reversing bus, jumping into its path and slamming his palm repeatedly against it to get the driver's attention. As the driver and the terminal official, while loading our luggage, discussed how stupid the two foreigners must be, we gratefully boarded. Sheepishly, we edged our way through the bus as it reversed. Not even the unanimous looks of disapproval we were receiving could dampen my sense of relief. My mood was further improved tenfold as we were escorted along the aisle of the air-conditioned bus by the low-altitude stewardess, who smilingly ushered us into our adjoining spacious seats, before offering us tea, coffee and biscuits. We had made it, and tonight's accommodation was going to be infinitely more luxurious than the previous night's hostel or the flight the night before that. This wasn't a bus; it was a plane without wings; and we were in First Class. This bus was even nicer than the 'luxury corporate cruiser' that had taken me on my first Roobarb trip arranged by Buz. Cathy wrapped herself in one of the courtesy blankets handed out by the stewardess to protect from the wonderful chill of the air-conditioning, and then reclined her chair to an almost horizontal position. She started to giggle.

"What's funny?"

"The wheels on the bus go round and round... seriously?"

After an hour of weaving through the Bangkok rush hour, the sun disappeared as abruptly as the city. As my eyes became accustomed to the moonlight I gazed out of the window, observing small settlements and night markets that appeared in the middle of nowhere as we flashed past, along with scores of scooters carrying three or four passengers at a time, or precariously balanced cargo as diverse as televisions and livestock. The bright moonlight dimmed, before disappearing completely behind clouds which gently began to release rain. This gentle shower quickly developed into a raging tempest. With face pressed against the window, I watched in amazement as the heavens opened like nothing I'd ever seen before; even the rain was different in Thailand. Soon the night was being illuminated by sporadic flashes of lightning as the storm raged above. Back down at ground level, as I continued to look in on the nightlife of rural Thailand as it rolled past my window, the bus slowed down to edge passed an overturned van and trailer. It had skidded off of the road in the storm, its load of boxed bananas strewn across the highway. A hundred yards further down the road another vehicle protruded from a ditch; its dazed driver clambering out of a window. Within the space of two miles we passed another four crashes yet, as the rain got harder, our bus seemed to be going faster and faster, only slowing to avoid debris from the catalogue of accidents that we passed. Cathy was blissfully ignorant to the carnage being reaped by the storm and was making up for two nights fitful sleep, happily curled up in the huge reclining seat that provided more than enough room for her petite frame. I felt as far from sleep now as I had done since our journey began. The dramas unfolding before me on every twist and turn in the road just made the adrenaline course through my veins with greater vigour. My attention was drawn back into the bus when the stewardess glided along the aisle, this time offering bottles of water, before slightly losing her sophisticated demeanour by hitching up her uniform's elegant pencil-skirt and precariously climbing onto the back of the driver's seat to reach the video player. The next eight hours saw the film Gladiator played three times in succession, dubbed in Thai, with German subtitles. Between the storm that continued to rage outside, and the Roman / Thai / Germanic on-screen rage of a father to a murdered son, husband to a murdered wife, who was sure to have his vengeance in this life or the next, I was destined for a third consecutive sleepless night.

11 - No Wolves (just snakes, elephants, dinosaurs and sharks)

"Ouch! It wasn't me."

I raised my arms to protect my face from the next blow. A sharp pain surged through my temple. As I lurched to my left and into Cathy, I drowsily realised that I wasn't being attacked by a vengeance seeking Russell Crowe after all; rather, I'd been rudely awakened by smashing my head against the window as the bus manoeuvred through the remnants of a road washed away during the night's storm. Squinting through the early morning daylight, I could see we were surrounded by lush forests and rocky hillsides. I had no idea how long I'd been asleep but as it was morning our destination had to be close.

"Cathy... wake up!"

How the impromptu off-road section of our journey had failed to shake anyone else from their slumber was beyond me, but she had to see this.

"Over there! Look... elephants... loads of them!"

I felt like a child on his first trip to the zoo.

"It's like a field full of cows... except its elephants... it's amazing!"

My insightful revelation finally prompted Cathy to open half an eye and nod her approval, before slumping back under her blanket. Now this was what I'd signed up for; fields full of elephants pretending to be cows.

After an hour of failing to spot more elephants, the bus started to pass makeshift shacks with increasing frequency before entering a town. Soon, the bus pulled into a car park and stopped.

"Cathy, wake up... we're here!"

It was nearly 6am. Apart from two dozen weary travellers departing the bus, Phuket Town was relatively quiet and, compared to Bangkok, it was positively tranquil. The two pale skinned tourists were the prize catch for the waiting tuk-tuk drivers and no sooner had our bags been removed from the undercarriage of the bus than they were being loaded into the back of a small open backed vehicle.

"You come with me, I take you to best hotel" said the smiling owner of the tuk-tuk eagerly.

He had shown an impressive turn of pace to win the five-yard-dash, claiming our bags ahead of the other drivers and, with them, the prize of the tourist rate fare. With trusty guidebook in hand, we showed him our map of the island and the village we wanted to go to.

"Kata... please take us to Kata" I said.

"Fantastic Hill Apartments in Kata" added Cathy.

We headed back out onto the road, this time holding on for dear life, for fear of sliding from the back of the tuk-tuk and onto the tarmac below. Before long, we were heading up a steep hillside through the lush forest, breathing in the fresh air and grinning from ear to ear as the cool breeze raced through our hair. As we neared the summit, our driver grumbled to himself in the universal fashion used by all drivers approaching a delay. If our pale skin, huge bags, lack of Thai language skills and general air of confusion hadn't given us away as tourists, then our whoops of delight and insistence at taking photos of the roadworks did the job. I didn't care; it wasn't every day that I saw a gang of elephants being used to clear a fallen tree from the road. The novelty of seeing elephants doing anything at all was still a long way from waning.

With the elephants completing their task, we continued on our way. On reaching the peak of the hill, we were welcomed by a breath-taking view across the western side of the island, a view that would send anyone from land-locked High Wycombe into a complete frenzy.

"The sea! I can see the sea!"

After two and a half days of travel, trauma and tantrums, we were finally here; down below, the Andaman Sea glistened for as far as the eye could see. All we had to do now was find some accommodation and then we could dump these bloody bags and let the holiday truly begin.

"Here. Here we are. This is a good place for you. Best place in Phuket... best place in all Thailand! You wait here one minute please."

We'd pulled up outside what was blatantly not even the best accommodation on the street, let alone on the whole island. Before we'd had time to protest, our driver disappeared inside the dilapidated building. Cathy and I looked at each other, rolling our eyes.

Our would-be accommodation fixer scampered back looking very pleased.

"Yes, yes... one room is available; you very lucky... lady-owner will show you now."

And with that, an old Thai woman of at least 85 years glided around the side of the building on a Vespa, pulling up in front of me. She patted the seat behind her.

"You go see now... you go with lady-owner."

"Yes, you go see!" encouraged Cathy, readying her camera.

I'd always fancied myself as a bit of a Mod, but this wasn't how I'd envisaged my first scooter ride. Cruising along the esplanade in Brighton in a sharp suit and fishtail parka felt more my style, not holding onto an octogenarian as we scattered startled chickens and stray dogs on a dirt track in Thailand. This was not a scene from Quadrophenia, not by any stretch of the imagination. By the time the old lady had managed to open the jammed door with a shoulder charge that belied her age, Cathy had walked down the track and joined us, happily enquiring if I'd enjoyed my ride. Before I had a chance to say "no", the woman beckoned us in to view a room that looked like it hadn't been inhabited, at least by humans, for decades. Having politely declined the room, I quickly began striding back up the track before anyone could get me back on the scooter.

Six crappy hostels later, our driver finally gave up on any hopes of a commission and dropped us at the top of a short, but extremely steep, driveway. We'd made it to Fantastic Hill. Upon seeing how nice the accommodation was in comparison to his recommendations, he at least had the decency to look a bit sheepish as he finally got the taxi fare that we'd agreed upon for the '20-minute ride' several hours before.

"Let me get you some breakfast" said Elle, the young woman who, along with her mother and sister, managed the small development of cabins.

Breakfast? It was only 8.30am, but after a third night of minimal sleep, followed by the morning's grand tour of Phuket flea-pits, my body clock was in disarray. But after eating nothing on the entire journey south, breakfast sounded like a great idea.

"Banana pancakes... my speciality."

Elle casually picked up a knife, walked over to the nearest tree, and cut down three bananas.

"Did you see that? I didn't know bananas grew on trees... did you?"

"Yes James... I did know bananas grew on trees."

Cathy spoke with a hint of sympathy in her voice. The tone she generally only used when I'd said something beyond my usual level of stupidity. I was too tired to care. Three days after leaving a frozen London, I was sitting in the morning sunshine of Thailand, eating the freshest banana pancake in the world.

After eating, I carried Cathy's backpack the final 20 yards to our room. Our new home was spotlessly clean, albeit basic, with just a bed and a bedside table, although that was immediately commandeered to house hairbrushes and an array of bottled lotions and creams. Most importantly, there was an adjoining en suite toilet, with a hole in the floor and a bucket for flushing, and a shower of sorts hanging from the ceiling. In my three days abroad, I'd already learnt that having a toilet in close proximity was the only luxury I needed, although having a private shower was hopefully going to help keep my blood pressure down too.

As Cathy busied herself, producing more and more stuff for 'her' table, I crashed out on the bed; finally drifting off for more than 30 minutes unbroken sleep. It was mid-afternoon before I awoke. Cathy was sitting on the bed next to me, reading through our travel guide.

"Good, you're awake... come on, let's explore!"

I'd had my longest sleep of the trip to date. Feeling all the better for it, I happily followed her out into the heat as she headed into the village to look around. It didn't take long to get our bearings; Kata wasn't huge. There was a choice of either following the solitary road around the bend and into the village, or straight on for the beach. It wasn't a difficult choice. As the sound of waves beckoned we quickened our pace, until something slithered across the path in front of us from the undergrowth and down into the gutter. My new found calm demeanour disappeared instantly.

"What the...? It's a snake! Cathy... it's a bloody snake! Cathy... Cathy?"

Giving a respectfully wide berth, I scurried down the hill towards Cathy, who had bolted 20 yards to safety the second she'd spotted it, leaving me as its only potential meal.

"Did you see it? It was three-feet-long!" I gibbered.

Cathy just nodded whilst struggling to light a cigarette. Stray dogs were definitely more to her taste, and I'd liked the elephants; neither of us was overly enamoured by our latest bout of wildlife spotting. After a couple of puffs, Cathy appeared to relax; I wondered if this would be a good time to take up smoking. I'd spent about 99 percent of the trip so far in a state of utter panic, and the remainder on the loo; not quite the chilled out lifestyle I'd envisaged before leaving England. Luckily, just yards down the track through a thicket of palm trees lay the Andaman Sea and a beautiful beach. We put thoughts of the snake behind us and headed onto the sand. Kicking off my trusty Gazelles, I tentatively stepped into the crystal clear waters. The mile long beach was just about wide enough to contain my smile. Surrounded by forest and sandwiched between two steep rocky hillsides that protected the bay and its small fleet of fishing boats, we had found our paradise; now this was what I'd envisioned.

"I didn't know the sea could be warm, did you?"

"It's about 100 degrees James … how would it not be warm?"

Cathy made a fair point, but my only experiences of the sea were from annual childhood holidays to visit the Scottish side of my family, up in Aberdeen. Aberdeen had miles of the finest sandy beaches you could imagine, but the North Sea didn't get warm, not even in the height of summer. So I'd always assumed that the sea was freezing, regardless of which beach it washed up on.

"I'm coming down here tomorrow, and I'm just gonna lie in it all day… and the day after that" I declared.

Striding through the gentle waves I vowed to become a chilled out beach bum, rather than the nervous wreck I'd so rapidly descended into since leaving home. As we reached the end of the beach and turned to retrace our steps, the sun started to drop from its lofty perch in the sky. Before we'd walked halfway back along the shoreline, it plummeted from view altogether. As it disappeared beyond the Indian Ocean, it created a beautiful orange tint across the water and painted the sky amazing shades of pink. This soon dulled into a purple hue, before sliding into the darkest imaginable blue, pierced by a myriad of stars. Within minutes the beach had been left in complete darkness, and the very second the sun disappeared a chorus of crickets hidden amongst the palm trees took their cue to strike up a song that would last the entire night.

As we hauled our weary legs back up the steep track into Fantastic Hill we could barely see a thing, having left the dim street lighting at the foot of the climb. Now, only the stars above offered any light. This truly was a different world from the one I'd grown up in. The sudden arrival of darkness was just another reminder.

"We need to take a torch tomorrow" gasped Cathy breathlessly as she fumbled in her bag.

"What are you looking for... your asthma inhaler or your ciggies?"

"Our key actually... there's a light above the door somewhere, hopefully the electricity hasn't been switched off for the night yet" she replied as we neared our cabin, rising above my snide remark.

Despite the darkness, we knew we'd reached the building - when I walked straight into it; instant karma delivered for my rudeness. Still unfamiliar with our surroundings, we slid our hands about the wall in search of the light switch, like apprentice mime artistes on the first day of training waiting to be unleashed upon real imaginary walls.

"Got it!" said Cathy triumphantly, bringing a dull glow to the doorway.

"What's that?" I yelped, spotting a dinosaur inches from her hand.

Stepping back, I lost my balance, ending up on my backside in a bush with my legs in the air, seemingly disturbing every insect in Thailand. The bugs instantly spat out a cacophony of noise in protest, rightfully annoyed at the clumsy sod who had invaded their home.

"Get me out! Get me out!"

Cathy practically had a laughter-induced asthma attack, before attempting to pull me back upright. But I was proving too heavy and was completely wedged into the bush.

"Hold on, I'll come round the other side" said Cathy, crying with laughter and thoroughly enjoying my second dose of karma. She grabbed my ankles and pulled them over my head, helping me to perform a less than graceful backwards roll out of the bush, leaving me lying flat on my face on the grass, covered in grazes and bites.

"That's it, I'm going home tomorrow."

I stormed into our room before ripping off my t-shirt and shorts in the shower. Yanking at the rope that dangled from the ceiling, I let the water rush over me and scrubbed furiously to remove any remaining bugs that had latched onto me. The water was warm at first, having been heated by the sun all day, but by the third pull of the rope had turned bitterly cold; cold enough to make me jump from the shower, but not cold enough to cool my mood. I marched out ready to start packing my things, but this was thwarted by the fact that I hadn't actually taken anything out of my bag since arriving early that morning. Instead, I did what any self-respecting 28-year-old man would do; I sat on the corner of the bed and sulked.

After ten minutes, Cathy nestled beside me.

"You know those 'dinosaurs'?"

She spoke gently, like a mother talking to her child.

"Well, they're actually called geckos, and they eat mosquitos. So it's quite cool to have them on the walls outside, and I'm pretty certain that they're more scared of you than you are of them."

I accepted her first point, but not the second.

"Just go to sleep babe, you'll soon get used to things... when I came to Thailand before I remember feeling the same when I first arrived, I promise... it will get better. Get some sleep."

Her calming words somehow managed to sooth my annoyance. Maybe she was right; I'd survived the snake and then the mini dinosaur, what could be worse? Before long I was fast asleep.

I awoke some time later to total darkness. Cathy had kissed me full on the lips, rousing me from my sleep, but now she appeared fast asleep herself. She must have been kissing me goodnight, which was surprising considering I'd been such a grump. I had no idea what time it was, or for how long I'd slept. I soon drifted back off.

"No... I'm not interested. It's too hot... let me sleep."

Cathy kissed me again, this time on my chest, then my shoulder, then with increasing speed, down my arm. On realising that Cathy was still asleep, and that it was something more fleet of foot that was getting amorous, I jumped up, thrashing my arms frantically against the darkness. I hurdled over Cathy to get to the light switch. The electricity appeared to be off for the night and so I felt my way back across the bedside table, through all Cathy's crap, until I found one of our small torchlights.

"Cathy... wake up please."

I spoke calmly, but with my bottom lip trembling.

"What?" she said groggily, shielding her eyes from the torch, despite it barely raising the light of a candle.

"What's that... that thing on the floor?"

Again, I asked coolly, now beyond tantrums and panic attacks, resigned to the fact that my world had descended into misery.

"Oh fuck!"

Cathy jumped impressively from her prone position and practically climbed up the wall, taking on the mantle of hysterical tourist that I'd been wearing so well.

"It's a cockroach, get it out, get it out!" she squealed, jumping up and down on the bed.

Rather than do as instructed, I jumped up beside her. We jostled for position behind each other in the corner.

"Kill it!" roared Cathy, with a venomous tone, whilst summoning enough strength to wedge herself between the wall and her cowardly boyfriend, leaving me exposed as her human shield.

"Oh god, it's moving! Kill it! Kill it!" she continued, leaving me in no doubt about what was expected of me.

"Whack it with your trainer!"

Screeched instructions continued as I crept towards the edge of the bed. With knees trembling, I gently set one bare foot down on the cool tiled floor, and then the other. Within seconds I was back up on the bed.

"Two of the bastards! I can't deal with two!"

Looking into Cathy's eyes, I could see there was to be no salvation in the trenches for me; I was going back over the top.

"James... kill."

At this point, I became more scared of my girlfriend than the cockroaches. This was a new side to her, and one that I didn't want to push. With one Adidas Gazelle firmly wedged onto each hand, I edged into battle; a modern day Gladiator, just like Maximus in the never ending movie I'd watched on the journey from Bangkok. Perhaps I crept into battle more akin to a Christian about to be fed to the lions, but I prepared to fight regardless. I took a step forward, they took a step back; I moved right, they moved left; like boxers prowling after the first bell, savouring the calm before the inevitable storm. I launched forward and, with eyes tightly closed, slammed both trusty Gazelles onto the floor before hurtling back up onto the bed.

"Did you get them?"

"How do I know? I had my eyes closed, weren't you watching?"

"I had my eyes closed too. I don't want to see you killing them... I just want you to kill them. Go see if they're under your trainers."

Oh no, I'd forgotten about my poor Adidas, which were now sitting exposed in the middle of the battlefield. What if I'd missed the little buggers and they'd captured my shoes?

"What if they've got inside?"

"Here... take this... burn your trainers" replied Cathy, handing me her cigarette lighter.

"What?"

What depths was this woman prepared to sink to? I had no problem burning two cockroaches to death but there was no way I was going to ruin my trainers so early into the trip, despite the fact they'd seen better days. I'd only ever thrown one pair of Gazelles away before their time, and that was when Sally Cinnamon had puked over them.

"No way... you only left me with three pairs to pack, remember? And these are the only Gazelles. There is no way I'm burning them... do I look like Jimi Hendrix?"

"Jimi burnt guitars, not trainers... torch them!"

"What about the room, we can't torch the room, we'll end up in jail."

I was far more concerned about losing my trainers than the prospect of burning down our room, but was getting desperate.

"What's to burn? The floor's tiled, there's no furniture apart from the bed, and I've got a bottle of water if that sparks up."

I was losing the argument, and my Gazelles. Once again I stepped down from the bed, edging towards the trainers. I couldn't see anything squashed on either sole so I grabbed a copy of the Bangkok Post and rolled it up before prodding at my shoes. I wanted to give the cockroaches every opportunity to face their destiny man to man or, at least, cockroach to man, without leaving my beloved Adidas as collateral damage.

"Burn them before they come back out!"

The despot was full of advice from her safe vantage point up on the bed.

I lowered my hand towards the trainers, dragging my thumb repeatedly over the strike wheel of the cheap plastic lighter before finally managing to ignite the flame.

"I'm so sorry... I love you."

"I love you too" whispered Cathy.

"Piss off, I wasn't talking to you, you heartless bitch... I was talking to my Adidas."

My trembling hand hovered over my trainers.

"Arghhh! The wall! They're against the wall! Get them!"

Cathy roared again, urging me forward into battle once more, this time waving the rolled up paper above my head like Excalibur. I slashed wildly against the skirting of the wall, this time with eyes open and confident that I'd destroyed the enemy, but before I could raise my weapon to finish them off they scuttled further along the floor, escaping under the door and out into the night. I grabbed a towel and dived headlong towards the foot of the door, ramming the towel into the void between it and the floor, creating an impenetrable defence.

"They've gone... and they aren't coming back."

"You did it! My hero!"

. Cathy jumped on top of me, rewarding her returning soldier with a lingering kiss.

"That was nice... much nicer than having the cockroaches crawling over my lips" I said when Cathy finally came up for air, instantly curtailing my moment of triumph, and sending my repulsed girlfriend scrambling for her toothbrush. Thankfully, the rest of the night passed without any further snake, lizard, cockroach or mosquito related incident.

The next morning saw a return to the beach. As Cathy dozed under a book, I decided to wade out into the bay and, although 50 yards out, the water was still only knee deep. Another 100 yards and eventually the sand underfoot dropped steeply away and I found myself up to my chin. A few steps further and I floated in the sea for the first time in my life, admittedly only six inches out of my depth but, as far as I was concerned, I was in the middle of the ocean. The sun was beating down on my skin and the salty water made floating easy. With the sea gently bobbing me up and down, I closed my eyes and listened to the waves lapping up onto the shore. My only concern was that I might fall asleep due to being so relaxed. Perhaps the dramas of the past few days were exaggerating how good this moment felt, but I couldn't recall having ever been this chilled out.

With a smile on my face I lay on my back, floating upon the shimmering Andaman Sea. I was finally living the dream for so long held in my head; on icy coach trips to watch Wycombe play away; in maths lessons at school; on Friday nights pushing trolleys in the rain; on long afternoons in offices. I hadn't dreamt about upset stomachs, uncomfortable flights or close encounters with snakes, mini dinosaurs or even American nymphomaniacs. But the sun? The sea? The sand? Yes, this was the life.

Then, without warning, it attacked me, tearing across my hip. In an instant my body tensed and I slid under, swallowing a mouthful of salty water. Panic stricken, I thrashed wildly in a vain attempt to find the surface. This was it; this was the end. Amidst my desperate flailing, I had a moment of clarity; 'Would the shark kill me before I had time to drown?' Mercifully, before I had time to find out, my head surfaced. I greedily gulped air into my lungs before hurling up a mouthful of seawater in return, followed by the remainder of my stomach's content. As I doubled over to wretch, my knees thudded into the sand, as I found myself closer to shore than expected. My momentum carried me over my imbedded knees and face first into the surf for another lungful of ocean, leaving me floundering in no more than a foot of water. I crawled back onto the beach coughing and spluttering, snot hanging from my nose, vomit drooling from my chin, and with my shorts hanging south of my backside. Four small children stood above me, laughing and pointing. Although not speaking any Thai, I'm pretty sure they weren't saying 'Look at the brave man, he must have swum for many miles to get here, fighting off sharks on the way'. Pulling up my shorts, I crouched into the surf and washed the sand from my face, before gingerly walking past my mockers and back to Cathy who was, thankfully, still asleep. This gave me time to rationalise what had just happened. Had I been attacked by a shark, or alternatively the rope anchoring one of the small fishing boats in the bay? I was unsure as events had unfolded so quickly. It was impossible to tell if the mark above my hip was from a rope burn or a tooth mark. The only logical conclusion was that it had been inflicted by a blunt, rope-shaped shark tooth.

Bravely, I decided there was no point in worrying Cathy with my latest near death experience and, as soon as she woke up, I suggested we head back to the village. Conveniently, it was also my dad's birthday and I wanted to surprise him with a phone call before he headed to work back in England, where, with the seven hour time difference, he would just be waking to the cold January morning.

"Ahhh, look at those cute little Thai kids waving" said Cathy as we left the beach. "They seem to like you, don't they!"

12 - Sun, sea and snow

"Hello? Mum... is that you? Can you hear me okay?" I mumbled into the telephone, feeling self-conscious in the tiny internet café at the foot of Fantastic Hill. It was silent inside, apart from the tapping on keyboards of five local teenagers staring into their hired by the minute screens. The high pitched scream that was returned down the line not only sent my head reeling from the receiver, but was also enough to stir the kids from their trance-like state, all swinging round and looking puzzled, except for the guy in the corner who hadn't appeared to blink, let alone move, since our arrival. At least the scream confirmed that the 15-digit number I'd dialled had indeed got me through to my folk's house on the other side of the planet.

"Are you okay? Is it nice? What's the weather like? Is it hot? Is everything alright?"

Eventually my Mum had to pause for breath, but not for long.

"It's so lovely to hear your voice... it sounds as if you're stood right next to me! Is Cathy with you?"

"Hiya!" shouted Cathy, leaning over my shoulder.

"I'm fine Mum... the flight was great, I loved Bangkok, the food's lovely, stomach is behaving, the beach is amazing, it's very hot... everything is great... just great."

I added some half-truths to the truths, along with a smattering of barefaced lies.

"Is Dad there? I just wanted to say happy birthday."

"Yes, he's standing next to me... you just caught him going out of the door! I'll pass you over... love you!"

Mum sounded as if she was about to explode with excitement.

"Love you too Mum" I replied, taking embarrassed mumbling to new levels.

"Hiya... you okay? Is it nice? What's the weather like; hot? Is Cathy okay? Is everything alright?"

These were already the most words I'd ever heard my Dad say on the telephone.

"I'm fine Dad. To be honest, everything's taking a bit of getting used to, but I'm getting there… Cathy is looking after me. It's bloody hot though … it must be 100-degrees at the minute. What's it like there?"

"There's an inch of snow… and it's still settling."

I could hear him opening the front door to inspect the weather for me.

"It's looking a bit dodgy for the Wolves game at the weekend if this carries on. They're expecting a sell-out crowd too, so they'll not want it postponed."

The FA Cup! Amidst my numerous traumas I'd forgotten about the upcoming match.

"I've seen a couple of the boys about… Buz was up the shops Friday lunchtime. He was rubbing his hands together like a little kid when I mentioned the game. He was asking after you. I saw Nick, Smudger and Beany going into The Falcon too; they said to say hello. Beany isn't going to the game… said he was working."

I wished my mates were around. We'd survived the roughest and grubbiest pubs in the country while following the Wanderers; Smudger would have dealt with the cockroaches for me.

"Yeah, Beany never goes to cup games. You tell them all to keep working hard… while I laze around on the beach!"

Forcing a laugh, I tried not to sound like a homesick little boy.

"I'd better go Dad, this is costing more than two nights' accommodation!" I said, looking to end the call. It was true; the call was expensive, but I didn't want to drop my guard, leaving my dad worrying more than he already was.

"Okay James, thanks for calling. Love to Cathy… you look after yourself… you hear me?" replied my dad, sounding a bit choked up himself.

"I will, I promise."

I was ready to burst into tears.

"Oh! I nearly forgot... Happy Birthday! Love you Dad! You take it easy on the way to work in that snow!"

As I put the phone down, Cathy looked at me and smiled; she didn't say anything, but just put a comforting arm around me. I assured her that it was just seawater still bothering my eyes.

"Come on... you can buy me some lemonade, then we'll head to the beach for sunset" said Cathy, tactfully providing an exit strategy as I wiped away a tear.

On the pavement, she paused for a moment.

"An inch of snow... and it's still laying? Suckers!"

I spent the remainder of the week slowly but surely settling into the hectic routine of a beach bum. Wake up; realise you don't have to get up; go back to sleep. Wake up again; stretch; open door; pick banana from tree; eat banana. Stroll to the beach; lie down; sleep. Wake up; realise you're on a beach; take a dip in the sea. If you can muster the energy, take a stroll along the shoreline; if not, have another sleep. Drink a little, eat a little. Repeat daily.

By Saturday, we had been in this routine for a full week, and I have to say that I was getting pretty good at it. My stomach issues weren't any better, but even they'd become part of the daily routine. I'd also come up with a simple solution; don't eat. The combination of the intense heat and my dodgy stomach meant I generally decided not to eat at all during the day, before having a small meal at one of the cafes in Kata each evening. After dinner I would wait for the stomach cramps, at which point I had five minutes to get home, where I could retire to the privacy of my own hole in the ground for the remainder of the night. The starvation diet and hours spent on the beach contributed to a drastic improvement on the way I looked. Inside, my stomach may have been a disaster zone, but outwardly, the excess weight that I'd carried upon arriving in Thailand was visibly dropping off. My skin was also beginning to bear a striking resemblance to that of the locals who worked on the beach.

I'd always tanned easily. My mum said it was on account of sunburn sustained as a baby in the beer garden of The Golden Fleece pub, around the corner from my Nan's house, which was where we lived until the council gave us the house I grew up in. 'We moved in on FA Cup Final day in 1974... Liverpool beat Newcastle' my Dad would often remind me; although he didn't seem to recall events of the day two years earlier outside The Golden Fleece. According to my mother, he had definitely been told to take me for a walk in my pram so that my grandad could get some sleep after his nightshift at the furniture factory. Whether it was due to sunburn as a baby or genetics, I was browner after a week under the Thai sun than I'd ever been after a summer playing football on the field over the road from my house. Cathy, on the other hand, was still portraying the 'English Rose' look, much to her frustration, as we arrived at the beach for another busy day.

"Maybe you didn't get burnt as a baby" I remarked.

"What?"

"You were born in Manchester weren't you?"

"Yes."

"There you go… your dad would have been perfectly safe to leave you in any Manchester beer garden… the pram's rain cover would have protected you for starters."

Cathy held her arm up against mine, and then settled back down into her sunbathing position, grumbling about the difference in colour.

"You'll catch up eventually; you were really brown after that summer you spent here before… I've seen the photos."

"I know… and I am getting a tan. Well… a bit of a tan anyway, but you look like the Thai boys! I'm not moving from this spot today. It's Saturday… I'm doing nothing."

"What… as opposed to your busy midweek schedule?"

Saturday? Saturday meant football and the FA Cup 4th Round; today was history in the making. I began to feel homesick for the first time in days; for the first time since speaking to my dad. I wondered if it was still snowing, and if the game was even going to be played. I wondered what the boys were doing too, before remembering that it was only 3am back in England. Buz would have got overexcited after work and gone straight out drinking with Nicko, peaking by 7pm before stumbling into the nearest takeaway, no doubt asking them if they did a home delivery service and, if so, would they deliver him home too, to save him a taxi fare. My old pal Jason would still be up and partying hard. I wasn't sure how he would be approaching the big match as, although he'd been watching Wycombe Wanderers Football Club for as long as I could remember, his dad supported Wolverhampton Wanderers Football Club, and had brought his son up the same way. Some people would see this as a 'can't win' situation, but Jason would definitely adopt the 'can't lose' attitude and would find a way to celebrate with one 'WWFC' or the other after the game. Tony would have been out drinking too, with Smudger and Lee, purely to calm their nerves; Tony probably wearing his lucky FA Cup hat in preparation. I guessed that the majority of the others would have taken it easier, saving their energy for the biggest FA Cup game in Wycombe's history and the celebrations that would follow in the unlikely event of a victory.

After a few more hours lazing on the beach, a swim in the sea and a stroll to the far end of the beach and back, I suggested to Cathy that we retreat to our room for a while until the sun lost its midday strength but, true to her word, she refused to budge, determined to accelerate her tan.

"I'm going to head back for a bit, do you mind?" I was beginning to feel nervous; a little about the football, but more about having been away from the loo all morning.

"Go find some shade brown boy... I need to catch up."

"Are you sure you don't want to come back... its getting ridiculously hot. I can feel my shoulders starting to burn... which never happens."

"I'm fine; just bring me a sandwich and lemonade when you come back down."

Cathy didn't move a muscle, intently concentrating on tanning. As I walked back up the hill towards the little village, the heat was unbearable; we'd been in town for a week, but this was far hotter than the previous days. Despite already being a stone lighter I felt really uncomfortable, so took a cold shower back in our room; due to the heat, this actually felt bearable for the first time.

Rooting through my bag for a clean t-shirt, I found the lightweight silky Wanderers shirt. I'd never been one for wearing football shirts anywhere but on a football pitch, but this seemed like the perfect time to start. It was Wycombe's big day in the FA Cup, and the shirt's long sleeves and bagginess would help protect me from the sun. All of my clothes were already a size too big; a habit I'd never grown out of thanks to the fashion inspired by The Stone Roses, Happy Mondays and The Charlatans. But an ever decreasing waistline meant everything was hanging that little more freely as the days progressed. Those bands also had a lot to answer for when it came to the various hairstyles I'd sported over the past decade, but as I stepped back out into the ferocious glare of the sun I decided that it might be time to take a couple of further steps to help me cool down; steps I'd considered unthinkable just a week before.

"Hello?" I peered through the windowless window frame, struggling to adjust to the darkness of the shaded room from the bright sunshine on the street.

"You cut hair? You cut my hair? You take it all off?"

I slipped effortlessly into my Thai accent. A toothless smile appeared from the tiny, wrinkle-faced old woman who was sitting in the corner on the floor, fanning herself with a giant banana tree leaf. Then she laughed. I wasn't sure if that constituted a 'yes' or a 'no', but I proceeded to step inside the hut as the old woman slowly got to her feet, still laughing and smiling.

"Zoom, zoom... all off" I said, running my clenched fist over my hair, whilst finding it impossible to speak properly.

This was met with more laughter before the old woman gestured for me to sit on a foot stool in front of a mirror. Two minutes later, ten years of carefully preened Madchester inspired hair was nothing but a memory and a heap on the floor. So this was what it felt like to be a sheared sheep.

"You like?" said the old lady, still laughing while rubbing her hands over my scalp.

"I liking very much... thank you."

I spoke while wondering what on earth I'd just done. The reflection in the mirror was barely recognisable. I rubbed my chin which, with its two days stubble, was now hairier than my head. Walking down the street, I wondered what my friends would think about my new haircut and dodgy Thai accent, deciding that I'd get away with the skinhead, but not the accent.

Now that my indie-boy hair was gone, it was time to take another massive step. Despite days of denial, deep down I knew I had to do something quite inconceivable; I had to discard my trainers and buy a pair of flip-flops. I took a deep breath and marched into the first market stall I saw selling touristy paraphernalia and picked up a pair of flip-flops with a rough Nike logo on them. My journey into the world of open-toed footwear would have been slightly easier to bear had there been some fake Adidas options, but this wasn't to be. "How much please?"

The young girl working on the stall looked no more than ten-years-old. Her English was better than my Thai, if not my English.

"350 Bhat."

"Okay, I'll take these."

"What? No... you haggle." The young girl looked confused. "How much you want to pay?"

"I... want... to... buy... these... sandals... please."

I spoke deliberately and loudly, while starting to count out the 350 Baht price.

"Okay, thank you. Have nice day."

The girl's mother swiftly took over, whipping the money from my hand. I couldn't help but notice her smirk. 'Shit, my hair must look really stupid' I concluded, whilst walking home with my flip-flops concealed in a bag. I still wasn't sure I could go through with it; I certainly wasn't prepared to wear them straight from the shop in public. No, this dirty deed would need to be done in private. But I wasn't in Wycombe anymore and, just like the haircut, the flip-flops felt pretty damn good as I practiced walking around the room like a small child clumping around in their parent's shoes.

I felt like a new person as I made my way back towards the beach. The faintest sea breeze now caressed my scalp and the loose fitting football shirt provided cooling protection from the sun. Okay, I'll admit it; my feet, freed from the heat of my trainers at last, felt amazing too. Topped off by my slimmer frame and tan, I couldn't help but admire my reflection in a shop window.

"Oh yeah, you're looking pretty damn cool Jamesyboy, if I say so myself."

'Pretty damn cool' disappeared whilst entering the shop to get Cathy's lunch, as I stubbed an unprotected toe, unleashing a world of pain in the process. Suddenly, the cool traveller dude swaggering down the hill reverted to the idiot who'd climbed it an hour earlier. The two minute walk to deliver Cathy's lunch turned into a ten minute limp.

"Here's your sandwich, miss." I sat down beside Cathy, casually sipping on a bottle of lemonade.

"What the...! What have you done!" she exclaimed, just managing to hold back from swearing, suddenly sitting bolt upright and fully alert.

"Nothing... I just needed to cool down a bit."

"Your hair, you haven't got any hair!"

"Yeah, I haven't got any trainers either." I raised my right foot, showing off my sandal and a bruised little toe.

"Fuck off!" This time Cathy failed miserably to conceal her astonishment. She leaned back and assumed a studious look, staring intently at me. Her eyes scanned me from head to bruised toe and back again. "I like it, yes... I think I approve."

She took the lemonade bottle from me, taking a deep gulp. "Do I look browner yet?" she continued.

"Well... you look redder, if that counts."

An hour later I was dispatched to the shade of the palm trees to replenish our lemonade stocks. There I found the drinks vendor sitting against a tree, seemingly asleep.

"Two lemonades?" he muttered, without appearing to open his eyes. "What team is that?" he inquired after eventually raising his eyelids, studying my Wycombe shirt intently.

"It's Wycombe Wanderers, from England."

I puffed my chest out proudly to show off the quartered blue shirt to its full glory.

"Wik... what? Who?" he replied, sounding very confused while leaning closer into my chest to examine the club crest.

"Wycombe Wanderers" I repeated, although this time with chest rather deflated at his complete lack of recognition.

"I support Liverpool. Robbie Fowler, Michael Owen, Sami Hyppia, Steven Gerrard. Do you like Liverpool? Can you beat Liverpool?" he replied, still studying my shirt.

"Yes... I like Liverpool. I saw them play once."

"Your blue team beat Liverpool?"

"Oh no... my team have never played Liverpool. They are a big team. My team are a little team."

"Premier League?" he queried.

"No."

"...League below Premier League?"

"No."

The drink seller's disappointment was palpable.

"...How many leagues in England?"

"Well, there are four professional leagues... they have 92 teams in total. Then there are lots of other leagues below that. They all get to enter the FA Cup. Wycombe used to be in the semi-pro leagues, but now..."

By the time I'd said 'Well, there are four professional leagues...' he'd turned to his ice box to hunt for more lemonade.

"So you never play Liverpool?"

"No. Wycombe never played Liverpool." I confirmed, wishing that this wasn't the case.

"Manchester... you play Manchester, yes?"

"Yes! We played Manchester City... we beat them!" I said, recalling the day Alan Hutchinson nearly got beaten up in his commentary box.

"United... Manchester United... Ryan Giggs, David Beckham. You play Manchester United?" he asked hopefully.

"Nope… not Man U either. We never play the teams in the Premier League. Not Liverpool. Not Manchester United. Not Arsenal. Not Chelsea… none of the good teams."

"Here… two lemonades" he said, dismissively.

As I made my way back across the sand to Cathy, he shouted after me.

"Liverpool plays Leeds tonight on television! Liverpool will win FA Cup. Robbie Fowler always scores the goals!"

I waved back, politely nodding in agreement.

"Fancy a hot date tonight Cathy? The drinks guy reckons Liverpool v Leeds is on the telly."

"Wow, how could a girl say no?"

We eventually retired from the beach once the sun had, again, dropped magnificently from view. Meanwhile, conditions were decidedly chillier back in High Wycombe, where the sun was just rising. The groundsman had awoken to find his football pitch covered by a deep layer of snow! The wintry blast that had visited the Chiltern Hills had put the highly anticipated FA Cup tie against Wolverhampton Wanderers in jeopardy as, along with the pitch, the car park and stadium approaches were also blanketed with snow. This would prove unacceptable to the safety officers required to sanction the game, even if the pitch could be made playable. The local radio station was contacted and soon broadcast a plea for volunteers to head to Adams Park, armed with shovels. The club chairman drove to the town's road-gritting depot and managed to commandeer two trucks to grit the stadium car park. Sanchez's assistant and several players, who hadn't been selected for the match, joined the ground staff and over 100 volunteers who had answered the call. After five hours of hard graft, the people of High Wycombe were able to claim at least one victory for the day; the game would go ahead; the stage was set for the biggest match in Wycombe's FA Cup history.

Anticipation had been growing around the town and the afternoon's match would be played before the stadium's first ever capacity crowd, with all available tickets having been sold five days prior to the game. This was unprecedented. One of the advantages of supporting Wycombe was that you rarely had to bother getting tickets in advance. Generally, when my friends and I took to our seats we could sit wherever we wanted, with feet stretched out upon the seat in front and arms resting on the seats adjacent; there was usually plenty of space.

Back in the evening heat of Thailand, we walked down the hill from our room to find a bar with a television to watch the Liverpool versus Leeds game. I wondered how Smudger would be getting on squeezed into a single seat, as our normally empty corner of the ground became swelled by the ranks of casual supporters, lured by the unchartered waters of the FA Cup 4th Round. Within five minutes it was likely he would be offending someone with his articulate vocal encouragement or unwieldy elbow throwing. Some of my pals would have been organised enough to purchase seats together. But most would have arrived at the ground fashionably late from the pub, as per normal, bemused by the hordes of additional spectators, as if arriving home from work and finding a complete stranger sitting in your favourite seat, reading your newspaper and hogging the television controls.

We had no such worries, and Cathy secured two prime seats in front of the television just as Liverpool kicked off in Leeds. As she made herself comfortable, I watched from the bar and ordered what seemed like our hundredth lemonades of the day. The clock behind the bar struck 10pm; while in a freezing Adams Park, the scoreboard clicked to 3pm.

Tony wearing his lucky FA Cup hat, Jason with his Wolves top hidden under a Wycombe scarf sat beside his dad Silver with his mop of mad-scientist hair, Buz about to get everyone back out of their seats again as he trouped off to the loo, Roger, Sharon, Jackie, Ian, Smudger, Bob and his daughters - already giggling at Smudger's antics, Mike, Nicko, Flipper and all the other Roobarbs, except for the overtime-grabbing Beany, took their places at Adams Park; all ready to witness the Chairboys kick their first ever ball in the FA Cup 4th Round. The Wycombe players stood facing their opponents from Wolverhampton, resplendent in Old Gold and Black; a strip that had become famous throughout Europe during the 1950's when 'The Wolves' had been crowned champions of England three times. And following a victorious series of matches against the elite of European football, hailed as 'The Champions of the World' by the press. Those heady days were long gone, but Wolverhampton Wanderers still carried a mighty weight of expectation from their fiercely passionate supporters. The noise they were making as kick-off approached suggested they were full of expectation that their Black Country heroes would soon dispose of these other upstart Wanderers who stood in their path, on the road to what they hoped would be a fifth FA Cup title in their illustrious history.

Wolves started the game in dominating fashion, eager to put their hosts on the back foot from the outset, spurred on by the vociferous support of the 2,000-strong Gold and Black Army, who were standing behind the goalmouth they were attacking. As ever, Martin Taylor stood ready to defend it for Wycombe. If Millwall had been a step up from Harrow Borough, and then Grimsby from Millwall, the start of this game served to confirm that Wolves would again be a more formidable challenge than what had gone before. Wolves looked to attack with pace down both flanks, aiming to stretch the Wycombe defence to breaking point. But the goal scoring centre-back heroes from the previous round, Paul McCarthy and Mark Rogers, stood strong in front of Taylor's goal with the ever-committed Jason Cousins and diminutive, but equally hard to beat, Chris Vinnicombe holding a firm blue line alongside them. Wolves finally found a chink in Wycombe's defensive armour after 35 minutes of trying. An opportunist effort looped from their forward Michael Branch's knee over a stranded Martin Taylor, only for the ball to hit the crossbar and rebound back into the relieved goalkeeper's arms, leaving the visiting supporters holding their heads in their hands, cursing such a near-miss. The Wolves supporters knew that an opening goal for their side would dampen the spirits of their hosts, sewing a seed of doubt within the minds of Wycombe players and supporters alike as to whether they could really compete equally with a club of Wolves' stature. Wycombe eagerly ushered the ball away from danger and advanced deeply into Wolverhampton territory. Within a minute it was the turn of the Wolves goalkeeper, Mike Stowell, to rely on the woodwork, with Wycombe's powerful forward, Andy Rammell, also being denied by the post. Having fired a warning shot against any complacency within the Wolves ranks, The Chairboys kept up the momentum, willed on by the unfamiliar roar of a capacity crowd who created a cauldron of noise whenever Wycombe mounted an attack, only to fall silent with fearful anticipation when the tide turned in favour of the Old Gold and Black. A minute after almost taking the lead, the Wanderers won a corner. Once again, the three sides of the ground surrounding the net Wycombe were attacking created a deafening roar. Martyn Lee carefully placed the ball, before sending over a cross that dropped invitingly onto the on-rushing head of McCarthy just eight yards from goal. He slammed the ball forward into the mass of bodies protecting the Wolves goal-line. Although Stowell was beaten, the ball didn't evade their highly rated defender Joleon Lescott, striking him in the most sensitive part of the body. The ball rebounded to Rammell, who coolly slotted it home, leaving Lescott prone in the back of the net with the football nestled beside him, only adding insult to painful injury.

Pandemonium erupted as the crowd saw the ball cross the line. Rammell celebrated by hurling himself into the mounds of snow which had been piled up against the advertising hoardings by the early morning volunteers, before being submerged under a pile of his teammates. The supporters stood at the front of the terrace leaning over the hoardings to embrace their heroes. If the goal had been scored 20 years before at the old Loakes Park, I would have been in prime position to jump from my place on The Wall and into the melee of celebrating Wanderers.

But, as was actually the case, I was blissfully unaware of the drama unfolding at Adams Park, instead having to settle for watching the heavyweight giants of Liverpool and Leeds on television. I sat there in my Wanderers shirt wondering what was happening back in Wycombe but, as half-time came and went, I was left frustrated as the Thai broadcaster didn't seem interested in mentioning how the other sixteen FA Cup ties were progressing.

Back in High Wycombe, the Blues were met by a barrage from Wolverhampton at the start of the second half who, despite their good play, had been stung by the Wycombe goal. Wolves were keen to cancel out Wycombe's lead as soon as possible, giving them time to push on for the victory that they were thoroughly expected to take home with them. Wycombe's cause hadn't been helped by Paul McCarthy being unable to return to the field after the break, having twisted his ankle. As the Chairboys defence looked to regroup, Wolves sensed blood and equalised following yet another marauding attack down the left-hand flank. A sense of inevitability fell over the crowds who had begun to believe that this cup run might reach the heady heights of the 5th Round. It was now the Wolves supporters who celebrated deliriously, their team striding back to the centre-spot for the restart with an added spring in their step. Wycombe manager, Laurie Sanchez, stood by the side of the pitch screaming encouragement, desperately trying to lift his players and reignite the belief that had carried them throughout the already wonderful FA Cup journey. As the players took their positions the crowd, too, began to lift. First, the regulars who supported the team week in, week out, rose from their seats; Smudger, Buz, Tony; all sitting apart for the day, along with other regular supporters dotted around the ground began to chant... "Come on Wycombe! Come on Wycombe! Come On Wycombe!" The minority grew, soon becoming the majority, and the stadium once again began reverberating with noise; the Wycombe supporters doing all they could to lift the team and drown-out the still celebrating Wolves fans. Sanchez also looked to wrestle back the initiative by making his final two substitutions as the game entered its final third, bringing on the veteran midfielder Steve Brown and a young loanee striker, Sam Parkin. If Wolves thought that Wycombe would buckle after finally succumbing to their pressure, they were wrong, and the Blues continued to give as good as they got, going close to regaining the lead on a couple of occasions.

Darkness had descended on the frozen Adams Park with ten minutes left to play and, as the floodlights illuminated the steam rising from the 22 battle weary players, thoughts around the ground began to turn to a replay at Wolverhampton's Molinuex Stadium. Any fatigue-induced errors now would prove fatal for Wycombe. FA Cup history was littered with heart-breaking underdog downfalls, driven by exhausted heroes falling just short of the line and being ruthlessly punished by mentally and physically superior opponents. Wycombe had control of the ball and worked it back to Martin Taylor, who again had been a rock defending the Chairboys goal. Taylor controlled the ball momentarily, giving his teammates a brief respite from their gargantuan efforts before sending the ball high into the air and deep into Wolverhampton territory. The Wolves defence sent it back towards the halfway line where Steve Brown was first to claim it. Still fresh legged, having been one of Wycombe's second half substitutions, Brownie strode forward on the left, midway into the Wolves half. Before Wolves had a chance to challenge, he whipped over a curling cross towards the penalty area. The ball spun through the air towards Wolves' Lescott and Wycombe's other late substitute, Sam Parkin. Lescott positioned himself between Parkin and the incoming ball. Parkin gambled, pulling away from Lescott just as they leapt to compete for the ball. As Lescott rose, he stretched every sinew but was unable to make contact with the ball, allowing Parkin the opportunity to direct it powerfully towards goal. The ball flashed from his head towards the bottom corner of the Wolves net, sending the keeper sprawling to his left. The ball evaded Stowell's fingertips and skidded over the line into the mounds of snow that still lay nestled in the back of the net. In an instant, Sanchez's substitutes had combined to swing the game dramatically back into Wycombe's favour with just minutes left to play. The terraces again exploded with unbridled celebrations and complete disbelief at the story that was unfurling. The Wolves fans, who had been so noisy and stood throughout the entire afternoon, sat back in their seats, silenced. As the clock wore down, the noise levels around the remainder of the ground grew increasingly. Now it was the Wycombe supporters who were all on their feet, willing the referee to blow the final whistle. Being so close to glory was almost unbearable for the faithful who, through many previous bitter experiences, knew that football could be the cruellest of mistresses, with perceived victory being whipped away in just a matter of seconds. Mercifully, the whistle was not long in coming, players and supporters alike celebrated wildly; the noise echoing through the valley, announcing to the town that Wycombe Wanderers had done it again.

As bedlam reigned at Adams Park, Cathy and I sat quietly in our deserted bar watching Liverpool score two late goals to put paid to Leeds United's FA Cup dreams, before strolling home at midnight ready for bed after what had been a very late night for us. Darkness came early and quickly in Kata, with day turning to night in a matter of minutes, heralded by the sun dropping from the sky like a stone. With no electricity in our room at night we had generally been in bed by 8pm each day, fooled into tiredness by the darkness. As we collapsed into bed after another exhausting day of doing nothing, High Wycombe was getting ready to celebrate. Not content with getting to the 4th Round, the Blues were going to give the 5th Round a go too. Back in July 2000, when the Extra Preliminary Round of the 2000-2001 FA Cup tournament kicked off, 610 teams had entered the competition, ranging from village amateur teams whose players paid for the privilege of getting a game, through to the billion dollar global brands such as Liverpool and Manchester United. Wycombe Wanderers were now down to the last sixteen.

Drifting off to sleep in the midnight heat, I was blissfully unaware of the amazing events that had transpired back home.

13 – Just a pair of charlatans

"James… are you asleep?"

"Yes. Why?"

"I'm ill."

Cathy was never ill. I was the one who got ill. If she said she was ill, then she meant properly ill. It was the dead of night. I couldn't see a thing.

"What's wrong?" I asked, while fumbling for a torch.

"I think I stayed in the sun for too long."

Now wasn't the time to say 'I told you so'; now was the time for sympathy and compassion.

"I told you Cathy! That was stupid today." Tiredness and worry had not combined to produce my finest hour. "I'm sorry, I didn't mean that… I'm just waking up. Where does it hurt?"

"Shoulders… chest… arms, legs, feet… even my stomach. But my shoulders and feet are worst."

I set one of our torches by the bed, and then pointed the other at Cathy's left shoulder as I knelt behind her to inspect the damage. Pushing her hair aside unveiled the worst sunburn I'd ever seen.

"Bloody hell! Your skin is literally bubbling up! You've boiled yourself!" I exclaimed with horror. "Did it not hurt in the pub watching the football?"

"It felt a bit funny, but I just thought it was my top itching. It's really burning now… I think I'm going to be…"

Cathy stumbled towards the bathroom.

"Oh god, I want a real toilet" she cried, doubling up in pain.

"Use the flush-bucket" I said. Bitter experience meant that I knew being sick into the flush-bucket was infinitely preferable to kneeling over the hole-in-the-floor toilet. The mere thought of it made me start to gag too.

The poor girl spent a wretched night toing and froing to the bathroom, whilst flitting between bouts of fever and chills. Apart from simply holding her hand, there seemed little I could do to comfort Cathy. I repeatedly soaked a couple of my t-shirts and laid them over her skin to sooth the burns, but even this was no use when the chills took over. Neither of us slept a wink, and I realised that it was tougher watching a loved one suffer than being ill myself. I felt bad that the start of our trip had been blighted by my dodgy stomach and tantrums. I made a mental note to stop being such a twat.

At first light, I left the room briefly to get drinking water and found Elle preparing breakfast. I told her about Cathy and she raced up to see her. Being a similar age, they had struck up a friendship at the breakfast bar where Cathy had generally been left to eat alone while her boyfriend suffered in the bathroom. Elle, being a girl, was of more help to Cathy in two minutes than I'd been throughout the night, racing away before returning with ointments and her mother, Mama Judy. The two women gently treated Cathy's skin. It looked as if this wasn't the first time they'd nursed a guest with sunstroke. Before leaving, Mama Judy gave her a motherly hug and then turned towards me.

"Why you let her burn? You look after her better!" she snapped, wagging her finger. There was no hug for me.

Cathy smiled and offered up a tired laugh, which made the telling-off worthwhile. After Elle and Mama Judy's visit, we both relaxed a bit. The creams applied had eased the pain, whilst the fever and sickness had both run their course. Sunday was spent dozing in the room after our sleepless night, with Cathy safely sheltered from the sun. The dramas of the day had pushed any thoughts of how Wycombe Wanderers had faired firmly from my mind. Upon waking on Monday, Cathy was much better. Any temptation for her to chase the sunshine again was helpfully removed by a rare rainy day, more akin to English weather than what we expected from Thailand. Around midday, Cathy decided that she was hungry, which was a great sign of recovery. She also wanted to get out of the room after 36 hours staring at the same four walls, and so disappeared to the shops. Although it was an overcast day, she took no chances, opting to wear one of my baggy t-shirts despite being a foot shorter than me, topped off with my floppy Stone Roses sun hat and her huge sunglasses which, between them, covered her entire face. She departed looking like a little girl who'd raided her parents' closet. Unscathed, she returned a while later bearing gifts, primarily 400 cigarettes for her, but also a couple of sandwiches for our lunch and a chocolate bar and newspaper for me; a reward for my limited nursing skills. Cathy soon tired after her shopping excursion, so we continued to lounge lazily on our bed, which doubled as our sofa and tripled as our dining table.

Back home I would flick through a newspaper in a matter of minutes, but today I was prepared to make reading the Bangkok Post last all afternoon. First, I looked at the front page to see what was going on around the world...

'TENSIONS MOUNT ON MYANMAR BORDER'

"Cathy, you're not expecting to visit the Burmese border while we're here are you?"

Cathy shook her dozing head. "Probably for the best" I muttered to myself.

'GENERAL PINOCHET PLACED UNDER HOUSE ARREST... PROTESTORS CLASH IN SANTIAGO'

"Hmmm, hopefully that will have calmed down by the time we get there."

'RIOTS IN DIVIDED KOSOVO CITY'

"Okay, that's not on our route, good."

'SHOOTING IN THE WEST BANK PROMPTS RETALIATORY STRIKES'

"Yep, we're not going there either."

'FALUN GONG FOLLOWERS BURN THEMSELVES IN TIANANMEN SQUARE PROTEST'

"What? That's awful. How long until we're in Beijing? Two months... great."

"Who are you talking to?" asked a disgruntled and half asleep Cathy, twisting around to face me.

"Sorry, I'm just reading the newspaper."

"Are you 5-years-old?"

"No, I'm 28."

"Do you want to try reading without saying the words out loud then? I'm trying to sleep!"

Turning my attentions back to my newspaper, I flipped it over to begin the in-depth reading of the sports section. The back page was primarily taken up with a report of Liverpool's victory in Leeds, Australia beating the West Indies at cricket, and basketball matches from America, all of which I read intently, and silently. Then I saw it.

'FA Cup 5th Round : Liverpool v Manchester City, Southampton v Tranmere Rovers, Leicester City v Bristol City, Bolton Wanderers v Blackburn Rovers, Sunderland v West Ham United, Tottenham Hotspur v Stockport County, Wycombe Wanderers v Wimbledon, Arsenal v Chelsea. Matches to be played weekend of 15th February'

"It says Wycombe" I whispered.

"It says Wycombe v Wimbledon!" I continued disbelievingly; my heart starting to pound.

"We did it! We beat Wolves! We did it! I don't believe it… we did it!"

By now I was bouncing up and down whilst still sitting crossed-legged on the bed.

"Cathy, we did it, we're in the next round! We bloody did it!"

"Well done" she replied sleepily, not offering up the enthusiasm Wycombe's achievement deserved.

"You stay here, I need to go out" I excitedly announced, scrambling over the convalescent.

In my haste to leave the room I found myself outside in a tropical downpour, wearing nothing but my shorts. I retreated and slipped into my flip-flops, before tearing through my bag for a shirt. Two weeks into our journey and I still hadn't unpacked. To be fair, there wasn't really any point as there was nowhere to hang anything anyway, and my zipped up bag at least offered my possessions protection from insects. I grabbed my Wanderers shirt again and one of the dozen plastic carrier bags I'd brought along 'just in case'. With Wycombe shirt proudly adorned and Bangkok Post wrapped in the carrier bag, I headed out.

The beach was deserted apart from one dripping wet westerner, wearing a Wycombe Wanderers football shirt and holding a carrier bag. I didn't care; I was stood on a beautiful beach, being pounded by huge warm raindrops and my football team had made history again. I kicked off my flip-flops and placed my shirt and newspaper under a palm tree, before running into the tumbling surf which had replaced the gentle millpond the ocean normally resembled. I splashed around and sang victorious Wanderers terrace chants while getting battered by the waves, celebrating as exuberantly as my pals back home would have done 48 hours before. My celebrations were loud enough to tempt a handful of curious locals out from their shelter to watch with bemusement as the rain eased. Amongst them was the drinks seller; as soon as I saw him, I waved and waded out from the sea.

"What you doing?" he asked as I bounded up to him; the two girls who worked in the noodle shack by the beach stepped back behind him, giggling to each other at my expense.

"I came to see you... FA Cup... Liverpool won. Wycombe boys won too! My team... the blue team!"

He continued to look at me as though I was mad, but I wasn't to be deterred.

"Look, next round... in the paper."

I unfolded the newspaper to reveal the 5th Round draw.

"What does it say?" he asked.

"Liverpool will play Manchester City. Arsenal will play Chelsea." I made sure I'd told him the teams he would recognise first. "And Wycombe Wanderers... that's my team... they will play against Wimbledon!"

He looked at the paper, then looked at me, then nodded approvingly, pausing thoughtfully before speaking.

"You want to buy lemonade now?"

"Erm, no thanks, I'm okay for now" I replied, a little crestfallen that my big news wasn't being so well received universally. Cathy had been ill so had an excuse for her lack of enthusiasm, but I'd really thought Drink-Boy would be impressed.

I put the newspaper away and wrapped my top around my neck in an attempt to dry it off, before trudging back towards the sea to walk along the beach. Wycombe Wanderers still weren't big news in Thailand, but in my world they had just done the impossible; I was happy to stroll along the beach lost in thoughts of home and my team, even if nobody else really cared.

Back home people cared though, as I found out the next day upon opening my Hotmail, discovering dozens of messages commenting on the game. This made me feel quite popular as, until now, my new email account had yet to receive enough messages to warrant a second page. The victory over Wolves must have sent the internet into near meltdown, as I now had to deal with a third page, let alone a second. Getting through them all was tougher than working for a living. Email-of-the-day went to Mike Roobarb, who had diligently typed out the News of the World's match report word-for-word 'because I can't work out how to do the bloody copy/paste thing'. Eventually I had just one more to open; marked 'Nov 2000 Examination Result Notification'. It wasn't by coincidence that this remained the only unopened message.

"Open it, come on!" urged Cathy, who was sitting looking over my shoulder, waiting her turn on the computer. "I'm sure you'll have passed."

"I'm pretty sure I won't have" I replied.

I wasn't understating my true expectations. The exam paper I'd been studying for was my nemesis. Until I passed it, I couldn't progress to the final set of four exams. I tried to comfort myself with the thought that I'd never wanted to be an accountant anyway. But, having spent five years putting myself through night school and even sacrificing seeing Wycombe beat Manchester City away in the league the weekend before my first set of exams, I really wanted to finish the job. Reluctantly, I clicked onto the email.

"Bollocks" I muttered, summing up the result perfectly.

"Wow, that's really crap isn't it?" commented Cathy.

"Yep."

"At least it wasn't even close to a Pass... that would have been really frustrating. I mean... if you'd just missed out by one mark or two... erm... oh you know what I mean."

With hindsight, I should have stuck around for the final half day of the revision course instead of going to the Harrow game, or stayed off the beer the night before with Scott and Sanj.

"Oh well, I'll get it next time. Shall we go eat?"

I really should have felt more upset, but being in Thailand instead of preparing to do 'the walk of shame' into work the next day, having to tell everyone I'd spectacularly failed my exam, seemed to be a fair consolation for such a dismal result. We strolled down the road to what had become our regular dining haunt, which we'd imaginatively christened 'The Indie Bar' due to the fact that the owner, a young Thai man, always played cool British indie music. We were on a tight budget and so, although we were on the most extravagantly extended holiday imaginable, when it came to the evenings, we kept things simple. Rather than going out drinking and eating in fancy restaurants, we just ate for necessity, and as cheaply as we could. Other plus points for the Indie Bar were that Cathy could get her beloved chips and it was conveniently close to our room if I had to make an emergency exit due to my temperamental stomach! As we weren't your average holidaymakers, we ate early before the street got busy. Generally, we were the only people around in the early evenings before the tourist trade picked up. As we approached, Indie-Boy was waiting, sitting on the step of his bar smoking. He waved from afar, doing all he could to make sure we didn't go elsewhere.

"Good evening... come in, come in" he greeted, while guiding us to the most prominent table by the window. "You go beach today? Getting very brown now!" he laughed, comparing my forearm to his which, much to the annoyance of Cathy, was by now pretty much the same colour.

Without waiting for us to order he brought over our now trademark two bottles of lemonade. Although entering a completely new world, I was already settling into the little patterns of habit that most people subconsciously draw small comforts from. The sudden removal of all such comforts upon arrival in Thailand had contributed to me initially freaking out so much, but each day was now becoming a more chilled out affair. Another couple of weeks on this curve would surely render me in a permanent state of blissful unconsciousness.

"I'll have a bowl of chips and a cheese and ham toasty please, but with no onions in the toasty" Cathy instructed Indie-Boy, who repeated her order word for word, whilst scribbling it down on his pad.

"Fried rice for me please... again."

Ten minutes later, after Cathy had performed the daily ritual of picking the unordered onions from her toasty, we tucked into our food. Barely eating anything all day made this a moment to savour. I'd always loved food but, despite this, my stomach's refusal to acclimatise to its tropical surroundings meant that the sacrifice of eating the bare minimum vastly outweighed the alternative, which guaranteed uncomfortable hours spent crouching over a toilet. I'd already forgotten that, for the best part of three decades, I'd been quite capable of eating normally without having to sprint to a toilet minutes later. This was the new norm and just another part of the travel experience.

After clearing our plates we took our time with our drinks, just listening to the music and watching the world go by out on the street, marvelling at the variety of objects, animals and passengers that could be transported by scooter. Even so, the bars and restaurants were still very quiet by the time we got up to leave. As we looked around to ask Indie-Boy for our bill, he dived back to his CD collection and fired up 'The Only One I Know' by The Charlatans. Automatically, I sat back down, unable to leave when one of my favourite bands was playing. Indie-Boy bounced over and asked if we would like another round of lemonades 'on the house'. How could we say no?

"You like this music! I put it on for you. I see your t-shirt!" he laughed. "You see this band play?"

I wasn't aware of what I was wearing so looked down and, sure enough, it was the old Charlatans t-shirt I'd bought nine years before at Brixton Academy, on the same day that Dennis Greene had scored all four goals for Wycombe away against Altrincham. I'd gone along with Jason, and we'd had a few early evening drinks to celebrate the Wanderers victory. As the warm-up acts finished, we edged our way through the massed ranks towards the front of the stage. Adidas trainer laces were tightly knotted and my watch was safely deposited into my pocket. Through bitter experience I knew finding a lost trainer after a gig was a real pain, and I'd already lost two watches in the melee down the front at previous Charlatans gigs. As the lights began to dim, signalling the imminent arrival of Tim, Martin, Rob, Jon and Mark on stage, an expectant hush fell across the crowd. Jason and I saw this as the perfect moment to start singing the praises of the goal machine Dennis Greene, as did someone across to the right side of the crowd, who joined in. Still singing, we edged further through the crowd to investigate, before converging with 'the third singer' in the mosh pit. In unison we all asked the obvious... "Are you Wycombe?"

Brief introductions were made with Jimbo until The Charlatans ambled onto the stage and kicked straight into the song 'Page One', prompting all hell to break loose for the next 90 minutes. The heat generated by 5,000 Charlatans fans when squeezed into Brixton Academy was pretty similar to that of an average Thai evening.

"Yes, we've seen the band many times" I told Indie-Boy, smiling as memories flashed through my mind of Charlatans gigs from Brighton to Blackpool with Cathy, Jason, and most of my mates, including Jimbo Roobarb on many more occasions following that chance meeting in Brixton.

"Cool. These drinks are free … you stay in my window… look cool and make place look busy, okay?"

…Free drinks? …The Charlatans? …In Thailand? We looked at each other across the table and toasted our newly found status as the official Ace-Faces of the Indie Bar.

"Cathy… am I looking cool?"

I gave my best Tim Burgess pout to passers-by, as we sat in the window, casually nodding to the beat of The Charlatans. The image would have looked a damn sight more authentic had I not succumbed to getting my Burgess-inspired mop-top shaved off just a few doors down the street. My budding PR career lasted 45 minutes before my stomach decided that playtime was over for the night; both the Indie Bar's and my own credibility would be severely put at risk unless I retreated to the sanctity of my bathroom; and fast.

14 – Wimbledon

As the small town of High Wycombe endured an epidemic of FA Cup fever over the next couple of weeks, with the Wimbledon game eagerly awaited, our Thai adventure meandered on. The sun continued to shine and we continued to do nothing more than sit on the beach most days, occasionally rising from our well rested laurels with touristy daytrips to islands and temples. Another stone lighter and skin several tones darker, I was beginning to wonder how I could string this lifestyle out forever. The thought of having to return to the real world again didn't seem overly appealing, nor did the thought of having to dust off the study books. Unsurprisingly, I managed to file these thoughts away in the furthest corner of my mind.

The world of work and study had been replaced by new mental stimulations. Cathy and I had become world-class Connect 4 players, having commandeered the frame that sat on Elle's breakfast bar. If the game had been elevated to its rightful position as an Olympic sport, we would be medal contenders. If it had been viewed as a respected battle of mental strength and strategic thinking akin to chess, we would surely be lauded as Grand Masters; mornings, afternoons and evenings came and went, all lost to epic tournaments.

Being on a tight budget ruled out expensive partying and meant that we mainly kept ourselves to ourselves. We had befriended Elle from Fantastic Hill, and would occasionally accompany her on what would, in normal circumstances, be mundane errands; but trips to local markets in a foreign land, far from the tourist path, provided great entertainment. Then there was Scouse John; the aging Liverpudlian hippy builder who also lodged at Fantastic Hill. If I could get away from my bathroom for long enough, watching his daily hungover rants at poor Elle for not having any HP Sauce to accompany his breakfast were a joy. Always with tongue firmly in cheek, he berated the poor girl as she cooked for him, but Elle just politely nodded and smiled as he vented his anger, before eventually choosing the perfect moment to render him speechless with a cutting one-liner regarding his excessive drinking or enquiries about where he'd spent the previous night. John lived in the small complex for half of the year, but never actually seemed to spend a night there. Most mornings, on our way down to the beach, we would encounter John staggering up the steep driveway to his room, struggling as if scaling the upper reaches of Mount Everest.

Sometimes he would be merrily drunk and would greet us accordingly; sometimes he was incapable of speaking, just raising an arm as we passed. Occasionally, he would be lying unconscious in a heap halfway up the hill, getting prodded by Mama Judy's broom or sniffed by an inquisitive street dog. No matter how bad a state he was in when he returned to base camp, you could set your watch by John appearing at the beach just before sunset, where he strutted along the shoreline in his tiny cut-off denim shorts. The other friendship we had formed provided as much conversation as the unconscious John; yet from our first meeting, Cathy had made friends for life. Joe and Bockie were young elephants who lived with their owner on waste ground behind Fantastic Hill. He had trained the elephants from birth to pose with the tourists visiting the restaurants of nearby Karon. They would lure the unsuspecting visitors in for a hug, and then practically pickpocket them by gently tapping the end of their trunks against pockets and handbags, before drawing attention to a multi-lingual sign informing the unassuming holidaymakers that they could pay for photographs and also for bananas to feed them. We had seen them in action when returning from some of our later evening walks on Karon Beach and, although the exploitation didn't sit comfortably, seeing them during the day just playing in their field was lovely. It's not every day you get a hug from an elephant or two on the way to get the morning's newspaper. Our Thai adventure was really in full swing and, day by day, I'd gradually got used to my surroundings and, to a certain extent, even the local wildlife. The one thing that was stubbornly refusing to embrace the adventure was my ever shrinking stomach, but despite now having spent a month unable to hold a meal inside me for more than an hour, it didn't seem like that much of a problem. And anyway, I was quite enjoying being skinny.

After another night spent squatting for England, I awoke to rays of sunshine squeezing through the slats of timber that formed the shutters on our glassless window. How beams of light could travel 93-million miles from the sun and yet still land directly onto my eyelids was beyond my comprehension, but it was nature's alarm clock and it did the trick. As was the norm, I was sprawled across the bed alone. Slowly, I swung my legs over the side of the bed to feel for my flip-flops, before grabbing the first t-shirt I could find and groggily hobbling out into the sunshine to find Cathy.

"Oh here he is… look, it's Diarrhoea Dave!" announced a very chirpy Scouse John.

"Good morning Sammy Shits… sleep well did we?" he continued.

"Ronnie Runs... come on down!" he added, failing to contain his hysterical laughter before, mercifully for me, losing his balance and falling from his stool beside Elle's open air breakfast bar, prompting our normally reserved hostess into fits of laughter herself, along with Cathy.

Despite slamming into the ground rather unexpectedly, and with a fair thump, John managed to keep his beer bottle perfectly balanced and didn't spill a drop.

"Bloody hell John, it's a bit early for that isn't it?" I said, while helping to heave him back onto his feet. The bright sun made it difficult to tell if his long hair was more blonde or grey, but his well-established moustache definitely suggested it was the latter.

"I'm still on it from last night lad" he replied, swaying gently from side to side with his eyes struggling to focus on me. He hadn't needed to tell me this; he reeked of alcohol.

"You need to get on it too boy" he continued, with all sincerity. "I'm never sick when I'm over here. You wanna know why? I'll tell you why... it's the booze. The booze kills the bugs. Even the mozzies leave me alone. A mosquito can smell alcohol in your bloodstream from 50 yards away. They know my blood is shite, so they stay away... it's true."

John then paused, turning his concentration to guiding his bottle towards his mouth, something you wouldn't believe could be made to look so difficult.

"Come on the lash with me tonight, your Cathy can stay here with Elle and Mama Judy. Liverpool are playing tonight... come on, I'll get you so wasted that your stomach won't know what's hit it."

He took another swig, this time managing to miss his mouth completely. Beer drooled from his chin onto his bare torso. He didn't appear to notice.

"Cathy... it's alright, I'll sort the fella out for you, trust me... it's strictly med... meda ... medina..."

"... Medicinal?" suggested Cathy. John was beginning to flag.

"John! Bed! Now!" Barked Elle from behind the counter, jolting him from his drink-induced slumber for long enough to stumble the ten yards back to his den.

His first snore could be heard a split second before the sound of drunken Scouser hitting mattress.

"Wow... good morning ladies" I belatedly said to Cathy and Elle, trying to bring some semblance of normality back to proceedings.

"This is why we buy rubber sheets at market the other day" explained Elle. "When that bad man get drunk, he acts like a little baby!" she continued, shaking her head. "That is why I never give him the HP Sauce he shouts for!"

I sat and watched Cathy finishing her breakfast, all the while deliberating the pros and cons of eating a slice of French toast. Eventually, after much thought, I decided that although I would have loved some, especially with the HP Sauce that Elle hid behind the counter, I'd much prefer to spend the day on the beach as opposed to in my all-too-familiar toilet.

"I take it you're out on the piss with Doctor John tonight then?" said Cathy as we ambled towards the beach.

"I wouldn't mind actually, but I'd end up spending a week's rent on beers. Plus I'm a bit out of practice" I conceded.

In all honesty, John wasn't a million miles removed from my Roobarb mates and, although Cathy had been a saint in putting up with my endless hissy fits about insects, travel arrangements and just about anything else you can think of, I was missing the banter I could only have with my friends back home. I loved the fact that Bob had been religiously printing out my emails each week, taking them down to the pub before home games and on the train to away matches to share with the Roobarbs who didn't have access to computers. It was nice to be there in spirit if nothing else. The previous week Wycombe had been playing away at Oxford in a League game, and the short trip by minibus had apparently been dominated by Ian reading intently between the lines of my email to discover non-existent hidden clues as to how much shagging I'd been doing, before regaling his own many tales of travel romances - again! Wycombe had beaten their local rivals 2-1, despite the fact that Tony had inexplicably turned up for the bus wearing his lucky FA Cup hat, which, after many years of false dawns, had finally brought some good fortune. Order had soon been restored when Smudger, Buz and Roger forcibly confiscated the bucket hat, safely stashing it away ready for its next outing at the following week's visit from Wimbledon. Wearing a lucky FA Cup hat to a League game was tantamount to waving goodbye to its magic and, with it, the FA Cup run too. I can only think that Tony had been in as bad a state from the night before as Scouse John and hadn't thought his actions through.

The sun had risen, slid across the azure sky and was starting its descent behind the Andaman Sea towards the chillier climbs of High Wycombe when Cathy said she was heading back up to the village to see Bockie and Joe before their Saturday night shift started. As I watched her disappear from the sand and into the shade of the palm trees she waved to somebody coming in the other direction. Sure enough, it was Scouse John ready to prowl the sunset-tinged surf, flicking his hair like a lion would its mane. Admittedly, this lion would no longer be the head of the pride and would have a few scars to prove it but, as with every evening, he'd sobered up enough to cruise the beach at sunset with chest proudly puffed out.

"Hiya John, how are you feeling?" I greeted my neighbour as he completed his return lap of the beach, just as the sun kissed the horizon.

John looked a bit confused, before sheepishly replying... "Alright our kid, how's it going? I was a bit battered last night... I didn't play up with Elle did I?"

"No, you were fine... you told me you'd cure my dodgy stomach though... with alcohol!"

"Did I? Sorry, I don't half talk some shite when I've had a few" he laughed, dropping himself down into the sand beside me to face the sea.

"Just beautiful isn't it?" he said admiringly, his face illuminated by the final glowing embers of the day.

John was right; the sunsets over Kata beach were amongst the most beautiful scenes I'd ever witnessed, and no two nights were ever the same. Along with the rest of the people still milling around by the beach as the sun finally sank into the sea, our conversation paused. A hush fell over the sand; no words ever felt important enough to interrupt the natural light show being played out before us.

"Where was your Cathy heading?" enquired John once the sun finally bid its farewell.

"She went to see those baby elephants."

"That pair of scallies? Bloody chancers they are… money making machines with trunks!" he sniffed, obviously not sharing Cathy's love of the elephants.

"One of the little feckers trod on my foot last year. I was limping for months… I needed my metal toe cap boots from home!" he added, going someway to explaining his less than complimentary opinion of Cathy's best friends.

"Do you work on the building sites back home then?"

"Yeah, six months on, six months off… that's off work and on the piss! I work like a dog for six months; I just go wherever the work is. I worked on the Channel Tunnel, Euro Disney, loads of motorway jobs; you name it… I built it."

"And then back to Thailand?"

"Yep, I work from April until the end of September… then I come here. I live like a monk over there… I don't touch a drop; I barely spend a penny; I kip on site and save my money. This is my home now" he said, with a doleful gaze towards the darkening horizon.

"What about family?" I couldn't help but enquire.

He shook his head. His lips appeared to tense under his white moustache.

"Not any more. I was married a long time ago, when I was about your age… two kids and all. I came back from three weeks offshore on the rigs and she'd shacked up with my best mate… my best fucking mate." John suddenly didn't seem like the happy-go-lucky bon viveur who spent his days in a hedonistic whirl.

"Bloody hell, I'm really sorry John, I didn't mean to pry." I quickly apologised, offering him an easy exit from the conversation which clearly still pained him.

"It's okay. I lost everything… my wife, my best mate, the dog… she even took my bloody wok."

He raised a rueful smile at the mention of his wok, before his expression gave way to an obvious sadness within.

"...But most of all, I lost the kids. They were just babies... two and one-years-old; they didn't need two dads around. They never knew who I was anyway. Things were different back then, you didn't have all this shared custody and seeing the girls at weekends and for holidays" he continued, sounding as though he was still trying to convince himself that this was truly the case. "I was always away working; working for them. And then that bitch just destroyed everything. I went a bit off the rails to be honest. Then a few years later my Ma passed away; I've not been back to Liverpool since the funeral. I'd go to Liverpool games away from home if they were playing nearby, and I always followed them away in the European Cup, but after a while I needed something else. I came out here for a two week holiday ten years ago and stayed for three months, then came back as soon as I could afford it. I'll stay for good one day... maybe get a girl, maybe get a bar too. I'm not stupid; I know the score here... I know the crack. I get drunk, I party with the girls, and I know they just love my money; but I get companionship here. England means nothing to me anymore" he concluded wistfully.

John had offered up more than I'd expected and, in lowering his guard, he just looked like a desperately lonely man who yearned for his long-lost wife and kids. His nomadic lifestyle now made perfect sense. I felt terrible for opening up old wounds and was intent on not pursuing the topic any further.

"Do you want to come and watch the football with me and Cathy tonight? It's FA Cup weekend; Liverpool don't play 'til tomorrow though. I'm hoping Wycombe v Wimbledon will be on" I said, looking to change the subject.

"Wimbledon? I'm not watching them bastards! I was there in '88 when they robbed us at Wembley... bloody robbed us!" he ranted.

It was good to see the old feisty John fire back into gear.

"Maybe tomorrow then... for Liverpool v Man City?"

"Aye... maybe lad, maybe. I feel like a big one tonight though, so I might go missing for a few days... y'know what I mean?"

Chuckling, he hauled himself to his feet and dusted the sand from his shorts.

"John... do you actually have any clothes?" I couldn't help but ask one more question.

"Only a t-shirt for the flight home lad!" he said, although his attention had already turned towards thoughts of the evening's adventures as he began to stroll towards the village.

Returning home, I reported back to Cathy about my conversation with John. After a month of no gossip, Cathy had been suffering withdrawal symptoms and although visibly annoyed that she'd not been there to direct further questioning, she was enthralled by his story and made sure that I recounted every detail. In return, all I discovered was that the elephants had fleeced my girlfriend for a bunch of bananas.

With the glamour ties of Liverpool versus Manchester City and Arsenal against Chelsea being shown live on the television back home the next day, as we set out for the evening I dared to think that Wycombe's match with Wimbledon might get shown in Thailand.

"So... there are just eight ties to be played. The big two are tomorrow... Sunderland are playing West Ham United in the early game tonight, which means there are only another five for Thai telly to choose from at 10 o'clock" I explained to Cathy, as we took the detour to the other end of the village, via the beach.

"Why are we on the beach?" asked Cathy, having not listened to anything I'd been saying, preoccupied with looking for Scouse John as we passed by the numerous bars he might be propping up.

"It's football night, I don't want Indie-Boy to see us going to the Footy Bar."

"What? We aren't under contract there you know" she replied, perplexed at the five minute detour.

Cathy was soon appeased by lemonade and a bag of crisps, as she sank into the highly coveted sofa that faced the three screens in the bar. Going out early had paid dividends; we would be watching the evening's footballing drama unfold in comfort.

"Perfect! Get comfy... it's only two hours until the Wycombe boys show the world what they are made of!" I said excitedly. Cathy devoured her crisps before moving onto the packet I'd bought for myself.

We endured West Ham beating Sunderland 1-0. Admittedly, the only enjoyment that could be taken from the experience was that the weather in Sunderland looked atrocious, raising ironic cheers from everyone who entered the bar. Nothing makes a holidaymaker happier than being reminded that they're sitting somewhere significantly warmer than their friends back home. As the game came to an end, the butterflies in my stomach started to take flight.

"Do you need the loo?" Cathy looked concerned, pausing by the table, ready to abort her trip to the bar.

"No, I'm just excited... it's only ten minutes to kick-off!"

I could barely contain my excitement. I still didn't know which game was going to be shown, but it had to be the Wanderers. Everybody loves an underdog story; surely the Asian networks would have thought about that when selecting their games?

"I've got some bad news..." said Cathy, placing our drinks on the table.

"What?"

But before she had a chance to explain, the channel switched from its studio based pundits across to its next broadcast.

"That's rugby. That's not football, that's bloody rugby" I gasped.

This wasn't part of the plan.

"Oi mate, excuse me... the telly is showing rugby; can you change the channel?" I called to the barman.

"Rugby now... Six Nations. No more football on today... rugby now; rugby later."

As he spoke he pointed the remote control towards the screens to change one to another sports channel. For a moment my hopes were raised, only to come crashing back to earth as the channel switch just meant we now had a choice of watching two rugby internationals. I dropped dejectedly into the sofa and knocked back my lemonade in a matter of seconds, unlike the previous three which I'd managed to stretch across three hours.

"Come on, let's go... I bloody hate rugby."

There were two reasons for my utter loathing of rugby.

Firstly, there was the one and only time that I'd endured a rugby lesson at school. My new PE teacher decreed that nobody could play for the school football team anymore unless they played for the rugby team too. He called me out from the reluctant crowd of trialists to help illustrate how to tackle. He threw me the ball and, before I knew what was happening, he launched himself at me, sending me crashing into the turf, the ball embedded in the pit of my stomach. With hindsight, I should have braced myself, but had just expected him to talk us through the required technique and maybe demonstrate with a gentle slow motion example. I wasn't in any pain as such, worryingly, I couldn't feel anything at all. I couldn't breathe, I couldn't move; I vaguely remember being able to blink. As I lay there looking up at the clouds, a gaggle of faces nervously peered down. My lack of movement gave the teacher the scare of his life too, as he pushed through the only scrum he would ever witness on our playing fields to check on me. I guess paralysing a pupil on his first day wouldn't have looked too good on the CV and, from that day forth, we never had to play rugby again.

Secondly, my dislike for the game was only reinforced by the blazer and tie wearing rugby players I had to endure during my college days. I've never quite got the wackiness of their 'sticking-your-genitalia-in-a-pint-of-beer-then-getting-your-mate-to-down-it' drinking games, nor the incessant songs that followed every game they played too. More annoying than that was the conundrum that I just could not fathom; what possessed pretty girls to fawn over these buffoons, parading with ties around heads and trousers around ankles? I, too, was a drunken idiot every Saturday night, singing incoherently, but at least I dressed normally and didn't drink my mate's penis-dunked beer; surely I represented a far more attractive option for a date on student-night at Pizza Hut? Thankfully, midway through my final year I met Cathy, who was more impressed by a decent indie-boy haircut than a vomit-drenched blazer. The fact that she also had a part-time job at Pizza Hut, which meant that every night was now pizza night, only sealed the deal.

As she finished her fifth packet of cheese and onion crisps, I cursed the rugger-buggers again; now I had a third reason to despise them. Imagine showing rugby internationals on television instead of Wycombe Wanderers v Wimbledon in the FA Cup 5th Round; utterly ridiculous.

With the teams poised to enter the fray, tension levels rose in the Adams Park player's tunnel, on the terraces, and in a small, but incredibly annoyed corner of a Thai bar. But one player stood ready to take to the field, just grateful for a brief release from the type of stresses that put all others into perspective. Steve Brown hadn't joined Wycombe's preparations on Thursday or Friday, as his 15-month-old son, Maxwell, was enduring a life-threatening operation to hopefully cure him of a chronic stomach problem that had blighted his short life. Brownie, at 34, had been a professional footballer for a long time, so when he told the Blues manager that he was okay to play, Lawrie Sanchez knew he could trust his feisty midfield general. Adams Park was once again packed to capacity with the people of High Wycombe increasingly falling under the spell of the FA Cup. Wimbledon themselves had experienced the ultimate FA Cup glory 13 years earlier, by shocking Liverpool and the watching world at Wembley in the Final itself. Wycombe's manager had forever ensured his place in history that day, by heading home the only goal of the match. Sanchez instantly became a Wimbledon legend; his goal ensured that Wimbledon would no longer only be famous for a tennis tournament and its fictional litter-picking bears. Twelve years a Don, Sanchez waved to the Wimbledon fans to acknowledge their salutations as he made his way to the dugout, but now intent on turning the tables on the most famous FA Cup giant-killers of them all. Football was a business, and his paymasters were now Wycombe Wanderers; any loyalties to the glories of his past were set aside, and for the next 90 minutes he would be focused on orchestrating the current day Wimbledon's downfall. The game started in a similar manner to those against Grimsby and Wolves, with the team from the higher division aggressively taking the early initiative, trying to rattle their hosts. Steve Brown, for one, was not a player to be easily rattled and, within 15 minutes had landed a crunching tackle on his combative opponent, Neil Ardley, who, like most of his teammates, had spent the majority of his career playing in the top division of English football. Wimbledon had only been relegated from the Premier League after a 15 year tenancy this season, and they fully expected to bounce straight back at the first time of asking. Despite Ardley's, together with his teammates, protestations at Brown's challenge, the referee gave Brownie the benefit of the doubt and gave no further punishment than a free-kick to The Dons. He wasn't so charitable a couple of minutes later when Brownie clattered Ardley again, this time brandishing a yellow card. Paul McCarthy soon followed Brownie into the referee's notebook, along with Wimbledon's million pound signing Darren Holloway. McCarthy was furious at a late challenge by Holloway on his teammate Jason Cousins (himself no stranger to inflicting pain) and so decided to help Holloway to his feet by grabbing him by the throat. If Wimbledon were to beat Wycombe they would need to do it using there Premier League quality as, judging by Brown and Macca's example, the Chairboys would not be bullied into submission.

Or maybe they would.

With 25 minutes gone, Wimbledon attacked. As several players vied for the ball, Blues goalkeeper Martin Taylor was kicked by the on-rushing Don, Mark Williams, just as Brownie conceded a corner. Williams was quick to apologise, leaving Taylor rubbing his thigh while preparing for the ensuing corner with a grimace on his face. To add insult to injury, Williams then rose highest to meet the resulting cross and powered a header into the Wanderers net. But Wycombe had come too far to just roll over and succumb to their guests and Keith Ryan soon smashed a left-footed effort towards the Wimbledon goal prompting their goalie, Kelvin Davis, into a flying save to preserve The Dons lead. The Wanderers fans agonised at the near-miss before applauding the effort, whilst from the other end of the ground, as is the nature of football, the relieved Wimbledon fans taunted Ryan.

Ryan had been playing for Wycombe since their non-league days and, along with the fiery Cousins and cultured winger Davie Carroll, helped to instil the spirit of the club to the younger, less experienced players now coming through. They had been there before the club had turned professional and, just like the thousands who cheered them on from the terraces, they knew what it was like to have a real job from Monday to Friday and, through this, the bond with the supporters was even greater; the fans lived their dreams through Ryan, Cousins and Carroll. Keith Ryan had earned the nickname 'Rhino' because of his combative style (okay, and it sounded a little like Ryan) but, just like a rhino, Ryan was thick-skinned and the taunts from the visiting Dons fans wouldn't unsettle him in the slightest. I was grateful that he possessed this attribute as many years earlier, when he had only been with the club for a couple of months, he stood watching a game on the terraces just behind me. I wasn't aware that he was there and spent the majority of the game, very loudly, telling anyone who would listen just how happy I was that he wasn't playing, and what an awful footballer he was. Maybe he took my criticisms on board at that early stage and used them to his advantage; who knows?

Back on the pitch the game was nearing the end of the first half, when the Wanderers' Michael Simpson was dispossessed on the halfway line. A quick interchange of passes saw Wimbledon bearing down on the Wycombe goal. Jason Euell drove forward before sliding the ball through the heart of the Wycombe defence towards his attacking partner, Patrick Agyemang, on the edge of the penalty area. Agyemang turned inside McCarthy's last-ditch lunge, opening up his body to face the Wanderers net and the on-rushing goalkeeper. Momentarily, the ball seemed to be rolling out of Agyemang's control but, stretching his long leg out in front of him, he just managed to get a toe to the ball, poking it beyond the despairing dive of Taylor and bobbling into the corner of the Wanderers net. It was now a two goal advantage that the high flying visitors would take into the half-time break. This late setback dealt a savage blow to the Wanderers, whilst on the flipside Wimbledon were heading into the break with a huge fillip to their own ambitions. The Wycombe players' shoulders slumped as the ball hit the net; on three sides of the ground, an air of inevitability that the magical FA Cup run was nearing its finale seemed to take over. Even the Roobarbs, who were again scattered amongst the capacity crowd, sat subdued as the referee blew his whistle to conclude the first half.

Sanchez spent the next 15 minutes trying to lift his team, but within seconds of the restart Wimbledon attacked again, smelling blood and looking to land a third and decisive blow. Thankfully, Taylor was equal to the challenge making yet another wonderful save; this time denying the Swede, Par Karlsson. This early escape seemed to spark the players and supporters alike into action; being two goals down felt bad, but conceding a third would have felt infinitely worse. Wycombe began to rally. They were again having as much of the game as their opponents although, buoyed by their two goal advantage, Wimbledon always looked confident and assured. Smudger was getting restless in the stands, constantly being asked to sit down, while trying to mind his language so as not to offend the old lady who was sitting in front of him.

"Sort it out Sanchez!" he bellowed, unable to contain his frustrations any longer, but impressively keeping his outburst civil.

At that very moment, Sanchez signalled to his substitutes and took the risk of making all three available changes in one fell swoop. Off came Andy Rammell, who'd carried an injury into the game, and the two wingers, youngster Martyn Lee and the veteran Davie Carroll. Neither youth nor experience had been able to unlock the key to Wimbledon's well-drilled defence as yet so Sanchez gambled everything, looking to somehow change the dynamic of the game. On in their places went Danny Bulman, Andy Baird and Sam Parkin, the hero of the previous round, following his late goal against Wolves.

"That's what I've been saying... get Parkin on" announced Smudger, feeling vindicated as he addressed the crowd around him.

The Blues turned up the pressure on their guests but couldn't get the breakthrough that their play deserved. With time slipping away, the two goals required to earn a replay seemed increasingly unlikely. Then, with just

18 minutes remaining, the goal that Wycombe had worked so hard for finally arrived. The game's first goalscorer, Williams, looked to slow the game down by passing the ball back to Wimbledon's goalkeeper, with the intention of Kelvin Davis then belting it deeply into Wycombe territory. Davis was a good keeper, but footwork wasn't his strong point; Keith Ryan charged towards him to try and force a mistake from a perceived lost cause. It was a long shot, but these were desperate times. Hurried into his clearance by the advancing Ryan, Davis could only lift the ball gently back towards the halfway-line. Parkin was first onto the ball, pushing forward down the left flank while the Wimbledon players were caught flat-footed, following their keeper's weak clearance. The crowd roared Parkin on as he looked to deliver the ball back into the heart of the Wimbledon goalmouth, but he began to slip as he stretched to cross it, leaving his pass under-hit and intercepted by the first line of defence. The on-rushing Wycombe forwards forlornly curtailed their runs into the penalty area, all except the tenacious Ryan who hurled himself into yet another tackle. This time Rhino managed to block the clearance. The ball ricocheted back into the heart of the penalty box towards Michael Simpson. Striking the ball first time as it span towards him, he didn't make a true contact, but at least managed to send a scuffed shot goalwards. Davies started to dive confidently to his left, but the ball took a deflection from the flailing boot of Wimbledon's Peter Hawkins - taking away what little pace the shot had, but also changing its trajectory, lifting the ball inches over the now desperate grasp of the keeper who was helpless to react. The crowd gasped as the ball gently looped over the keeper towards the goal, bouncing two yards from the line, and then again at the base of the goalpost. With Davis stranded on his knees, the players of both teams could do no more than watch as the ball travelled along the white line, clinging to it like a gymnast on a beam, spinning wildly for what felt like an eternity, before finally falling in The Chairboys' favour by veering into the net.

A poor back-pass, a scuffed clearance, a weak cross, a blocked second clearance, a mis-hit shot, an ill-timed deflection and a fortuitous ricochet; it was a scrappy goal, but nonetheless one worth its weight in gold, drawing raptures from the Wanderers support. Smudger's two flailing arms were joined by 18,000 more around Adams Park, whilst on the away terrace the other 2,000 hands were raised to faces in horror, as the crowd prepared for what would surely be an excruciatingly tense final 15 minutes. The game's momentum had turned. Just as Wimbledon's second goal had taken the winds from Wycombe's sails, Simpson's goal had whipped them back in The Blues favour; now a hurricane of hope was threatening to destroy all of The Dons prior good work. Passes became crisper, movement more decisive and tackles stronger. The underdogs were now in the ascendancy and the calm assurance of the visitors was being torn apart as they found themselves subjected to constant pressure.

In the midst of the frenzy, Wycombe's Mark Rogers went down injured. Rogers was a tough Canadian who had paid his own way to England to pursue the dream of becoming a professional footballer. This bloody-mindedness also summed up the way he played, and if Rogers was on the floor, then he was really hurt. The injury couldn't have happened at a worse time for The Blues, as it gave Wimbledon a respite when they were desperately clinging to the ropes, and looking likely to succumb to a knockout blow. As Rogers was helped from the field it dawned on everyone that Wycombe had already made their quota of substitutions; they would now need to find the elusive equaliser with only ten players against Wimbledon's eleven. The crowd roared on the ten men with renewed vigour, doing all they could to become the extra player themselves by creating a cauldron of noise to inspire their heroes. At every opportunity the Wanderers continued to pour forward; Steve Brown sent a high cross deep into the penalty area, looking for the heads of Baird and Parkin, along with Rhino and Macca who'd both abandoned all defensive duties. The cross evaded all of Brownie's intended targets, but as it dropped towards The Dons defender Hawkins, he couldn't be sure if any of the Wanderers aerial threats were lurking behind him ready to pounce, and so cautiously opted to guide the ball behind for a corner kick. Unfortunately for the luckless defender, he only succeeded in looping the ball gently up in front of his goalkeeper rather than out of play. Maybe it was a momentary lapse in concentration, or just nerves, but Davis instinctively plucked it out of the air, rather than trying to clear the ball without illegally using his hands following his defender's intervention.

"Back-pass!" screamed 9,000 Wycombians simultaneously, not that the referee needed any help in spotting the infringement; Davis was stood holding the ball like a guilty child caught with his hand in the cookie jar.

"Ten yards Ref, get them back ten yards!" bellowed Buz and Tony, as is obligatory of any self-respecting football fan when a referee is organising a free-kick. Although with the infringement taking place so close to goal, for the Wimbledon players to be ten yards from the ball would have meant asking the front row of their supporters sitting behind the net to vacate their seats. Instead, the referee tried to organise the chaotic scene with the entire Wimbledon team lined up on the goal-line, interspersed with several Wanderers players hell-bent on disrupting the defenders to create a chink in the wall's armour. Whilst all of this was going on, Kelvin Davis tried to figure out the best place to stand, before squeezing himself into the middle of the mass of bodies. Steve Brown stood two yards behind the ball, poised to blast it goalwards from Michael Simpson's tapped pass. Simpson twice tried to tempt a break in the wall by pretending to knock the ball to Brownie. This only succeeded in giving the defenders two opportunities to sneak a few inches forward, by which time the referee had also had enough of Simpson's antics and had given up pushing the wall back. By the time Simpson eventually touched the ball to Brownie, the white-shirted wall was already upon him, bearing down like a wave devouring a surfer, making it impossible to find a route through to goal. The ball rebounded from the wall, bouncing high and away from the penalty area sending the Wimbledon supporters leaping into the air with relief, confident that the danger had been averted. The ball dropped to Wycombe's Sam Parkin on the edge of the box. But with his back to goal and being tightly marked he had no option but to pass the ball even further from the danger zone, back to Chris Vinnicombe who, by now, was the only Wanderer still defending. Vinnicombe chipped the ball high into the sky, back into the Wimbledon penalty area where their defenders were rushing out en mass, aiming to leave the Wanderers stranded behind them in offside positions. As the ball hurtled in, it clipped a Wimbledon head. Vitally, the slight touch meant that the three Wycombe players behind the defensive line were no longer in offside positions, completely changing the complexion of play as they eagerly bore down on the dropping ball. Steve Brown reached it first, just before the desperate charge of Kelvin Davis clattered him leaving Brownie in agony on the ground, but not until his flicked shot had steered the ball through the keeper's legs and into the empty net, giving the Wanderers an equaliser!

As Brown kept his promise of getting a goal for his poorly son, the stadium erupted again; three sides in unbridled joy at the sight of their team coming back from the dead, the other incredulous at the referee's decision to allow the goal to stand when at least three Wanderers attackers, including the scorer, appeared to be offside. The Wimbledon players and management team also showed their disgust, surrounding the referee and his linesman to berate the decision, driven by fury as victory slipped from their grasp. All the while, Steve Brown remained prone on the pitch amid the chaos getting medical support from Wycombe's physiotherapist, whilst back over by the dugout his assistant frantically tried to bandage up Mark Rogers to enable him to see out the remaining minutes on the pitch. When order was finally restored, Rogers bravely hobbled back onto the field with Sanchez despatching his wounded defender with the brief to 'be a nuisance'. With

Wimbledon in shock, the Blues remained in the ascendancy and continued to push for what would prove to be an unlikely and famous winner. That opportunity never came though, and Wycombe players and fans alike were more than delighted to rescue a draw against their illustrious opponents, who trudged away from the field feeling as though they had been defeated, having for so long been in the ascendancy themselves.

The supporters, too, began to slowly disperse. Smudger was eager to rejoin the Roobarbs in the bar to celebrate, but with the capacity crowd in attendance he would have to wait. As he stood there impatiently, the old woman who had been sitting quietly in front of him for the entire match turned and smiled, before gesturing at him to lean forward towards her.

"Well, they got out of fucking jail today, didn't they?" she whispered, before chuckling to herself and shuffling off down the stairs, leaving Smudger, for the first time in his life, as the shocked recipient of foul language on the terraces.

Back in Thailand, Cathy was asleep and I was squatting for England, whilst thinking about Wycombe, sad in the knowledge that, by now, realistically they would surely be out of the FA Cup.

15 – A chill wind in paradise

"Will you give it a bloody rest James!" snapped Cathy, before turning over on her beach towel to expose her back to the midday sun.

"I mean it; I'm not going back in there... how could they not show the football?"

"For the final time... the Six Nations rugby would get more viewers than Wycombe bloody Wanderers!"

"Rugby is shite... end of..."

We'd been bickering for hours. Another night spent in the bathroom hadn't helped my disposition and, as ever, Cathy was bearing the brunt of my grumpiness. Being a mature, self-respecting man, I stomped down to the shoreline. Looking back over my shoulder, Cathy didn't appear overly bothered by my dramatics, so I took a detour into the village when I reached the far end of the beach, rather than retracing my steps. I was sure that any prolonged absence would make her realise that I had been right all along. Where the sand met the street, I put my t-shirt back on, not yet having adopted Scouse John's minimalist dress code when away from the beach. Even the smallest t-shirt I'd packed, while listening to the Grimsby game back in my bedroom a month before, now looked ridiculous on me. Since arriving in Thailand, hand washing my clothes had stretched my t-shirts a little, but my ever decreasing frame was certainly the main factor. To prolong Cathy's punishment a little further, I decided upon some retail therapy, in the form of a t-shirt that actually fitted.

The market was at the far end of the street. As I meandered up the dusty track, carefully dodging mopeds as they whizzed through the village, I saw the barman from the Footy Bar. He was busily chalking up the 'what's on' sign that sat on the sidewalk outside the pub. He looked up and shouted across the street to me...

"Football back tonight my friend, see you later!"

I smiled and waved back, feeling a bit guilty about my planned boycott. A couple of doors along, I waved through the window to my 'hairstylist', receiving back a toothless smile. A few moments later another voice caught my attention...

"Hello Charlatans! I thought you and Red Hair go home! I see you tonight… we'll play some tunes, yes?"

This time it was Indie-Boy unloading crates of beer from a dangerously overladen tuk-tuk. Again, I replied with a wave. Inside, I was thrilled at getting acknowledged by both guys, but played it cool. At least the pale skinned elderly German tourists who were walking along the street just a few yards behind me would think I was a hardened traveller, even if my girlfriend knew that I blatantly wasn't. Buoyed by this new found popularity, I confidently bounced into the clothes stall and picked out a 'medium' sized t-shirt rather than an 'extra-large' for the first time in ten years. The Germans ventured in behind me and started looking around too.

"350 Baht please" said the same little girl from my awful flip-flop bartering episode.

"200 Baht" I replied confidently.

"325 Baht please" countered my young adversary.

"No, I pay you 200 Baht."

I'd been in town a month now; and seemed more popular on Kata High Street than I'd ever been in High Wycombe's equivalent. I wasn't going to get stung again and, besides, I needed to make back some of the money I'd overpaid on the flip-flops.

"310 Baht. No less please" the girl said politely.

"200 Baht. That's all."

The little girl of about ten-years-old suddenly looked a lot younger. Her eyes welled up with tears.

"Hey… you pay the girl! What is wrong with you?" said the German woman sternly as her husband shook his head in disgust.

"Here… here you go, 310 Baht for the t-shirt… and keep the change… 40 Baht for you" I stammered.

I was mortified. My newly acquired confidence had been wiped away almost as quickly as the little girl's tears upon receiving her 40 Baht bonus.

"Shame on you!" muttered the miserable German cow, followed by something similar, no doubt, from her husband in his native tongue. I scuttled away from the scene as quickly as possible.

Back down on the beach and with my composure partially restored, Cathy was back sunning her front when I delivered an 'I'm sorry for being a twat' lemonade and crisps peace offering. Having suddenly become a pariah with the latest influx of German tourists, I thought a thawing of relations with my closest ally a sensible option.

"I think we should go back to the Footy Bar tonight... it's wasn't their fault that the rugby was on all the sports channels."

Cathy was yet to speak, but had accepted my gifts all the same.

"What about the Indie bar; are we hiding from matey-boy in their again then?" replied Cathy snootily.

"No, we should probably pop in and see him too... maybe we could go out early and have dinner and a game of pool there before the football" I casually suggested.

"A game of pool? Have you won the lottery?" mocked Cathy, taking full advantage of me being in the doghouse.

To avoid the risk of falling out again, I let her teasing wash over me before heading down to the sea to let the waves do the same.

Bathing in the surf, my thoughts drifted to home and thoughts of what my friends would be doing. Six o'clock on Sunday morning? I guessed that Buz, Nicko and Smudger would be asleep on their sofas having been unable to make it up the stairs after the post FA Cup drinks. Lee and Ian would still be dancing in the 100-Club. Beany the gas man would probably be raking in the triple rate overtime, especially as it was FA Cup weekend as, for some reason, he didn't do FA Cup games. Jason would certainly still be out and about somewhere and his dad, Silver, would be awake and putting Jason's football kit into his van, waiting for the call to a mystery location to pick up his rapscallion son, which would then be followed by the weekly race against time to get him to his Sunday League match before kick-off. Despite having partied all night, he'd still be the best player on the pitch, just like every week.

Later that afternoon, Cathy and I readied ourselves for our big night out. Dinner from the 'pre-theatre' menu and some games of pool at the Indie Bar awaited, before an FA Cup double-header in the Footy Bar.

"What're you doing?" I asked Cathy, alluding to the fact that she was modelling my new t-shirt, as I came out of the toilet for what would hopefully be the last time for several hours.

"I think it looks good" she replied, looking down admiringly at herself.

"It's a bit long for you."

"I could wear it as a dress."

"A very short dress though" I said, by now realising that I had a fight on my hands to get my new t-shirt back.

"It must be too small for you, surely?"

Cathy reluctantly handed over the shirt, now taking her turn to have a sulk upon seeing her slimmed down boyfriend fitting nicely into it.

"Oh my god, I hadn't realised you'd lost that much! Your mum would have a fit if she saw you!"

Having sensed the opportunity for a whole new wardrobe, she then slipped on my Wanderers shirt. The blue quarters hung from her like an oversized sack, with its hem and long sleeves reaching beyond her knees.

"Maybe with a belt?" she suggested hopefully, receiving nothing more than a shake of my head.

One World Cup-style shirt swap later, we were ready for our hot date.

Hot date or not, a hard fought 2-1 victory on the pool table was still celebrated with glee, and the fried rice that followed tasted all the better for it. Cathy didn't seem too bothered about her loss though, and happily demolished her now obligatory 'chips with a cheese and ham toastie... no onions please', just as soon as she'd removed the onions. Soon after, we said goodnight to Indie-Boy and headed in the direction of our room, before taking a sneaky left towards the beach instead of a right back up the hill.

"Do we really need to take the detour?" Cathy protested. "The Footy Bar is literally six doors down the street!"

"Ah, come on… a walk on the beach won't hurt" I replied, still not wanting to appear disloyal to Indie-Boy.

As we strolled hand in hand past the posh hotel that sat at the far end of the beach, the old German couple came walking from the other direction. Both were practically snarling as they passed, despite Cathy nodding politely.

"Did you see the faces on that pair? Miserable bastards! It makes you wonder why some people bother going on holiday" she hissed as they disappeared into their hotel.

A minute later, and for the second night in a row, we managed to grab the prized front-row sofa, mainly on account of being the first people arriving at the Footy Bar (excluding the barman and the hostesses who waited tables and socialised with the clientele). Despite our minimal spending, the girls seemed to really like Cathy and me. There didn't seem to be many people of our age frequenting the place, and the Thai girls, with their jet-black hair, loved Cathy's red locks. They seemed to enjoy having a guy in the bar who they didn't have to flirt with too.

Midway through the first half of the Arsenal versus Chelsea game, I realised that Cathy hadn't returned from the bar. A quick glance behind me showed that she was playing more pool, this time with the girls from the bar. This proved to be a win-win situation; I got to watch the football in peace; Cathy got to enjoy some female company; and most importantly, nobody seemed to have noticed that we weren't spending any money. Thierry Henry and Sylvain Wiltord had put Arsenal 3-1 ahead late into the second half before I saw her again. My undivided attention on the football was broken by high-pitched hysterical laughter from behind me, closely followed by the stomping sound of Cathy approaching, precariously balancing a tray of drinks and wearing one of the girls' eight inch high platform stilettos.

"…Your drink sir."

Carefully, she set a drink on the table before tentatively manoeuvring a ten-point turn like a giraffe on ice, and heading back towards her adoring audience of Thai girlfriends who were cheering her every awkward step. Bemused, I tried to process what had just happened, before sinking back into my football bubble to watch Arsenal see out the remainder of the game, securing their place in the Quarter-Final of the FA Cup. The game finished just as the raucous cackle from Cathy's trial run as a bar hostess eventually died down. We were still the only punters there and so the bar fell into relative silence; that is, until the television show returned from its post-game commercial break, adding Arsenal's score line to the list of Saturday's results.

"They drew! They drew! They bloody drew!"

I jumped up from my seat triumphantly before tripping over the low table that sat in front of the sofa. Cathy's clumsy tottering was spectacularly surpassed as I stumbled over the table, ending up lying on my back, as if poleaxed by my rugby-loving PE teacher. For a moment I lay there stunned, looking up at the ceiling fan whizzing around above me. A grazed shin and a very public fall from grace would normally lead to a surge of embarrassment, but not when you've just seen that your team have earned a very respectable and unexpected draw in the FA Cup.

"Wee-kaaam One-Dress, did you hear that? He said Wee-kaaam One-Dress!"

Shouting and pointing at the television from the floor, I received nothing back but looks of utter bewilderment from the barman, his hostesses and even my own girlfriend.

"We drew 2-2! Wycombe Wanderers drew! I can't believe it!"

I continued ranting with an inane grin on my face, not speaking to anyone in particular.

Two hours later, Liverpool's international superstars had knocked four goals past Manchester City to join Arsenal in the draw for the last eight, and still I sat staring at the screen, smiling from ear to ear. Technically, my beloved Wanderers were in the 6th Round draw too. Okay, they had the small task of somehow beating Wimbledon in the replay back on Wimbledon's home turf, but still, for now they were in the draw for the next round.

'Wycombe Wanderers, in the draw for the 6th Round of the FA Cup?' Just the thought of it was enough to send me into another fit of giggles.

"James, let's go... I think you're starting to freak people out" whispered Cathy, gently tugging at my arm and guiding me out of the bar, which at some stage during the Liverpool game had filled up considerably behind me.

I awoke early the next morning. Cathy was still asleep, the temperature had yet to reach unbearable and I hadn't been to the toilet once during the night; all of these factors led me to believe that I might still be asleep. Then my thoughts turned to the previous night; Cathy the bar hostess in platform stilettos? Wycombe drawing with Wimbledon? Yes, I concluded that I was definitely just dreaming. Then I noticed the bruise on my shin - the coffee table; that jump for joy; the results on the television.

"I'm awake, it's all true!"

When Cathy eventually stirred, she too discovered an injury from the night before, in the form of a swollen ankle following her high heeled escapades. Her ankle had stiffened overnight and she could barely walk, which meant I was dispatched down to see Elle to procure breakfast in bed for my injured trainee hostess. I treated myself to some scrambled eggs in the morning sunshine to celebrate the Wycombe result, and also the fact that I'd managed to make it through a whole night without a dodgy stomach. I'd felt drunk on euphoria in the bar, but the fact that my head felt clear as I devoured my breakfast suggested that I was indeed hangover free.

"Elle, check this out" I said, drawing her attention away from the French toast she was preparing for Cathy, towards the shambolic wreck of a man tentatively making his way up the driveway.

For every step taken forward, John took at least three to the left or right. It was painful to watch; painfully funny. As we marvelled at his drunken ascent I quickly passed the HP Sauce bottle back to Elle to hide. A minute or so later, the intrepid mountaineer reached the summit of Fantastic Hill, steadied himself, flicked his hair from his face and raised his arms out wide before closing his eyes. Elle and I looked at him and then at each other, puzzled, both fully expecting that our next move would be to peel him back up from the floor.

"Elle, Elle... my belle. I need some food... can you make it for me now? My beautiful Elle" sang Scouse John, surprisingly well, to the tune of 'Michelle' by The Beatles.

As ever, John's entrance had been nothing short of spectacular. He staggered wearily across to Elle's breakfast bar, leaning against it with his elbows and dreamily gazing across to Elle with his chin cupped between his hands. John was on the charm offensive.

"What you sing to me, you drunk man?" snapped Elle with a mock frown.

"It's the feckin' Beatles!"

John pulled himself upright before staggering back a step.

"Help! I need somebody. Help! Not just anybody... Won't you take me down, cos I'm going to, Strawberry Fields, nothing is real... There are places I remember... Isn't it good? Norwegian Wood... Altogether now! We all live on a yellow submarine, a yellow submarine, a yellow submarine!" roared John, confusing the hell out of Elle with an impromptu Beatles medley.

"It's The Beatles Elle, you've heard of The Beatles haven't you?"

Elle nodded without looking up, busying herself in the kitchen.

"Oh yeah, I knew the Beatles me like... cracking lads, I drummed with them a couple of times. I went to school with George and Paul; played in the same footy team as John when we were kids; and I went out with Ringo's cousin. Lovely lass she was, that Karen... erm, no... was it Karen? What was her name again?"

His sentence trailed off as he started to question his memory.

Elle looked at me and I shook my head dismissively. I wasn't sure exactly how old John was but, despite his haggard demeanour, I didn't believe that he was quite old enough to have been in Paul McCartney's class at school, let alone the rest of his dubious story. He'd previously told me that Bill Shankly had tried to sign him for Liverpool as a youngster, but he'd just started an apprenticeship on the docks. Either John was prone to telling the odd tall story, or he was Merseyside's greatest 'nearly man'.

"Elle, you know you're the only girl for me... but you need to get me some HP Sauce lass."

John appeared to have forgotten about Ringo's gorgeous cousin.

"Here is black coffee. Here is runny egg sandwich. Sit down and eat. No falling off stool today."

"Elle, come on darlin'… get me some brown sauce and I'll marry you. I'll take you away from all this. You know you love me too Elle!"

"You take me where? Bad bars in Patong? Pattaya?" questioned Elle sarcastically.

"I'll take you around the world Elle; just like Toby Trots over there and his Cathy."

As he pointed in my direction, John wobbled on his precarious perch, saved from falling by the worktop behind him.

"HP Sauce. I just want some brown sauce Elle" he whispered again, as Elle angrily wiped up the coffee he'd managed to spill following his latest battle against gravity.

"Speaking of Cathy, I'd better take her this breakfast. Thanks Elle!" I said, having become distracted by the latest instalment of Scouse John's drunken ramblings.

"Hey, John… did you see Liverpool last night? They won 4-2. Wycombe drew with Wimbledon… we might get you in the next round!" I added, wearing my FA Cup smile again.

"What? Your shower-of-shite will never grace the same pitch as the greatest football team in the world!" he roared, before standing, ready to burst into song again.

I took this as my prompt to head back to my room, leaving Elle to listen to John's rendition of the Liverpool anthem 'You'll Never Walk Alone'. Back in our room, Cathy was lying with her swollen ankle raised up on a mound of bedding.

"Ooh, that looks sore."

"I can barely walk."

"I've seen you in heels twice before… and you fell over on both occasions."

"That's bollocks!" Cathy wasn't impressed.

"There was your sister's wedding… when you collapsed at the altar, just as she turned to walk back up the aisle!"

"Come on! That wasn't the heels, it was stupidly hot in that church and I fainted!" countered Cathy.

"Fair enough" I conceded. "I still wish someone had videoed the vicar casually stepping over you though... he didn't want to miss being in the photos! That was so funny... well, you know what I mean... it wasn't funny... not at the time obviously" I quickly added.

"... and the other time?"

"... when you went down on the dance floor at the college ball."

"It was 7 o'clock in the morning! It was FA Cup Final day and we'd been drinking for 19 hours! Who didn't fall over that night?" replied Cathy, again putting up a strong case for the defence.

"That's true" I acknowledged.

"Those shoes were ridiculous last night though. I don't know how they can wear them every night. The whisky didn't help either" she added sheepishly.

"Whisky?"

"The girls were knocking it back... so I joined in. It was all free, so why not?"

"Why not indeed!" I agreed, before adding... "Why don't I carry you down to the breakfast bar... you can have a black coffee with John, maybe sober up together?"

"Is that him I can hear singing 'Ferry across the Mersey'?" queried Cathy.

"Oh yes, he's on fire this morning... you should go and ask him about his mates, The Beatles."

Cathy wasn't going anywhere though, and her foot remained raised up on its perch all day. I would have got some ice to put on it, but it would have melted by the time I returned from the mini-market's freezer in the village. Instead, the day was spent like most of our evenings, playing 'Connect 4' and reading. In our bid to spend as little money as possible we had avoided alcohol (apart from Cathy's freebies the night before), and our 'wild' nights out consisted of a few lemonades in the Footy Bar at the weekends. For the first couple of nights after our arrival, we had sat in our room, each reading our own books by torchlight, but Cathy suggested we should read together.

That way, we would have something else to talk about apart from how hot it was, how much I was missing home, and how many times I'd been to the toilet. With hindsight, I can see why she was willing to try anything. I wasn't so sure though; protesting that I was a really slow reader and hadn't read out loud since my English Literature classes at school. That had always been a high pressured situation, nervously waiting to get jeered and pelted with screwed up sheets of paper by the rest of the class whenever a word was mispronounced. Inevitably, Cathy had won the argument by pointing out that I was happy to read the newspaper football reports out loud, even when she wasn't asking or, indeed, wanting me to. So after a bit of cajoling and Cathy agreeing that we would start by reading the only book that I had brought along for our six month trip, we were ready to commence our very exclusive book club. I'm not sure how many highbrow book clubs have discussed the merits of Bez from The Happy Mondays autobiography, but after the first chapter (when I realised that Cathy was a far more forgiving audience than my old classmates), I started to enjoy it. Bez's tales of sex and drugs and rock'n'roll were followed by a slushy romance (which I got more emotional about than Cathy), and then by a fast-paced Carl Hiaasen crime caper. In just over a week, I'd read more books than I had in the past decade.

Tuesday morning saw Cathy manage to limp down the path to catch up with her pal Elle at breakfast, but she was still hobbling badly. There was no sign of the fifth Beatle though, so it was a chilled out start to a blisteringly hot day. After an hour spent chatting with Elle, she hopped back to our room to rest her foot again. I wanted to get out for a while having spent the previous day cooped up, so told Cathy I was going to get a copy of the Bangkok Post. Tuesday was the day that reported all the weekend's sporting action from home, and I hoped that the mighty Wanderers may get a mention for their draw against Wimbledon.

"Can you get me some shampoo and conditioner?" asked Cathy, just as I was halfway through the door.

"What about all that crap on the table you bought from Boots in Wycombe?"

"That's not shampoo and conditioner though, is it?" she reasoned. "They run out quicker."

"Give us your money then, I'm not buying shampoo every bloody week."

"What money?"

"What do you mean, 'what money'?" I mimicked.

"I haven't got any money."

Her response was quite matter-of-fact.

"Well, get some at the bank later. I'm serious. I'm not buying you bloody make-up for another five months!"

"I'm serious too... I haven't got any money" she repeated. "I spent the last on my 400 cigarettes. They were a bargain though... 14 quid... would have cost me 70 back home."

Cathy's third attempt at telling me that she had no money left for the remainder of our time in Thailand, Hong Kong, China, Australia, Easter Island, Chile and New York finally started to resonate. I wasn't best pleased.

"You're kidding me, right?" My voice raised a decibel or two.

"You said you were paying for everything."

"Yeah, I meant 'everything' as in flights, rent, trips, food... all that stuff... not cigarettes and sodding conditioner! Well I'll tell you this... you'd better ration those smokes lady, because there's no way I'm wasting my money buying you more!"

Our ramshackle door almost left its' hinges as I stormed out, slamming it behind me.

"Anyway... shampoo and conditioner are not make-up!" yelled Cathy defiantly behind me.

Despite the 100-degree heat, a frosty chill filled the air around Kata that day. I was prone to bouts of sulking and Cathy was as fiery as her red hair. This was by no means the first big disagreement we'd ever had, but it was the first time I didn't have the refuge of my folks place to stomp off too. Instead, I marched to Kata beach to walk off my frustrations, then thrashed around in the waves for a couple of hours.

A morning spent messing around in paradise can do wonders for your mood, and I started to walk back towards our room as the sun reached its scorching peak before remembering that diplomatic relations were currently strained. Wanting to avoid further confrontation, I kept walking beyond Fantastic Hill, across to the neighbouring Karon Beach, saying hello to our elephant friends along the way. Karon Beach stretched on forever, and by the time I reached its far end I was eager to get out of the sun for a while. Hungry and conscious that I was a long way from my personal squatting hole, I found a little beach café and ate a sandwich in the shade before using 'the facilities'. I still didn't fancy going back to the room to continue fighting with Cathy, and after a month of being constantly together, an afternoon apart was probably long overdue. I bought a newspaper and a bottle of water before making myself comfortable on the beach for the afternoon. I turned straight to the back page, and there it was, at the foot of the column titled 'English FA Cup'...

'... and Wycombe Wanderers earned a commendable draw against ex-champions Wimbledon.'

It was hardly an in-depth report on the Wanderers brave comeback, but I was mesmerised by just seeing those familiar words in print so far from home. As a child, I'd eagerly studied the local paper for the latest Wanderers news; I never thought I'd be doing the same while sitting on a beach in Thailand. Just underneath the ten word report on the game from Adams Park was cause for further excitement; the draw for the Quarter-Finals.

'Leicester City v Wycombe Wanderers or Wimbledon, Southampton or Tranmere Rovers v Liverpool, West Ham United v Tottenham Hotspur, Arsenal v Bolton Wanderers or Blackburn Rovers. Ties to be played on 10th and 11th March 2001'

My heart sank.

"Oh that's not fair!" I blurted out loud like a child, startling a couple sunbathing nearby.

"FA Cup draw... Leicester away... no chance" I explained, shaking my head in disgust.

The sunbathers gathered their belongings and moved off further down the beach.

I was gutted. Surely by now we had done enough to deserve a glamour-tie. I'd hoped for Liverpool, Arsenal or Tottenham, possibly West Ham; a tie that would attract a massive crowd and a big payday for the club. But no, we get an away tie against Leicester City who, despite being one of the top teams in the Premier League, weren't exactly a world-renowned team that the drink-selling boys on the beach would support. It wasn't the household name we'd deserved, but a top six Premier League team all the same who, having been drawn out of the hat first, would no doubt slaughter us on their own pitch at Filbert Street. After my initial disappointment, I comforted myself with two points. Firstly, I was holding a newspaper showing the draw for the Quarter-Finals of the FA Cup and, by some miracle, Wycombe Wanderers were in it. I'd dreamed of this since I was five-years-old, so reminded myself that I should really make the most of the moment. Secondly, after next week's replay at Wimbledon, the draw would be hypothetical anyway, as Leicester would be playing host to Wimbledon, and Wycombe's temporary place as an FA Cup Quarter-Finalist would be erased from the footballing history books forever.

Another spectacular sunset past and, as darkness fell, the beach cleared of tourists. I, too, was about to depart on my long walk back along the beach to Kata, when a dozen locals walked down to the shoreline. They started calling to the fishermen who were 100 yards out to sea on four long wooden canoe-like structures. I couldn't understand what they were saying, but they all seemed happy, and there was lots of laughter between those on shore and those out in the boats. I wondered what they were discussing; maybe the draw for the FA Cup Quarter-Finals? The guys on the beach then split into two groups, walking in opposite directions in the surf until they were 300 yards apart. Not being in any hurry to get back to Cathy, I sat back down and watched curiously as one from each group waded out into the waves before returning pulling ropes over their shoulders. Their pals soon waded in behind them, and then both groups took on the form of tug-of-war teams, battling against the Andaman Sea. I couldn't work out what they were doing, but became completely engrossed regardless. Eventually, both teams backed slowly from the water, heaving upon the ropes with all their might. The anchor-man of the closest team to me looked around and shouted something in Thai. I turned to see who he was talking to, but there wasn't anyone else left on the beach but me. Seeing my obvious confusion, he shouted again, this time in English...

"Don't watch... come help!"

Tucking my newspaper into the back of my shorts, I walked down to the group. The anchor-man thrust the rope into my hands.

"Laak! Laak! Pull! Pull! That's it!" he encouraged, before reverting to Thai; raising hysterical laughter from his pals, presumably commenting upon the free labour he'd just press-ganged.

I had no idea what we were doing, but I was enjoying the experience regardless, and soon joined in with the chanting that accompanied each and every hard earned backwards step further up the beach. Singing along with them reminded me of being back on the terraces with my mates, and in my head I imagined that it was actually Smudge, Buz and the rest of the Roobarbs who were on the rope with me. Some ten minutes in, my arms were screaming at me to stop, but there was no way I was going to provide further reason to laugh at the tourist. A minute later, when the rest of my body was beginning to agree with my arms, a cheer went up as the first sign of netting attached to our ropes came into view above the waves. I looked across to the other team who were also way out of the surf by this stage, and they too had netting attached to their ropes. My anchor-man tapped me on the shoulder and pointed to our left, indicating that we were to start walking diagonally up the beach towards the other group, while continuing to heave the ropes further from the water. As our two groups got closer, the wet ropes and netting got heavier. Thankfully, further reinforcements were recruited as we went on, and after an hour of dragging the huge net into a tight circle, the two teams finally met, 100 yards back from the shoreline. Everyone dropped the ropes and dashed excitedly back towards the sea, where the four fishing boats were now beached, surrounded by hundreds of sea birds hovering in hungry anticipation above. I followed behind and upon reaching the net found everyone eagerly inspecting the catch that had been unwittingly dragged alive from the ocean. Half of Karon soon appeared behind us to stake their claim on the catch, but not before my tug-of-war comrades had taken their pick.

"You take fish!" prompted my new workmates, waving several still squirming specimens in front of me.

"No, really, it's okay... you can have mine" I insisted, imagining the uncomfortable hour long walk back to Fantastic Hill carrying a freshly caught fish.

After washing my hands and face in the cooling ocean, I waved goodbye to the fishermen and made my way back up to the street. Hot and thirsty after my first hours work for two months (and my first hard-labour for many years) I needed a drink, and so ventured back into Karon. With its three streets compared to Kata's one, Karon felt like a sprawling metropolis, especially when illuminated after dark. I found another internet café, and decided to email my mates to tell them about my day spent on the beach staring at the FA Cup draw and my impromptu fishing experience.

16 – Underground, overground, wombling free

'… *So that's been my day! If I don't write again beforehand, I hope you all have a brilliant night in Wimbledon next Tuesday, remember to raise a glass and to give the mighty Wanderers a cheer for me. Wish I could be there. Right, I'd better head off to start rationing Cathy's cigarettes… I reckon she needs to get down to three a day if she wants them to last until we get home!*

See you in June.

Stoodent James'

"Ah, bless him" said Bob, handing the email to Ian, "…he's hurting not being here, isn't he?"

"He'll be hurting after all that rope heaving. He's never done a day's work in his life! Bloody student!" laughed Teddy.

"I can't believe he hasn't come back for the replay" added Smudger, opening his second cider of the journey as the train pulled into Beaconsfield en route to London.

"From Thailand?" laughed Bob, "Just to watch Wycombe?"

"Yeah… why not? It's the 5th Round… we won't ever go this far again, will we? This is a once in a lifetime thing" replied Smudger.

"Maybe he'll come back for Leicester in the next round" suggested Bob.

"Yeah right, we've got to beat Wimbledon first!" scoffed Smudger.

"Well, we'd better beat them; I've already promised Laura and Abby that Daddy will take them to the Quarter-Final… it was the only way I could get them to stop crying at bedtime last night. They weren't happy when they found out that they still had to go to school instead of 'on the train with Smudger the famous drinker'!"

"Bob-mate, you should have let them skive off" added Smudger the famous drinker.

"Oi! Oi! Here's a question for you... who do you think is more upset about missing today... Jamesy or Bob's little girls?" asked Buz, addressing the whole carriage.

"It's a tough one, that!" answered Lee. "Here's another... whose most pissed off; Jamesy about missing the cup run... or Cathy, having to listen to him going on about it?"

"Seriously though, I'm surprised he hasn't come back" maintained Smudger, by now crushing his second empty can and rooting around in his carrier bag for a third.

"I don't think Cathy would be best pleased if Jamesy said they were coming home just for the football, do you?" chipped in Pat.

"Sounds like he's getting pissed off with her anyway" added Ian, looking up from my email. "He's probably been 'playing away' left, right and centre by now... I remember when I was in Thailand... I was on this overnight train with five gorgeous Dutch girls and..." Ian continued, before getting shouted down by the entire Roobarb travelling party.

The 11am train was empty apart from my mates, who had all seen fit to take a day's holiday to fully enjoy seeing the Wanderers that evening. Big games always dictated that several hours' quality drinking time was required in preparation. Tonight promised to be as big a game as anyone supporting Wycombe Wanderers had ever seen, and so it had made perfect sense to set off on their two hour trek to Wimbledon's South London ground nine hours before kick-off.

"Look at this" announced Buz, pointing to the email again; "Jamesy thinks the game's next Tuesday. The muppet's in for a surprise in the morning!"

As the Roobarbs roared into London, I crept silently into our room. Thankfully Cathy was already asleep. I carefully climbed over her and curled up, facing the wall; we could sort out our disagreements later. Exhausted from my day on the beach I, too, was soon fast asleep.

The Roobarbs may have been the only Wanderers fans on the 11am train, but the advance party had seen reinforcements steadily joining their ranks as they meandered through the regular 'away day' drinking haunts of London. By the time they eventually reached the Selhurst Park stadium, they could have been mistaken for believing they were back in High Wycombe; there were Wanderers fans everywhere. Wimbledon had never been the best supported team. Despite over a decade of unprecedented success in the Premier League and winning an FA Cup Final, their following had remained primarily the loyal local supporters from the London Borough of Merton, and attendance-wise, they continued to live in the shadow of the London giants; Arsenal, Tottenham, Chelsea and West Ham. Selhurst Park was a large ground shared with Wimbledon's landlords, Crystal Palace. Wimbledon never filled the stadium, and so the replay with Wycombe hadn't been made an all-ticket affair. Nobody was sure how many supporters Wycombe would take. I'd been travelling to watch Chairboys away games since I was young and, generally, there could be anything between 50 and 500 of us cheering them on; for very big games we might take 1,500. As Tony pulled out his lucky FA Cup hat, with the Roobarbs characteristically arriving just moments before kick-off, he did so to the cheers of over 5,000 fellow Wycombians roaring their team onto the pitch with a deafening ovation.

"Bloody hell! Listen to that!" exclaimed Buz, looking up at the massed ranks of Chairboys and Chairgirls who lined the full length of the pitch. Like most teams, Wycombe's supporters always made more noise at away games. I'm not sure if it was the alcohol, the additional effort it had taken to get to the match, or just that the passion of the more fanatical supporters wasn't getting diluted by some less enthusiastic fans who only attended home games but, for whatever reason, I generally grew up being unable to speak properly on Sundays and Mondays following Wycombe away games. Any lingering doubts on the terrace that Wycombe couldn't continue their brave cup run were washed away on the tide of noise coming from the away section of Selhurst Park. Wycombe had over half of the supporters in the stadium, and it sounded more like the entire crowd. Logic evaporated on the wave of expectation.

Since the weekend, the Wimbledon camp had been telling anyone who would listen in the media that they'd been robbed by a terrible refereeing decision at Adams Park. Their manager, players and supporters all viewed this evening's replay as a formality, but also as an opportunity to dispatch Wycombe in style, a team who they deemed undeserving of a second chance. Lawrie Sanchez, on the other hand, had gathered his players in the dressing room before the game and told them that Wimbledon had had their chance. He reminded them that Wimbledon had been two goals ahead and then blown it. This was Wycombe's time. This was probably their only chance to get to an FA Cup Quarter-Final, and Sanchez sent his team out urging them to take that chance. No matter how pumped up the Wycombe players were by Sanchez's words or the reception they received from the vociferous wandering thousands, Wimbledon were no mugs and they knew that, if they executed their own game plan, their pedigree should surely see them prevail.

Wycombe were no longer respecters of reputation though, and they picked up from where they had left off at Adams Park; by attacking. Steve Brown soon had Kelvin Davis frantically backpedalling with an audacious lob from 30 yards, forcing the goalkeeper to tip the ball over his crossbar to avoid conceding an early goal.

If the volume had been hovering at '10 out of 10' when the Wanderers supporters had welcomed their team onto the pitch, then Brownie's long range effort had forced them to turn it up to 11. The Blues fans were doing everything in their power to push Wycombe into the ascendancy, and the Wimbledon players must have wondered if there was anybody in the ground actually supporting the home team. Inspired by the travelling thousands, the Blues attacked again. Nothing came of the advance though, and the ball was cleared by The Dons' Ardley, grateful to relieve the pressure that had been mounting since kick-off. On the halfway-line the scorer of Wimbledon's second goal from the first game, Patrick Agyemang, shielded the ball into Gareth Ainsworth's path. The winger outstripped the Wanderers defence for pace, bearing down on the visitors' goal. Just two touches and 50 yards later, he coolly slid the ball under Martin Taylor and into the net. There was nothing the Blues keeper could do; from nowhere, Wycombe Wanderers were a goal down after just 12 minutes.

At last the Wimbledon faithful had something to cheer about and, having endured a barrage of noise from their visiting counterparts, they boisterously celebrated the goal and taunted the travelling Chairboys. Without hesitation, the Wanderers supporters rallied again, desperate to raise their players and to drown out the newly awakened home crowd. The battle was easily being won by 'the old Bucks boys' on the terraces, but on the pitch Wimbledon went in for the kill. Ainsworth surged forward again, this time sending a diagonal pass into the penalty area towards Agyemang. Martin Taylor bravely took a whack from the on-rushing forward in the process of snuffing out the danger, inadvertently sending the giant forward spiralling through the air like a rag-doll. Again the crowd responded, roaring their approval at Taylor's victory in this latest of personal duels, which was indicative of clashes being fought all over the pitch. Despite being willing to do battle with the physical nature of the Wimbledon side, Wycombe continued to try and play good football on the muddy and heavily rutted Selhurst Park pitch. Paul McCarthy began another Wanderers raid by taking the ball from his goalkeeper on the edge of Wycombe's penalty area, before sending a slightly wayward pass up the left flank towards Keith Ryan on the halfway-line. Rhino stretched to divert the ball past his marker, finding Danny Bulman just inside the Wimbledon half. The stocky midfielder bustled forward, shaking off his opposing number to create just enough space to allow him to release a shot from 30 yards. A lunging block took all the venom from his effort, but the ball fell invitingly on the edge of the Wimbledon penalty area for Andy Rammell. Rammell struck the ball sweetly with his left foot, low and hard towards the corner of The Dons net, forcing Davis into a fine flying save down low to his left. But Davies could only palm the ball into the path of Davey Carroll who launched himself at the ball, slamming it past the still recovering keeper before being mobbed by his delighted teammates and sending the Blues fans into raptures; something he'd been doing regularly for the previous 13 years. After 32 minutes, the Wanderers had once again hauled themselves back onto level terms.

As half-time approached, Wycombe continued to give as good as they got, growing in self-belief following their equaliser. But on 40 minutes the Blues target-man, Rammell, hobbled off with an injury. Then, just moments later, his replacement, Andy Baird, was scythed down and also had to be carried off. Adding insult to injury, the referee only produced a yellow card for his assailant, Mark Williams, already the villain of the piece, having scored Wimbledon's opening goal at Adams Park just seconds after kicking Martin Taylor. The Blues support bayed for a sending off and, after applauding the stricken Andy Baird from the field, first turned their ire towards Williams and then to the referee as he brought proceedings to a close with a shrill blast of his whistle. As he followed the player into the tunnel from the pitch, the referee disappeared to a chorus of boos from the furious Wycombe faithful.

The crowd needed the 15 minutes respite as much as the players, and with the huge travelling contingent from Wycombe completely overwhelming the meagre refreshment facilities that had been opened for them, most folk spent the break in queues that weren't moving debating the merits of the game so far, with friend and stranger alike. As the players came back out onto the pitch, Buz (who was no closer to the toilets than he had been at the half-time whistle), reluctantly had to resort to the old trick he had mastered two decades earlier on the terraces of Loakes Park; Pisser was back.

The second half commenced in a similar fashion to the first, with both teams fully committed to gaining victory. The referee soon felt the wrath of the Wanderers supporters again when he booked their midfielder, Michael Simpson, for an innocuous foul. If Simpson's misdemeanour was worth a yellow card, then surely Mark Williams's challenge on Andy Baird had been worth ten years in jail with no parole. With 20 minutes remaining, disaster struck. Simmo challenged for another loose ball and the referee blew his whistle. Again, the crowd yelled in frustration, arguing that no foul had been committed. Seconds later, frustration turned to incredulity as the referee reached for his back pocket.

"He's sending him off!" gasped Ian.

He raised his hands to his face in astonishment; a motion that was being replicated by the 5,000 supporters all around him, and by the Wycombe players. As Simmo trudged disconsolately from the field, Wanderers stalwarts Keith Ryan and Jason Cousins rushed up to the dejected figure, as much to pump themselves up emotionally as to offer their commiserations. With head bowed, Simpson departed, passing by his manager Sanchez who was already looking out beyond him and barking instructions to his remaining ten men, throwing his arms around manically to help illustrate the tactical adjustments that he wanted. This perceived travesty just stoked the fire within the Wanderers supporters further, and they continued to drive their team on with a non-stop wall of sound.

Despite losing two centre-forwards to injury and being down to ten men, the Blues continued to battle tirelessly for the final 20 minutes. Half an hour's extra time loomed when the home team pushed forward one last time. Marcus Gayle charged down the left wing towards the bye-line in front of the home fans, before sending over a dangerous cross to the near post. Paul McCarthy jumped to head the ball clear, but was fractionally beaten to it by The Dons' fresh-legged substitute, Wayne Gray. The Wimbledon striker could only send the ball sailing gently into his supporters behind the goal, who collectively slumped back onto their heels, resigned to the game now going into extra time. One of Gray's teammates raised his hand to make a token-gesture appeal for the referee to award a corner, but even the ball-boy sitting just a yard behind the net was already handing the ball back to Wycombe's goalkeeper in anticipation of a goal-kick. As Gray began to pick himself up from the muddy surface alongside his aerial combatant Macca, he glanced up towards the referee to see if he'd somehow gained his side a corner. He couldn't believe what he saw, and instinctively looked back down towards the ground to conceal his astonishment; the referee was inexplicably pointing towards the penalty spot! A momentary shock-induced silence fell across the entire stadium, before the Wycombe players began to swarm around the official and the two sets of supporters burst back into life to make their very different emotions known.

As the Blues players protests were ushered away by the referee with a dismissive wave and a shake of his head, they looked close to tears. After eight sterling performances against Harrow, Millwall, Grimsby, Wolves and Wimbledon, it seemed cruel beyond comprehension that the dream was finally to be killed by a handball that only one person out of the 10,000 in Selhurst Park had actually seen. Why did that solitary person have to be the bloody referee? The Roobarbs, along with everyone else in the ground connected to Wycombe just looked at each other, dumbfounded. Tony pulled his lucky hat down over his face, Smudger kicked the pitch-side hoardings in frustration and Buz tried to hide his pain by jokingly suggesting that they might still make the last train home. Some people shouted, some cursed, some prayed, some wept, but most supporters just looked at each other, totally crestfallen. All around, people shuffled nervously. There was nothing the Roobarbs could do; there was nothing that Sanchez could do for his team; for nine of the remaining ten players on the pitch, there was nothing they could do either; everything was now down to a duel between Martin Taylor and Wimbledon's Neil Ardley.

As Ardley placed the ball on the spot, Jason Cousins approached to give him and the referee a further piece of his mind, before Ardley stepped back to the edge of the box to begin his run-up. With the Wycombe supporters, players and officials muttering "Come on Martin" in unison, Ardley struck the ball firmly and low towards the right of Taylor who flew in the same direction, palming the ball away to safety with both hands. The communally whispered "Come on Martin" became a roared "He's saved it!" Seconds later, the ball gently found its way back into the keepers grasp. Outwardly, Taylor appeared to remain the calmest person in the stadium as the Wycombe supporters exploded into riotous celebration. Flipper and Nicko surged down the aisle before dancing beside the pitch; Pat and Bob fell over the seats in front of them, still hugging each other. Tony temporarily lost his hat, and Buz was sure he was about to have a heart attack. Taylor launched an adrenalin-powered kick high and long into the Wimbledon half and as his opposite number, Davis, collected the ball at the other end of the pitch upon its re-entry into the earth's atmosphere, the referee blew the full-time whistle. The Wanderers players punched the air as if victorious, having dodged yet another bullet, before rushing en mass to thank their saviour, Martin Taylor.

"There's no way we're getting home tonight!" laughed Roger, shaking his head in disbelief, before giving Buz a huge hug. The friends had been watching the Wanderers for over 30 years together, but they'd never seen anything like this.

The two managers gathered their respective players around them to try and inspire yet another push for victory, while their assistants worked frantically to refresh exhausted limbs. The Wanderers players, in particular, had already given everything for the cause, again reaching new levels just to compete with their higher division opponents. Those demands had only intensified upon the dismissal of Michael Simpson. As the euphoria of Taylor's dramatic last gasp penalty save receded, the harsh reality of now having to face another 30 minutes against Wimbledon's 11 men started to sink in.

"This is going to be bloody tough" admitted Smudger.

"I don't fancy a penalty shoot-out" said Tony, nervously adjusting his lucky hat.

"Penalties are the best we can hope for" suggested Little-Wanker.

"The little toss-pot's right" added Teddy, "...they've already kicked Rammell and young Bairdy off the pitch... where's a goal coming from?"

"Yeah, Baird gets stretchered off and that dirty bastard Williams is still on the pitch, yet Simmo gets sent off for nothing! The ref's a joke!" blasted Flipper.

"He is crap" agreed Nicko, "...but if he's giving handball against Macca for that ridiculous penalty decision, then surely he has to send him off too? He'd already been booked. I'll tell you what... I wouldn't fancy extra time with just nine players ... we've still got a chance!"

"Whatever we do, we need to keep it tight at the back. Teddy's right; I can't see us getting a goal... if Wimbledon score, well... basically we're fucked" concluded Ian succinctly.

Moments later Teddy and Ian looked at each other again, nodded, and together said..."We're fucked."

Within 20 seconds of restarting the game, The Dons substitute Gray was again at the centre of the action. The ball was fed though to him on the edge of the Wycombe box and with his back to goal, he took full advantage of the tired defenders around him, using his strength and speed to break free from the blue shackles before poking the ball past Taylor to score.

Suddenly, small town dreams were replaced by big city realism deep in South London; a goal down, a player down, no substitutions left and, with 29 minutes to go, the players had already given everything. Would we have been better just losing to that last minute penalty? This could turn into a rout. Wycombe didn't deserve that, not after everything they'd been through. Along the terrace, these thoughts flew through the mentally exhausted minds of the Wycombe faithful. They were voiced quietly amongst small pockets of friends, or just held privately, as suddenly, everything had gone wrong. Even the bravest boxer can't climb from the canvas after one blow too many, and this was real life, not a Rocky movie.

Also in real life, the last train doesn't get held back if you're running a bit late; you miss it and get left stranded. Muted conversations about travel times back to central London were starting to circulate, and it was becoming evident that this unexpected extra time was going to severely complicate getting home. Thoughts of logistical issues temporarily invaded the brain, as what had just happened on the pitch was too painful to bear. Buz, who'd been successfully failing to coordinate Roobarb travel coherently for years, soon refocused the minds of the Roobarb amongst the crowd.

"Don't worry about getting home… we'll go home tomorrow, or walk; forget about it… this is do or die time! Come on Wycombe!" before urging the crowd around him to join in his chanting.

Within seconds, 5,000 were once again singing as one, roaring on the football team that they loved; "Come on Wycombe! Come on Wycombe!"

The Wimbledon supporters could only watch on sheepishly with admiration. If this was to be the end of the road, then so be it; the people of High Wycombe were going to send their team home in style.

But the floodgates didn't open, and Wycombe remained just a goal adrift as the minutes ebbed away, thanks in the main to yet another stunning save from Taylor with just five minutes remaining. As in previous rounds, Sanchez pushed defenders forward as time began to run out. It was time to risk all again, as without a goal the cup run was coming to an end. As the clock ticked the Wycombe supporters refused to allow the home fans to be heard, despite the hosts finally beginning to raise their voices after two hours of relative silence as the scent of victory grew increasingly pungent. With seconds to go, the noise level generated from the away stand was spine-tingling and just encouraged those singing to get louder as they built to a crescendo, which looked likely to signal the end of the road for the Wanderers. The players were inspired by this support, despite being physically spent, and chased the ball like dogs in the park, trying to force an error from their opponents who, with their goal advantage and a player extra on the pitch for the past hour, were confidently knocking the ball around as the minutes remaining dwindled to seconds.

The Dons continued to pass, and Wycombe continued to chase. In the centre circle the Wimbledon midfield turned the ball back to defence, and then again back towards Davis in goal to launch the ball high into the sky. Danny Bulman, as he had done for the previous 120 minutes, first chased midfielder, then defender, and then goalkeeper. Danny was a youngster who'd made his debut alongside the likes of Keith Ryan, and his play had been heavily influenced by Rhino's never-say-die attitude. Bulman's tenacity, combined with the ball taking a wicked bobble from the uneven surface as it arrived at the goalkeeper's feet, led to another scuffed clearance from Davies. On the halfway line, the ball was met by Wycombe's left-back, Chris Vinnicombe, who knocked it forward immediately, knowing there was no time to build steadily from the back. The ball fell to Sam Parkin, who had become the Blues third centre-forward of the day following the earlier injuries. He picked up the ball midway into the Wimbledon half and instinctively looked to run towards goal. The well-marshalled Wimbledon defence were in attendance in numbers, only allowing Parkin to travel sideways across to the left flank. He avoided one challenge and then another without creating a better position, before turning back towards goal with a clever step-over that left a third defender floundering in his wake. This gave Parkin the room to cross the ball into the penalty area, where Bulman was still lurking. Bulman shot wearily from the edge of the box but, before the Blues fans had a chance to release their groans of disappointment, the ball rolled into the path of Paul McCarthy who, from the edge of the six-yard box, threw himself at the ball and redirected it past the despairing Kelvin Davis to score another equalising goal for Wycombe.

Once again, pandemonium reigned on the terraces, and the luminously clad stewards who had circled the pitch in the dying minutes looked at their supervisors for guidance. The details of their temporary assignments hadn't mentioned the possibility of getting hugged by 5,000 delirious football fans or the opportunity for overtime pay. In the commotion, seeing his team pegged back by Wycombe for the second time of the evening and for the third time in four days was too much for Wimbledon's manager, Terry Burton, who vented his frustrations at the referee, complaining that Macca's goal should have been ruled out for offside. Having had to endure a similar rant at Adams Park just days before, the referee lost patience with Burton and showed him the red card that he should have brandished to Mark Williams 75 minutes earlier. Sanchez just watched on, his calm façade belying the drama that was unfurling. With Burton dispatched to the stands the referee promptly restarted the match, before almost immediately blowing the full-time whistle. As at Adams Park, and again just 30 minutes previously, the Wycombe players and supporters celebrated as though they had won the match, having cheated certain elimination right at the death for a third dramatic time. In comparison, the Wimbledon players couldn't believe what had just happened. The initial 90 minutes at Adams Park hadn't been enough to separate the teams, nor had 120 more at Selhurst Park. This epic battle would need to be decided by a penalty shoot-out.

The referee briefly went through the motions of telling both teams the rules of the shoot-out, although everybody in the ground already knew them; there would be five shots for each team; if a winner couldn't be decided following those, there would be a sudden-death situation, with one penalty for each team until a victor prevailed. The Wimbledon supporters cheered as the referee carried the ball towards the penalty area in front of the massed home support.

Wycombe's hero from Saturday, Steve Brown, was the first to take the long, lonely walk from the halfway-line to the penalty-spot. He did so to jeers from those behind the goal, but these were more than matched as his every step was accompanied by the Wanderers supporters chanting "Brownie! Brownie!"

Brown placed the ball, took a breath, and then despatched the ball fiercely into the top right-hand corner of the net. Davis guessed the correct direction to dive, but could get nowhere near the ball.

1-0 to Wycombe.

Those behind the goal fell silent as Brownie cupped his hands to his ears to mockingly signal that he couldn't hear their taunts anymore, before turning first to Martin Taylor with a clenched fist of encouragement, and then towards the Wanderers fans who continued to chant his name.

Any perceived advantage that Wimbledon thought they would gain from shooting towards their fans soon felt nullified as a chorus of boos echoed around the stadium from the Blues fans. Kenny Cunningham was the first to run the gauntlet. His walk from the halfway-line appeared to be a lot further than Brown's as he was heckled mercilessly by the Chairboys support. Cunningham looked relaxed as he placed the ball. He took just one step back before casually chipping his penalty goalwards. Taylor turned to watch the ball thump against the top of the post, before bouncing back towards the deflated Cunningham. Taylor punched the air and again, the banks of Wycombe supporters exploded with delight. For the first time in the whole tie, Wycombe led.

Jason Cousins marched forward like a man on a mission. He set the ball on the spot before taking a long run-up and blasting the ball straight into the middle of the net. If Kelvin Davis hadn't dived out of its path, I fear the ball would have just ripped straight through him, such was the ferocity of Cousins' effort.

2-0 to Wycombe.

With a broad smile of relief Jason saluted the supporters and took the acclaim of his teammates. This was an understated celebration in comparison to that which followed the goal he'd scored for Wycombe at Wembley in the FA Trophy Final a decade before. That day, the younger, more excitable Jason had smashed his free-kick into the net before jumping up onto the eight-foot-high barrier that was supposed to stop supporters invading the pitch. They weren't designed to stop players invading the stands though, and Jason nearly impaled himself as he celebrated with the fans atop the steel fence.

Jason Euell quickly eased any panic within the Wimbledon ranks, clinically despatching his penalty low past Taylor's outstretched hand.

2-1 to Wycombe.

Next up was Keith Ryan. "Rhino! Rhino! Rhino!" reverberated around the ground as Ryan confidently jogged up to the spot. Just like Cousins before him, he sat the ball purposefully and then charged forward, striking it straight towards the middle of the goal. Unlike Cousins, though, Ryan launched the ball high, sending it whistling over the crossbar and deep into the jubilant Wimbledon supporters behind the goal. The pain on Ryan's face was clear to see, and he cut a dejected figure as he hauled himself back towards his teammates, struggling to look them in the eye. Cousins was the first to reach his long-term teammate, and escorted him into the bosom of his team.

The loudest cheer of the night from the Wimbledon contingent soon followed as Marcus Gayle sent Taylor the wrong way, giving The Dons an equalising goal.

All-square, 2-2.

Danny Bulman stepped up fourth for the Wanderers. Danny liked to have a shot when opportunity arose, but accuracy was not something normally associated. He placed the ball and, without looking up, quickly took three strides back followed by a jump and three paces forward, slamming the ball into the top corner before Davis knew what had happened. He then ambled back to his teammates having made penalty-taking look like the easiest task in the world.

3-2 to Wycombe.

Jonathan Hunt followed for Wimbledon, with the pressure intensified following Bulman's success. Hunt drove the ball low and hard towards the corner of the net. Taylor's dive gave momentary hope, but the pace and accuracy of Hunt's delivery once more brought The Dons level.

3-3.

Sam Parkin approached the ball for Wycombe. He had already scored the winner against Wolves, and the youngster's short-term loan from Chelsea's youth squad 'to gain some experience' had so far done just that, beyond anyone's initial expectation. Now he was about to experience the pressure that only a penalty shoot-out could muster; something that couldn't be replicated on a training ground. How would the youngster react? Cometh the hour, cometh the man; like Brown and Bulman before him, Parkin despatched a spectacular shot fiercely into the uppermost corner of the net; penalties that no keeper in the world could save. Taylor and Davis could have defended the net together against these three penalties and they wouldn't have been able to save them.

4-3 to Wycombe.

With just one of the ten penalties remaining, Neil Ardley stepped forward for Wimbledon. Taylor stood confidently on the goal-line, having already prevented Ardley from sending The Dons through by saving his earlier 90th minute penalty. If he could repeat the feat, Wycombe Wanderers would be victorious.

The Wanderers section of the ground buzzed with anticipation, whilst behind the goal an air of impending doom prevailed. Earlier, Ardley had seen Taylor dive low to his right to thwart him. Should he shoot the same way? Should he go for power over precision? Everyone in the stadium pondered the conundrum facing Ardley as he placed the ball. Taylor guessed that he would shoot the same way, but Ardley outfoxed him by sending his shot into the opposite corner. Wimbledon breathed a collective sigh of relief, no one more so than Neil Ardley. The two teams reconvened in their collective huddles to prepare for the stakes to be raised even higher; sudden-death loomed.

4-4.

Chris Vinnicombe stepped up next for the Blues. He was a great defender, but had never scored for Wycombe before. Even when his teammates had tried to address that by letting him take a penalty against Oxford earlier in the season, he'd missed the opportunity. Any doubters need not have feared though, as Vinnie smashed the ball expertly into the top left-hand corner, leaving Kelvin Davis rooted to the spot. He couldn't contain his delight, and saluted the Wycombe fans who returned their gratitude loudly.

5-4 to Wycombe.

Darren Holloway then fired Wimbledon level with the minimum of fuss, despite needing to score, calmly sending Taylor to the right and the ball to the left.

5-5.

If the sight of the seasoned professional Chris Vinnicombe approaching the ball had worried some Wycombe fans then seeing young Ben Townsend, who'd only played a handful of games, caused outright panic. Sam Parkin may have risen to the occasion despite his tender years, but at least he was a centre-forward who would go on to earn his living by scoring goals. Ben was not a goalscorer, and had proved the point during the game by spurning a golden opportunity. But again, the Wanderers supporters were left cheering on the brink of glory as Townsend showed nerves of steel to slot the ball safely home.

6-5 to Wycombe.

Wayne Gray became the seventh Wimbledon penalty taker and fourteenth in total. Having scored in extra time, he looked assured and wrong-footed Taylor to calmly keep his team in the FA Cup. Taylor screamed at himself, becoming frustrated at not managing to get a hand on any of the shoot-out penalties faced thus far, despite getting close on several occasions.

Tied at 6-6.

Defender Jamie Bates stepped up next. He had scored Wycombe's opening goal in this whole adventure, eight games ago against Harrow Borough, and was one of the more experienced players in the squad. Bates didn't stand on ceremony, taking just a stride before striking the ball. He looked uncomfortable from the outset and clumsily bobbled his shot along the ground. His shot lacked both precision and pace, and gently found its way into the midriff of a grateful Davis, who hadn't looked close to saving any of Wycombe's previous seven penalties. Bates shook his head and berated himself as he ambled back towards his teammates who were quick to put their arms around him, offering well-intentioned but empty words. Penalty shootouts always needed a fall-guy, and it looked like Jamie Bates was going to assume the dubious mantle.

6-6, still.

Peter Hawkins strode forward with a spring in his step following Bates awful miss. Suddenly the Wimbledon player had the opportunity to be the hero of the evening, safe in the knowledge that even if he missed, his team would still be level.

Again, the chants of "Taylor! Taylor!" rose, this time with a hint of desperation.

Hawkins confidently positioned the ball and stepped back, visualising what he was about to do. I'm sure his visualisation didn't reflect the reality of the outcome though, as his shot followed a similar path to that of Jamie Bates. Taylor dived to his left, actually past the ball, but he managed to stretch his foot back just enough to stop its momentum with the tip of his boot, before spinning round to grasp the ball and preventing it from squirming over the line.

And still the score remained at 6-6.

Wycombe had dodged yet another Wimbledon bullet. Surely after the two games that The Dons had somehow contrived not to win they would soon run out of ammunition?

Paul McCarthy, despite his mounting tally of crucial FA Cup goals, had not wanted to take a penalty, hence only being ninth in line. But moments before, as Hawkins lined up his potentially game-winning shot for Wimbledon, Macca would have given anything to still have the opportunity to take one. Hawkins' miss had given McCarthy that chance, and he now gratefully strode forward with head held high. Kelvin Davis looked alert, reinvigorated by his save from Bates, and launched himself to his right as Macca approached the ball. Macca appeared to readjust his stance at the last second upon seeing Davis flinch, and he steered the ball safely into the centre of the net.

7-6 to Wycombe.

There seemed to be some confusion in the Wimbledon ranks following McCarthy's penalty and a delay in the next player walking forward.

"It's the keeper! It's their keeper look!" exclaimed Smudger, drawing everyone's attention to the strange sight of Kelvin Davis stood over the penalty-spot.

"I don't believe it!" cheered Tony, finding it hard to believe that the goalkeeper, who's kicking had been the weakest aspect of his performance throughout both games, had been chosen ahead of two outfield teammates. All around, the Blues fans readied themselves to leap into the air upon Davis sending the ball high, wide and handsome. The two goalkeepers glanced at each other, and then Davis locked onto the ball and drilled it low and hard into the corner of the net past the outstretched arm of Taylor. Davis had kept his team's hopes alive with a fantastically converted penalty; he wheeled away in delight to face his teammates.

7-7.

"Oh no!" cried Tony, "now Taylors taking one... this is ridiculous!"

"Surely not?" muttered Buz.

"He has to... he's the only player left isn't he?" suggested Smudger.

"Bloody hell, you're right!" said Nicko. "What happens after that then... do they just go round again?"

The conversation was soon drowned out as the familiar chant went up again... "Taylor! Taylor! Taylor!"

Davis and Taylor shared a wry smile at the absurdity of proceedings as they crossed to swap places; Davis assumed his more familiar position between the posts, with Martin Taylor looking somewhat out of place, preparing to take his penalty. Without hesitation, Taylor ran up to the ball and powerfully side-footed it low towards the left-hand upright. Davies flew after it, but couldn't match the speed that Taylor had put into his shot. It was Taylor's turn to celebrate and he turned towards his teammates with both fists pumped triumphantly.

8-7 to Wycombe.

"Taylor! Taylor! Taylor!" continued the thousands of Wycombe fans with increased vigour, having now seen all ten of their players take a penalty. Taylor's goal now meant that, once again, Wimbledon needed to convert to remain in the tie.

The chants of "Taylor! Taylor!" became mixed with booing as more Wycombe fans became aware of Wimbledon's tenth penalty-taker.

"Williams you dirty bastard, you shouldn't even be on the pitch!" screamed Flipper, summing up the general sentiment. Mark Williams had adopted the role of pantomime villain for his crude challenge that had seen Andy Baird carried from the field earlier, and also for his clash with Taylor at Adams Park that had led to him scoring just moments later. With his shirt splattered with mud and blood, he indeed looked the part as he placed the ball on the spot, prompting the booing to reach an ear-splitting intensity. He charged towards the ball, leaving Martin Taylor in no doubt that he was going for power over precision, so the goalkeeper just stood his ground with arms raised, attempting to create as large a barrier in the goal as possible. Williams hammered the ball forwards, but like Keith Ryan earlier, failed to keep the ball under control and sent it hurtling over the crossbar.

Final score: 8-7 to Wycombe.

Taylor rushed forward arms aloft, his teammates sprinting, hobbling or being carried towards him, resulting in a mound of bodies bouncing joyously as one in the middle of Selhurst Park. The ecstatic group then turned and ran towards the hysterical fans who had supported them throughout the epic evening, providing vocal encouragement beyond compare to any previous game in the Wanderers 114-year history.

The remainder of Selhurst Park emptied of shell-shocked Wimbledon fans almost as quickly as it took their vanquished team to depart the scene, but the Wanderers players and staff continued to celebrate alongside the Wycombe fans, savouring an incredible victory. When the players eventually started to retreat across the pitch towards their dressing room, still being acclaimed by the astounded Wanderers following, it was past 11pm.

"We need to find an off-licence quick" declared Buz as the Roobarbs left the stadium, following the crowds towards the nearest train station. "I think we might be stuck here until morning!"

17 – Moving on

The train that departed from Selhurst Park 20 minutes beforehand had offered its passengers a slightly better chance of catching the last High Wycombe-bound train out of Marylebone, but there hadn't been any Wycombians on it. Instead, it had been packed with Wimbledon supporters holding sombre post-mortems on their teams exit from the FA Cup. The 2,000 or so Blues fans who hadn't travelled by car or coach had willingly traded away all hope of catching the last train home, but sticking with their team until the end had brought the reward of witnessing, undoubtedly, the greatest victory in the clubs history.

After the evening's nerve-shredding drama the Roobarbs were thirsty, ensuring that one lucky off-licence received a late night sales boom. With history rewritten and refreshments in hand, most of the party were not overly concerned about hatching a plan to get home. Carriage after carriage echoed with chants hailing the Wanderers' famous victory, intermingled with muted talk of estimated arrival time at Marylebone and alternative back-up plans. There was talk of hiring minibuses, strangers clubbing together to share taxis, calling up friends who lived in the city, and diverting to Baker Street to get the later train out to Amersham, which was at least closer to home than London.

"I'm up for a party at Marylebone all night! Who's with me?" announced a jubilant Tony, mustering a chorus of cheers from the majority of the carriage.

Whether that was bravado or not, the air of joviality became slightly tempered as the train ground abruptly to an unscheduled halt between stations, deep beneath the city. Mention of 'the Baker Street option' became more prevalent as the train stubbornly refused to move on, costing valuable minutes. When it eventually jerked back into action, everyone knew that the ten past midnight last train home would be long departed. This prompted a significant exodus at the next station by those exploring the 'Amersham is better than nothing' escape plan. More through inertia than a tangible Plan B, the Roobarbs stayed put, slumping wearily into the vacated seats.

"First train is just before six in the morning" advised Buz.

"Not sure we've got enough beer to last until then" grumbled Smudger.

"Don't worry about that Smudge, we'll find somewhere to get more. London's the city that never sleeps" stated Flipper optimistically.

"Isn't that New York?" queried his brother Adam.

"I'll call your mother, she'll come and get us" said their Dad, John.

"Yeah, good luck with that!" they both scoffed back at him, unconvinced.

"Anyway, you're our dad, you need to look after us... pay for a taxi!" replied Flipper, trying to prompt some parental responsibility.

"Yeah, that's a good point" said Darren, looking at his own dad, Teddy.

"Shit-a-fucking-brick... Flipper's twenty-bastard-eight! You're twenty-sodding-four! Sixty-frigging-quid? You can pay for the bloody taxi... you little wanker!" retorted Teddy in his usual eloquent manner, supported by a nod of agreement from John.

"I'll have to get a taxi" conceded Bob. "I've got work in five hours."

"I know... those that are getting taxis can sell their beer to those who are staying up here all night... then everyone's a winner!" concluded Tony, before bursting back into a victorious rendition of 'We are the old Bucks boys' that soon reverberated throughout the train until it arrived beneath Marylebone.

Around a thousand supporters made their way through the labyrinth of tight passageways and onto the escalators that led upwards to the Marylebone Station concourse. Once back up at ground level, they found that the night which couldn't get better was, indeed, about to get better. Due to the huge numbers of people who would be left stranded following the delayed conclusion to the game, the London Transport Police had instructed the train operators to hold back the final few trains until the Wycombe fans had been given the opportunity to return to Marylebone. As the news spread, the normally civil train station became a boisterous football terrace, and a spontaneous chant soon echoed around the old Victorian building so loudly that it could be heard by those supporters who had opted for 'Plan B' and were standing a five minute walk away at Baker Street, waiting for the Amersham-bound train. "We're going home, we're going home, we're going... Wycombe's going home!"

Wycombe Wanderers didn't have nights like this, and normally the last train waited for no man. This was, indeed, a night that would never be forgotten. The delayed trains gently pulled away from Marylebone and, at last, the Chairboys could begin to relax and take stock of what they had just witnessed.

Nicko, Buz, Jason and Tony spent the entire 45 minute journey walking up and down the train like politicians on a 'meet and greet', shaking hands, exchanging stories and starting chants with anyone willing to humour them and some 'City' types who weren't. Anyone who had just been out in London for the evening and had planned on getting the normally empty midweek last train home must have wondered what had hit them, as the standing room only carriages were as busy as any of the rush hour commuter trains that had left the city many hours before. Flipper, Adam and Darren happily sat and drank, alongside their dads from whom they'd learnt such skills. Bob, Les, Lee, Sharon, Roger, Jackie and Mike all tried in vain to get some sleep in preparation for somehow returning to the real world early the next morning, although this proved more difficult than they'd expected, due to constant wake up calls from Tony who thought it hilarious to keep advising 'the next stop's Wycombe, you'd better wake up.'

"Let's all go round to Beany's and wake him up! He'll have plenty of drink in the fridge" suggested Tony as the Roobarbs walked out of High Wycombe station at approaching two in the morning.

"I'm up for that!" declared Nicko, "This'll teach him for never going to Cup games... what a night to miss!"

"Sod that Tony, I'm going home... I start work in a few hours!" reminded Bob.

"Yeah, I'm knackered too" added Mike, "but make sure to say hello to Beany from me!"

"Who's got a computer at home?" asked Buz, "Someone had better email Stoodent James too!"

"What's the time in Thailand? He'll probably be up by now!" said Sharon, as the Roobarbs hugged, kissed and staggered their separate ways after the best night of their lives.

By the time the Roobarbs were finally crawling into their beds, I was being rudely awakened by a slamming door; a slam that allowed me to gauge Cathy's mood. If my first wakened moment of the day had confirmed that my girlfriend was still annoyed with me for not buying her hair conditioner, then it was closely followed by a second that reminded me I was still annoyed with her too, for not having any money to buy hair conditioner; or anything else for that matter. I'd hoped to wake up to Cathy gently cuddling up to me, whispering that she was 'sorry about the money thing'; we'd then kiss and make up, before getting on with our lazy lives. Cathy generally had to make the first move on the road to reconciliation, on account of her boyfriend being an obstinate idiot, but it appeared that hair conditioner was not a subject to be trifled with lightly. I'd been furious the previous day, but after a period of solitary reflection and a rare decent night's sleep, my rage was gone and I just wanted everything to be back to normal. I'd known deep down that Cathy would have no money; after all, she never had any money, and had never claimed any different. Despite this, due to being stubborn and prone to a sulk, I wasn't about to throw an olive branch down to Elle's breakfast bar, where I could hear our host talking with Cathy and Scouse John.

"Morning" uttered Cathy tersely as she came back up to the room following her breakfast.

"Morning" I replied equally abruptly. This was followed by a long uncomfortable silence, which I eventually escaped by disappearing to sit in the toilet. It wasn't until I was there that I remembered that there wasn't actually a toilet seat to sit on, or anything else for that matter. Typical; this was the first time in over a month that I didn't need to 'go', yet I found myself hiding out surrounded by the same four walls that I'd become so familiar with; every crack, every chipped tile; I knew them intimately. I stood there for a couple of minutes, before going through the motions of filling the water bucket and chucking it into the hole in the floor as if I'd really been using the facilities, before walking out past Cathy, whose face was, by now, hidden deeply between the pages of a magazine.

"I'm going for a walk" I said, before treating the door to yet another slam. Yes, I'd teach her a lesson for storming out of the room and slamming the door on me; by storming out of the room and slamming the door on her.

"Alright Winnie the Pooh lad, how's it going?" quipped John as I passed him on my way down to the village. I waved and smiled, but wasn't in the mood to stop for small-talk following the frosty start to my morning, especially with the likelihood of further cold fronts moving in throughout the day.

It was only 9am, which was early for me to be wandering the streets. The combination of my dodgy stomach and the intense overnight temperatures had led to many a broken night's sleep. Added to the fact that we genuinely didn't have a reason to get up in the morning, this explained why I'd seen a lot more sunsets on our trip than sunrises. None of the market stalls were open and even the beach was deserted, despite it already being a gloriously sunny morning. That was fine by me, as I liked being the only person in this little slice of paradise. For now, it was all mine.

After a couple of lengths of the shoreline I headed back into the village, deciding to check in at the internet cafe at the foot of Fantastic Hill to see if I'd had any replies overnight from the Roobarbs. As I approached, there seemed to be a hive of activity outside. "Come in, come in" encouraged Elle's sister, "We open as normal" she insisted, while sticking a homemade '*OPEN*' sign to the door.

The small room was empty except for one member of the computer-geek gang who had been there on my first visit to call my dad on his birthday. Thinking about it, the guy had been sat in his regular corner seat every time I'd visited. I sat down at one of the terminals and noticed the table was pulled back from the wall, making the room even more claustrophobic than usual. Apart from the ventilation grate that sat at the top of the wall being missing, nothing else seemed to be different.

"It's all okay, we make small change today" assured Elle's sister again, noticing that I was looking around the room inquisitively.

She looked slightly uptight behind her forced smile, rather than her normal laidback self. I wished that I could remember her name, but in my sleep deprived state following our arrival from Bangkok, I hadn't been paying attention the day Elle had introduced her. Now it was too late to ask again, having chatted politely to her every couple of days for over a month. As I waited for the computer to start up, I peered through the window to try and see what the dozen workmen outside were up to, but they'd all disappeared from view. I couldn't see them, but I could hear them laughing and joking, accompanied by a constant tapping sound coming from the wall in front of me. The chipping seemed to be coming from all angles and the noise soon became incessant, sounding as if all the workmen were joining in. As ever, the computer was proving infuriatingly slow and I was about to give up when the hammering suddenly abated. I tapped in my Hotmail password whilst enjoying the relative silence before, again, getting distracted from the screen. A pickaxe tied to a rope was being manoeuvred through the ventilation cavity from outside, directly in front of me. Enthusiastic chatter then ensued on the other side of the wall, before I heard a familiar word I'd been chanting the night before on the beach with the fishermen.

"Laak!" cried the workmen, and the pickaxe (which was not dissimilar to 'the oldest pickaxe in the world' that Mike had stolen from Northwich Victoria) was suddenly pulled taught against the wall. Three 'laaks' later and the wall began to wobble gently, after the tenth 'laak' it started to fall away from me, still completely intact, before being caught by twenty-four raised Thai hands which then dragged it six yards back before leaning it against the side of the steep driveway.

I sat in stunned silence as the workmen outside looked into the room and smiled, a couple saying 'hello' in their best English. Elle and Mama Judy were stood just above them on the Fantastic Hill driveway watching proceedings, with Elle's sister shouting a progress report up towards them from behind my shoulder. I looked to my left, but geek-boy hadn't even flinched, still totally fixated on his screen. As I looked back outside and waved up to Mama Judy, the workmen started to lay breeze blocks to the front and back walls, extending them out towards the driveway. I couldn't be sure if the team were attempting a world record for the 'fastest ever building extension', but I certainly felt as though I was watching a time-lapse video. If I'd been in the library in High Wycombe on one of the public access computers, the room would have been evacuated on safety grounds if a light bulb had required changing, but as this was Thailand my surprise was short lived, and I cast my eyes back to my screen, scanning the list of emails.

"Cool, one from Mike, one from Bob", I mumbled, before looking across at the subject column.

Mike… *'Unbelievable!'*

Bob… *'Get in!'*

"I wonder what's unbelievable. How much Mike hates his job? How envious he is of my trip? Maybe something Christine or the kids have done to annoy him?" I pondered the options as I opened his email, not realising just how unbelievable the content was going to be.

It took me a moment to process the news.

'He's only sent this about an hour ago… that's 3 o'clock in the morning back home. He say's we beat Wimbledon… but the replay's next week? What does he mean... a reserve game or something? Why would he be telling me about a reserve game?'

I flicked to Bob's email. Scanning rapidly through it, my heartbeat began to race as I struggled to take in the salient points.

'We bloody did it Jamesy'... *'We were thinking of you mate'...* *'8-7 on penalties'...* *'Even Taylor scored a penalty!'...* *'I've broken a rib from celebrating Macca's last minute equaliser, Pat has too'...* *'Leicester City here we come!'*

This had to be a hoax, a cruel hoax... the bastards were winding me up. I opened another screen, tapping impatiently on the table as it slowly whirred into life. I logged on to the BBC and immediately clicked into the 'Sports' section.

'Dons devastated by Wycombe' read the headline.

My hands began to shake and tears pooled in my eyes before streaming south onto the table. I'd nearly cried on my first visit here after speaking to my folks on the phone, but there was no stemming them now and, quite frankly, I didn't care. A couple of the workmen (who were already plastering the freshly laid blocks while the walls were still being extended beyond them), had paused momentarily to watch the foreigner crying. With a smile on my face and a thumbs-up signal I looked at them and simply said "Football!" before returning to my bubble, oblivious to the sun that was now beating down on me through the roofless annex, or the building site that surrounded me. "I have to tell Cathy" I muttered before shutting the computer down and paying a very confused looking Elle's sister.

Halfway up the driveway I about-turned and rushed back down to the village, before returning to Cathy with peace offerings.

"We did it! We beat Wimbledon, we beat Wimbledon!" I blurted excitedly upon crashing back into our room, only to find it empty. Before I had time to get concerned by the fact that Cathy might have left me, I heard the familiar sound of a bucket of water getting sploshed in the bathroom.

"What's up?" asked Cathy curtly, still in fighting mode.

"We did it! We beat Wimbledon! We beat Wimbledon!" I repeated, not tiring of hearing the words.

"No way!" she laughed, instantly dropping her icy tone.

"I've got you crisps and chocolate to celebrate… and these too, I got two of each… I reckon they'll be cheaper in Thailand than anywhere else" I said, dropping bottles of shampoo and conditioner onto the bed. "I'm not buying you cigarettes though… I draw the line at that."

Cathy didn't protest, and with that, normal service was resumed; all thanks to a Wimbledon footballer called Mark Williams missing a penalty.

"James, why do you stink of fish?" asked Cathy, as we left the room together for an afternoon on the beach. But before I'd had a chance to explain my impromptu fishing trip to Karon beach the previous night, her attention was diverted to the internet room's extension. "That wasn't there last night!"

"That wasn't there an hour ago" I replied.

Our 'Wycombe are in the Quarter-Finals' beach party was curtailed somewhat by gate-crashing jellyfish, and so without the ocean to cool us down, we headed home earlier than usual to retreat from the sun for a siesta. At Fantastic Hill there were 12 workmen with the same idea, all snoozing in the shade of Mama Judy's banana trees. Before downing tools, they had somehow managed to complete a tiled floor, two plastered walls and a roof. All that was now missing was the wall that had been pulled down earlier that morning and, currently, there were six builders fast asleep on that. Back in our room we, too, had fallen asleep for several hours, only to be awoken by the sound of the workmen who were once again in heated discussion. Peering out of the window we saw that sunset was almost upon us, so quickly headed back towards the beach for nature's daily grand finale.

Having witnessed the builders in action throughout the day, the sight of them precariously lifting the wall that they'd pulled down earlier and dropping it onto freshly laid foundations didn't surprise me. I did raise an eyebrow, however, as they made their finishing touches. I wasn't overly confident that the two guys who'd been given the thankless job of squeezing mortar onto the sides of the wall, as it was eased back into place would be going home with all their fingers still intact. Thankfully, as we progressed down the track towards the beach I didn't hear any screams, which I took to be a good sign. When we heard a distant triumphant cheer a couple of minutes later, I was sure that all was well and that the job was complete.

After another meal spent trying to make the Indie Bar look busy, we looked in on Elle's very proud sister and her expanded emporium. We found that normal service had resumed; geek-boy was still transfixed in his corner, and the rest of the geek-crew were also back, along with six more terminals in the extension. From the outside, the freshly resurrected wall looked no different, apart from the two tree trunks wedged between it and the ground for support. I reassured myself that this was just a precaution, but also made a mental note to not frequent the 'new seats' for a few days.

I was up early again the following morning, this time rushing to the village to pick up an early edition of the Bangkok Post. I opened its pages there and then on the counter, while waiting for my change. There it was, on the back page; official confirmation in black and white...

'TRANMERE AND WYCOMBE REVIVE CUP MAGIC'

"That's my team that is" I said proudly, pointing to the word 'Wycombe' that sat atop the page in big, bold characters. I'd got excited just seeing the team's name printed in the previous rounds results, but this was seven paragraphs over two columns; and with a headline too!

"Thank you, please go now please" prompted the cashier nervously, after I'd recited the entire report. The shop had been empty upon my arrival, but I now appeared to be causing a queue.

As I turned ready to apologise, I received glares from my two favourite German tourists and so, instead, just smiled my most annoyingly inane smile and walked off proudly with newspaper tucked under arm.

"So Mike and Bob weren't winding you up then" giggled Cathy, studying the newspaper report back at Elle's breakfast bar. "And it's a pity we aren't heading to Bangkok this week, look... we could have had our picture taken with the FA Cup!" she added, alluding to the picture which accompanied the report, showing a Malaysian woman holding the famous trophy aloft. "It says it's on a tour of South East Asia, before heading back to Britain for the final at Cardiff's Millennium Stadium in May. The FA Cup is going to be in Bangkok next week!"

"How can you have the FA Cup Final in Cardiff? You might as well play it in Bangkok! Wales? My arse!" complained Scouse John.

"Well, they can't play it at Wembley, it's been flattened!" I reminded him.

"Fair point that, Ivor Imodium... as it goes, I'm sniffing around for some work there when I go back. I always dreamed of playing at Wembley!" roared John. "Tranmere got through as well? Bloody hell... a nice little local derby for them then, against the greatest football team in the world! Tranmere nil... Liverpool four... that's my prediction. Here's another for yer... 'Leicester six... Wycombe Wanderers nil'. Place yer bets ladies and gentlemen, place your bets!"

"You might be right John, Leicester are flying this year; sixth in the Premier League... plus home advantage... we couldn't really have got a worse draw" I conceded.

"You never know, you could get lucky. Anyway, it could have been worse... you could've drawn Liverpool... now, they really would destroy you!" replied John, before giving us another rendition of 'You'll Never Walk Alone'.

We might have been missing the photo opportunity with the FA Cup in Bangkok but, regardless, we would be back in the Thai capital soon enough. Our extended beach holiday was rapidly coming to an end, and the pace would soon be changing significantly with a month spent on the move, travelling through China. Just like children coming to the end of the long summer holiday from school, we started to squeeze all the things we'd planned to do over two months into a hectic final fortnight. Visits to temples and boat trips to exotic islands became more frequent, as we explored the paradise on our doorstep. Cathy discovered that sunbathing on a boat skipping across the waves at a rate of knots was the ideal way to keep cool whilst also maximising tanning opportunities, as she tried in vain to get remotely close to my skin colour. These journeys were often accompanied by dolphins and flying fish swimming alongside the boat and, just when you thought that the sun and sea had exhausted the wonderment available on any given day, over the horizon would appear dots of land that soon grew into towering sheer limestone karsts that jutted vertically out of the water. Upon arriving amongst these stunningly majestic mountains in the sea, the tourists and crew alike would always fall silent. There were no words, in any language, to do these natural wonders justice; it started to make sense as to why film producers had long sought the area for creating stunning movie backdrops. We visited Phang Nga, which had brought eastern exoticism to James Bond's 'The Man With The Golden Gun' in the early 1970's, and also Maya Bay and Koh Phi-Phi, which just the year before our visit, had once again treated the outside world to Thailand's wealth of unbridled beauty by providing the location for 'The Beach'.

Back in bed after our trip to Maya Bay, I busily scrawled illiterate ramblings into my diary. I'd never been one for keeping a journal but, with a memory like a sieve, I was keen to record my thoughts and details of the day while travelling. It had taken me 28 years to grab this opportunity, and I knew it was a 'once in a lifetime' adventure. A few minutes spent writing each evening, before retiring to spend the night squatting in the loo, would at least allow me to dip back into a different world, years from now when I was older, fatter and paler.

"You could turn your diary into a movie... 'The Beach - The Sequel'" mocked Cathy, as I struggled to cram my musings into the tiny pocket diary I'd stupidly opted to use before leaving England.

"Hmmm, I'm not sure. 'The Beach' had torrid affairs with French supermodels, murder and mind-bending drugs. 'James on the Beach' would mainly focus on Connect 4 tournaments, bedtime book club and South East Asia's largest stash of Imodium" I replied. "I can't see Leonardo DiCaprio winning any Oscars for that... can you?"

"She isn't a supermodel, she's an actress" pointed out Cathy. "You said you didn't fancy her when we went to the pictures."

"What are you talking about?"

"'Affairs with French supermodels'... that's what you said. You fancy the actress."

"I don't fancy her."

"Why did you say she was a supermodel then?"

"I thought that you'd said she was a model as well as an actress... I dunno."

"Yeah, a model... not a supermodel."

"Fine, I stand corrected. Virginie Ledoyen is just an actress and a model, not a supermodel" I backtracked.

"You know her name! How do you know her name? You can't remember anyone's name! You love her, you bloody lecherous pig! I can't believe you know her name" Cathy exploded, teetering on the knife-edged arête between 'jokingly' annoyed and 'proper' annoyed.

"Cathy… when I sell the film rights to Hollywood, I will stipulate that you get played by Kate Moss… she's English… and a supermodel. Okay?" I calmly replied, before closing my diary and departing to the bathroom, locking it firmly behind me, just in case. As I squatted, I cursed Virginie Ledoyen and her big brown eyes, her beautiful smile, dark flowing locks, toned figure and undoubted wonderful personality.

Just as the last grains of sand in the hourglass appear to flow faster than the first, our final days until departure quickly disappeared. A penultimate football night in the bar had seen Liverpool win the first major trophy of the season with a League Cup victory over Birmingham, driving John to discover new levels of drunkenness at Elle's breakfast bar the following morning. A trip into Phuket Town had reserved us seats on the VIP bus back up to Bangkok the following Wednesday, and as we entered our final weekend, we were determined to make the most of our time. Having spent the previous week like real holidaymakers, cramming in as much as we could, we were ready to revert back to our simple Kata lifestyle… beach, Indie Bar and, as it was Saturday… a final visit to the Footy Bar.

Despite the tourist season being all but over the sun shone fiercely onto the beach all day, and Cathy embraced it fully, striving for a final 'holiday burn' to take with her into China. After an early dinner in the Indie Bar, a marathon pool session awaited Cathy and her Thai girlfriends in the Footy Bar, as I made myself comfortable to watch Manchester United face Leeds. An unprecedented second dinner was consumed to distract me through the England versus Scotland rugby match that followed, before the main event of the evening, Leicester City versus the mighty Liverpool in a top-of-the-table Premier League clash. Liverpool entered the game fresh from the previous week's League Cup glory, sitting in third position in the league, whilst also progressing nicely in both European competition and the FA Cup. Leicester, meanwhile, were also enjoying their status as a top six Premier League team. A victory over Liverpool would send them up to the heady heights of fourth place and, with a home tie against the minnows from Wycombe Wanderers just seven days away, a place in the FA Cup Semi-Final also looked a formality.

Ironic cheers once again filled the Footy Bar as the screen switched to a wintery scene in Leicester, as we basked in the warmth of the Thai evening. Leicester City soured my mood slightly though, with an ominously well-deserved 2-0 victory over Liverpool.

"Please don't let them humiliate Wycombe next week" I prayed.

Back home in Fantastic Hill, my decadent two dinner, ten lemonade fuelled night on the tiles soon took on a different meaning altogether, as I literally spent the whole night on the tiles of the bathroom floor. Concerns about Wycombe Wanderers well-being were soon overshadowed for thoughts of my own, as my body found ways of demonstrating its discontent from varying orifices. It was 1am by the time we got home after the Leicester versus Liverpool game, and Cathy was soon asleep having had, I suspect, a few nightcaps at the pool table with her Thai friends. I, on the other hand, finally drifted off curled up in a ball on the bathroom floor, too exhausted to crawl through to the bed and pretty certain I'd be needing the hole in the ground beside me again soon enough anyway. Even by my standards, this was a rough night, beyond compare with anything the previous couple of months had thrown my way. As my stomach finally showed some mercy, a restless fever-driven slumber took over, and I found myself back on the coach to York as a child, trying to sooth my nausea by pressing my head against the cool glass of the coach's window. We beat York, and then Altrincham in the next round. Then in the fifth round, it wasn't York who visited Anfield, the home of Liverpool, the most successful team in English football; it was the brave semi-professionals of Wycombe Wanderers. My hero, Mark West, was leading the attack for Wycombe, Buz was pissing on the terraces and there was Scouse John, singing 'You'll Never Walk Alone' from across the fence in the Liverpool end.

I awoke, with my cheek plastered to the cool bathroom floor as Cathy banged the door against my back. "Are you okay?" she asked, "Have you been there all night?"

"I really feel like crap" was all I could muster as I gingerly got to my feet and shuffled past her towards our bed.

"You need to see a doctor, this is getting ridiculous!" spat Cathy with equal measures of frustration and concern.

"It's the heat... I don't think my stomach can handle the heat. I'll be fine when we get to China."

"James, you need to see a doctor... shall I ask Elle to call one?"

"No. I don't want to see some foreign doctor who's going to stick pins and needles in me to cure a dodgy belly" I stubbornly argued.

"Fine, suit yourself... I'll get you a bottle of water" she said. "I'm going for breakfast... I want to see Elle telling John off again. He sounds lashed up this morning, did you hear him? He was singing 'You'll Never Walk Alone' again a minute ago!"

Sunday completely passed me by. By the time I awoke darkness had returned and I was feeling too weak to seek out food. Besides, I'd rather starve than have a repeat performance of the night before. Monday morning arrived, thankfully without any further drama, and for the first time in my life, I had to make a concerted effort to eat.

"So, the bus leaves on Wednesday afternoon, correct?" I asked Cathy, while toying with scrambled eggs on toast.

"Correct."

"Okay... I'll eat this, and then I'll hang around near the loo for a bit, just in case. Then let's hit the beach. Tonight I'll eat again, but then that's it until Bangkok... total starvation. I can't be dealing with being sick on that journey" I declared, having formulated a simple plan that would hopefully get me to Bangkok in one piece, whilst also allowing me to enjoy our final couple of days, free from the captivity of the bathroom.

"Do you not think it might just be easier to get some drugs from a doctor?" reasoned Cathy.

"Oh crap... we lost at home to Port Vale look, 1-0" I said, using my newly acquired newspaper to change the subject. "And that's after getting beaten away against Peterborough last week too. Those Wimbledon games must have really knackered them."

A late afternoon visit to the internet room confirmed my suspicions.

'It's all gone a bit wrong mate. We haven't got any forwards left! The Wimbledon replay has left Rammell and Baird injured, poor Bairdy is out for a year. Devine and McSporran were already out for the season, and young Sam Parkin's loan is finished and we can't get him back. It's a bloody disaster. You'd better come home mate; you and Oggy might be playing up front against Leicester at this rate! (It's the only way you would get in the ground as well... they've only given us 3,000 tickets for the away section). The lack of players meant that we even had a trialist make an appearance on Saturday in a league game... Roy something or other... anyway, he wasn't 'Roy of the Rovers', that's for sure... he was crap and we lost again. Typical Wycombe... the biggest game in our history is on Saturday and we haven't got enough players!

Right, better get back to work.

Everyone says hello... love to Cathy,

Bob'

'Bob's right, they could play me and Oggy up front' I thought to myself.

Admittedly, neither of us had progressed far beyond Division Five of the High Wycombe Sunday League in our playing careers, but it couldn't be argued that we had been the undoubted attacking superstars of the Wycombe Wanderers Independent Supporters team a few years back. This was a team that started playing when Bob and Sharon from our Roobarb rabble had somehow got roped in to setting up a new Wanderers supporters club. Somebody thought it would be a good idea to arrange a match against fans of Wycombe's opponents before our respective clubs did battle that afternoon. Initially, there was a lukewarm response from the Roobarb fraternity. We weren't overly keen on mixing exercise with pleasure and were also rightfully concerned that these morning games would eat into our drinking time. But with Bob struggling to muster much of a team, those of us who did actually play football begrudgingly volunteered to make up the numbers required, lured by the promise of a brand new Wanderers kit that had been cajoled from the then Wycombe manager, John Gregory. Like children on Christmas morning, we eagerly tore open the packaging to get to the immaculate Wanderers strip, before proudly trotting out onto the pitch masquerading as our heroes. Luckily, as we warmed up for the first game and I cast my eye across the field to our opposition, it appeared that we had been pitched against a group of like-minded individuals whose best days were behind them. It soon became apparent that at least half the players on either team had never played football before, but were just keen to represent their team in any way possible, playing as passionately as they supported; at least until they ran out of steam, which for most was after about ten minutes. A good time was had by all, and both sets of supporters were soon back where they belonged, safely ensconced in a pub an hour or two before the real football kicked off. It was decided we would play some more games, but only, as Bob pointed out "...if you thieving sods hand the new kit back!"

We played host to teams from all over the country and, regardless of the results, the games would always end with lots of drinks en route to the stadium to watch the professionals that afternoon. Then we inexplicably got talked into playing a game away from home, when Wycombe were scheduled to play at Plymouth Argyle. What we should have done was say, "no thanks, when we have weekends away, we really like to make the most of it, so we won't be in any state to play football." Failing that, we should have prepared like a proper football team, and ensured that we were in our hotel beds early on the Friday night prior to our Saturday morning game. As it turned out, triumph truly can come through adversity; and suspected alcohol poisoning. Despite eleven hangovers, several bouts of public vomiting, and the game being played on the coldest, most exposed, wretched football pitch on the planet, we managed to beat the Plymouth supporter's team 12-0. Some might say it was 13-0, due to a bizarre argument that raged between the Plymouth goalkeeper and Nobby, the most reluctant member of the Roobarbs to get roped into playing, and also the least argumentative person in the world. The keeper was adamant that he had conceded yet another goal, whilst Nobby tried to assure him that the ball had only ended up in the back of the net due to a large rip in its side. This all happened as the game was reaching its conclusion. The referee looked at his watch and, upon realising that pub opening time was approaching, took the executive decision to blow the full-time whistle while the debate continued.

If Lawrie Sanchez had seen our finest hour down on the coast in Plymouth where, between us, Oggy and I had scored ten goals, surely he would now be preparing to make us offers to come to the Wanderers' aid. I maintain to this day that Oggy wouldn't have scored his nine of those ten goals if I hadn't been there to bear the brunt of the workload.

In his small office, tucked away under the stand at Adams Park, Sanchez had been making a decision not dissimilar to my deluded dreams. He sat ruing the list of injuries that had decimated his attacking options, alongside Alan Hutchinson, the Club Secretary and, at times, over-enthusiastic commentator on Wycombe's away games for local radio.

"Any luck getting someone in yet boss?" asked Hutch hopefully, having popped his head around the door of the manager's office for the umpteenth time.

Wycombe were in a desperate position, and Sanchez had been calling around all his contacts gained from 25 years in the game. Everyone who'd become available seemed to be cup-tied, having played for one of the 602 teams that had already been knocked out of the competition. Sanchez had even tried to lure footballing legends out of retirement. The England international and Arsenal's record goalscorer, Ian Wright, had recently hung up his prolific boots following one injury too many at his final club,

Burnley. Sanchez called him to offer one last hurrah, but the injury that had prompted Wright to leave Burnley had yet to heal fully. Gianluca Vialli, who had played centre-forward for Italy, Sampdoria, Juventus and Chelsea, was offered the opportunity to add Wycombe Wanderers to that prestigious list, but he too politely declined. These were world-renowned footballers; the only player better than those to ever grace a Wycombe Wanderers shirt was George Best, and technically he was only wearing a Wanderers second strip as a member of the International XI that had been invited to Loakes Park to play against Wycombe in the proud old stadium's final game, before it drew its final curtain in 1990.

"I don't know, Hutch" replied a perplexed Sanchez, "there must be someone out there who wants to play in an FA Cup Quarter-Final! Send out a press release or something... stick it on Teletext... just say 'Wanted, centre-forward, must not be cup-tied'!"

Lawrie Sanchez's primary objective had been to get Alan Hutchinson out of his office. But Hutch did as instructed, and Wycombe's plea was loaded onto Teletext, for all of Britain to see.

Only one person answered the call, and he wasn't of Wright or Vialli's ilk; more an unemployed footballer born in Belfast and raised in Ghana who had, until recently, been eeking out a living by playing in Finland. He saw the advert and called his agent. The agent in turn called Sanchez.

"Look, we haven't even got time to see him in training. Just send him to the ground for 11 o'clock on Saturday and we'll bring him on as a sub. Tell him to ask for me or Alan Hutchinson at the reception desk. He'd better not be a clown though, as it'll be me who ends up looking like a mug!" said Sanchez reluctantly. "What's his name again? Roy what?"

The months had become weeks, the weeks had become days, and now the day had become hours. We took what felt like a month's supply of bananas around the corner to the elephants, Bockie and Joe, before taking a final walk down to the beach and back up the street to bid fond farewells to the drink seller relaxing against his palm tree on the beach, the Footy bar staff, my hair shaver, and the Indie Bar owner, all of whom were reminded to look out for Wycombe Wanderers on Saturday night in the FA Cup, although I still wasn't sure that the old lady with the hair clippers had ever understood a word I'd said. As we reached the top of the street, I told Cathy that I had one more stop to make.

"I'm going to buy that 'Travel Connect 4' game in the market... and I'm not paying over the odds again" I informed her determinedly.

As I walked in, I could see the little girl's eyes light up. I was sure she'd be ready to turn on the tears again if negotiations weren't going her way. I walked past her and greeted her mother instead, asking what the price was.

"450 Baht please."

"Ooh, that is expensive... it's very small look, it must be cheaper than that, surely?" I replied, delivering my well-rehearsed line perfectly, complimenting it with a feigned look of surprise and disinterest.

"400, I give you for 400 Baht" countered the woman with equal assurance. She was a professional after all.

"I can't pay that much. Look... 'big Connect 4' costs 450 Baht... 'Travel Connect 4' is only half the size! I think 250 is a fair price" I reasoned, taking both versions of the game from the shelf, and holding them up to illustrate my point.

The little girl looked up at her mum. She knew I'd played a good shot there, and as her mother rolled her eyes, I knew that she thought so too.

"300, I can't go lower than 300."

'300 Baht? Wow, I wasn't expecting that! That's a bargain' I thought to myself. But 'cry-baby' had duped me out of 40 Baht over the t-shirt... what the hell, I was leaving town in an hour anyway.

"No, that's too much. I'll pay you 260 Baht. That's a good price" I offered, trying not to blush.

"No! I can't give you for 260 Baht! 300 Baht, no less!" laughed the woman, admiring my improved technique, but not budging any further.

"Okay, nevermind... I'll buy one in Bangkok tomorrow, on Koh San Road. Thanks anyway."

I'd delivered my big line, then followed it up with a courteous nod, before turning to leave.

"260! 260 is good price! I'll wrap for you!" conceded the flustered woman, having seen the apprentice finally become a master.

Cathy nodded her approval from the street, looking impressed. But as I began to count out my cash, I soon lost my cockiness upon realising that I only had 200 Baht on me. I checked all six pockets on my 'travel day' combat shorts, more out of panic than for dramatic effect, but eventually had to concede defeat.

"I'm really sorry. I thought I had more money on me. I've only got 200 Baht" I mumbled, absolutely gutted about missing out on the little game that I thought would see us back up to Bangkok and through many hours travelling across China. Again, I turned to leave, but this time with genuine intent, and my tail firmly between my legs.

"Very good! You too good at this now!" laughed the woman again, this time emphasising the point by applauding. "200 Baht, I give to you for 200 Baht."

At last! I'd finally won a bartering joust; it was time to move on. Following tearful hugs with Elle, Elle's sister, Mama Judy and even Scouse John, we felt as if we were leaving home and everything that we knew, for the second time in two months.

18 – Bonkers in Honkers

With two months of travelling under my tightened belt, the chaos of Bangkok didn't seem so intimidating upon our return. Perhaps our 5am arrival helped to ease us back into the bustling city too. Koh San Road was still asleep, apart from those either arriving or leaving. This was fine with us; we weren't in a rush and had two days to kill before flying to Hong Kong with nothing particular to do. So we dumped our bags under the very table that we'd clung to like a life raft with Mark on our first night in Thailand, and parked ourselves until the street began to stir into life. We booked into the same crappy hostel that we had used back in January, having convinced ourselves that now we were hardened travellers, the place wouldn't feel half as bad as it had the first time round. We were sadly wrong and, if anything, it was worse than we'd remembered. On the plus side, we were able to book a room for just the two of us this time, without having to take in a total stranger for good measure. After 18 hours travelling, albeit mostly on the luxurious VIP bus, I needed a shower and some sleep. I was ready to sleep first, shower later, but when Cathy made her way to the communal shower room I figured that to save any potential incidents later, I'd be wise to go at the same time.

Sleep was never going to be a long affair as the temperature rose and the city got noisier, and it wasn't long before another sensation took over my body and mind, something I'd never truly experienced until arriving in Thailand; hunger. After three days of fasting to ensure an uneventful journey to Bangkok, I was ravenous, and headed downstairs to work my way through the tourist-friendly menu. I may have been sick since leaving Heathrow, but I was born with a very active sense of gluttony, and given a highly desirable menu and nowhere to go for two days, I was happy to take a few risks. After all, I'd lost three stone; that was like credit in the bank for a usually tubby lad like me. If anything, I 'needed' to be a greedy bastard just to get my strength up for the next leg of our journey. That's what I told myself, and I didn't need much convincing.

A couple of hours later we were about to enter the Royal Palace for a touristy look around when I doubled up on the pavement. My ill-conceived 'feed your way back to health' combination of omelette, pizza, and chocolate pancakes may, with hindsight, have been slightly ambitious, and they all now voiced their disapproval in the form of the mother of all stomach cramps.

"Cathy... we're about 20 minutes' walk away from the hostel, and I reckon I've got about five minutes until Armageddon... I know it's hot, and I know you don't run, but believe me... we need to run, and bloody fast."

I might have returned skinnier, browner and more chilled out, but Bangkok was going to serve up the same memories for me second time around; mainly crouching over the actual shit-hole in an utter shit-hole. The next day I told Cathy to head off and do some sightseeing if she wanted, but I was staying close to home after our impromptu jog through the city the previous day, but she was happy to hang around the local area with me. We were both ready to leave Thailand behind, and besides, she said that she couldn't desert the birthday boy.

Growing up in High Wycombe, I'd never been overly excited about visits into the dark, concrete world of the Octagon Shopping Centre which adjoined its ugly twin, the bus station. The only highlight was running off and exploring in the toy section of Murrays department store, but even that had been curtailed at an early age when my Mum had lost me and my little sister. We didn't even realise that we were 'missing' until our names were announced over the tannoy. This prompted my sister to cry and me to follow suit, knowing full well that this was going to result in a smack from our mum. Opposite Murrays was Boots, the familiar pharmacy store that graced every city and town across the land. I was petrified of going into Boots, as I always saw bigger boys and girls, mainly girls, getting taken away by the Police. I had no concept of what shoplifting was, and just assumed that the Police arrested random children there. I'd grown up with a deep distrust of the place based on this, but when I saw the familiar 'Boots' sign jutting out amidst the chaotic jumble of hostel and bar signs above Koh San Road, I thought it was a mirage.

"Cathy, look! It's a Boots!"

Eagerly, we dodged the dogs, bikes, mopeds and tuk-tuks to cross the busy street, before entering the little slice of home. Lip gloss for Cathy awaited, and for me, enough Imodium to last the next four months provided the most exciting birthday present I'd received in years.

Most of the day was spent sitting outside cafés showing off our tans, and despite not being able to compete with mine, Cathy was highly excited to be darker than most tourists who passed by. I know this as she made a point of telling me, every time somebody walked past; every time without fail, despite us being on the busiest street in Thailand. Then, as the sun began to set on both the day and our Thai adventure, we ducked into one of the many internet cafés along the street, which seemed gargantuan in comparison to the newly expanded Fantastic Hill operation down in Kata. My Hotmail box was full of birthday wishes, excitement about the Quarter-Final that was now just a day away, along with some last-minute details about our trip around China.

"There're going to be six of us travelling together... three guys and three girls... we're to meet in the foyer of the hotel in Hong Kong on Sunday evening" I recited.

"Cool, female company at last! No offence" replied Cathy.

"Everyone seems sorted for FA Cup tickets tomorrow. Oh, hold on, that's sad... Pat's not going; his Dad's passed away, so he isn't bothering" I continued, scanning the many emails from my mates.

"Oh no, poor Pat. That's terrible" said Cathy, leaning across to see the email on my screen. "You know what... I think I'll email my Dad at work."

"Good shout... I'll email my Mum; she'll print it out to show my Dad tonight."

Within seconds of sending the email to my mum, I got an excited reply.

'Hi, are you there?' it read.

'Yes... in Bangkok!' I replied.

'Lovely! Happy Birthday! Are you both okay?'

'We're fine, flying to Hong Kong in the morning.'

'Watching the game in Hong Kong?'

'Yes, will watch it in a bar or at hotel... can't wait!'

'Brilliant! I saw Buz on Industrial Estate yesterday, he's VERY excited! Have to go now, got to go to a meeting. Be careful in China. Love you!!!!!!!'

'Okay, bye Mum. Love to Dad and Paula.'

"The internet is clever isn't it?" I said to Cathy as we walked back towards our hostel.

"What about it?" she asked distractedly, more interested in people watching than what I was saying.

"Well... just everything really... like talking to my mum just now, and looking at websites... like seeing the best way to get to the hotel tomorrow and pictures of it. It's just all very clever" I explained, although Cathy wasn't really listening. "I remember the first time I ever saw the internet" I continued.

"Really? When was that? What did you look at?" asked Cathy, finally hearing something of interest.

"It was when I got the job in Lane End."

"The job your lesbian girlfriend got for you?"

"Yeah... but she wasn't really my girlfriend, or a lesbian, not at the time. Anyway, they got the internet loaded onto a computer at work and everyone gathered around me to watch" I recalled.

"Why did they get you to look first?"

"I don't know. Maybe because I was the most junior there... I think everyone was a bit scared of what might happen."

"And what did happen then?"

"Well, I clicked on the internet button and it came up with a list of options, I think it was all magazine names. All the bosses were there, so I let them all discuss it first."

"And?"

"... and then I clicked on 'Playboy'."

"Wow... and an internet pioneer was born" Cathy sighed. "Come on; give me some money so I can buy you a birthday beer."

By lunchtime the following day, Thailand was but a memory as our plane touched down in Hong Kong. In contrast to the slap-dash magic that pervaded Thailand, we were met by an ultra-modern airport which rose symmetrically on reclaimed land from the South China Sea. Unlike our bumpy passage into Bangkok, we were seamlessly whisked into the heart of Kowloon via a speedy rail link. When we reached the end of the line, underneath the bustling city, we were transferred to a minibus and soon driven up to ground level for a whistle-stop tour of the city's grand hotels, dropping off other visitors along the way. Impossibly, Kowloon made Bangkok look tranquil by comparison as we peered through the minibus window; buildings rose so high that we couldn't see their tops. People swarmed from every direction and the overload of neon signs fought for our attention, welcoming us into a cauldron of chaos. Before long, we were the only passengers left on board as the van pulled up outside a more modest looking hotel. In comparison to the 5-star hotels we had stopped off at en route, it wasn't in the same league, but after two months in Thailand on a very tight budget, there was no containing our excitement upon entering the air-conditioned room.

"Look at the bed!" screeched Cathy, before bounding onto it. "Oh my god, it's heavenly... that's it... I'm not moving all day" she purred.

I closed the door behind me and dropped the bags, watching her bouncing for delight. Beside the door was the light switch. I turned it off. I turned it on. I turned it off again and then back on. Without speaking, we both stared admiringly at the various light bulbs around the room as they exploded into light, before dispersing just as quickly; tonight, our little torches would be getting the evening off.

"Electricity!" we exclaimed appreciatively, as if we'd been transported through time from another era.

"Cathy, come here... you've got to see this" I said, my voice trembling.

"I'm not moving from my bed. What is it?"

"Please. It's better than the bed... I promise you!"

Tempted by curiosity, Cathy gasped and fell to her knees with her hand over her mouth in utter disbelief at the wonderful sight as I held the bathroom door open.

"Oh it's beautiful. It's just beautiful!" she cried.

"You go first" I said.

"No... I couldn't. You go... go on... I'll watch" she offered, as the pair of us became increasingly emotional.

So as Cathy held the door and looked on admiringly, I took three tentative steps forward, before turning around. We looked at each other, smiled and gave a knowing nod of acknowledgment as to how much this moment meant, then I gently sat down on the toilet seat.

Following a period of reflective silence, I was finally able to speak.

"I don't believe this... it's even got a flush!"

"No bucket!" added Cathy, joyously. "Do you think it flushes paper?" she added, almost not daring to believe what she was suggesting.

We both frantically looked around the bathroom for any instructions to the contrary, but could find nothing.

"Shall we try?" dared Cathy.

"I can't do it, I can't" I pleaded. This was all becoming too much. I stepped back out into the doorway. "Go on... you try it."

The sound of water gushing from cistern to pan, then flowing freely away down the drain heralded whoops of unconfined joy.

"There's hot water in the taps too! I'd forgotten about hot water!" I proclaimed, as this voyage of discovery continued at the washbasin.

"Hot water? I'm having a bath... right now" announced Cathy without hesitation, launching towards the bath taps.

Moments after the groans of ecstasy had died down from the bathtub as she submerged herself in bubbles, I heard Cathy once again call through to the bedroom.

"James... what's that noise?"

"That? Oh nothing important, that's just our... television!" I tried to reply casually, before breaking into unabashed excitement. The simple life had been good, but this had proven to be the most wonderful ten minutes imaginable.

Having wallowed in western opulence for a couple of hours, we ventured out to explore ever further east; firstly through the bustling streets, before discovering the relative tranquillity of Kowloon's promenade that looked out across Victoria Harbour to Hong Kong Island and its indomitable high-rise skyline. Just like our first sighting of Kata beach, the panorama was jaw-droppingly spectacular. The waterway, which separated Hong Kong Island from its Kowloon District on the Chinese mainland, was littered with hundreds of vessels varying from huge cargo-laden tankers, to tiny dinghies racing across the choppy waters. In between, a dozen green and white ferries danced between the two parts of Hong Kong.

"Let's go over!" suggested Cathy, full of wanderlust, pointing across to the island.

"What, now? Why don't we go tomorrow? Let's just get our bearings a bit today… besides, we need to find somewhere to watch the football."

Shaking her head dismissively, Cathy strode off towards the terminal where a ferry was just docking.

"Wait for me!" I shouted, before scurrying to catch up.

Once on board I was glad of her gumption, as the ride across the bay was exhilarating, offering ever changing views of both coastlines. The breeze and the waves buffeted the small ferry as it ploughed its way through the water, leaving Kowloon receding into the distance and Hong Kong Island looming ever larger.

"I could stay on here all day" I shouted, struggling to be heard above the sound of the engines. As I took in our dramatic surroundings, I half expected James Bond or Bruce Lee to come up on deck, looking for a ruckus.

Disembarking on Hong Kong Island, Cathy was in full-blown tourist mode and, after the amazing ferry ride, I was happy to follow her lead. She marched into the city following her guide map until we reached the funicular Peak Tram which hauled its way up the hillside to Victoria Peak, allowing us stunning views back across the island towards Kowloon. With the Peak visited, we returned to sea level in the business district to find Hong Kong Park, which sat nestled like an oasis amongst the towering cathedrals of commerce. Our Thai adventure had never really felt like a holiday, more a ridiculously lazy way of life, but within six hours of being in Hong Kong, we were already well on the way to ticking off most of Cathy's 'to-do' list. Hong Kong Park provided a respite from the noise of the city and, once ensconced in its giant aviary, we could have been sitting in a remote jungle rather than one of the world's most populous cities. The aviary was situated in a naturally forested valley within the park, and its huge sweeping netting towered high above the trees, leaving its 80 varying species 'free' to soar through the sky. The scale of the project made it easy to forget that these birds were actually being held in captivity. One captive made its own silent protest, by crapping on my shoulder from a great height, much to the delight of Cathy and a group of small children on a school trip.

"It's supposed to be good luck" pointed out Cathy, between fits of laughter.

"How was that remotely lucky? What possible positive can I take from getting shat on by a bloody Toucan?" I grumpily replied. "Come on, it's nearly 5 o'clock... let's get back to Kowloon... we need to find a bar for the match."

As we set sail back across to Kowloon, numerous groups were congregating on Platform 2 at High Wycombe train station, eight time zones to the west. The 9am train to Birmingham was due any minute, and the air was full of anticipation as to what the daytrip to Leicester would bring. True to his word before departing for the Wimbledon replay, Bob had brought along youthful reinforcements in the form of his daughters, ten-year-old Abby and her little sister Laura, who was eight. It was Abby who announced the imminent arrival of the train, long before the Station Master, as it curled into view from the east.

"Smudger... you sit there. Buz... you sit next to him" ordered Abby, while directing her sister into the seats opposite their bemused travel companions. "Do you know how to play 'Paper-Scissors-Stone'?"

"Pass me a beer Smudge, this is going to be a long journey" sighed Buz.

As the train was preparing to pull away, a figure dashed across the platform, just managing to squeeze through the shutting door.

"Oi Oi! Look who it is!" exclaimed Tony, as Beany breathlessly joined the party.

"Alright lads, room for one more?"

"What are you doing here?" asked Tony.

"What do you mean?" replied Beany innocently.

"It's the FA Cup!" chorused Bob, Teddy, Little-Wanker, John, Flipper, Adam, Jimbo, Ian, Oggy, Nicko, Mike, Buz, Roger, Jackie, Sharon, Les, Nobby and Smudger.

"You never go to the cup games" concluded Laura, pausing before adding... "my daddy said you're too tight to pay for the extra games."

Beany slumped into a seat to hoots of derision, before taking consolation from his first cider of the day.

"I didn't think you were bothering today Beany?" queried Bob.

"I've got Pat's ticket, he wasn't up for it after the funeral and everything... said he was just going to spend some time with his mum."

Driving down Amersham Hill and over the railway bridge into the town centre, Pat passed directly over the Roobarb travelling party, as the train headed out of the station towards the Midlands. A couple of minutes later, he was sitting at his mum's kitchen table as she busied herself at the stove.

"Patrick, isn't today that big football match everyone's been gabbing about?"

"Yeah, it's Leicester away in the FA Cup. Wycombe Wanderers in the quarter-finals... unbelievable" replied Pat, while looking at the local paper's match preview.

"So what are doing here then?"

"Nah, I'm not bothered Mum. It's too soon after Dad... I'm happy spending the day with you."

"Don't be so frickin daft son. I don't want you here making the place untidy!" she said matter-of-factly, delivering a mug of tea and a plate of toast to the table, before diving back to her frying pan.

"Besides, yer Dad would be annoyed thinking that you missed the big match because of him."

"Well, it's too late now, I gave Beany my ticket... the boys will be on the train already, they were leaving at nine."

"Beany? But he never..."

"... never goes to the FA Cup, I know" said Pat, completing his mum's sentence.

"Nothing ever stopped you going to football before... not even when you were supposed to be banned after that altercation with the eejit goalkeeper... I'll never forget the look on your father's face when he opened the paper to see you and the footballer on the front page, looking like a pair of Bruce Lee's doing the Kung-Fu!" chuckled Pat's mother.

Hearing his mum laugh raised Pat's spirits immensely.

"That was 15 years ago!" he protested. "You're right though, I'll go down to Adams Park later... they've got a big screen set up for those who couldn't get tickets. Is that bacon nearly ready?"

Three hours later, and still stuffed from breakfast, Pat gave his mum a loving hug... "I'll leave the car here mum and pick it up in the morning if that's okay. I'll take you out for lunch, yeah?"

"That would be lovely son, I'll see you tomorrow" she replied, as Pat wandered off towards town. "Oh Patrick!" she shouted after him... "At least I won't have to worry about you fighting the goalie today then!" while waving her son off to football, as she'd done for the best part of 30 years.

It was only a short walk into the High Street, where he found plenty of folk adorned with Wanderers scarves and shirts milling around the pubs nervously, all dressed up with nowhere to go. Before Pat had even got to the bar, he received a friendly tap on the shoulder from Jason.

"Hiya Pat, you going up to the big screen? Let me buy you a Guinness mate... here's to yer old man."

Jason and Pat may have been about to take their first sip of the day, but the Roobarbs who'd travelled to Leicester were, it's fair to say, already 'well oiled' and holding court in boisterous fashion in a pub close to Filbert Street, the home of Leicester City. Songs normally reserved for the privacy of a steamed up minibus on long journeys home, and generally only sung for the benefit of keeping our designated driver awake, were getting belted out and shared with others. All teams have songs that endure through the years, and the Roobarbs had proudly continued the tradition of singing songs from generations past. As ever, Buz was happy to take the lead whenever an audience became available; conducting proceedings, albeit slightly precariously, from the top of a table.

"Right… listen up… this one was sung as the young men of High Wycombe marched off to World War One!"

"We are the old Bucks boys,

We make a hell of a noise!

Give us a tanner,

And we'll mind our manners,

We are the old Bucks boys!"

"… and this one is from the early Sixties" he continued, ignoring repeated calls from behind the bar to get down from his makeshift podium.

"We all agree, Maskell is better than Yashin,

Horseman is better than Eusebio…

And Hendon are in for a thrashin'!"

"One more! I've got one more! This is the Roobarbs own contribution to our history! We wrote this… well, along with The Kinks" he passionately declared. Laura and Abby giggled in anticipation of Buz either falling flat on his face or being told off again by the barman.

"There's a crack up on the ce-eee-eiling,

And the kitchen sink is le-eee-eaking,

Out of work and got no mo-onnn-ey,

Sunday joint of bread and ho-onnn-ey.

What are we living for?

WYCOMBE WANDERERS IN DIVISION FOUR!"

"Hold up… I'm not done yet" protested Buz, as the bouncers politely advised him to get off of the table immediately. "There're three more verses yet… Jamesy knows them; he made them up. Jamesy! How does the next bit go again? Where's Jamesy?"

"Shagging in Thailand, you daft sod!" shouted Ian.

"No, he said he would be in Hong Kong for the game" added Bob, pulling out the last email I'd sent home. "It's 8 o'clock at night there… he'll be in a worse state than you Buz!"

Bob was right, I was in a state, but it was a state of panic rather than drunkenness.

"I can't believe we couldn't find a sports bar" I complained to Cathy for the umpteenth time, as I sat on the bed, waiting for her to come out of the bathroom. "How much longer are you going to be?"

"Not long… just enjoying having a proper bathroom… and a shower… and a mirror… and a hairdryer. I'm sure we'll find somewhere this evening."

Back out on the street darkness had descended, but the overload of neon advertising hoardings and shop signs meant that we stepped out into a dazzling, illuminescent glare that took some getting used to. The cool chill in the air also took me by surprise, leading to a quick retreat to dig out a pair of trousers from my bag for the first time in two months. Kowloon was proving to be the only city in the world without an Irish Bar and, after exploring dozens of streets to no avail for a bar showing sports, we found ourselves approaching the promenade again. Temporarily, all thoughts of finding somewhere to watch the game disappeared as we turned the corner onto the boardwalk, into full view of the harbour. During the day, the Hong Kong City skyline had been stunning, but now, with the miles of skyscrapers sitting in front of the moonlit mountain ridge illuminated, and with their neon signs reflecting down onto the shimmering waters of the harbour, the marriage of the geographical and architectural was simply breathtaking.

"Wow" I eventually managed to summon up.

"Wow" agreed Cathy, equally spellbound.

Sometimes words aren't necessary, so we just continued to stand and stare. It could have been for minutes, it could have been for hours, but either way, the impact of the view never diminished.

Back in England, in the gardens of a hotel just outside Leicester, Wycombe Wanderers goalkeeper Martin Taylor was also quiet. It was midday and the team were taking a leisurely walk around the hotel grounds following their pre-match meal. Training was done; the tactical meetings were done too. Now, all the players were falling into their specific routines as the countdown to the biggest game of their careers, an FA Cup Quarter-Final against Leicester City, continued. Some disappeared into a world of music, some joked around to release nervous energy. Martin Taylor just walked quietly at the back of the group in reflective mood. Facing Leicester City, in the biggest game of his career, this was a case of history repeating.

Having served his apprenticeship as understudy to England's most capped international, the legendary Peter Shilton, Taylor had taken over the mantle of being Derby County's first choice goalkeeper. Fame and fortune beckoned as Derby led Leicester City 1-0 late in the First Division play-off final at Wembley Stadium on 30th May 1994, with the prize of promotion to the Premier League the following season awaiting the victor. Just two days beforehand, the Roobarbs had been in the iconic old stadium to witness Wycombe Wanderers beat Preston North End in the Third Division equivalent, providing a fairy-tale ending to their first ever season in the Football League. Taylor's Derby County were on course to emulate Wycombe's earlier triumph on that Bank Holiday weekend, when Martin came to claim a simple cross, but instead found himself bundled over by a Leicester forward. The blatant offence was inexplicably missed by the referee, and Leicester equalised. The games momentum turned instantly, and Leicester scored again; promotion was lost. After the game, having seen a replay of Leicester's equalising goal, the referee sought Taylor out in the bowels of the famous stadium to apologise for his error. On such decisions lives can be changed. The following season, instead of gracing Old Trafford and playing against Manchester United, Martin Taylor and his Derby teammates ended up playing in the more modest surroundings of Roots Hall, the home of Southend United. By rights, Taylor and his Derby teammates shouldn't have been there, but it was on that fateful night in Southend that he suffered his career threatening leg injury. After two years of rehabilitation, his shot at the big-time was gone. Martin Taylor had unfinished business with Leicester City.

Two hours later, the Wycombe players were again out walking; this time inspecting the Filbert Street pitch, before heading back to the sanctity of their dressing room to change into their unfamiliar second choice kit of red and white quarters, to avoid a clash with the home teams traditional blue.

"I can't believe there are no sports bars... any bars. Where are the bloody bars?" I ranted.

"Let's ask someone" suggested Cathy.

"But everyone's Chinese, I didn't think Hong Kong would be so Chinese... it used to be British until recently, didn't it?" I reasoned, failing woefully to take into consideration that Kowloon was actually on the Chinese mainland and had, in reality, always been predominantly Chinese, with the greater western influence being felt back across the water on Hong Kong Island.

"Of course it's bloody Chinese!" snapped a weary Cathy. "We've walked for miles... let's just go back to the hotel. There's still the hotel bar, plus we've got our own telly remember!"

"Our telly! Of course! I'd forgotten about that! Let's get back to the hotel!" I replied excitedly. "I can't believe I didn't think about that. I'm such an idiot sometimes."

"Yes, you certainly are" muttered Cathy, as she struggled to keep up with my determined march back to the hotel.

Upon reaching the hotel bar, it soon became evident that we wouldn't be watching the game there. The glitzy wine bar was a tad more formal than the Footy Bar in Kata Bay; its prices were less appealing too. Thankfully, we'd spotted that there wasn't a television screen before ordering drinks that would have cost more than a week's rent back at Fantastic Hill.

In High Wycombe, Pat and Jason were in the supporters club at Adams Park. The surroundings may have been familiar, and also many of the faces milling around, but there were definitely a few things amiss; no away supporters, no teams, not even an actual game. Despite this, they were treating their pre-match routine with the respect it deserved, and after a rough few weeks for Pat, there wasn't any better company than Jason, a guy who had a gift for lifting a room with his infectious dedication to having a good time. A good time was also being had by all in Leicester. Buz had finally been talked down to safety from the edge of the table, but after a period of calm (whilst the game had been previewed on Football Focus on the pub's television), Beany had now taken over, strutting along the rows of table-tops in the pub, sending glasses crashing with every step while doing his best Mick Jagger impression. As soon as the first chords of 'Jumpin Jack Flash' had belted out from the jukebox, Bob had ushered his young daughters to the exit. He was fine with them seeing the Roobarbs in fine fettle, but the thought of them arriving home and saying "Mummy, guess what... we all got kicked out of a pub because of Beany" didn't fill him with joy. And, inevitably, although Beany's Mick Jagger routine was indeed impressive, it did usually end with him being asked to leave, if not all of us.

"Daddy, why aren't we waiting for the others?" asked Abby, as they made their way towards the floodlight pylons towering over the surrounding rooftops.

"It's going to be really busy today... so I want to get you in the ground and settled early. Leicester are a much bigger team than Wycombe, and the ground is twice as big as Adams Park... so we have to sit where we're told today, and you can't run around the terraces like you do at Wycombe, okay?"

"Daddy, why did everyone shout at that man on the telly earlier, was it because he had a moustache?" asked Laura.

"Mark Lawrenson? No! It wasn't because of his moustache" laughed Bob.

"Good, because Roger's got a moustache too, and that would have made him sad" she added.

"It was because Mark Lawrenson said 'Wycombe should just enjoy their day out'... and that annoyed everyone... what he meant was he doesn't think we can win, he was being a bit patronising" explained Bob... "But don't repeat what you heard everyone shouting."

"What is 'patronising'?" replied Abby.

"Can I have a moustache?" asked Laura.

"What does wanker mean?" added Abby.

"Look, we're here!" replied a relieved Daddy, quickly changing the subject.

Even though they'd stopped off at another pub en route to the ground after the inevitable 'Jagger' related eviction, the rest of the Roobarbs had taken to their seats before Bob, despite his best endeavours, could persuade poor Laura to do likewise.

"It's too high up Daddy! It's too steep... I want to go down... I'm scared" sobbed Laura, who had been crying hysterically for the past 20 minutes, ever since finding their seats at the back of the stand along the side of the Filbert Street pitch. This hadn't been a problem initially, when there were only a few hundred people in the ground, but now there were 22,000 and a fair few were waiting for the drama to unfold on the pitch by watching the high altitude stand-off between two little girls and their increasingly perplexed father.

"I want to go home, get Mummy to come and pick me up!" demanded Laura.

"We aren't in Wycombe Laura; Mummy's a two hour drive away. The game will be finished by the time she gets here… sit between Abby and me, it'll be fine" pleaded Bob.

"No, I don't want to sit next to you… I want Smudger and Buz!" screamed Laura, at last managing to stop crying, but still refusing to sit down.

"Don't worry love, the game will start in a minute; look, here come the teams" said the old man who had been sitting silently on the other side of Laura.

Laura froze with embarrassment at the stranger's interjection, before a roar enveloped the ground welcoming the teams. The combination of the two sent Laura scurrying back along the compact aisle, past her big sister and into her dad's arms as she once again burst into inconsolable tears.

"Come on Laura love… give the players a cheer with me. Look… there's Tony, Beany, Les and Teddy standing over there; they're all cheering. Can you see Tony waving his lucky FA Cup hat? And look below them, down near the front… there's Smudger thrashing his arms about already. You see… you don't want to be sitting next to those big elbows, do you?" comforted Bob.

Laura wiped her tears away and ushered her sister to move one seat along, next to the old man, before standing on her seat and joining the rest of the 3,200 Chairboys in supporting their team, "Come on Wycombe! Come on Wycombe!"

Back in High Wycombe, my dad shuffled into my old room, sat himself down on my old bed, turned on my old portable radio and smiled at the memory of my packing dilemmas the night Grimsby were vanquished three rounds before. "Come on Wycombe" he whispered towards the radio.

"This is weird" said Pat, as he and Jason took their seats amongst nearly 4,000 other ticketless supporters at Adams Park, looking across the pitch to a giant screen that was parked in front of the managers dugouts, on the back of a lorry trailer.

"It is, isn't it?" agreed Jason. "What's the point in cheering? They can't hear us up in Leicester!"

"We can't just sit here quietly though, I'll go mad" pondered Pat.

"Here, this should sort us out" whispered Jason, stealthily sneaking a small bottle of rum from his jacket pocket. "Well... it's a special occasion isn't it?" he reasoned.

Up on the screen, the camera zoomed in on Martin Taylor in the Wanderers goal. His calm exterior hid a pounding heart and a steely determination to finally take his revenge on Leicester City. The referee, Steve Bennett, blew his whistle and the game kicked off, prompting roars from 7,000 Wanderers fans sitting in two stands, 100 miles apart. "Come on Wycombe! Come on Wycombe!"

"Come on... come on... it's got to be on somewhere" I muttered back in Hong Kong, as I sat on the edge of the bed, frantically pressing the television remote control buttons with increasing intensity.

At 11.15pm, and having gone through all the channels for the tenth time, I finally conceded that China wasn't showing the Leicester City versus Wycombe Wanderers game, or any other football match for that matter. I cursed my rotten luck, and the bird that had crapped on me earlier in the day; the feathered precision bomber certainly hadn't brought me any good fortune. If only our stay in Thailand had lasted a few days longer, I would have been happily sitting in the Footy Bar, watching Wycombe Wanderers. Deflated, I reluctantly turned the television off and joined Cathy under the unfamiliar weight of a duvet, where she was already drifting off following our hectic day of travel and sightseeing. I punched a groove into my pillow before closing my eyes and resting my head. The day had taken its toll on me too, and before I'd had time to repeat a second silent chorus in my head of "Come on Wycombe!" I too was asleep.

19 – Leicester

I awoke with a start, eyes dancing across the darkened room as I struggled to get my bearings. A dull glow warmed the blackout curtains, suggesting it was morning already. Tired from the previous day's exertions, I hadn't moved a muscle during the night, and if it wasn't for dawn's early light subtly filtering into the room, I would have been sure that I'd barely closed my eyes moments before. I felt the duvet on top of me and remembered that I was now in Hong Kong, with its views from the promenade and the bathroom with a proper toilet. Then my heart missed a beat; the football! If I could find an English news channel, hopefully I'd find out the score. I slid out from under the duvet, so as not to wake Cathy, and perched on the end of the bed in front of the television. Flicking through the channels, I eventually stumbled across a football match. The commentary was in Chinese, and the match graphics in the corner of the screen were equally alien to me, but it looked like a game from Europe. In fact, the stadium looked very English. It also looked very familiar; it looked like Filbert Street. I'd seen it just the week before in Thailand, when Leicester City soundly beat Liverpool 2-0. Yep, that was Leicester in their traditional blue and white. And then my mind registered.

"That's… no… it can't be… it's Wycombe. I don't believe it… it's Wycombe."

First I thought it, then I mumbled it, and then I screamed it.

"Cathy… it's Wycombe!"

Cathy sleepily hauled herself up against the headboard and smiled at the sight of her freshly turned 29-year-old boyfriend looking more excited than a child on Christmas morning.

"It's Brownie, look!" I yelled as the camera focused on Steve Brown, "…and Danny Bulman! Look, it's Danny Bulman… on the telly… here in Hong Kong… look!"

"Yes James, I can see it… I get it!" laughed Cathy.

For almost a minute, the screen showed Leicester's keeper waiting for the ball to be retrieved from the crowd. I realised that this wasn't a brief highlights package just showing goals. I also noticed that none of the players looked overly battle weary.

"This is weird… it's like a live broadcast… it must be a full-length recording… I can't believe this!"

A couple of moments later, a small graphic flashed up in the corner of the screen, it was just legible underneath the local networks Chinese lettering.

"Look at that! *'LEIC v WYC 0-0 05.00'*… its nil-nil, and they've only played five minutes! They've held them out for five minutes… that's superb! Come on Wycombe!" I roared as, unlike Jason and Pat, I was undeterred by the fact that my support couldn't be heard 6,000 miles away back in Leicester.

Wycombe appeared to be starting the game very well, and any casual Chinese viewer would have found it impossible to differentiate the Premier League high-flyers from the team languishing in sixteenth position three divisions below.

Since my first visit to Loakes Park as a four-year-old, I'd revered the men wearing the Oxford and Cambridge Blues of Wycombe Wanderers and although, today, their shirts were quartered with red and white, I once again felt a swell of pride rush through me as I watched those representing my town. As a child, there had been nothing more special to me than a Wycombe Wanderer. It was a feeling that had never left me, even as I'd grown into adulthood and found myself supporting Wanderers who were my own age. I'd met an ex-player called Kevin Day through my university studies, and helped out on a children's training camp with another, Simon Stapleton. Hardly household names; but when opportunity had presented itself, I could barely bring myself to speak to them. They were from a different world; they were Wycombe Wanderers, not mere mortals. And then there was the Steve Guppy encounter; the greatest sporting moment of my life.

I was 18 and enjoying the fact that, unlike school, college hours were few and far between. It was a Wednesday afternoon and, with nothing particular to do, I'd trodden the familiar path across the street from my childhood home to Fernie Fields, a sprawling council recreation ground. As a child I'd wake up at the weekend and eagerly dive across my room to the window to see if any of my mates were already 'over the field' setting up makeshift goals with jumpers and sticks, or scouting for a patch of grass devoid of dog crap. Alan, who'd inadvertently introduced me to the HR girl Becky, was always first, closely followed by Jason (who was now sitting watching a giant screen down at Adams Park swigging rum). We'd played football on 'Fernies' almost every day without fail for 13 years, but now that our schooldays were in the past, Alan and Jason had ruined it by getting proper jobs. For now, I would have to make do with practising on my own. I did a few laps of the pub league pitch that only came alive at the weekends, and took some shots into the un-netted goalposts, before looking up to notice someone jogging around the park's perimeter with a ball seemingly glued to his foot. After retrieving my ball from the bushes following a wayward shot, I turned back towards the pitch to see the footballing jogger completing his lap and coming back towards my pitch.

"Can I knock some crosses in to you?" he shouted over.

"Erm, yes... no problem" I managed to blurt out, as I kicked my football towards him.

It was Steve Guppy, Wycombe Wanderers flying winger, one of the most exciting players I'd ever seen grace a football pitch. It was an opinion shared by many older and wiser Chairboys too, and although Guppy hadn't managed to progress through the ranks at professional outfit Southampton, since dropping into the part-time game with Wycombe, he had been nothing short of a revelation.

"You start out at the edge of the box, and I'll drop it towards the back post, okay?" he yelled over casually.

"Cool" I replied, feigning equal casualness, but in reality, my legs were turning to jelly.

As I took up my position, a flurry of thoughts raced through my mind.

'I'm playing football with Steve Guppy... the Wycombe Wanderer Steve Guppy!'

'If I do well, he could get me a trial. Yes! He'll tell the manager about me... this could be my chance!'

'Don't be stupid, you're crap, remember? Ah, but 'Gupps' doesn't know that!'

'Concentrate... just concentrate you idiot. Whatever you do, don't make a twat of yourself... just head the ball.'

'He's hit it... eyes on the ball... keep your eyes on the ball, don't let 'Gupps' down.'

"Ouch! Ooh... bollocks!" I cursed, having risen towards Guppy's whipped-in cross, before closing my eyes as the ball smashed fully into my nose.

"Are you okay mate?" asked Steve as I rubbed my nose and wiped away the tears that infuriatingly were forming in my eyes, no matter how hard I tried to stem them.

"Yeah, I'm good... I just lost track of the ball in the sun."

"Are you sure? Well thanks anyway, see you around."

"Don't go! Take some more, I'm fine, honestly!" I pleaded somewhat desperately.

"Alright, I'll do some in-swingers from the other side... so, erm, the sun doesn't get in your eyes."

Twenty minutes later, Steve Guppy had perfected his in-swinging corner and I'd scored a headed hat-trick that I'd never forget. There's no need to recall the other two dozen efforts I'd sent high and wide of the goal. The headache that lasted for the remainder of the day was but a small price to pay. And now, ten years later, here was Steve Guppy again, playing for Leicester City, an England International and one of the stars of the Premier League, pitting his wits against his old friends and teammates, Keith Ryan and Jason Cousins. Unfortunately for the Chairboys, it was fellow international footballers and superstars such as Robbie Savage, Muzzy Izzett, Matt Elliott, Gerry Taggart and Ade Akinbiyi who would be on the end of Guppy's crosses today, and not some star-struck kid in the park.

Despite their friendship, Cousins was in no mood to show any generosity towards his old teammate, and had picked up a yellow card within the first 20 minutes. There were few referees in the land who didn't know how to spell 'Jason Cousins', and it was fairly certain that today's official, Steve Bennett, had also reserved spaces in his notepad for the names 'Steve Brown' and 'Robbie Savage'. Neither was renowned for ever 'giving an inch' and as the game flowed freely from end to end in its early stages, both combatants had left their painful marks on the game, and each other.

As the first half progressed, Wycombe continued to impress, buoyed by the confidence gained from the heroic double-header with Wimbledon. Leicester were, again, a step up in class, but Wycombe had created as many opportunities as their hosts, and the few chances the Chairboys defensive line failed to snuff out were dealt with by the ever dependable Martin

Taylor. I leapt from the bed as Danny Bulman sent a powerful shot zipping across the grass towards Simon Royce's near post, providing the Leicester goalkeeper cause for concern as he dived low to his right to palm the ball behind for a Wycombe corner. From the corner, Wycombe's latest temporary attacking loanee, George Clegg, headed another chance just over the bar, prompting me to instinctively try to head the ball with him.

"You know you're not playing, right?" Cathy pointed out. "Who's that who did actually head the ball?"

"I've no idea; we don't have any strikers at all out there!" I replied, upon seeing the familiar figure of utility man Keith Ryan leading the line alongside his far from familiar partner, Clegg.

"That's nearly half an hour gone... if we can just contain them until half-time" I muttered, worrying that Wycombe's audacity at nearly opening the scoring might sting Leicester into action. But the Wanderers continued to hassle Leicester's players into mistakes, whilst remaining calm whenever they had possession. "We're playing really well you know" I commented, feeling a mixture of emotions; excitement at seeing my team, and pride in how well they were playing, but also a sense of dread of the inevitable moment when their concentration would lapse and this magical spell would be broken by clinical Premier League execution.

"Go on Brownie!" screeched Cathy, pulling my attention fully back to the screen as the Wanderer crunched into Savage, leaving the Leicester midfielder rolling around on the floor, protesting towards the referee with an expression that suggested that he'd never seen a tackle before. "I hate that Robbie Savage and his girly long hair... the gobby twat" she continued. I didn't take my eyes from the screen, but nodded my agreement.

In the stadium, Smudger and Nicko were once again out of their front row seats screaming at Savage in a similar vein to Cathy, although with somewhat more 'industrial language' thrown in, as Mr Bennett waved his yellow card in Brown's direction. They only ceased their volley of abuse as Steve Guppy jogged over to retrieve the ball from directly in front of them.

"Alright Juppy mate!" applauded Nicko.

The winger looked up, slightly bemused; maybe because it wasn't that common to be greeted so warmly by the opposition's supporters, or possibly at Nicko's inability to say the word 'Guppy' properly.

"Stevie Guppy... you're a Wycombe legend mate" added Smudger.

Guppy smiled back, before preparing to kick the ball back into play.

"Why can't you say 'Guppy?'" continued Smudger, turning to Nicko.

"What do you mean, 'Why can't I say Juppy'?"

As soon as Guppy turned away, the ceasefire ended and the Wanderers supporters around Nicko and Smudger reignited their chorus of indignation directed at Robbie Savage.

Laura turned to her sister and giggled, "Listen, they're singing that song again... like they did about the man with the moustache on the telly at lunchtime."

At Adams Park, Jason was giggling too. "There's no way Brownie or Cousins aren't getting sent off today... both booked and it's not even half-time yet!" he exclaimed, before leaning down into his jacket for another wee snifter of Jamaican Rum.

"I know, but there's no need to look so happy about it!" rebuked Pat.

"I'm just saying" replied Jason.

"You've had a bet on it, haven't you? You can't do that! That's treachery!" laughed Pat.

"Admittedly, I've had a little bet on one of them getting a red card" confessed Jason, rather sheepishly. "But I've also got a tenner on Wycombe to win at 10-to-1 though."

The heat was soon taken off Jason as the 4,000 sitting around him rose to roar their disapproval at the screen. It was Steve Brown's turn to hit the deck, as Savage lived up to his name, seeking swift retribution. Unimpressed, but not looking overly surprised, Mr Bennett added Savage to his list of cautioned players. The Wanderers supporters inside Filbert Street were even more vocal in their indignation and let Savage know, in no uncertain terms, what they felt about him. Looking around first to check that even Daddy was getting involved, Laura and Abby happily joined in the latest chorus of 'Robbie Savage, you're a wanker, you're a wanker'... a delightful little ditty that followed the colourful character around all the grounds that he played in. Boos soon turned back to cheers as Vinnicombe dispossessed Savage, with the ball falling to Brown who sent it rocketing through the air from fully 25 yards towards the top corner of the Leicester net. This time, Royce had to stretch high into the air to desperately claw the ball away from danger, for another Wanderers corner. The longer the game had gone on, the better Wycombe had played, and as they and their supporters grew in belief, an air of restless disquiet filled the remainder of the ground. This was mirrored on the face of the Foxes' manager, Peter Taylor, and, as the referee brought the first half to a goalless conclusion, it was the Leicester players and supporters who were most relieved to hear the whistle.

Laura and Abby both accepted a sweet from the old man sitting beside them. Jason studied his various betting slips against the half-time scores being announced over the Adams Park tannoy. Buz hopped uncomfortably from leg to leg in the queue for the Filbert Street toilets. My dad went to tell my mum the score and to get a cup of tea. Cathy declared that she was going to find what breakfast the hotel offered. Peter Taylor frantically tried to snap his team out of their sluggish slumber. And Lawrie Sanchez continued to drill into his Wycombe players what they needed to focus on to achieve one of the biggest upsets in footballing history. I remained perched on the edge of my hotel bed, watching Chinese adverts and pinching myself, just to check that this was really happening.

During the half-time interval, the cloud cover above Filbert Street had darkened considerably and, as the second half commenced, it did so under a torrential downpour that only added to the drama unfolding on the pitch. Undeterred by the monsoon, Lawrie Sanchez continued to prowl the small technical area afforded to him in front of the Wycombe bench. With his hair plastered to his head and his trench coat soaked through, he continued to coach his team from the side-line, seemingly oblivious to the atrocious conditions. Fired by Sanchez's passion and the persistent wall of noise from the travelling thousands, Wycombe continued to press, refusing to allow their opponents any time to settle on the ball. George Clegg jostled Andrew Impey for the ball just inside the Leicester half before being out-muscled and falling to the ground. As had been the case from the very first minute, before Impey had been given any opportunity to bring the ball under control, another figure in red and white, Michael Simpson, was upon him and dispossessed the outnumbered defender. Impey instinctively dragged Simpson down to prevent him starting yet another Wanderers foray into Leicester territory. With a free-kick awarded, Wycombe were able to set up for another well-rehearsed set piece which, against the skill of their Premier League opponents, offered the Wanderers perhaps their best chance of scoring. The aerial threat of all three centre-backs, Bates, Cousins and McCarthy, was sent forward to join with Clegg and Ryan on the 18-yard line, and all were being bumped and barged by equally statuesque Leicester defenders. Back out on the side-line at the scene of Impey's crime, Steve Brown hovered over the ball, waiting to send in a cross as his teammates took up their positions. As he launched the ball forward, Bates dashed towards the near post while Clegg pulled away from the goal with Ryan, all three taking their markers with them. At the same time, Cousins and McCarthy continued to move closer to goal. Cousins advanced towards the near post and McCarthy drifted in behind him. These coordinated movements left McCarthy with just one defender to deal with as the ball fell towards him on the six-yard line, where he manoeuvred in front of Ade Akinbiyi, allowing a clear sight of the ball as it dropped into the danger zone. McCarthy launched forward and headed the ball past Royce, who could do nothing but stand and watch as the ball skidded from the rain soaked turf and into the net.

Macca lay on his back in the Filbert Street mud, with fists clenched in delight as his teammates bundled on top of him. Over 7,000 Wanderers fans in two football stadiums exploded into delirious excitement, hugging friend and stranger alike, whilst my dad dropped my radio before shouting down the stairs to let my mum know the good news. In Hong Kong, I'd fallen to my knees in front of the television and let out an unbridled primal scream.

"There's 40 minutes to go… we've scored too early" I quickly told myself, doing what all long-suffering football fans do, in preparing myself for the worst; a subconscious act of self-preservation.

From the kick-off Leicester added urgency to their game, driven by a desperate sounding 85 percent of the packed stadium. But Wycombe's dedication to the cause only increased, and with the goal they'd yearned for now secured, they found yet another level of resilience which none of their supporters thought possible. Again, defenders sacrificed themselves, throwing bodies between goal-bound efforts and the Wanderers net, and Taylor, as ever, continued to stand firm whenever his brave defensive wall was breached. Leicester became increasingly anxious and, ten minutes after going behind, a dejected Robbie Savage limped from the field to be replaced by Darren Eadie. The Wanderers fans roared their approval; Brownie had won the gladiatorial battle of the midfield enforcers, which felt almost as significant as McCarthy's crucial goal itself. The clock continued to tick and with just over 20 minutes remaining, all the noise in the ground was coming from the Wycombe supporters who were beginning to dare to dream.

Leicester started another advance towards the Wanderers goal from inside their own half, with the Northern Ireland international Gerry Taggart striding forward, weighing up his attacking options. The fresh-legged Eadie raced from the centre of the pitch into space on the left, just outside the Wycombe box, leaving Steve Brown tracking Muzzy Izzett. Brownie paused for a split second and watched as Taggart slid the ball into Eadie's path, beyond the chasing Michael Simpson. The momentary lapse was all Izzett needed, and he sprinted away from Brownie, into the Wanderers penalty area in anticipation of Eadie crossing the ball. From Taggart's pass forward, Eadie crossed the ball with his first touch and Izzett gleefully slid it into the gaping net past the stranded Taylor. In a matter of seconds, 68 minutes of unparalleled effort was undone. The Leicester players embraced Izzett and, along with their supporters, let out a collective sigh of relief as normal service was resumed; their third tier guests put firmly back in their place.

For 18 minutes, Wycombe Wanderers had held a lead, and for that short time everyone connected with the club, either professionally or emotionally, had envisaged the team walking out for an FA Cup Semi-Final. It was a silly little dream that every supporter would have had as a child, and for those 18 magical minutes, we had all been transported back to that childlike state, free from the burdens of adulthood. But as Izzett equalised, he also pulled us back into the harsh real world of mortgage payments and crappy jobs to return to on Monday. Just for a moment, a collective pang of embarrassment immersed the Wycombe faithful, who'd foolishly allowed themselves to become intoxicated by the belief that impossible dreams could come true. But if football fans stopped believing at the first bump in the road, then the game wouldn't have become the planet's most popular sport, and the Wanderers who represented the people of High Wycombe wouldn't have been in their 114th year of existence. As the Wanderers restarted the game, surely feeling like mountaineers who'd had the summit of Everest in their sights only to slide back to Base Camp, all they could hear were the chants of the Wycombe fans, singing through sheer bloody-mindedness to drown out the Leicester goal celebrations.

Immediately though, the rollercoaster of emotions risked veering from the tracks altogether. Inexplicably, the Blues midfield lost the ball straight from the restart and Martin Taylor found himself faced with Adi Akinbiyi bearing down on goal, with his stunned defenders powerless to assist. A roar of anticipation reverberated around the stadium and the Leicester manager almost jumped out of his skin with disbelief, as his fortunes looked to be swinging from potential defeat to likely victory within a matter of seconds. Martin Taylor stood tall and strong, before rushing towards the striker as he prepared to shoot. Akinbiyi saw his effort smothered by the imposing frame of the keeper and, as quickly as the opportunity had presented itself, it was gone. Instantly, the disappointment of conceding the equaliser dissipated from the Wycombe players, as Leicester squandered the golden opportunity to score a rapid second with the best chance of the game. The supporters who had travelled from Buckinghamshire continued in their refusal to let the 19,000 home fans wrestle the initiative away from the Wanderers, and roared their heroes into every tackle, and the players, following the costly wobble, responded to them. Lawrie Sanchez, too, urged his players forward, knowing that a replay would be a wonderful reward for his side but that, realistically, Leicester would surely raise their game back at Adams Park. Today was Wycombe's opportunity. There were just 15 minutes to go, and his team still had all to play for. Sanchez called his assistant Terry Gibson to prepare two substitutes. Keith Ryan and George Clegg had battled tirelessly up front and, as instructed by Sanchez, had chased down the Leicester defenders at every opportunity, not giving them a second of peace. This first line of defence had meant lots of rushed and wayward passes, allowing the Wanderers midfield a fighting chance to break up the majority of Leicester's advances before any danger was presented. The exhausted front pairing had given their all, and so Sanchez looked to replace them with Stewart Castledine, who was normally a midfield player, and Roy Essandoh, the unknown quantity procured from Alan Hutchinson's tongue-in-cheek Teletext appeal for a striker.

"Just chase around up front… keep the ball away from our end… although a goal would be nice" encouraged Sanchez with deadpan calm, as the pair stood ready to enter the fray. Clegg reached them first, and the eager Castledine raced onto the pitch. Keith Ryan wearily followed, unstrapping the captain's armband and handing it to Essandoh.

The substitute, who had only joined the club a week before, looked at the armband sheepishly as he trotted onto the pitch, before deciding to pass it to 'the crazy guy' Cousins from defence.

"You'd better have this… I don't even know everyone's names!" he said, before taking up his advanced position.

Essandoh looked around the packed stadium and at the international centre-backs, Taggart and Elliott, who were now stood either side of him, sizing him up, before snapping into game mode as Martin Taylor launched forward a goal-kick towards him.

"Ooh, he's nice... I've not seen him before" cooed Cathy, re-entering the room.

"That's Stewart Castledine... he's okay, but he's not a striker... and the other one? I haven't got a clue about him" I replied, just as the television zoomed in on the stranger to announce his presence. Beside the Chinese letterings on the screen flashed up the name 'Roy Essandoh'.

"Roy Essandoh" read Cathy. "Nope... I've never heard of him."

"Me neither, it must be the bloke Bob mentioned in his email. Bob reckoned last week was going to be his first *and* last game" I added, fearing the worst at seeing Wycombe bring on an out-of-position squad player and a complete stranger.

"I got you some cake... the breakfast buffet is brilliant... it's just fried rice and noodles, and then cake!" continued Cathy.

"Not now... I feel sick, we can still win this!" I told her, again not taking my eyes from the screen.

"Really? What's the score?" she asked, sounding surprised.

"It's one apiece. We scored first, but Leicester just equalised. Your mate Savage has gone off injured though."

Cathy sensed the seriousness of the situation, and jumped onto the bed behind me to watch the remainder of the game, while refraining from asking any more questions. After five minutes of frantically chasing and harrying the Leicester defenders, Essandoh and Castledine were able to catch their breath as Wycombe were awarded another free-kick in a dangerous position, just ten yards back from the Leicester corner flag. Up jogged the three central defenders to join their forwards again, as the Blues looked to create more havoc in the Leicester goalmouth. The rainclouds dispersed and sunshine flooded into Filbert Street as Steve Brown swung over the cross, which was more akin to a corner kick than the deep cross that had led to McCarthy's earlier goal. The Leicester defence, though, made no mistake this time around, and Matty Elliott headed the ball back from whence it came. Brown controlled the ball and, before Steve Guppy could get close enough to make a challenge, he swung the ball back towards the congested goalmouth. This time, his hurried cross didn't have the required power or trajectory, and the ball failed to clear Stefan Oakes who, as the second line of defence behind Guppy, was stood a couple of yards inside the penalty box. The ball reached Oakes at an awkward height and smashed against his flailing left arm.

"Handball!" screamed the thousands of Wycombe fans, who had clearly seen the Leicester player's infringement. The Wanderers players, too, screamed at the referee and linesman, fully expecting their appeals to be met by the referee pointing towards the penalty spot. But, as the protests from both pitch and stand became more desperate, the referee did nothing. Oakes, yet to hear the shrill sound of the referee's whistle, hammered the ball away from danger, before Ben Townsend kicked it out of play to prevent the on-rushing Steve Guppy breaking clear for the home team. As the ball crashed into the advertising hoardings, Sanchez marched out of his designated area, storming past Townsend and Guppy towards the linesman, who had surely had the best view in the entire stadium of the incident, and yet had not signalled to the referee that a penalty should be awarded. Sanchez, like his players and supporters, was furious, and confronted the startled linesman. The referee sprinted over to usher him away, but not before the livid Sanchez let both match officials know exactly what he thought of the decision or, more appropriately, the lack of one.

"That's fucking bollocks! You've cost us the game!" he roared at the linesman, who just looked away as if in denial that the confrontation was even happening. No matter in which direction the official looked, the Wanderers players were there, venting their fury; the stadium had become a cauldron of dissent aimed at him. There could be no denying that his decision had not been met kindly by the normally placid folk of High Wycombe.

Back at Adams Park, Pat had forgotten that he couldn't be heard up at Filbert Street, and was remonstrating with the video screen in a similar vein to Lawrie Sanchez, who was by now being escorted from the arena by the referee having been shown a red card for dissent, much to the delight of the relieved Leicester City supporters. To be fair to Sanchez, if you're going to get sent off for dissent, then you may as well do it in style. A few choice words aimed at a match official will often merit a manager being issued with a red card, but at least Sanchez would have got his money's worth out of his dismissal when the inevitable fine dropped through his letter box from the Football Association. His unprecedented 50 yard march along the touchline took everyone in the ground by surprise. His actions reflected the feeling of his players and every Wanderers fan in the ground. With just ten minutes remaining in the biggest game in the club's history, and having already made his key substitutions, maybe Sanchez knew exactly what he was doing with such a dramatic demonstration. The linesman must have realised that he had made a mistake, the referee probably did too. If any of the Leicester players had still been in any doubt about the Wanderers' ambitions, then they too got the message from watching Sanchez's last contribution to the afternoon's proceedings. Wycombe weren't looking to go home with a draw; they were looking for a victory. All around the ground, everybody knew that this was what they deserved. Most importantly, as Sanchez reluctantly disappeared down the tunnel, his players knew what their manager expected.

Having demonstrated his passion and conviction to the cause, Sanchez, just like the 4,000 supporters sitting in Adams Park and the two sitting in a Hong Kong hotel room, could now only look on helplessly in front of a television screen, tucked away deep under the stand at Filbert Street.

"I bet they edit that bit out on 'Match of the Day'!" giggled Cathy, referring to Sanchez's venomous outburst.

"They shouldn't dub it out though... because Lawrie's right. If that had been up at the other end, I bet the linesman would have flagged for a penalty. He's completely bottled it!" I complained, missing the humour in her comment completely as the tension of events became almost too much to bear.

"Yeah, well at least most people in China wouldn't have understood what he was shouting anyway... which is probably for the best!" pointed out Cathy, before adding "The sun's coming back out in Leicester, look."

"Yeah, and I'd like to stick that linesman's flag right up where the sun don't shine" I hissed, just as Nicko and Smudger were informing the flustered official of the very same desire.

The minutes ticked away, and both sides continued to strive forward. Tactics had gone out of the window, and the three divisions and 53 league positions that separated the two sides now counted for nothing. Wycombe had defied the nation's expectations and, more importantly, Leicester City's, proving that on their day they could compete with the best. But this had to be Wycombe's day, as Leicester were amongst the country's best. This was realistically the Wanderers' one shot, and deep down, I knew that Leicester would approach a replay at Adams Park with a confidence that Wycombe couldn't play this well again. Any thoughts of a replay soon disappeared, though, as Leicester won a corner with just a minute remaining. The loudest Leicester roar of the afternoon grew amongst the local supporters as Steve Guppy purposefully placed the ball beside the corner flag.

"Don't do this to me Juppy!" pleaded Nicko.

"No… not you Gupps… please don't make me hate you" groaned Buz, remembering the many goals that Wycombe had scored from Guppy corners on their rise from semi-professional also-rans to proud members of the Football League.

"I can't watch" Tony said to Beany, sinking down into his seat for the first time during the game. He pulled his lucky FA Cup hat down over his eyes for good measure, despite being surrounded by other standing supporters who were already shielding him from view of the looming corner kick.

"Isn't that him who you taught to take corners?" asked Cathy.

"What? Erm, yeah… kind of."

"So it's your fault if they score then" she helpfully pointed out.

Thankfully, for all Guppy's technical prowess, Martin Taylor was his match, and managed to punch the devilishly executed corner over the bar. As the exhausted Wanderers regrouped to defend the next onslaught, all sides of the sold-out stadium notched up the vocal encouragement to a deafening level. The Leicester fans who, for most of the game, had seemed even more lacklustre than those representing them on the field, at last tried to help their team over the finishing line, while tucked away in a corner, every Wanderers supporter, man, woman and child continued to will their heroes on. Over the years, the Roobarbs had stood on half empty terraces across the country cheering on our team, on many occasions being told to 'shut up' or 'mind your bloody language' by less vocally engaged Blues fans, but not today; today there were 3,200 Roobarbs, and if some hadn't been quite as vocal when the game kicked off, at some point during the afternoon, they had been inspired; maybe by Brownie's refusal to be bullied by Savage, or Macca's heroic challenge to deny the long haired midfielder a certain goal just before half-time. Then there was the youngster, Ben Townsend, who had marshalled the legendary genius of Wycombe's most successful graduate, Steve Guppy. As had been happening throughout the whole FA Cup adventure, all over the pitch players were rising to levels of performance beyond anyone's expectation. On the field the players had, once again, given everything they had and, in the stand, the people of High Wycombe were feeding from this. The 3,000 sounded more like 30,000, and no matter how the Leicester fans tried to wrestle the vocal dominance back, they couldn't do it; the Wycombe Wanderers faithful refused to be beaten, just like their football team.

With the allotted 90 minutes expiring, the decibels rose ever higher as the impenetrable red and white defensive wall broke down yet another Leicester advance. For the entire game there had appeared to be more Wycombe players on the pitch than their Leicester counterparts. They had defended together to stifle Leicester's creativity; battled as one in midfield to out-muscle Savage and Izzett; and when opportunity presented itself, defender, midfielder and forward alike had attacked the Leicester defence with menace. Carried by the roar of the frenzied supporters standing just feet away from him, Michael Simpson summoned the last of his reserves to power forward from the halfway line deep into enemy territory along the touchline, leaving Leicester's Icelandic international, Arnar Gunnaugsson, trailing in his wake and trying to hold the Chairboy back. The banks of Wanderers supporters soon saw their barrage of disapproval turn to cheers, as referee Steve Bennett finally gave a decision in Wycombe's favour.

I punched the air with relief.

"Oh thank god! Time's up surely? Just stand over the ball... run the clock down... hold it in the corner... I can't believe it, we're gonna do it! We're going to get a draw!" I triumphantly yelled.

The Chinese commentator announced 'My-kaal Seem-saan' to the watching Asian millions as he readied himself to take the free kick.

"No Simmo! Just hold it by the corner flag!" I pleaded with the television screen, as it became obvious that Simpson was preparing to whip the ball into the heart of the Leicester penalty box.

Simpson didn't hear me and fired the ball into the melee of bodies loitering with intent around Simon Royce's goal. Essandoh and Cousins drifted towards the far post, with Bates and Castledine moving towards the near post looking for a flick-on. But the ball bypassed the pair, leaving McCarthy in an aerial dual with the on-rushing goalkeeper, who refused to let Macca get the better of him for a second time. Royce powerfully fisted the ball away from his area and it bounced repeatedly, further towards the centre circle.

"Get there Danny! Get there!" I screamed desperately, as Danny Bulman came into view on the screen, just ahead of Steve Guppy. When he'd been a Wanderer, I'd seen Guppy pick up the ball close to Wycombe's corner flag and then proceed to outrun the entire opposition along the full length of the pitch before casually slotting the ball past the goalkeeper. I wanted Danny Bulman to kick the ball as far out of Filbert Street as was humanly possible.

Again, the Wanderers weren't listening to me. Bulman launched the ball high into the sky, but back into the Leicester box, rather than out into the terraced streets surrounding the stadium. Jamie Bates was the nearest Chairboy to the ball and backtracked with eyes focused as it began to fall on the far side of the penalty box, just six yards from the touchline. He rose above his marker and powered the ball back into the heart of the penalty area towards Roy Essandoh, who leapt and headed the ball, making a perfect connection.

For a moment, everything stopped.

The ball flew from Essandoh's head with a resounding thud, slapping against the rain soaked net, sending a spray of droplets hurtling into the front row of open mouthed Leicester City supporters, their faces contorted with horror. The ball dropped to the ground, gently bouncing once then twice, before nestling on the turf. The silent split second of utter disbelief then exploded into pandemonium.

In a heartbeat, the player who no one had ever heard of became the most talked about footballer in the world; television and radio commentators relayed the drama to their audiences and news agencies across the globe received wires proclaiming...

'ENGLAND... FA CUP... GOAL... WYCOMBE WANDERERS... ESSANDOH... 90 + 2 MINUTES'

Essandoh knew he'd scored the moment he connected with the ball and, as the world around him took a moment to process what he'd done, he raced towards the side-line wheeling his arms in delight, bouncing back towards the halfway line in front of the rolling sea of smiles, waving arms and bodies, all seemingly transcended to a higher plain. He was eventually dragged to the ground by Jason Cousins, who grabbed Essandoh's shirt and proceeded to shake him enthusiastically to within an inch of his life as the adrenalin levels amongst the Wycombe players and supporters alike threatened to spiral wildly out of control. The rest of the team immediately descended on the pair like a pack of ravenous prairie dogs bearing down on their prey. Brownie tore off his shirt and waved it triumphantly in the air, as normally conservative middle-aged men with far less athletic physiques did likewise in the stand. The impossible was happening, and all logic was being thrown out of the window. Under the Filbert Street stand, Lawrie Sanchez turned away from the television pumping his clenched fists triumphantly in the air, before heading out of his temporary detention centre to peer back through the players tunnel, as if to double check that what he'd just seen being relayed on the screen was actually what was happening out on the battlefield from which he'd been banished.

Smudger and Nicko could barely move for the weight of fellow supporters jumping on them as they leant over the advertising hoardings just feet away from Essandoh, who was equally incapacitated due to Cousins well-meaning assault. Further up towards the back of the Wanderers enclosure Bob was throwing Laura in the air like one of her rag dolls, and Abby was waving to her in fits of laughter from a similarly lofty vantage point three rows in front, having been passed around the joyous crowd like a Brixton Academy crowd surfer. Buz and Roger found themselves down at pitch level from their tenth row seats before their feet had touched the ground, screaming hysterically. All along the terrace, friends were spotting each other momentarily and waving manically, before being swallowed up again by the next swaying wave of wild celebration.

As some semblance of order began to reappear, pockets of supporters peeled themselves from the corrugated roof (quite literally in the case of Bob's daughters) and returned to their seats. Tony and Beany were using their seats, but only to stand on, as they precariously continued to dance for joy. Beside them, Les was close to having a heart attack; not so much due to the excitement of Wycombe's most important ever goal, but due more to the sight of Teddy's infamous Farrah trousers letting him down as he, too, jumped for joy as Essandoh sent the ball crashing into the Leicester net. By the time the goalscorer's joyful salute to the crowd had been so unceremoniously curtailed by Jason Cousins, Teddy's trousers had unwittingly fallen around his ankles. Having watched the Wanderers for the best part of 60 years, Teddy wasn't going to let an ill-timed wardrobe malfunction distract him from joining in the celebrations, so there he stood, jumping up and down wildly with arms aloft and his ample belly proudly bouncing above a rather spindly pair of legs that hadn't seen daylight in many a year. Thankfully, for Teddy and the entire watching world, due to his movement being constrained by his collapsed trousers, he hadn't managed to jump up onto his seat beside Tony and Beany, who were about to make their international television debuts.

In Hong Kong, I was on my knees in front of the television, screaming incoherently. Behind me, Cathy was using the bed as a trampoline and taking photographs of the television. This surreal dream (for this must surely be a dream) couldn't get any more ludicrous; then the camera panned away from the mass of red and white muddied shirts on the pitch, and up into the delirium in the crowd; zooming in on two dancing goons, with smiles from ear to ear.

"It's Tony!" I yelled disbelievingly. "And Beany too!"

There were my friends, 6,000 miles away, on television, singing and dancing.

"There's Les too!" exclaimed Cathy.

"Is he laughing or crying?" I said.

"Both I think... he's pissing himself laughing, look!" giggled Cathy, having no idea that just out of camera shot, Teddy was struggling to manoeuvre himself into a position to pick up his disgraced Farrah's, driving Les to a laughter-induced hernia in the process.

Back at home, my loyal transistor radio, which for years had furtively relayed countless school night football matches to me whilst hidden under my duvet, lay in pieces on the bedroom floor; my dad having dropped it again as Alan Hutchinson sent a high pitched scream across the airwaves to announce Essandoh's goal. Down the hill at Adams Park, Jason and Pat were running around the pitch deliriously, punching the air for joy, Jason waving a betting slip in his clenched fist.

"Please leave the field of play sir" requested a solemn faced steward.

"Are you joking?" challenged Pat, having never been a huge respecter of any form of authority, let alone an orange jacket clad teenager sent up from the local recruitment agency.

"Please leave the field of play sir. It is an offence to enter the field of play during a match" the steward repeated robotically.

"Look... look around you... this isn't 'a field of play', is it? Not today... it's just a bloody field!"

The steward looked confused, paused for a moment, nodded and shrugged, then left the pair to continue their celebrations.

As the camera moved away from the dancing Roobarbs back in Leicester, boos started to echo around Filbert Street. Steve Brown was being escorted from the field by Steve Bennett, the referee. Brownie had a pained expression on his face and was holding his hand across his eyes; Bennett was saying something to him as they walked, but didn't look overly comfortable.

"Is it over?" asked Cathy, sounding confused.

"I don't know what's happening" I admitted, returning to the bed from my goal celebration knee slide.

"I don't believe it... he's sent him off!" I gasped, upon seeing Brownie embraced on the touch-line by Terry Gibson, who was now deputising for the already banished Sanchez.

I thought I was going to be sick. I physically, nor mentally, had any capacity left to cope with any further drama; and now, that pantomime villain dressed in black, who'd already denied my team a blatant penalty and then sent off our manager, was now sending off Steve Brown just seconds after we'd scored. His crime; taking off his shirt to reveal a vest with a message to his sick son who, having spent the majority of his young life in hospital, was watching his daddy play football for the first time.

If at lunchtime 50 Wanderers fans had sung 'Mark Lawrenson... you're a wanker' in the pub, and then 3,200 had serenaded Robbie Savage similarly during the match, Steve Bennett was about to hear it from every football fan in the country, and then, when the background to the story was reported more widely, he'd hear it from the entire world; now that's quite a feat of 'wankerness'.

'We can't lose now' I reassured myself, as Leicester restarted the game and pressed forward, three minutes into injury time. 'They haven't got time to score two... worst case scenario? A replay... yes, we've got a replay at the very least'.

My heart threatened to punch its way out of my chest and my fingers trembled uncontrollably, my mouth suddenly became devoid of moisture and breathing no longer felt like a subconscious act. Sometimes, no, most of the time, watching your chosen football team is no fun whatsoever, even when they are on the cusp of their most famous victory.

The next minute was the longest of my life, but Leicester could only manage one more effort that barely threatened Martin Taylor's goal before Mr Bennett signalled the end of the game, triggering further scenes of mass jubilation in the Wanderers section of the ground and disbelieving silence from all other quarters, as Leicester City found themselves on the receiving end of one of the biggest and most dramatic giant-killing episodes in the FA Cup's 120 year history. Roy Essandoh collapsed to his knees on the Filbert Street pitch, in shock at the life-changing moment that had just occurred. I, too, found myself back down on my knees, screaming, crying and laughing all at the same time, as Cathy jumped on me in a 'Jason Cousins-esque' style. The triumphant Wanderers team were joined on the pitch by their injured teammates, substitutes, and all of Sanchez's management team, as hoards of cameramen descended upon them, eager to capture the images that would be splashed across the front and back pages of the Sunday newspapers the following morning. As the thousands of Wycombe supporters created a joyous backdrop to the images being captured on the pitch, Laura tugged at her dad's coat.

"Daddy, the old man with the sweets... he's crying now, do you think he's scared like I was?" she asked, looking concerned.

"No, he's fine love, the football's made him cry, that's all" he bent down and told her, before returning to singing the praises of the team.

Laura peered past Abby again to look at the old man, but wasn't overly convinced with her dad's reassurances, and so edged past her big sister and tapped the old man gently on his hand. Leaning forward, she whispered in his ear... "It's okay, I think we won." This seemed to do the trick, and the old man gently dabbed his eyes with a handkerchief before slowly rising from his seat to join Laura, Abby and Bob in one last salute to the Wycombe Wanderers who had just sent shockwaves throughout the sporting world.

The atmosphere and emotions in Leicester were being mirrored back at Adams Park and, as the initial explosion of euphoria began to subside, Jason sat trying to work out how much Essandoh's goal and Steve Brown's sending off in that crazy last minute had earned him. Beside him, Pat sat surrounded by 4,000 celebrating supporters but, for a moment, alone in his thoughts. It had been a rough couple of weeks beyond compare, but his beloved football team had come through for him today and, for now, they had gifted him a reason to smile again.

Eventually, the players began to depart the scene of their victory. The supporters who were lucky enough to have been there to witness it reluctantly began to make their way out of Filbert Street to embark on the journey back to High Wycombe, to join up with the thousands who would be waiting for them to continue the party all over town. As they left the ground, they were congratulated on their victory by hundreds of bitterly disappointed Leicester fans who had turned up expecting to witness a procession as Leicester City went through the formalities of knocking out the lowly Wanderers. But instead, they had seen their team deservedly beaten, and they could have no complaints at the game's outcome; rather, only a sense of envy at how their counterparts from Buckinghamshire must be feeling.

Back in the Wanderers changing room, the party was only just starting, and the players now took the lead in belting out the supporter's favourite chants; if ever there was a moment fit to sing one's own praises, this was surely it. As his teammates continued to celebrate, Martin Taylor sat quietly in a corner of the dressing room. With his face buried into his green goalkeeper's jersey and giant gloves, he sobbed uncontrollably. If revenge is a dish best served cold, then he'd just delivered it to Leicester City Football Club directly from the freezer. After seven years of pent up frustration, Martin Taylor was an FA Cup Semi-Finalist; he couldn't turn back the clock to right the wrongs of the Derby County v Leicester City play-off final, nor the events that had transpired so painfully thereafter, but this career defining moment would, at last, allow him to close that chapter of his life.

20 – In shock, in Hong Kong

It was only 10am and yet it already felt like the longest day of my life; our first full day in Hong Kong and Wycombe Wanderers had just knocked Leicester City out of the FA Cup. It's safe to say I was feeling emotional.

"Come on, let's get out there and explore!" urged Cathy.

I sat on the hotel bed, still staring at the television which was now showing a Korean baseball match. I wasn't really aware of the baseball, all I could see was Roy Essandoh's header powering into the Leicester net, and Tony and Beany dancing in the crowd.

"But Beany doesn't go to cup games" I mumbled to myself.

"What's that?" asked Cathy.

"Beany... he doesn't go to cup games."

"I thought that when I saw him dancing on the telly!" replied Cathy.

"My knees are knackered" I moaned, finally noticing the carpet burns I'd picked up whilst sliding across the room to join Essandoh and Cousins as they celebrated on the television.

"It serves you right! You went crazy... I'm surprised nobody complained. Now come on... let's go ride the ferry again!"

I don't have a great recollection of the rest of the day's proceedings. I followed Cathy around while proudly wearing my Wanderers shirt; I nodded occasionally during one-sided conversations, but generally spent the day oblivious to one of the world's most exciting cities as we explored it. As we ambled home in the late afternoon sun, I was still in a world of my own until Cathy tugged at my arm.

"James! Are you even listening to me?" she hissed, "I said 'aren't you going to go in and get a copy?'"

"Copy of what?" I asked, slightly bemused.

"I knew you weren't listening... look at the headlines in the window!"

"Oh my god! Cathy... have you seen this?"

There in the shop window hung the day's newspaper covers. Across the front page of the Hong Kong Mail tabloid was a picture of the Wanderers celebrating on the Filbert Street pitch, with a bold headline that simply said *'STUNNING'*. Beside it was the traditionally laid out broadsheet, The South China Morning Post, with the somewhat wordier *'ESSANDOH GOES FROM ZERO TO HERO IN SPLIT SECOND – HIS NAME WILL BE SPLASHED ALL OVER THE PLACE (IF THEY CAN SPELL IT RIGHT)'* taking pride of place (and a lot of space) on the back page.

"Do you want some sweets to celebrate?" I offered, before disappearing into the store.

Upon leaving the shop with both of the newspapers, along with another written completely in Chinese script, I'd reached new levels of shock.

"What is it?" asked Cathy, looking concerned. "Has something bad happened back home?"

She snatched the bundle from me and scanned the front pages for clues as to my demeanour.

"Liverpool" I whispered.

"Liverpool?" echoed Cathy.

"Liverpool... Wycombe drew Liverpool in the Semi-Final. Look... 'Wycombe Wanderers versus Liverpool, Arsenal versus Tottenham Hotspur'... I hadn't even thought about the Semi-Final!"

"Well, that's that then... you'll get slaughtered" said Cathy, matter-of-factly.

"You said that about Leicester... and Wimbledon... and Wolves... and Grimsby. Did you say it about Millwall too?" I replied defiantly.

"Come on, we need to get back... we're meeting the rest of the group in the bar at six" she responded, without giving my argument the slightest credence.

Back in the hotel, Cathy busied herself in the bathroom in preparation for the evening's introductions and pre-trip briefing. I sat cross-legged on the bed, fawning over the newspaper reports that I'd spread out all around me.

"Does this look nice?" asked Cathy, modelling her third potential outfit.

"Yep, lovely" I responded.

"Will you at least look up before you answer?" she snapped back.

"What?" I replied, looking up, albeit a question too late.

"How long are you going to paw over those newspapers? I mean... that one's in Chinese! What was the point of buying that?"

Cathy just didn't get it. This wasn't the local newspaper I'd eagerly awaited each Friday as a child and this wasn't a report about plucky non-league Wycombe knocking out Division Four giants Colchester United in 1985, or the daylight robbery that followed two rounds later after that long cold trip to York. If the chubby little lad on the coach that day had known that some sixteen years later, his Wanderers would be battling their way into the Semi-Finals of the FA Cup, and that he would be in Hong Kong to witness it, he'd be expecting his grown up incarnation to buy every scrap of proof available.

"I'm ready, what do you think?" asked Cathy, 30 minutes and four more outfits later.

"No wonder your backpack is so bloody heavy... that's what I think" I mistakenly said out loud, before quickly adding... "Nice, you look nice."

"What are you going to wear?"

"I'm going down like this" I said, gesturing to the combat shorts and my increasingly well-worn Wanderers shirt, which I'd been wearing all day. "We're on holiday, this isn't a job interview" I protested. Cathy shook her head in disgust.

As we waited for the elevator to arrive at our floor, Cathy read through the email we'd printed in Thailand again... "Alf is the tour leader... Alf doesn't sound very Chinese, does it? Then there's a 'Jane', and a 'Mick and Kris'... they must be married... ooh I'm excited, a bit nervous too!" clapped Cathy, indeed looking both excited and nervous.

"Being part of a group's going to be weird isn't it? I hope we get on with them" I replied.

I'd not given much thought to the possibility of being stuck with a bunch of idiots for the next three weeks. Now I was starting to feel a bit nervous too. Exiting the elevator, there didn't seem to be anyone potentially looking like a Chinese tour guide called Alf, so we did what came naturally; we found the bar, looking decidedly under-dressed for the glitzy surroundings.

"I'm going to have a look around in the lobby; maybe we were supposed to meet there... get me a Diet Coke please" instructed Cathy before disappearing, leaving me to order possibly the most expensive soft drinks on the planet. Two months' worth of lemonades in Thailand hadn't cost much more than two Cokes in this bloody hotel. I sipped tentatively at my drink, knowing full well that it needed to last the entire evening, until I heard Cathy coming back into the room.

"This is my boyfriend James" she said as she approached, accompanied by a guy of about our age, refreshingly dressed as shabbily as me.

"G'day mate, I'm Alf" he said, with a beaming smile and a firm handshake.

"You're Australian... I thought you were going to be Chinese!" I blurted.

"You're not exactly what I was expecting either! Strewth!" laughed Alf, pointing to the photo attached to my Chinese visa in his hand. "Where's your hair gone? Where have your cheeks gone? And look at the colour of you! You know what... I saw you in the lobby this morning... I noticed your footy top... it didn't even cross my mind that you were this guy in the picture!"

This was a good start; we were hitting it off with Alf immediately, and soon any concerns about our other travel companions would also be laid to rest. Mick and his wife Kris soon joined us, and they were equally affable; a laid-back American couple, a fair bit older than us but, again, within minutes we were laughing and joking. Cathy seemed to have met a kindred spirit in Kris, or maybe she was just revelling in the opportunity to talk to somebody else apart from me. The final member of our troop, a Londoner called Jane, joined us a while later in something of a fluster.

"Hi, sorry I'm late; I thought we were meeting at half past six. I was in the bath ten minutes ago looking at the joining notes, and I just said to myself 'Shit! I'm late'... what a first impression. Oh, I'm Jane by the way, pleased to meet you!"

'Cool, Jane swears too, I'm sure we'll get on' I thought to myself.

I hadn't been sure what to expect, but after two months of going solo, it would have been awkward to end up on a three week jaunt around China with people like the miserable German couple I'd repeatedly failed to impress in Thailand.

Alf spent 30 minutes telling us about our itinerary and how we would be on the move constantly. His eyes lit up as he passionately told us about the places we would be visiting. If any of us hadn't been excited before, we certainly were now.

"Planes, trains and automobiles! Get used to them... and throw in some bikes, buses and boats too! China is the craziest place on Earth, and I'm going to show you everything... the good, the bad and the ugly. Now, enough with the film title clichés, who fancies a beer?" he concluded.

"Sod that, two Cokes has nearly bankrupted me at the bar!" I cursed.

"No mate... this is the budget tour! You lot go and sit in the lobby, I'll nip round the corner to the grocery store to get some cans in. This hotel is just to ease you in gently... don't get me wrong, everywhere we stay is clean, but it'll be pretty basic."

Cathy and I looked at each other; we'd got used to 'basic'.

Minutes later, as the five of us sunk down into the hotel lobby's plush leather sofas, Alf reappeared and plonked a dozen cans of Chinese beer onto the table.

"Are we okay to drink these here?" asked Kris nervously.

"Absolutely, hotel lobbies will be our friend over the next few weeks. When we've got time to kill between travel connections, you'll be glad to make yourself comfortable" Alf replied, before leaning in and whispering... "Most of them have 'sit down' toilets for a start."

"I'm in" I said, adding my complete commitment to Alf's plan to find western style toilets wherever possible.

"He's had a rough couple of months... in the stomach area" explained Cathy helpfully. "He's lost about three stone."

"What's a stone?" asked Mick and Kris.

"14 pounds" answered Alf.

"So 42 pounds?" gasped Kris.

"I'd love to lose three stone" Jane sighed.

"You've lost over 40 pounds? Shit!" said Mick.

"Yep, 40 pounds of shit... quite literally" Cathy continued, to roars of laughter. This was more information than anyone needed, but there wasn't much I could say, so I helped myself to a beer.

"Cheers everyone... to China!" I toasted, blushing heavily beneath my tan.

"Seriously, have you seen a doctor?" asked Alf, putting his tour leader hat back on for a moment.

"No, I think it was the heat in Thailand... I wasn't used to it. Plus I ate a dodgy burger at Heathrow Airport before we left England."

"You've been away for two months though, right? Mate, that's not food poisoning! You should get it checked out" Alf advised.

"I'll be fine... I'll wait until I get to Australia next month. That's if I have any more problems, I'm sure I'll be fine."

"Basically, he doesn't want to see a foreign doctor" chimed in Cathy again.

I tried to give her a 'for the love of god, will you please shut up!' stare, but Cathy was by now in full on gossip mode with Kris and Jane, and they were all happily discussing my toiletry issues as if I wasn't there.

"He thinks they'll stick pins in him."

"What like a voodoo doll?" laughed Alf.

"All that acupuncture stuff... I don't fancy it" I replied sheepishly, cursing Cathy under my breath.

Any initial misconceptions that the group may have formed about me being a cool and hardened traveller were now being flushed away faster than one of my bouts of diarrhoea. To make matters worse, Cathy proceeded to recount the various nicknames Scouse John had given me back at Fantastic Hill.

"Diarrhoea Dave... Sammy Shits... Ronnie Runs... Winnie the Pooh... Ivor Imodium... Toby Trots... what else was there James?"

Mercifully, Alf brought an end to proceedings as we emptied the last of the cans.

"Listen, everybody get a good night's sleep... we'll meet back here at 2pm tomorrow, then head for the airport, okay?" he said before turning to me... "Oh, and you make the most of your lovely bathroom tonight, Winnie!"

Back up in our room, Cathy was in high spirits having met our travel companions, and from her two cans of beer. I, on the other hand, was sinking into a sulk.

"Did you really have to go into so much detail? It's embarrassing!"

"Oh don't be such a grump, it's no big deal" Cathy retorted.

"We'd never met these people before! Now they'll all be going to bed singing 'Burning Ring of Fire'. Mick and Kris are probably sitting in bed saying 'what was the boy's name again? Was it Dave? Winnie? Toby? Ivor? Sammy? Ronnie?'" I grumbled, only cutting off from my rant upon hearing the telephone ring.

The telephone; this was a new experience; we hadn't heard a telephone ringing for a couple of months.

"Who is it?" I asked, looking towards Cathy as the ringing continued.

"How do I know?" she replied, giving me her 'you're an idiot' stare. "Maybe it's the hotel manager, complaining about all the noise you made watching the game this morning."

She'd said it in jest, but as we both pondered the thought, it sounded increasingly feasible.

"Let it ring out" I whispered, as if whoever was calling could already hear us.

"No, it might be important" Cathy whispered back. "Pick it up!"

"Hello" I mumbled into the handset.

"James! Is that you?"

"Mum!"

"Hi James... listen to this!" shouted my Dad, before there was a temporary lull.

"...which one is the play button again?" I heard my parents muffled tones, before the unmistakable voice of a very excited Alan Hutchinson began screaming into my ear.

"Yesssssssssss! Yesssssssssss! It's in! I can't believe it! It's in! Who was it? Who's that? No! No way! I don't believe it... it's Essandoh. Roy's scored! Surely that's it? We've won! We must have won! Blow the whistle referee! Blow the bloody whistle!"

The hairs on the back of my neck stood up as I listened to the tape recording of Hutch describing the glorious moment as Wycombe scored their winning goal, in his own unique commentary style.

"That's brilliant! I love it!" I shouted back down the phone.

"Did you know? Did you know the score?" My mum sounded almost as excited as Hutch.

"I saw it on the telly... Chinese commentary and all! I saw Beany and Tony dancing in the crowd too!" I replied, inciting further excited shrieks from England.

"I thought Beany didn't go to FA Cup games?" said my Dad, suddenly sounding more serious.

"Are you both okay?" asked my Mum, "Have the shits cleared up?"

"No they haven't!" shouted the eavesdropping Cathy.

"Oh dear... listen, we'd better go, this'll probably cost a fortune. Love you both. Bye! Love you!" shouted my mum. "Up the Blues!" added my dad, before the phone went dead.

What perfect timing. There was I, about to go to bed in a sulk; it was no way to end such a momentous day; the greatest day in my football team's history. Forever the most famous football team from Buckinghamshire, but for today and the next few weeks, the world would want to know who Wycombe Wanderers were; the team that would face Liverpool in the FA Cup Semi-Final. I crashed out on the bed with a smile, knowing that whatever dreams awaited me, they couldn't match the unbelievable reality of the past 24 hours. I was in dreamland before I'd even closed my eyes.

21 – Welcome to China

The group met, as planned, the following afternoon, before being whisked to the airport. This was going to be fun; all the trials and tribulations of logistics and planning connections now fell upon Alf's shoulders. It was time for him to earn his money, while I immersed myself in China. With the promise of many long journeys on the horizon, we dived into the airport's bookshop, as Alf advised it was our last opportunity to buy anything in English. We then made ourselves comfortable in the departure lounge and waited for Alf to tell us what to do next. Before we had even checked in, I'd completely checked out; I didn't know exactly where we were going, which airline we were flying with, or even what time we had to be at the gate; I had more important things to think about.

"What books did you get, Kris?" asked Cathy.

The inaugural meeting of the 'Tour of China' book club promptly began; with everyone's new purchases being discussed, along with a host of other books brought from home. Romantic novels, Chinese travel guides and historical dramas all featured, along with trashy showbiz magazines from both sides of the Atlantic. Cathy, Mick, Jane and then Kris had all taken their turn, before Alf held up 'Complete Mandarin: From Beginner to Intermediate'.

"I'm more 'intermediate' than 'beginner'" he assured us, before adding, "but if I lose this, we're in trouble!"

All eyes then turned towards me.

"What about you James... what's in the bag?" asked Jane.

I'd hoped my bag of purchases might go unnoticed from its hiding place behind my rucksack, but alas it hadn't, so I slowly pulled out the two British newspapers I'd purchased, each at ten times their face value.

"This is the football team I support" I explained, holding up the first back page in front of me like a child presenting during a school assembly.

'ESS-CLUB HEAVEN' read the headline, beside a photo of Roy Essandoh rising to score his now famous winner. "It's a play on words... like the band 'S-Club Seven'... his name is Essandoh, hence the 'Ess' and he's sent the team into heaven with his goal."

When I'd seen the headline, I'd nearly keeled over in the shop with excitement; the extortionate price for a two-day-old newspaper hadn't even crossed my mind. But now that I was explaining it out loud, it didn't sound quite as impressive as Alf's Mandarin language studies or Mick's 'History of Genghis Kahn'. To be fair, even Cathy's 'Hello' magazine now seemed to carry more journalistic merit.

"S-Club Seven? I don't think we have them in the States" remarked Kris, trying to find something to say about my lacklustre book club contribution.

"You're not missing much Kris, they're a talentless pop band" replied Cathy, while giving me a sarcastic smile.

'How dare she tarnish the good name of pop princess Rachel Stevens' I thought to myself, but this wasn't the time or place to start another argument.

"And on this one... we made the front page!" I added, unable to conceal my pride at Wycombe Wanderers becoming the talk of the country.

'WYC-KED' read the headline, focussing on the referee's heartless sending off of Steve Brown amidst the last minute goal celebrations. Upon explaining how Brownie had been dismissed for taking off his shirt to show a message to his poorly young son, I at last managed to garner the group's attention, and so confidently flipped the paper around to display the back page, which focused on the footballing side of the story... 'WYCOMBE... WE SAW... WE CONQUERED!'

"That's where I'm from... High Wycombe... Wycombe... 'we came'... do you get it?"

"We came, we saw, we conquered... just like Genghis Kahn, right?" laughed Mick.

There; my newspaper and Mick's history book weren't that far apart after all.

"I read about that game on the internet yesterday... it made it into our American sports news, the guy who won the game came from nowhere, right?" said Mick.

"I watched it in the hotel, what a game, what a result" added Alf. "Ahhh... I guess that was you I heard screaming!"

Cathy rolled her eyes. "Don't encourage him, please! This is all I've heard for the past two months!"

"That's our gate number up guys... let's go" said Alf, bringing book club to an abrupt end, just as I was starting to enjoy it.

Looking around, we were the only westerner's boarding the plane, and queuing didn't seem to be very high on anyone's agenda. A smartly dressed businessman pushed between Cathy and me just before we reached the ticket desk. The wrinkle that always appeared at the top of her nose when she was about to kick-off was already in evidence when the queue-jumper leaned back and drew a throatful of mucus up into the back of his mouth, before turning his head and casually spitting the contents of his gullet onto the carpet besides Cathy's feet. As he turned back, he unleashed a flatulent roar, wiggled his backside in appreciation, then picked up his briefcase and handed over his boarding pass to the stewardess; just as if nothing had happened.

"Welcome to China" laughed Alf, leaning forward between us.

For the first time in seven years I watched as Cathy stood frozen to the spot, speechless.

Following a short flight, we landed after sunset into the People's Republic of China, full of anticipation at what the, for so long, secretive and mysterious country had in store for us. Whatever that might be would not be revealed immediately though, as by the time we reached our hotel, it was nearing midnight. The following morning, I eagerly pulled open the curtains to get my first glimpse of China. It was underwhelming. A grey, drizzly morning looked back at me, and the surroundings, along with the weather didn't look too dissimilar from home. Having only checked in hours before, we were on the move again very early to travel to our next destination, Yangshou, which was a five hour boat ride upstream along the Li River. The route meandered its way through stunning cliffs and peaks, interspersed with agricultural land being worked by muscle-bound water buffalo and curious farmhands, who watched us watching them as we drifted along the river. The scenery was stunning, and the low hanging patches of cloud that hugged the mountains only added to the air of tranquillity that pervaded our surroundings. Only the sound of the small boat's engine ploughing its way through the still water broke the silence, along with the odd local tourist organising their friends for a photo opportunity on the deck. After the madness of Bangkok and Hong Kong, the stark contrast felt all the more amazing.

Both Mick and Jane had arrived at breakfast with big cameras draped around their necks and were now putting them to good use, busily scuttling around the deck, eager to capture the multitude of breath-taking vistas. Cathy and Kris had taken up residence on a bench under a canopy offering shelter from the sporadic drizzle that was threatening to become increasingly heavy. I just stood staring out across the valleys, trying to commit as much to memory as possible.

"What do you think then?" asked Alf, who was flitting between us all, but mainly just leaving us to our own devices.

"It's stunning... it's simply stunning" was all I could muster, having fallen under the spell of the peaceful stillness.

"It's a real shame about the weather though; we can only see the first row of hills. Believe me, on a clear day they are just stacked up, row after row for as far as you can see."

"This will do for me! I love it. Even the drizzle and the cool breeze, it's wonderful. I never thought I'd get to see a place like this in person" I continued.

"Ha-ha! Mate, that's brilliant... I've never heard anyone praise the rain before! Still, you Pommies love your rain!" laughed Alf, happy to have an easily pleased customer on his hands.

"I guess after the heat of Thailand, the novelty of cooler climes hasn't worn off yet!" I agreed.

"By the way, you're causing quite a stir with the local tourists... I don't think they've seen a guy wearing shorts since they left school!" Alf informed me.

"You're kidding?" I asked, noting that I was indeed the subject of a conversation from across the boat. The group of five middle-aged Chinese tourists smiled and nodded when they saw me look over, so I smiled and nodded back.

"No, seriously... they don't wear shorts over here. It gets stupidly hot in the summer too, but they never wear shorts; it's crazy."

As Alf completed his sentence, one of the Chinese gentlemen came across and said something to me. I automatically looked at Alf.

"They want a photo" he smiled.

"Oh, sure... I'll take their picture" I replied.

"No, they want a picture with you!" he smiled.

"With me?"

Before I knew it, I was surrounded by the locals, all standing proudly to attention and smiling at Alf who was readying the camera. Five firm handshakes later, the happy band retrieved their camera and returned to watching the landscape drifting away behind us. Cathy and Kris provided a mock round of applause, whilst Mick and Jane both asked me for a picture too.

"That will be 50 Yuan each please" I joked, before turning to Alf who was looking very amused.

"What did they say?" I asked.

"It turns out it wasn't your shorts that were the attraction... they've never seen 'a blue eyes' with such dark skin before!" explained Alf. "My Mandarin is getting better, but I wasn't really sure what to say to them... I'll look up 'it's a two month sun tan' tonight!"

"That's a tan?" remarked Mick.

I pulled out my passport, to show my pre-travel complexion.

"Wow!" he replied.

"No! That's not you!" protested Kris upon seeing my passport photo, much to Alf and Cathy's delight.

"You really did lose three stone, didn't you!" added Jane, "Although some of that was the awful mop of hair, surely!"

Cathy just smiled at my embarrassment.

Several hours further along the river, we arrived in Yangshou, a beautiful little town sat upon the riverbank and surrounded by giant karst peaks. As soon as we'd checked into our hotel Alf told us to meet back down in the lobby; we were going on a bike ride.

"A bike ride? I haven't been on a bike since I was about ten" sniffed Cathy.

"I'm not really a bike rider either... I'll just stay here" added Jane.

"No-no-no! Where's your spirit of adventure? I'm here to show you China; I can't show you it all from trains and buses. Everyone... out front in ten minutes... no exceptions" demanded Alf.

Once outside, Alf marched us through the town centre, where it was becoming obvious that we were as of much interest to the locals as they were to us.

"I really don't fancy this" grumbled Cathy, as we had various cycles sized up against us.

"It'll be fine. You never forget how to ride a bike... we'll be out in the countryside in a few minutes anyway, away from all these prying eyes" I reassured her.

But, contrary to the old saying, it turns out that you can forget how to ride a bike, and Cathy was proving it. Somehow, we managed to manoeuvre our way through the streets that led to the outskirts of town, avoiding collisions with the diesel-belching trucks and mopeds that darted past at alarming speeds.

"Okay; I'm going to take you through the countryside to see some beautiful spots now; no more roads, we can take it real easy" said Alf, trying to cajole some enthusiasm from the still to be convinced Cathy, who appeared to have taken on board some of the sulking tips I'd been displaying for the past couple of months.

We were soon out amongst the fields, down by the river bank. I was holding back to keep Cathy company as she was still struggling. Mick and Jane were constantly finding more subjects to stop and photograph. So thanks to water buffalo ploughing fields, labourers in traditional pointed conical hats crouching to pick crops, and the abundance of scenic panoramas, we never fell too far behind. Cathy was finally mastering the art of peddling when we caught up again, beside a small hut amidst the farmland. A woman was sitting at the door watching over an ensemble of the cutest little children imaginable, while their parents worked the field. She waved and smiled as Mick gestured for approval to take a photo. Just as we got back onto the bikes, several other women appeared from the fields and rushed into the hut. Moments later, they charged back out waving postcards and cans of Coke at us.

"Hello! Postcard? Hello, hello... postcard?" they repeated, each choosing a cyclist to target.

We politely declined and set off again, but the local entrepreneurs were not to be denied, proceeding to give chase whilst continuing with their sales pitch; "Hello! Postcard? Hello, hello! Postcard?"

The faster we pedalled, the faster they ran, but all concerned seemed to be enjoying the chase.

"They won't give up!" advised a smiling Alf, as he guided us down a path to view an ancient irrigation system still being used by the farmers to transport water from the river up to their rice crops, far from the riverbank. Our pursuers looked glad of the rest, and sat happily talking amongst themselves beside our bikes, while we went to explore, but as soon as we set off again, the truce was off, and they began to chase again.

We hit a downhill section, and Cathy took full advantage of it, speeding past the rest of the group. She'd now mastered balancing and pedalling, but not slowing down when approaching a bend. Unfortunately, she soon received, quite literally, a crash course, tumbling from the bike onto the dirt track.

"Are you okay" I asked as Cathy dusted herself down.

"I was just starting to enjoy that!" she said, more embarrassed than upset.

"Ooh, your hand is bleeding" said a concerned Kris, her motherly instincts shining through, while the rest of us were focussing more on the bike for signs of damage.

One of the farm girls pulled out a tissue and began wiping the graze clean, before another produced a plaster and gently placed it on Cathy's hand. She stepped back and smiled, admiring her first aid skills, before looking at Cathy and saying "Hello! Postcard?"

This brought a roar of laughter from everyone, especially her sales associates, who knew that the deal was done; they couldn't possibly be denied any longer.

Back at the hotel, following rejuvenating showers, we headed out for dinner. Alf was keen to take us to his favourite restaurant and, as he was the only one of us who could say more than "hello" in Mandarin, we were all glad to follow. The little restaurant was completely empty. Alf poked his head through the unlocked door and shouted "Ni hoa!"

"I could have done that. That just means hello" whispered Cathy.

"Betty? Elsa?" Alf shouted again, and then banged his fist against the door.

"I could have done that!" I muttered back to Cathy.

The banging had triggered some activity, and a light flickered into life from the back of the room, before two young local women came into view.

"Alf! Hello my friend!" greeted one the girls warmly, giving Alf a hug.

"You woke us up!" added the other, yawning her way into a welcoming smile.

"Welcome everybody, come in and sit down... let me get you drinks and the menu while we get kitchen ready. I'm Betty, this is my sister Elsa."

"I'll have a beer" replied Alf. "Beer?" he prompted, gesturing to Mick, and then Jane, who both nodded.

"A Coke for me, please" said Kris.

"Me too" added Cathy.

Alf looked at me and, crumbling to peer pressure at the first hurdle, I replied "Yeah, beer please."

As Alf walked up to the bar, chatting with Betty, Elsa pulled a couple of tables together for us and produced some menu's... "Pick what you like... it all taste good!" she confidently informed us, before disappearing into the kitchen of the little restaurant which was colourfully decorated with murals covering walls and ceiling alike.

Much to our relief, the menu was in English. It also had an extensive list of western favourites alongside a host of oriental dishes.

"I really want the pizza and chips" said Cathy apologetically.

"Me too" replied Mick, "...do you think it would look bad?"

"We'd look like real tourists, wouldn't we?" agreed Cathy.

"We are real tourists" I pointed out, hoping to sway the general consensus back towards pizza, but as Elsa reappeared with her note pad, Kris ordered a local chicken dish and Cathy followed her lead. Jane 'went local' too, leaving the men no place to go but down the eastern side of the menu. Elsa then went up to the bar to get Alf's order on her way back to the kitchen.

Alf carefully carried back a tray of drinks and we toasted our first day's adventures in China. My initial impressions of the group had so far been upheld and, as we'd meandered along the Li River earlier in the day, I'd had decent conversations with everyone. Mick and Kris had already blown away any misconceptions harboured about Americans not having passports, having travelled to dozens of countries on similar trips to this. They were very chilled-out and, as veterans of group tours, appreciated that a good rapport with their travel companions would only enhance the experience. Between Kris and Mick's social skills and the fact that Cathy and I had nothing left to speak to each other about after two months sitting on a beach together, there was no danger of Alf and Jane being left stuck with two cliquey couples.

"Let me get a picture of our first supper!" said Jane, leaning down to her bag to get her camera. "Oh, hold on, I need to change the film again... bugger! Mick... do you have a spare roll of film with you?"

"You need to get one of these Jane" replied Mick, "...its digital... no film."

"Mick loves anything techie!" said Kris apologetically, shaking her head.

"It's the future!" protested Mick. "Look, it's got a screen... you can view your shot as soon as it's taken, so if it's no good, you just delete it. Here are my photos from today" he added, turning his camera around and proceeding to display his snaps of the Li River and our bike riding exploits.

"There's one of you and the 'Hello postcard' girls Cathy!" I giggled, as we reached the end of Mick's impromptu presentation.

"Here's to the 'Hello postcard' girls" said Alf, raising his glass.

"The 'Hello postcard' girls!"

The beer tasted good, and was going down all too easily.

"We should have got a digital camera before we left home" said Cathy.

"Nah, it's just a gimmick... it won't catch on. Anyway... have you seen the price of them" I replied discretely.

Before long, Elsa and Betty reappeared with bowls of steaming rice and noodles for us to share.

"Getting stuck into the local grub? Good on yer!" remarked Alf.

Our various chicken, fish and vegetable dishes soon followed. Everything looked gorgeous and after our cycling exertions, we were ready to tuck in, but out of politeness held back as Alf's meal still hadn't appeared.

"Don't let it get cold guys, dig in... mine will be a bit longer, I always order the same thing here... it takes a while."

Alf hadn't let us down with the restaurant choice. The food was amazing, and a cut above the Chinese takeaway offerings back home in England.

"Here you go Alf; tropical pizza and fries... enjoy!" said Elsa proudly, as Betty delivered a second round of unexpected drinks.

"What?" asked Alf, looking up from his first mouthful of delicious looking pizza to find ten eyes trained upon him. "Listen, its local food all the way from here on in... get it while you can, that's what I say! One more thing... I definitely recommend the apple pie and ice cream for dessert!"

All six dishes proved to be a resounding success, with empty plates all round proving the point. Many tales of previous travels were shared, and laughter accompanied the food with every mouthful. Mick told crazy stories about Mexico and tequila whilst Kris tried to stop him; Jane recalled a hen party from hell in Spain; Alf talked about Nepal and the Himalayas, and I talked about my trip to Northwich Victoria in the boot of a car and spending all my football money on Charlatans memorabilia. Before I could elaborate on more Wanderers related stories, Cathy got up and said she was going back to the hotel. Jane was ready to head back too, and then Kris pulled on her jacket, prompting Mick to reluctantly rise from his seat.

"I'm staying for while" said Alf, "a few of the other guides come and hang out here later... you're welcome to join us; they're a really nice bunch."

"You stay James, but I'm knackered from the bike ride... my legs are starting to stiffen up already" said Cathy.

"Okay, I'll have another beer... just until Alf's pals turn up."

I would happily have gone back to the hotel, but now that an official pass had been issued, it seemed rude not to accept it, and besides, Alf was proving great company and would willingly talk about football all night given half a chance. Soon the restaurant started to fill up, mainly with groups of Chinese tourists and, before I knew it, another four pints had been consumed and the other tables were emptying again. By the time the last diners had left, Alf and I had been joined at the table by Elsa, along with another guide and a local artist who'd introduced himself as 'Forrest... just like Forrest Gump'. Apart from my new pal Forrest, who asked if I'd ever been to his cousin's restaurant in Bristol, the rest of the group were mainly conversing in Chinese, which was fine by me, as I too was beginning to struggle to speak English. After seeing the final stragglers out, Betty locked the door, and placed shot glasses and a sinister looking bottle on the table. She then pulled up a chair and squeezed in between me and Forrest.

"So James, how do you like China so far?" she asked, filling the shot glasses as she spoke.

"I love it" I slurred.

"And my restaurant?"

"I love it."

"Hey... what about my paintings on the walls?" asked Forrest, peering past Betty and prodding my shoulder. "I did all this" he continued, now leaning back and spreading his arms out wide, gesturing towards the walls and ceiling in general.

"I love it. I love it all Forrest... Forrest? Where did Forrest go?"

"The ceiling looks good from down here" commented Forrest.

"Forrest, time for you to go home I think" said Betty, looking down to the floor, where Forrest was lying flat on his back, still firmly seated in his upturned chair.

"One more drink with my English friend James, then I'll go. One more drink... just to stop the room spinning" he replied before reverting to speaking Mandarin for another three rounds. He spoke in Chinese, I spoke in English, but we continued to enjoy each other's company until the bottle was empty. The emptying of the bottle coincided with Forrest slumping into a drunken slumber at the table.

"Alf... I think Forrest's had enough" I slurred.

Alf just nodded, not looking much more alert than the unconscious artist. With this lull in conversation, I pushed back my chair and stood, ready to visit the toilet. Within seconds I decided to sit down again as survival instincts kicked in; the lower I was to the ground, the less distance I had to fall. Forrest had been right after all; the room was indeed spinning. At the second attempt, I managed to stumble my way to the small bathroom, but for all my might, I couldn't open the door. When pulling and banging didn't work, I took to swearing at the door, until Betty came to investigate. She leant past me and gently slid the door along its rail with one finger.

"Oh... sorry Betty, I didn't realise it was a slider" I said sheepishly. "I think I'm a bit drunk."

This suspicion became a certainty as I tried to manoeuvre myself into position above the Asian style toilet. Two months of practice in Thailand hadn't prepared me for trying to squat whilst drunk. Eventually, I staggered back into the restaurant using Forrest's brightly decorated walls for support. Forrest was still asleep, with his head slumped down on the table; Elsa had assumed the same position, while Alf and the other guide he'd been talking to were heading out of the door that Betty was preparing to lock behind them.

"Wait for me!" I mumbled as I reluctantly let go of the wall and unsteadily crossed the room in the general direction of the door.

"I thought you'd gone!" said Alf, putting a supporting arm around my shoulder although, as we started on the short walk back to the hotel, I wasn't sure who was holding who up. Back in my bed, Cathy was fast asleep and the room continued to spin.

22 – Keep on keeping on

I awoke to a world of pain. Drums and firecrackers exploded in my skull. Even before opening my eyes, I knew the room was still spinning. I scurried to the bathroom, just making it to the porcelain hole in the floor before vomiting. The stench of stale alcohol rose to greet me as I knelt shaking, a cold sweat dripping from my forehead. The noises in my head just got louder and louder. I gingerly shuffled back to the bedroom and opened the window, eager to breathe some fresh air into my pickled body. Easing my head out into the cool, misty morning air, I looked down and received the shock of my life; an old woman was staring back up at me; from inside an open coffin.

'What the fuck!' I screamed (thankfully only in my head), as I fell back from the window to hide behind the curtain. I convinced myself that I hadn't just seen a dead woman staring at me, it had to be an alcohol-induced dream. Slowly, I peeked back through the curtains, but she was still there, being slowly carried up the hill, followed by dozens of people, all wearing white and all walking backwards. I didn't believe what I was seeing but, regardless, I couldn't pull myself away from the macabre spectacle. I crouched and rested my chin on the window frame, watching as the procession advanced into the mist that loitered above the river. As the funeral cortege disappeared into the distance and the sound of the accompanying firecrackers and drums quelled, I retreated back to bed. No sooner had I closed my eyes than there was a loud rap on the door.

"Wakey wakey guys, breakfast in 15 minutes... then we're out on the bikes again! There's no lie-ins on this trip... you'll have plenty of time to sleep when you get to Australia!"

"Alf sounds lively this morning... what time did you two get back?" quizzed Cathy.

"I've absolutely no idea" I replied, before rushing back to the bathroom.

"Are you okay? Has the bug come back?"

"I'm not sure... it might be something I ate. I'll see you downstairs... I think I'll give breakfast a miss."

Following another 30 minutes spent cowering on the bathroom floor, I managed to put on a façade of sobriety and joined the others outside the hotel. The cold air soothed my pounding head somewhat, but a return to bed was all I could think of.

"Morning James, did you get woken up by that noise this morning?" asked Kris.

"I thought a bomb was going off, it was crazy" added Mick.

The firecrackers, had they been real? What about the dead woman? I wasn't sure what I'd seen and what I'd dreamt. As I pondered, Alf interjected.

"It was a traditional funeral procession. I've read about them, but never seen one until this morning... it was quite something. The firecrackers and drums are to ward off evil spirits. As a display of grief, all the mourners follow the casket whilst walking backwards."

"Wow, I wish I'd seen it" replied Mick.

I wanted to say that I had, but opening my mouth risked more vomiting.

"You okay buddy?" asked Alf, as we set off on the bikes again.

"I'll tell you when I sober up" I confessed, as the bike wobbled precariously beneath me.

The cool wind rushing through me as we picked up speed gradually helped to quell my hangover, and by mid-afternoon I was beginning to enjoy the beautiful surroundings again. This joy was short lived, though, as Cathy repeated her involuntary cornering dismount, ending up flat on her face in a muddy puddle. There are times when the odd mishap can be laughed off and you carry on regardless; alternatively, there are times when the mission needs to be aborted right there and then. Looking like a mud covered swamp beast, Cathy got back to her feet and started kicking the partly submerged bicycle. For her, the bike ride was over.

A calming bath, a change of clothes and two chocolate bars later, Cathy was ready to face the world again. At dusk, we headed back out onto the Li River with local cormorant fishermen, as precariously perched guests on their tiny rafts to watch their birds diving into the water to collect fish for them. The ancient skill, which had been passed down through the generations for a thousand years, was amazing to watch. The orange glow of the oil lamps hanging from each rickety vessel gently illuminated the river to dramatic effect, along with the odd flash from Mick and Jane's cameras. As the fisherman thrust their poles deep into the riverbed to propel us along, I was certain that at least one of us would be getting another soaking. I prayed to the gods of the river to take me before Cathy, as she really wouldn't be happy to ruin a second set of clothes in one day, but ideally, if we could sacrifice Jane, Mick or Kris instead, that would be preferable. Somehow, the five logs that were bound together below me didn't let me down; another benefit of my Thailand weight loss to be grateful for.

"The fishermen sell their catch around the local restaurants" said Alf, who was waiting for us back on dry land, "Who had the fish last night? Well, this is how it was caught."

"That's amazing... but I'm still having the pizza tonight!" replied Cathy, to nods of agreement all round.

"I'll just have a coke please Betty" I said shamefacedly, once back in the restaurant awaiting our pizzas. "Well, we've got another early start in the morning, right?" I added, although in truth, the mere thought of alcohol sent a shiver down my spine.

Back in High Wycombe, Smudger was also waiting, but not for a pizza.

"You've plugged it in haven't you?" he asked from his perch on the bed.

"Yes Smudge, I've plugged it in" replied an increasingly frustrated voice from under the table. "Pass me down the instructions again" said Tony.

"Is it done yet Tone?" shouted up Smudger's mum from the foot of the stairs.

"No, I think I'm missing a cable" Tony called back.

"No internet bride for you tonight then son!" she shouted back up, laughing.

"Yeah, thanks for that Mum" grunted Smudger, as laughter emanated from under the desk. "Piss off Tony!"

"She's right though mate... no internet porn for you tonight! I need to get another cable" explained Tony.

"I'm not interested in internet porn! I want to email Jamesy, don't I?" Smudger protested. "I need to do that CV thing too."

"Get James to do your CV for you... he's done sod all since Christmas... the bloody student tosser" moaned Tony.

"I saw his mum and dad down at the football ground the other day... getting tickets for the Semi-Final" said Smudger.

"Will he be back?"

"No, the tickets were for them... they said he'll be in Australia by then. He's in China now."

"I reckon he'll come back. Surely he won't miss Liverpool?" mused Tony.

"Sod that! He'll jinx it! And I'll tell him that in my email" scoffed Smudger.

"I'll come back and sort this out after work tomorrow Smudge."

"Alright mate, thanks. Tony... when it's working... it will have the internet porn though, won't it?"

Waking up the following morning hangover free was a joy; more than compensating for the fact that it was only 6 o'clock. Our stay in beautiful Yangshou was coming to an end and we were due to fly west to Kunming, but not before visiting the local markets. The marketplace offered an assault on the senses, with explosions of colour in the flower market competing with aromas from the numerous food stalls and spice stands. Alf became the centre of attention as crowds twenty deep surrounded the barber's chair that sat outside in the central square. Roars of delight grew amongst the jostling crowd as his face and head were lathered in preparation for being given a very close shave. The barber revelled in the attention, theatrically wielding his razor high above his head before expertly bringing the blade down onto Alf's scalp. The crowd began to disperse as the barber's concentration turned to Alf, rather than his razor juggling antics, and it became evident that any bloodletting looked increasingly unlikely. Before long, only those dependent on Alf's wellbeing remained. There hadn't been much hair on Alf's head to start with, so it shouldn't have been a surprise when, very quickly, he was towelled down and released from the chair. The barber turned and beckoned to me and Mick with his razor, looking for his next client, but we were both quick to back away, although Mick left with a cracking photo of what looked like a madman bearing down upon him with a cut-throat razor. The girls had already started to enter the next part of the market as Mick and I waited for Alf to settle his bill. When Alf joined us, he looked around for the ladies.

"They've just gone through there" I said, gesturing towards a tented bazaar.

"We'd better go and get them" he said, striding off purposefully. Mick and I looked at each other, shrugged and followed.

"Maybe it's where they sell the women" Mick joked, as we tried to keep up.

I wondered how much I could get for Cathy, and if it would cover the cost of a return flight from Australia and a Semi-Final ticket. Just then, Cathy came bouncing towards me with an excited smile on her face.

"You've got to come and see all the puppies... they're so cute!"

True enough, there were hundreds of puppies in cages and I had to admit, they were very cute, despite the constant yapping. They also looked in far better condition than the flea-ridden strays that roamed wild in Thailand.

"There you are!" gasped Alf, looking a bit concerned as he pushed through the crowds to get to us. "There's something I need to mention..."

Just as he spoke, the cage of the little golden ball of fluff that Cathy was currently fawning over opened and the little dog was unceremoniously yanked from view. Cathy looked up confused; Alf shook his head and made a chopping gesture.

"This is China... a different culture, and different views on food" he reasoned. "To them, it's just a furry four legged animal, just like a sheep or a cow."

Tears welled in Cathy's eyes.

"Let's get back to the minibus, it's time we headed for the airport anyway" said Alf with perfect timing, before Cathy had any opportunity to try and buy all the dogs in the market.

"Keep on keeping on!" remarked Mick, gesturing in the direction of the bus.

He was right; it was just a week since I'd left Thailand, yet it felt like I hadn't stopped for breath since. I'd loved every minute though and, with Alf at the helm, the next couple of weeks promised nothing but more adventure as we travelled through this crazy country, so different from my own.

At the airport we all checked in early and together, but still managed to get seats spread throughout the plane. Cathy was bitterly disappointed to find that her 'Row 1' seat didn't constitute an upgrade, and by the time I'd fought my way back to Row 54, I realised I might have a problem; my ticket was for Row 55, which by my reckoning meant I would, at best, be sitting in the toilet, as Row 55 didn't appear to exist. As the remainder of the plane's passengers settled into their seats for take-off, five concerned western faces peered back through the cabin, while I stood nervously watching three airline staff arguing in an animated fashion around me. A plan of action appeared to have been agreed. Each took a section of the plane and began rechecking everyone's ticket. I wasn't sure how this was going to locate Row 55, but was just grateful that I hadn't yet been thrown off the plane. I was also glad to see Alf talking to one of the crew and he didn't look overly concerned, offering me a hopeful thumbs-up from halfway along the fuselage. All attention was soon drawn towards a heated discussion between two stewardesses and an old woman sitting five rows ahead. The third steward soon joined the party and he began shouting. The old woman, who must have been in her eighties, was then helped out of her seat and marched from the plane, with the steward continuing to shout at her the entire length of the aisle until they reached the exit. As she disappeared from view, the two hostesses turned and smiled sweetly, gesturing for me to take the vacated seat, as if nothing had happened. Within seconds of strapping on my seatbelt, the plane roared into life and we hurtled down the runway. I wasn't entirely convinced that any of us were on the right plane until we arrived inside the Kunming Airport arrivals terminal after midnight. Alf assured me that the old lady had simply gotten onto the wrong plane, but I wasn't confident that the steward hadn't just looked for the least threatening passenger to bump from the flight. I did feel a tinge of guilt, but then again, she probably had just got on the wrong plane; because that happens all the time, right?

"What time is it?" I murmured whilst attempting to remain asleep the following morning.

"Ten past six" replied Cathy.

"What day is it?"

"Saturday."

"Where are we again?"

"A hotel."

"Seriously, where are we?"

"Kunming... Southwest China."

"Seeing as you're so on the ball this morning... anything else I should know?" I added sarcastically, having peered out from the sanctuary of the duvet to see Cathy already dressed and sitting with her back to me at the dressing table, brushing her hair.

"Well, it's the capital of Yunnan Province; it's known as 'the City of Eternal Spring' due to its pleasant climate and flowers that bloom all year long. It boasts a history of more than 2,400 years. Today it's the political, economic and cultural centre of Yunnan Province, as well as the most popular tourist destination in southwest China... and we're meeting the others for breakfast on the 2nd floor in approximately three minutes time."

"What?" I replied, having had my sarcasm well and truly rammed back down my throat.

"It's all in here" said Cathy, tossing our guide book onto the bed. "Apart from the bit about breakfast... 2nd floor remember... I'll see you down there."

I ambled into the hotel restaurant 20 minutes later and, as I approached, a waiter wished me good morning and ushered me across to Cathy, Mick, Kris and Alf.

"Morning all, how did he know I was with you?"

"Tall, western looking... look around, we're the only foreigners here" observed Alf.

"Where's Jane?" I asked.

"Jane doesn't do breakfast" laughed Kris.

"Right, listen up" said Alf, putting on his rarely used official tour leader voice, "we'll be getting accompanied by our first State guide today. His or her job is to ensure we enjoy our stay in the area... or in other words, to make sure we spend an allotted amount of time, and hopefully a lot of money, in the official Cultural Centre. Basically, it's an overpriced gift shop for tourists. We have to go... that's part of the deal we sign up to, to be allowed to run these tours... but you don't have to buy anything. They always offer tea, which is free, and the toilets are always clean... so it's not all bad!" he summed up. "Now, make sure to grab some water from the buffet table... it'll be warm out there in the Stone Forest today... see you outside in 10 minutes... I'm going to get Jane moving."

Ten minutes later a coach pulled up outside the hotel, carrying a smartly dressed young lady wielding a clipboard, looking every inch a representative of the State.

"Good morning ladies and gentlemen. On behalf of the People's Republic of China, I would like to welcome you to Kunming, the Eternal City of Spring."

With that, my own mine of information, Cathy, looked round and gave me a knowing 'I told you that!' grin.

"My name is Ginger... but I am not Ginger Spice."

Excellent, the comedy was being thrown in for free.

It was a three hour drive to the Stone Forest and, before long, Ginger had finished her official script and sat amongst us, turning from State sponsored robot into a normal human being. After an hour, the bus pulled over beside a small settlement in the middle of nowhere. Alf had asked Ginger if we could take a small detour, so that Mick could get some photos.

"Welcome to Seven Star Village. This is a very small place... not really for tourists, but you can go look around anyway, but we must leave again in 20 minutes please" instructed Citizen Ginger.

Mick and Jane raced off, camera's at the ready, while Kris, Cathy and I followed. Alf stood by the bus talking to Ginger. The hamlet was tiny and the houses were little more than shacks, built with mud and straw walls, with corrugated roofs. There were plenty of chickens roaming around, but a distinct lack of people made for an eerie atmosphere. As we walked down the dirt track that cut through the heart of the settlement, we turned a corner and heard the universal sound of a school playground. There, about 50 yards ahead, Mick and Jane were being mobbed by two dozen immaculately dressed young children, as their teachers looked on, laughing. Mick was crouching and the children were taking turns to look through his camera back towards us as we approached. The zoom lens was causing huge excitement amongst the youngsters. As they saw us, lots of the little girls ran forward; they swarmed around Cathy, much to her delight, completely ignoring me and Kris.

"I think it's your red hair!" laughed Kris, as we stood back to avoid getting trampled by Cathy's new found fans. Sure enough, as Cathy knelt down to say hello, the girls all started to touch her beautiful shiny henna red locks.

"It was her hair that first attracted me, too" I confessed to Kris.

As we inched our way towards Mick and Jane at the school gates, we could see that Jane was getting the same celebrity treatment as Cathy, and her tight blond curls were being met with equal adoration. Before we left, each child, none of whom looked older than seven, took a turn to introduce themselves, using perfect English.

"Hello, my name is Peter; what is your name?" asked one boy.

"Hello, my name is James" I replied, using the best pronunciation of my life.

Alf and Ginger eventually came looking for us, and the school teachers called the children back to class. Immediately and without protest, they formed a boy's line and a girl's line, but couldn't resist from turning back repeatedly to check that we were still there. As we walked away, the children broke ranks again, and waved to us all the way back up the track, chanting "Bye-bye Jane, bye-bye Cathy" repeatedly.

"I think that was the best moment of my entire life!" Cathy gushed as we boarded the bus. Two hours later, as we arrived at the Stone Forest, both she and Jane still had grins from ear to ear.

I hadn't been sure what to expect from a stone forest but, sure enough, we found ourselves walking through a forest of stones. Stacked limestone towers protruded from the ground for as far as we could see down the hill, into the valley, and across to the horizon.

"It's like stalactites... just without a cave on top" I suggested, as we squeezed our way between two boulders, only to find ourselves surrounded by ever more magnificent rock formations.

"Stalagmites... you mean stalagmites" replied Cathy.

"I mean the pointy things in caves, what's the difference anyway?"

"Mites crawl up, tights fall down" said Alf.

"Stalactites, they hold on tight! Stalagmites, they might gain height!" sang Kris, sealing the debate in Cathy's favour.

"Okay then, it's like a world of stalagmites, just without a cave" I replied, wishing I'd not said anything in the first place.

Around the next turn in the natural maze of stones, we encountered a Chinese group being whipped into quite a frenzy, taking turns to leap in an attempt to touch an overhanging rock. Ginger was quick to inform us that it was deemed incredibly lucky to touch the rock. Despite the vociferous encouragement and increasingly long run-ups that the party were taking, nobody was getting remotely close to succeeding.

"Show 'em how it's done big guy, you've got at least a foot in height on this lot" whispered Alf, as we stood watching at the back of the huddle. Alf then shouted something to draw everyone's attention in my direction, and a gap instantly opened up in the crowd between me and the rock. The locals cheered initially, before a hush of anticipation fell over the scene. Jane and Mick steadied their cameras, and Cathy giggled next to Kris. I sprung forward with each step being met by a clap from my audience as if I was an Olympic high-jumper approaching the bar. A fourth step and then a fifth led to a leap; I closed my eyes and extended my arm as high as I could stretch it, crashing it onto the rock as I peaked.

"Ouch! Bloody hell!" I yelped, as I landed to an eruption of applause and two dozen Chinese hands patting me firmly on the back.

"It's your turn to be the superstar now!" laughed Cathy, as I lined up for a group photo with my new Chinese friends underneath the 'lucky leap' rock.

"I think I've broken my wrist" I cursed, having completely underestimated my height advantage over the locals. "How's that funny?" I moaned as Alf came towards me laughing.

"They're calling you Magic Johnson!"

"Like the basketball player?" I replied.

"Yep, I'm not sure if it's for your skin tone or your jumping prowess!"

"You'll all be catching me up today though. It's scorching hot, isn't it?"

If our foreign appearance hadn't drawn enough attention already, the bright red sunburn displayed by Jane, Alf, Mick and Kris the following morning ensured we'd be stared at constantly during our final day in Kunming. Despite being a bustling Chinese city, westerners were conspicuous by their absence wherever we explored. Cathy took on nursing duties, having become the master of all sunburn soothing tricks after her experiences in Thailand, before we took off to explore the city and its surrounds ahead of the 18 hour train journey overnight to Leshan, to the north in Sichuan Province. I would have been content to stand on the overpass just ten yards from the hotel all day, marvelling at the thousands of cyclists pedalling their way through the city's thoroughfares, but that would have denied the population of Kunming the opportunity to marvel at the scarlet faced tourists. Instead, we explored the People's Park and more markets (dogs appeared to be off the menu in Kunming, thankfully) during the morning, before heading to the Bamboo Temple, high on the forested hillside that overlooked the metropolis. Again, Mick and Jane found a multitude of photo opportunities amongst the beautiful temple and its numerous depictions of Buddha, but despite the big Buddhas, small Buddhas, seated Buddhas, reclining Buddhas, gold laden Buddhas and carved wooden Buddhas all being incredibly beautiful, our time in Asia was beginning to leave me with a case of Buddha burn-out, so as the rest of the group explored, I found a quiet spot outside the temple and watched the crazy world rushing about, back in the urban sprawl that had taken over the valley below us. The tranquillity of the temple seemed a million miles removed from the city, rather than just a 20 minute taxi ride.

By mid-afternoon, I was again lugging Cathy's backpack across town towards the train station. Eighteen hours on an overnight train? I didn't like the sound of this at all. Even with good company and Alf dealing with all the details, 18 hours was a long time. Would my stomach hold out for that long? It had been relatively settled for a few days, excluding my Yangshou hangover, but that didn't count. Had Scouse John been right after all? Maybe all I'd needed to kill the bugs was a skinful of alcohol; and between them, Alf and Betty had certainly administered that medicine in ample measure. At the station, Alf collected our tickets and then directed us to a small supermarket on the central concourse.

"The food's a bit hit-and-miss on the trains, so stock up now. Hot water is provided throughout the journey, so noodle pots are your best bet" he advised.

"Crisps... let's find the crisps" said Cathy, before disappearing with Jane closely in tow.

"Cathy would eat nothing but crisps if left to her own devices" I remarked, as she started to fill her basket. "...and I think she's about to prove it."

The rest of us continued to follow Alf's lead religiously, and headed in search of noodles.

"Bloody hell!" I gasped as we turned the corner.

The whole aisle was stacked floor to ceiling with pots of dehydrated noodles.

"How do you choose!" laughed Mick, shaking his head at the hundreds of options available.

'This is a student's dream' I thought to myself, recalling college days powered by Pot Noodle budget meals. Incapable of making decisions for ourselves any longer, Kris, Mick and I just picked up whatever Alf had, and made our way to the checkouts, where Cathy was waiting with enough chocolate and crisps to feed the entire train, if not the population of Kunming.

The platform was a chaotic scene, but as the train pulled into the station, my concerns about how all the people were going to squeeze on board started to ease. This was the longest train I'd ever seen, surely a mile long, and far removed from the three carriage Marylebone Express that served High Wycombe. As the train stopped, for as far as the eye could see, and in complete synchronisation, each carriage door opened and out jumped a uniformed attendant standing to attention, saluting. Again, this was not something you generally saw on British Rail away days with Wycombe Wanderers.

Our home for the next 18 hours seemed very comfortable; there were four bunks in a cabin, so the girls and Mick had a whole compartment to themselves, while Alf and I were to share the adjoining compartment with a couple of locals. After dumping our bags, Alf and I joined the others in their cabin, to while away the hours by watching the Chinese landscape passing us by and starting an epic competition of the dice game, Yahtzee. This proved more group friendly than the one-on-one combat of Connect 4. There was plenty of time for conversation too and, before long, the topic inevitably turned to sport. Alf talked about Australian cricket and Spanish football, then Mick and Kris waxed lyrical about the Green Bay Packers, the famous American Football team that dominated the town they lived in, and Cathy talked about Norwich City, her hometown team ardently supported by her brother and brother-in-law, before confessing that her allegiances lay with Manchester City, like her Dad.

"Manchester City? I've only heard of Manchester United" said Mick, much to Cathy's dismay. "United are the number one team in England, right?" he added, now raising my ire.

"Man U are not the number one team" I corrected, before reeling off the list of facts that every schoolboy in England could recite. I couldn't recall such details as the dates of the Industrial Revolution or when the Spinning Jenny was invented, but when it came to football, I was on solid ground.

"Champions of England... Liverpool 18... United 13" I said, as if reading the classified football results.

"Champions of Europe... Liverpool 4... United 2."

"Liverpool's 'the number one team' without doubt" I concluded.

"United are catching them though" chimed in Cathy.

"Not for much longer... their manager Alex Ferguson is 60; he'll be packing up before long; then United will be finished" I replied. "Fergie's a genius... I'll grant you that... he's our version of your Vince Lombardi" I added, likening the United boss to the legendary Green Bay Packers coach to help Mick and Kris's understanding.

I wasn't a Manchester United fan, but Fergie had been Aberdeen's manager when they toppled the Spanish giants, Real Madrid, to rule Europe when I was young. The party my Dad and his fellow English based Aberdonian friends held after the game would never be forgotten; so in our house, Fergie was revered.

"So what about Liverpool; are they still good?" asked Mick.

"They're still up there; they won the League Cup a couple of weeks ago and are going strong in Europe too."

"They're going to win the FA Cup too, don't forget! They've got an easy game in the Semi-Final!" laughed Cathy.

The next few hours were spent explaining the wonderful adventures of Wycombe Wanderers in this year's FA Cup, along with their less prolific exploits over the previous 114 years. I don't know if it was due to my informative lecture on the glorious 'Pride of Buckinghamshire', but everyone opted for an early night, catching up on sleep after our hectic first week tearing around China.

When we dropped our bags in our Leshan hotel early the following morning, we were glad of the sound night's sleep on the train, as a minibus was already waiting for us outside, along with our next local State guide. Another Ginger introduced herself, and started recounting facts about the highlight of the day's itinerary; a trip to see Dafo, 'the biggest Buddha in the world'.

"Didn't we see the biggest Buddha in the world in Thailand?" whispered Cathy.

"I think that was the biggest reclining Buddha... maybe the biggest reclining golden Buddha... or was it the biggest reclining golden Buddha that lived in a cave?" I replied.

"Do you think all the guides are called Ginger" Cathy said, trying to contain a fit of giggles.

Alf leaned over from the row behind, "In China, on the first day at school, the teacher lines up the new intake and goes through the alphabet, giving each child a western name" he explained.

"So that's not her real name then?" replied Cathy.

"No! She would have been seventh in the line at school that day! Anna, Betty, Cathy, Doris, Elsa, Fanny, Ginger, Ida... that sort of thing... it's generally old fashioned names" Alf continued.

"What's old fashioned about Cathy?" snapped Cathy.

Alf was saved by the minibus pulling up and parking beside the river.

"This way please, time to meet Dafo" declared Ginger, leading us down to a small boat.

Before long, we were sailing again, this time on the confluence of the Dadu, Min and Qingyi rivers.

"How long until we get to the Buddha?" asked Kris.

"Erm, I think that might be the big boy just ahead" I casually replied, just as a 70-metre high cliff carving came into view around the bend.

"Wow!" was the general consensus, as Dafo towered above us.

"Now that really is a big Buddha" Cathy said.

"Yep, it's not gold, it's not reclining, and it's not in a cave, but it is big... I'll grant it that" I agreed.

Back on dry land, Dafo's size became even more impressive as we found ourselves approaching the intricate carvings on the top of the Buddha's head, along the cliff top.

"There's a path down his side; be careful though" warned Alf, while posing for a photo beside a sign written in English.

'WATCH YOUR STEP - IF YOU FALL, YOU WILL DIE'

The sheer scale of Dafo meant that, as we tentatively edged our way down the carved steps beside his earlobe, our western novelty temporarily waned, and all eyes, be they Chinese, American, Australian or English, were firmly trained upon the giant Buddha meditating before us. Once we had negotiated the stairway down to the riverbank, even Mick's fancy camera couldn't frame a shot of us alongside Dafo in his entirety, so we had to settle for a picture stood next to the toes on his right foot, and even those were as tall as me.

"Ginger, that was one mighty Buddha" I remarked as we said farewell to Ginger number two, back at the hotel that evening, my Buddha love restored.

23 – Pandas and the Libertine Buddhas

As the town of Leshan began to stir at first light, we were already leaving it behind on the journey to Chengdu. It was too early for conversation and the six of us were taking full advantage of the spare seats on the minibus, strategically placing our luggage in the aisle to create makeshift beds. Jane was asleep before we'd left the town boundary and Kris wasn't far behind. With the road getting bumpier, Alf and Cathy now had their noses in books and Mick's camera was primed by a window, ready to capture anything of interest as we drove through the agricultural heartlands of the Chengdu Plain. I'd been wide awake and full of excitement from the off; today we were going to visit China's most successful ambassadors, the giant pandas. Today was also the day I'd fulfil the promise I'd made to my seven-year-old self; a promise made just after my mum had thrown my beloved panda, Mr Bamboo, in the bin. I maintain to this day that a stuffed toy cannot catch head lice.

"Yes! I got it!" yelled Mick, clenching his fist in triumph before turning to show me the shot he'd just captured. The photo was certainly one to be proud of; five farm labourers crouching in a row picking crops, barely visible but for their straw hats pointing up towards the mist that hung between the field they tended and the mountains beyond.

"I'll have a copy of that one if you don't mind!" I replied, "That's not a rice paddy though is it? I wonder what they're harvesting."

"It's tea" Alf answered from the front of the bus.

"Tea? I thought tea came from India" I responded innocently, causing raised eyebrows from all corners of the bus. My long suffering girlfriend wasn't quite as charitable as our travel companions though.

"'For all the tea in China'... you've heard that saying before, right? 'For all the bloody tea in China!'" she muttered, while throwing a 'stop embarrassing me' glare.

"Oh yeah, I have heard it... I'd never given it much thought though" I continued, not picking up on Cathy's desire for me to stop talking. "So, they grow a lot of tea here then?"

"Yeah, a third of all tea comes from China" replied Alf. Cathy tutted and turned away in disgust. "India makes about a quarter though... so you were right about that" added our guide generously.

"That's a lot of tea bags" I thought to myself, before Cathy's increasingly venomous stare made me realise I'd continued speaking out loud.

After three hours spent driving through tea plantations we arrived at our destination; a small research centre in the mountains dedicated to protecting the increasingly rare giant panda population. Waiting at the gate was a smartly dressed young man holding a tell-tale clipboard, "I think I've spotted our guide for the day!" pointed out Jane as we exited the bus.

"Good morning! Welcome to Panda Centre. My name is Alf; I will look after you today. We begin here at Panda Centre, and then visit local cultural centre before arriving at your hotel in Chengdu."

'Our Alf' introduced each of us in turn before 'Chinese Alf' asked us to follow him to the entrance; locked wrought iron gates no more than four strides away. This obviously didn't take too long, but it took 15 minutes of increasingly agitated screaming from Chinese Alf before a caretaker appeared with the key. The first port of call, once inside, was the toilet for Cathy and Jane, who'd struggled to contain fits of giggles as we'd awkwardly witnessed Chinese Alf's confident State Representative demeanour rapidly crumble. His light hearted shouts had soon descended into outright rage as he shook the gates manically. The casual amble of the cigarette smoking caretaker, who looked thoroughly unimpressed with Chinese Alf's protestations, only added to the risk of Cathy and Jane having an accident. A brief but frank discussion was being held between Chinese Alf and the caretaker as the gates were finally opened. For a tantalising moment it looked as if we would be witnessing a full on fist fight, but as Mick readied his camera the pair separated, the caretaker retreating towards his den shaking his keys tauntingly and Chinese Alf responding by waving his clipboard.

"I'd score that as a dishonourable draw" whispered Mick, drawing further giggles and nods of agreement from all.

Things didn't get much better as we entered. Both Alfs looked around anxiously as something appeared to be missing; pandas. Chinese Alf, who'd only just begun to regain any semblance of composure, was again showing the early signs of a nervous breakdown but, more worryingly, our Alf was also looking concerned.

"Normally there are pandas in here" he said, pointing to the large forested pit beside us. Cathy, Kris and Jane had already begun to explore other enclosures and looked back with a collective shrug of shoulders to confirm that they too were having no luck. We all knew that pandas were an endangered species and that sightings of them in the wild were rare, but we hadn't considered that they might be just as elusive in the conservation centre. After five minutes of nervous foot shuffling, a high pitched squeal came from behind a thick clump of bamboo and instantly both the Alf's smiled. A grunt followed the squeal and a pair of pandas padded out through the thick vegetation into view, seemingly discussing the pressing matters of the day. Immediately, cameras kicked into action. If nothing else, I was sure that by travelling all the way to China to see some pandas, I'd proved to my mum beyond any doubt that she should never have murdered Mr Bamboo.

After 30 minutes of wandering around the other enclosures, where more pandas were making themselves known, Chinese Alf rounded up the group, keen to move us on to 'the amazing local cultural centre'. Everyone stood around, not wishing to be the one to tell him that we wanted to stay longer; after all, the guy hadn't had the greatest of starts to the day.

"What's at the cultural centre?" enquired Mick eventually, breaking the awkward silence.

"Many wonderful things" replied Chinese Alf, "... ornate paintings, precious stones and jewellery... and even a workshop where you can see the ancient skills being carried out by master craftsmen."

"So basically the same tat we see every day at the 'clean toilet and cup of tea' break" I whispered to Cathy.

"That sounds great Alf, but maybe we could just spend another 20 minutes with the pandas... we don't get this opportunity back home" replied Mick, using diplomacy I could only admire.

I leaned towards Cathy again.

"Sod this! I didn't come all this way to spend less than an hour with the pandas... you go that way, I'll go this way... they can't leave if they can't find us."

Cathy nodded, she knew this had been one of my main reasons for visiting China. Besides, she didn't need asking twice to cause a bit of mischief. Mick and our Alf clocked what we were doing immediately and smiled as, unlike Ginger the First, Ginger the Second, or any of the other guides who'd joined us on our trip so far, Chinese Alf wasn't ingratiating himself to anyone.

For the next two hours the pandas were entertained by humans playing a game of cat and mouse. The others soon joined in as Chinese Alf again resorted to waving his clipboard and shouting as his schedule slipped further behind plan. Even the caretaker joined in after a while, deliberately feeding the hapless guide false information to keep him from our trail. In return for our dedication to the cause, the pandas rewarded us with a show of their own; play fighting, running and climbing trees in a 30 minute burst of activity, the like of which Alf had never seen on previous visits.

"To be honest, it's no wonder pandas are an endangered species... they're the laziest little bastards you could ever wish to meet" Alf confessed. "Normally, you're lucky to see them just lying there stuffing endless shoots of bamboo into their gobs... but this has been amazing... I bet they sleep for the next 24 hours to recover!"

The caretaker was leaning over his spade beside us. He laughed and muttered something, to which we all turned to Alf for a translation.

"He said the pandas must like you; he reckons even he's never seen them messing around like this!"

With this revelation, we beamed with pride at our good fortune, just as Chinese Alf, looking a broken man, finally caught up with the whole group.

"Please, please, we must leave now... you can see panda paintings at the cultural centre!" he said through gritted teeth and a very false smile.

Right on cue, the beautiful pandas seemed to run out of energy and began to retreat into the bushes to sleep. Climbing back onto the bus, Alf patted me on the back and said "Did you enjoy that?"

"Yeah, it was brilliant. Thanks for playing along" I replied.

"No worries mate... that was the most rewarding game of hide and seek I'm ever likely to have!"

After a toilet break and another free cup of tea, Chinese Alf had no trouble rounding up his party to leave the cultural centre that afternoon and we were soon in Chengdu, the capital city of Sichuan Province. We would only be in town for one night, so Alf told us we had to experience the local specialty; Chengdu hotpot.

"Ooh, I love a hotpot, that's a Lancashire speciality too, my dad makes it sometimes" remarked Cathy, as we walked through the bustling city to the restaurant.

"Yeah, I think this is a bit different from what they make in Manchester" laughed Alf.

The restaurant was huge and almost full as we were escorted to our table. Every table was of a uniform shape and size; square and fixed to the floor, with a large hole in the middle. As the waiter approached, Alf gestured for six beers.

"Don't we get menus?" asked Kris.

"No need, just one dish on the menu here... Chengdu hotpot" replied Alf. "... and here it comes."

A waiter carefully manoeuvred a boiling cauldron down into the hole in the table. We all leaned over, peering into the steaming vat; it looked like the inside of a volcano. Even the steam that rose to meet our curiosity stung our eyes, the chilli-infused vapour being so intense. Our waiter soon returned, this time delivering a tray of raw meatballs, chunks of chicken and vegetables. Alf proceeded to tip the lot into the fiery red sauce, which was continuing to bubble due to a stove built into the table.

"Now we wait for the food to float to the top. When it does, it's ready to eat" Alf explained solemnly.

None of us looked overly enthusiastic as we gulped from our beer bottles and waited. Eventually, morsels began to rise; Mick went first, trapping a piece of chicken expertly between his chopsticks and thrusting it straight into his mouth without hesitation. He chewed, we watched. He swore, we watched. He started to sweat, we watched. In hindsight, Mick had the right idea; the only thing worse than a fear of the unknown is a fear of the known. And now we had to at least try something, knowing full well that we'd soon be joining him in a Sichuan Peppercorn-induced hell.

"I say we all go in together" suggested Alf as we sat there silently. Silent, that is, apart from Mick, who could be heard cursing under his breathe while using a napkin to wipe away the beads of sweat that continued to abandon his polluted body.

"On three; ready? One... two... three!" said Alf, whilst proving that no matter what the situation, peer pressure can make people do the stupidest of things.

"My ears are bleeding" I soon gasped, shaking my head from side to side.

"Fuck!" screamed Cathy, incredibly loudly, managing to find the only western word that the rest of the packed restaurant understood, before finishing her bottle of beer and moving straight on to Jane's. Jane wasn't there to protest, as within seconds of putting the chopsticks to her lips she'd politely said "excuse me" and walked out of the restaurant.

Alf was trying to hold himself together but, like Mick, was sweating profusely, his shaven head glistening under the restaurant lights. "Who's going in for more then?" he challenged.

"Piss off, I think I'm going blind" I cried.

"Okay Alf... looks like it's just me and you then" said Kris quite calmly.

She looked completely unscathed from her first mouthful, and expertly hooked a second from the cauldron and devoured it. Alf looked shocked, but Kris had called his bluff, so in he went for round two. He didn't suggest a third.

Maybe it was the aftermath of the hotpot or just the 5.30am start the next morning, but nobody opted for breakfast in the hotel before beginning the five hour drive to Dazu, which Cathy's travel guide informed us was famous for its rock carvings.

"What do the carvings depict then?" I asked, although feeling pretty confident that I knew the answer already.

Cathy smiled. "You'll never guess."

The five hours felt like ten, so we were glad to stretch our legs upon arriving in Dazu, where we were greeted by Polly, unsurprisingly a smartly dressed girl with a clipboard.

"Welcome to Dazu everybody. This is my hometown and I am very proud to be your guide today, and also very proud to show you the rock carvings that we have here. There are 75 sites around the area, with over 50,000 statues and over 100,000 inscriptions... so we will be very busy!"

After our experiences with Chinese Alf the previous day, Polly's enthusiasm was a breath of fresh air, but surely she was exaggerating... 50,000 statues? Alf must have read my mind, as he nodded to confirm the numbers.

"Our exceptional series of rock carvings date from the 9th to the 13th century. They are remarkable for their aesthetic quality, their rich diversity of subject matter, both secular and religious, and the light that they shed on everyday life in China during this period. They provide outstanding evidence of the harmonious synthesis of Buddhism, Taoism and Confucianism" Polly continued, as we strode into a valley to be faced by a rock overhang that had been carved into, admittedly, the most ornate reclining Buddha imaginable.

"You might need to translate again for me today... Polly's English is way better than mine!" I whispered to Alf, as we chased our guide, who was marching onwards at a cracking pace.

After a couple of hours, we stopped for a picnic lunch. We were grateful to collapse onto the grass as the sun beat down, all exhausted by trying to keep up with Polly who hadn't stopped talking. Her boundless passion, combined with the depth of knowledge she had for the carvings, meant that we were all doing our best to reciprocate. But there must be a limit to the level of appreciation any one person can dedicate to rock carvings of Buddhas, and I was certainly nearing my threshold. Mick was soon asleep under his sunhat; Jane and Kris were embracing the midday sun, while Cathy sat in the shade smoking a cigarette.

"You all look very hot and tired" said Polly, "... but do not worry, this afternoon we will visit the many caves of the park... the caves will keep you cool... they too are full of many carvings."

With the best will in the world, and despite all of us enjoying Polly's company, after a couple more hours of looking at stone carved Buddhas my mind drifted to a far off place; a place where, although they couldn't boast 100,000 carvings, they did have a chair museum and a football team in the Semi-Final of the FA Cup. I began to wonder where in High Wycombe was suitable to carve an ornate tribute to the mighty Wanderers, concluding that the side of the bus station was probably the best bet as West Wycombe's Hellfire Caves were too far out of town. I'd not had a chance to check emails since we'd embarked on our whistle-stop tour of China nine days before, and could only imagine the level of excitement that would be growing back home. Would any of our forwards manage to recover from injury before the big game? Andy Rammel, Sean Devine, Jermaine McSporran, Andy Baird; surely one of them would be fit to face Liverpool?

I didn't know how long I'd flipped out for, but as my attention returned to China, I was standing at the entrance of yet another cave, just as Polly was imparting more knowledge upon my friends inside. I edged my way back up to the group, and just caught the end of Polly's delivery.

"...this cave depicts the various Buddhist hells... some of the carvings are... erm, what is the correct word? Very... liberal."

I felt bad for not paying attention, so tried to make up for it by asking a question.

"Liberal you say? So the carvings are of a political nature?"

I'd heard the word 'Liberal' and through word association had instantly thought, 'Liberal, Labour, Conservative... she's talking about politics'. Polly looked both flustered and confused, falling silent for the first time all day. She gestured for me to go into the cave and find out for myself. I'd been wrong; she hadn't been referring to anything political. The cave was basically a 1,400-year-old shrine to hundreds of pornographic carvings. Men, women and animals of all descriptions, intertwined in every combination you can imagine, and then many more that you couldn't possibly imagine. No wonder Polly had blushed when I'd tried to ask a sensible question. Polly had saved the Hell cave until last, so mercifully I didn't have too long to concern myself with making any further ill-timed comments. Disappointingly, the gift shop didn't appear to have a section dedicated to the porn cave, as it would have provided the perfect postcards to send home to the Roobarbs.

We were all sad to be waving farewell to Polly as our minibus pulled away from Dazu. She had been, by far, the least officious of our State guides and a pleasure to meet, although we weren't so reluctant to leave the 50,000 Buddhas behind. As Alf stood at the front of the bus in true tour guide fashion, he assured us that, from here on in, the Buddha count would significantly start to drop. Our next stop was the famous Yangtze River, and a cruise eastwards through the famous Three Gorges (I'd never heard of them, but the guide book advised that they were famous), which would end at the construction site of the Three Gorges Dam project. To me, this didn't sound overly exciting; yes, I'd always dreamed of exploring far off lands, but I'd never envisaged that this would include a guided tour of a construction site. Mick on the other hand, couldn't wait to see it.

"The dam's going to be the world's largest power station... it should be an awesome spectacle" he eagerly informed me. I still wasn't convinced.

"The boat doesn't set sail until 10 o'clock tonight, so we'll stop in Chongqing first for dinner. Who's up for more hotpot?" said Alf.

Five blank expressions stared back.

"Only kidding... there are lots of noodle vendors who set up on the street... I'll be eating at one of those, but there's a small foreign restaurant you might be interested in visiting... it's called 'McDonalds'."

Signs of life magically returned to Alf's weary troupe.

"That sounds heavenly" replied Mick.

"Chips... they will have chips won't they?" asked Cathy.

"I hate McDonalds, I never eat there" hissed Kris, before adding "... but hell, I'm having a Big Mac and fries!"

I, too, spent the rest of the bus ride to Chongqing dreaming of burgers but, upon arrival, and seeing Alf give instructions of where to find the restaurant and how to point to the pictures on the menu to communicate with the local staff, I decided that leaving my brain turned off and following Alf to a roadside noodle stand was the easier option. Jane said she wanted to try a local noodle dish she'd read about in her travel guide but I suspect that, deep down, she was just being lazy too. Cathy looked like a child going for a birthday treat with her parents as she raced off with Mick and Kris, leaving me with Jane and Alf on a dusty street corner that hardly seemed the ideal spot to pitch a noodle stand. As we waved the McDonalds hunters on their way, a man had appeared across the street, somehow managing to transport a couple of tables, a dozen stools, an old oil drum and a cauldron to his patch, all on a wheelbarrow. Further down the road, other street vendors were already open for business. Jane and I followed Alf to a busy stand where about twenty men looked up at us in fascination, whilst continuing to slurp from the noodle bowls they were hunched over. Despite being on a relatively well-trodden tourist path, we had been stared at wherever we'd been since venturing behind the bamboo curtain. As had been the case throughout China, when we smiled back at our noodle-sucking observers, they didn't react at all; not a smile in return, no acknowledgement of our attempted interaction; it was quite unnerving and something I couldn't get used to. We grabbed three stools and sat slightly away from the table, which was already full.

"This guy needs a bigger wheelbarrow... fancy only bringing one table!" Alf joked as we waited for our food. It wasn't long before steaming bowls of noodles were proudly placed on our laps by the beaming cook. Rather than going back to his cauldron, he stood inches from us with his arms crossed, waiting for us to eat. Suddenly, the silence that had accompanied the stares upon our arrival turned into excited chatter; Jane and I both looked to Alf for reassurance that we weren't about to get murdered.

"They're betting on who'll finish the noodles first!" said Alf, with a smile. "'Straw hair', 'brown hair' or 'no hair'... that's what they're calling us, the cheeky sods!"

As we snapped our chopsticks apart and prepared to eat, our audience left their seats and surrounded us for a better view. The fact that we knew how to handle chopsticks seemed to cause great surprise amongst them and it appeared that bets were being altered as we tucked in. One thing that I'd found in China was that a crowd generates a bigger crowd, and by the time we'd unceremoniously sucked and slurped our way to the bottom of our bowls, there were a hundred people watching. Alf had triumphantly raised his bowl onto his head long before Jane or I had got close to finishing. It soon became obvious who'd wagered on 'no hair'. No sooner had the cheers and jeers died down, when all eyes turned to me and Jane, and a secondary market on whether 'straw hair' or 'brown hair' would finish next came into play. What the gamblers didn't know was that 'brown hair' hadn't been at his fighting weight for several months now, and was never likely to be a real contender in the race. Although I'd undoubtedly cost a fair few of our audience their betting stakes, nobody seemed too cross with the outcome, and whereas we'd arrived to stony silence, we departed to applause and hefty pats on the back. Arriving back at the bus, Cathy, Mick and Kris seemed to be floating on air, high from the effects of burgers and fries.

"We got extra fries to take out for you all... but we had to eat them. Sorry!" confessed Kris.

"I've never enjoyed food more" confided Cathy.

"I've never been more proud to be American" mocked Mick, "McDonalds... our gift to the world!"

Two different culinary experiences, but six contented diners headed down to the banks of the Yangtze, ready for three days on the water; and the prospect of a lie-in at last.

That silly notion was crushed at 6am the next morning, courtesy of a wake-up call from the ship's captain over an incredibly effective tannoy system. It turned out that Alf, not wanting to spoil the elation of the previous night's dining experiences, had omitted to tell us that we were signed up for an excursion at the crack of dawn. Mick and Kris knocked on our cabin door as we prepared to depart. Mick looked as tired and dishevelled as I did; we'd both struggled to find our sea legs during the night's journey eastwards through the Yangtze's choppy waters.

"Have you heard where we're going this morning?" Mick whispered, "A-B-T... another... bloody... temple."

The next three days saw us cutting through the heartland of central China upon the waters that had already flowed nearly 3,000 miles from the glaciers of the Tibetan Plateau; another 1,000 miles would see them reach Shanghai and finally the East China Sea. Our first river cruise in China had been a morning spent on a small tug boat carrying just a dozen tourists, but this vessel, which spent its life cruising the Yangtze, was a different beast altogether, carrying hundreds of passengers. The one similarity with our earlier river trip was that, again, we were the only westerners on board.

The daily excursions to temples and small towns were enjoyable enough, along with the adrenalin filled transfers to and from the ship, which involved clambering aboard some of the least seaworthy vessels imaginable. But the most striking images along the route were not the spectacular gorges which towered above the river, nor the rapids or wind tunnels that they created. Littered all along the steep river banks were large towns with hundreds of buildings; schools, factories, shops, homes; all completely deserted. Beside them, rising ominously from the water's edge, were huge black and white signs clinging to the hillsides, creating a giant height gauge. First a '20m' sign and then ten metres above that, beyond a cluster of trees, a '30m' sign which sat parallel to the heart of the town we were now passing. The '40m' sign was above all but a few grand looking houses that sat overlooking the settlement below.

"They're going to be riverside apartments before long" said Alf, "...and then the masses will be looking down on them" he added with a rueful smile, pointing further up the hill to the bulldozers that were clearing trees just below the ridge. "Another year or so and the town below will be under water... all part of the Great Dam project. So take it all in Jamesy, because if you ever come back to China, this will all be gone."

"So, all the people in these towns we've been passing, they don't have a choice? They just have to move?" I asked.

"Yep... if they're lucky, just up the hill like this place, but if they aren't so fortunate they'll get displaced completely."

I tried to imagine the River Wye getting dammed back home in High Wycombe, and then everyone getting told to move. To be fair it would take a long time; the Wye wasn't quite in the same league as the Yangtze and someone would have to find it first as, in their infinite wisdom, the town planners in the 1960's had decided that the area would be better served if the river flowing freely through its heart was diverted under a slab of concrete and the Brutalist architecture of the bus station and shopping arcade.

"They reckon it will stop flooding further downstream and create better shipping lanes. The dam is going to generate about ten percent of China's electricity too... or so they say" continued Alf, sounding sceptical.

"I don't know... it seems wrong to mess with nature on this scale. But what do I know? I'm just a backpacker with a suntan!" I surmised.

Looking at all the ghost towns and the thought of the scenery we'd passed soon to be lost forever, it seemed crazy. The notion that a government could completely transform what nature had taken millions of years to create seemed even crazier. Alf snapped me out of my ponderings with a tap on the shoulder.

"That's mankind mate... we're just trouble! Anyway, we can't do anything about it, so come on, we'd better get ready for dinner... the final night on board is always 'party' night. Are you any good at singing?"

Singing? I could hold a tune on the terraces, but I wasn't sure how that was going to help me through another bowl of rice and chicken. Before I could ask Alf what he meant, he'd disappeared below deck.

As we sat down for dinner, there was a definite air of excitement in the room. The dining hall was completely full and, whereas on the previous nights we'd had a table to ourselves, tonight we were sharing with two smartly dressed gentlemen; one roughly my age, the other in his sixties. The younger introduced himself and then his father. They were Japanese and had tagged the cruise to the end of a business trip. His English wasn't great and he struggled to understand our replies, so the conversation soon petered out. We did our best to compensate for our limited communication skills with smiles and hand gestures, before Alf cemented relations with the universally understood ritual of filling our Japanese friends' empty glasses from our beer bottles. The older man looked very embarrassed and sheepishly raised his hand as if to say 'no thanks', but in unison we raised our glasses for a toast, insisting that they join us. As I'd found on my drunken night in Yangshou with Forrest, Betty and Elsa, alcohol can definitely help overcome language barriers and, before long, our guests seemed more relaxed in our company. Chants of 'Gan Bei' became increasingly regular after Alf gave a language master class in how to say 'cheers' in Chinese to his American, English and Japanese pupils.

As food began to be served to other tables around the room, our anticipation grew. Roars of approval were greeting the food in the same way that my dad and I used to welcome a steaming bowl of macaroni cheese to the table after walking home from Loakes Park on wintery Saturday evenings. For the majority at our table, the dish proudly laid before us proved something of an anti-climax.

"Is that what I think it is?" asked Cathy.

"Do you think it's a claw of some description?" replied Jane.

"Yes" said Cathy.

"Then yes, I conclude that it is indeed what you think it to be" uttered Jane, adopting her courtroom lawyer's manner.

Our Japanese elder politely gestured to us all to dig in, but even Alf declined, chicken's feet being a delicacy that even he'd failed to embrace during his time in China. Our new friends couldn't believe their luck, and happily dived into the bowl with relish. Things got better as the main courses were served; lots of rice and noodles drew sighs of relief from the western fraternity, and the meat dishes looked promising too. We all filled our plates, before pausing politely to wait until everyone was ready to tuck in. Again, the Japanese father turned to his son, whispering something into his ear. Junior, looking equally as sheepish as Senior, leant forward to speak.

"My father has noticed that none of you has taken the head of the chicken... would you mind if he selected it?"

"Go ahead… it's all yours. Please take it" I replied enthusiastically, confident that I spoke on behalf of my companions when I said that we had no yearning to eat the head of a chicken, staring eyes, beak and all.

The son nodded to his father, who bowed his head in thanks to the rest of the table, barely able to conceal his excited smile. He promptly hooked the chicken's head expertly between his chopsticks and slammed it down onto the edge of his plate, splitting its tiny skull in two, before passing half across to his son, who then explained to us that they regarded the brain as the best bit of an animal.

"Well, I regard the breast as the best bit" I replied, before ramming a tender piece of chicken into my mouth.

"Amen to that brother. We all love the breasts!" shouted Mick, prompting a clip around the head from his wife. This needed no translation, and prompted laughter from our Japanese companions.

Alf's initial act of friendship, offering a couple of glasses of beer for our reserved guests, had been repaid by four further rounds by the time the dishes were cleared from our table. Our Japanese elder's jacket was off and his tie loosened. Gone was the respectable businessman who'd sat down less than two hours earlier; we were now sitting with the life and soul of the party. Somewhat unsteadily, he rose to his feet, boisterously applauding as yet another eight bottles of beer arrived at the table.

"Bloody hell, your mates would love this guy!" laughed Cathy.

"I'm beginning to love him myself" I replied.

No sooner had he sat back down than he was up again, cheering even louder.

"Oh my god! That isn't a… that isn't… no, oh surely no?" gasped a gobsmacked Jane, no longer sounding the polished London lawyer of five beers before.

"Jane, do you believe that to be a snake in a bottle of wine?" asked Cathy.

"Yes" replied Jane.

"Then yes, I do indeed believe it to be what you think it to be" mimicked Cathy, sounding disturbingly more like Maggie Thatcher than a lawyer.

"Snake wine!" stated Japan Junior, as his dad waved the bottle above his head, generating applause from the surrounding tables.

"Is it safe to drink?" Kris leaned across the table and asked Alf.

Alf concentrated on pouring another glass of beer before looking up and shrugging.

"Yes. Well, mainly yes. Normally yes. It depends how long the snakes been in there... the ethanol from the alcohol nullifies the snake venom."

"The what?" replied a horrified Kris, not looking overly reassured.

"...the venom... the snake venom. I think it'll be fine" continued Alf.

"Well, we turned down the claws, and then we turned down the brains... it would be rude to turn down the snake wine too, right? It's a case of three-and-out where I come from" reasoned Mick.

Mick had confessed to me that he'd been gutted at missing the late night drinking session in Yangshou; he was doing his best to ensure we ended the boat trip with a bang.

"What do you think?" asked Cathy, slumping down in the chair beside me.

"Sod it... I'll be on the toilet all night anyway... I'm going for it. I mean, you'd eat the worm from a bottle of tequila, wouldn't you?" I reasoned.

"No. I hate tequila... and remember that time you drank tequila all the way home after Carlisle away?" said Cathy, recalling the night that had nearly brought our relationship to a premature end after I'd been sick all over her bed; and her.

"That wasn't my fault... I was young and Buz made me do it, I couldn't back down!"

"You could've backed down... and you should've backed down... you always blame poor Buz."

"All in!" commanded Alf, rising slowly to his feet. "Let's make some memories."

"Memories? After tonight I don't think we'll remember a damn thing" grumbled Kris.

All eight of us raised our glasses and toasted the pickled snake that was looking up at us from the now drained bottle on the table.

24 – Sick

It's hard to imagine a sorrier looking party ever having passed through the Three Gorge Dam Project's visitor centre, than that which skulked through the next morning. Maybe it was the rancid snake wine that had almost caused synchronised vomiting at the dinner table or the six pints of beer each beforehand. Maybe it was the further four that were required afterwards, just to rid our mouths of the disgusting taste and the numbness that it had left in our throats. If the snake had risen from the bottle and bitten me with all its venomous might, it couldn't have been a worse experience than drinking the wine it bathed in. No wonder the locals called it 'snake piss'.

The night had ended with the Japanese dad singing karaoke on top of the table with his tie around his head like a hachimaki bandana. Not to be outdone, Alf had led the audience with a rambling version of Frank Sinatra's 'My Way', which appeared to be the one western song that everyone aboard knew. Thankfully, the combination of too much beer, shots of Sake rice wine and the hideous snake piss meant that I only had the vaguest recollections of my unsuccessful attempt to get the ship singing 'Made Of Stone' by The Stone Roses. Not even when I'd seamlessly transitioned into The Charlatans 'The Only One I Know' had the bemused crowd joined in.

"'The Only One I Know'? More like 'the only one who knew the words'!" teased Jane as we waved goodbye to the Yangtze for the final time.

"At least you could have joined in, Cathy" I moaned.

"How could I sing? I couldn't even speak by that stage... besides, I was dancing with Old Man Japan... he liked your singing!"

"I liked the last one" chimed in Kris. "We are the old Bucks boys... and we make a hell of a noise! Give us a spanner, and we'll mind our manners... we are the old Bucks boys!" she sung softly.

"It's 'tanner', not 'spanner'... a good effort though Kris. Much better than my loyal girlfriend could muster when it mattered last night, isn't that right Cathy dearest?"

By lunchtime, our communal hangover had eased just enough to allow us to make a dent in yet another gargantuan banquet, laid on for us in a hotel adjacent to the train station from which we were departing later that afternoon. The rotating table spun the food at about the same speed as my head was still spinning but, as ever, I was willing to see if food could prove to be a remedy for my hangover. The food, the western toilets and the sumptuous leather couches which adorned the hotel lobby seemed to do the job and by the time we prised ourselves away from the sofas some three hours later to catch the overnight train to Luoyang, all of us were feeling rejuvenated.

The journey started well, and we found ourselves in a similar set up as before; a cabin of four, with two sharing the adjoining compartment with other travellers. Mick and Alf stowed away their luggage in the other cabin, before joining me and the girls for games of Yahtzee, noodle eating, book reading and learning Wycombe Wanderers terrace chants. I fell asleep easily as darkness fell, curled up on my top bunk safe in the knowledge that, for this journey, I was sharing with the girls. This meant I could relax; not having to keep one eye on any strangers who might be sharing with us.

Sometime later, I woke up.

It was pitch black as I tried to sit up, only succeeding in banging my head against the ceiling which proved to be a lot closer to my bunk than anticipated. Slumping back onto my pillow I tried to work out if I was awake or just dreaming that I felt like shit. I hoped it was a dream and closed my eyes. What felt like moments later I awoke again upon hearing noises; train doors opening; a conversation in Chinese; train doors closing; the train starting to move; yes, I was awake for sure this time. The churning in my stomach was still there too. I decided to visit the toilet, figuring it would save me having to get up again later. Becoming more accustomed to the darkness, I hauled my legs over the side of the bed and slid down to ground level, before tiptoeing across to the door. I edged along the corridor, only to find the toilet locked. Within seconds the conductor responsible for our carriage jumped out from her cubby-hole opposite and eyed me up and down suspiciously. She soon established that my language skills were non-existent, and I discovered that gesturing that I wanted to use the toilet by holding my crotch wasn't the greatest idea either. The unimpressed attendant disappeared back into her den and grabbed a well-thumbed sign.

'ALL TOYLET IS LOCK 15 MINIT BEFORE AND UNLOCK 15 MINIT AFTER STOP AT STAYSHUN'

I smiled and nodded, before heading back along the corridor to my bunk. I still needed the loo and I still didn't feel great, but tiredness was my overriding sensation; I was soon back under my covers.

Maybe it was minutes, maybe hours, but the next time I awoke I knew straight away that I wasn't dreaming. No, this wasn't a fire drill, the alarm bells ringing in my head weren't so much on Red Alert, they were at Defcon-One and signalling imminent attack. I launched myself from the bunk to the door in one movement, just making it out into the tight, dimly lit corridor before vomiting all over the window just inches from my face. I didn't stop to survey the damage as I knew it was only the start; all I could focus on was bouncing from wall to wall towards the refuge of the toilet. I was sick four more times on the 20 yard journey.

"Oh please no, don't be locked... you bastard!" I cried, frantically grappling with the door-handle.

Feeling the pit of my stomach ominously tense up again, I bundled into the next carriage, hoping to find an unlocked toilet on the other side. All I found was a packed Third Class carriage and despite the ungodly hour, everyone was awake; I felt like a stranger who had just swaggered into the saloon bar at high noon, looking for a gunfight. There was a moments silence as I made my clumsy entrance into the smoke filled compartment. The carriage was crammed full of tense looking card schools, a man holding a cage full of chickens and others sitting upon luggage of every size imaginable. I stared at them, and they all stared back; the nicotine haze filled my senses and triggered the next attack. I doubled over and was sick again, all over the floor.

This was a new low.

The months of crouching over the hole-in-the-floor in the privacy of our Thai shack suddenly became cherished memories; now here I was, stood in nothing but my Wycombe Wanderers shorts and a sweat-soaked t-shirt on a train in the middle of China, puking my guts up in front of a hundred faces, all devoid of any emotion. They just stared at me, no wincing with disgust, no laughter at my expense, not even a sarcastic round of applause. Barring shitting myself, things couldn't get any worse. I looked down wearily to my bare feet, which were stood in a pool of vomit, raised my hand in a gesture of apology and turned to trudge dejectedly back to my own carriage. I was immediately stopped in my tracks by the carriage attendant. If she had looked unimpressed at my 'I'm just looking for the toilet' crotch-holding gesture before, her face was now like thunder, greyer than the military style uniform she wore with aplomb. I also couldn't help but notice the force with which she was gripping the mop that rose from a bucket on the floor beside her. I shamefacedly took the mop and started to wipe it over the pool of vomit, still not raising a reaction of any kind from my bemused but captivated audience. After ten seconds of watching me push my freshly regurgitated insides from left to right and back again, the attendant screamed at me and yanked the mop from my grasp. This at last drew a collective gasp from the fascinated onlookers. She angrily started to fumble with a set of at least 50 keys, before unlocking the toilet door and shouting at me again. I like to think she was thanking me for my help in attempting to clear up the carnage, but deep down, even in my feverish state, I assumed that she was calling me the Chinese equivalent of 'a complete wanker'. When she then whacked me across the back with the mop, I was left in no doubt.

Pathetically, I shuffled past her and into the toilet. She slammed the door behind me and I locked it before slumping down onto the ground, ready for the next bout of bile to burn its way to the surface. You really know you are in a bad way when lying on the floor of a train's Third Class public toilet offers a step up from your prior predicament. Bereft of energy, and exhausted by my body's violent reaction to whatever was upsetting it, I just lay motionless, letting random thoughts flitter in and out of my mind.

Was it too late to just give up and go home?

Would I manage to get a ticket for the Liverpool game?

How long would it take for the others to notice I was missing?

Was the train lady still standing outside waiting to give me another whack with her stick?

Had Tim Burgess prophesised my downfall in The Charlatans song 'Page One' when he wrote the line 'The moods of a foreigner and the beatings of a train conductor'?

Sometimes, no matter how old you are, there's nothing else to do but sit there and cry for your mum to come and make things better. After an hour of tears, vomiting and vain attempts to recall happier times, there was a gentle knock on the door. It wasn't my mum, but the next best thing.

"James, are you in there?"

Cathy had come looking for me as it was just 30 minutes until our 4am arrival in Luoyang. Although the nausea had mercifully subsided, I struggled to walk down the corridor to our compartment, Cathy having to help me.

"Jesus, it stinks out here" she moaned as we progressed slowly.

"I was sick."

"You were 'sick' sick?"

"Yeah... really sick."

"Where?"

"There... then down there. There... and even up there" I offered feebly as we stepped over a trail of tell-tale damp patches of scrubbed carpet and went past freshly wiped windows.

We arrived in Luoyang on time and not a moment too soon. I was really struggling and felt as though I'd been hit by a train rather than travelling on one. I had no strength whatsoever and could barely support myself as we walked out of the station. Cathy even offered to carry her own rucksack for once, leaving me to drag my wheelie-bag, but even that was proving too much. Alf came to the rescue and helped me to a waiting taxi. Fifteen minutes later, having demonstrated high speed drive-by vomiting to the innocent early risers of Luoyang, I collapsed into a hotel bed and drifted into a restless fever-driven sleep. I awoke four hours later, to Cathy gently nudging me and whispering my name.

"James, it's time for the trip... did you want to come?"

"What? Where are we?"

I struggled to come to my senses. 'This isn't a train... did I dream last night up?' I thought to myself, before the piercing pain running through my ribs gave me an instant reminder that my woes of the night before hadn't, alas, been a dream, but rather a very real nightmare.

"No, I need to stay in bed, I'm too ill" I eventually replied grumpily.

"Sorry, I didn't know whether to wake you or not... it's just I know you wanted to see the monks doing the martial arts thing... it's the Shaolin Temple visit today."

"I don't give a shit if it's Bruce Lee fighting Hong Kong Fuey and the Karate Kid... I'm too ill. I'm staying right here" I snapped.

True to my word, that's where I stayed for the next two days.

25 – The Warriors meet a Wanderer

It was with trepidation that I returned to Luoyang train station to start the six hour journey to Xi'an. Being greeted by a polite nod and a smile from the conductor as we passed in the corridor (rather than a forearm smash with a broom handle) helped to put me at ease, as did being fully clothed when nipping to the loo. I couldn't have enjoyed a tedious, uneventful train journey more if I'd tried. The bright lights of Xi'an city centre greeted us as we arrived after dark and the group soon disappeared to explore the city, eager to stretch their legs after a day cooped up on a train. Weak after a third day without food, I opted to take advantage of our upmarket hotel instead, and headed for an early night.

The wonders of a good night's sleep had rejuvenated my spirits when I awoke early the following morning. Cathy was nothing but a curled up ball, buried deep beneath the duvet, so I carefully crept across the room and took a peak through the curtains where the faintest chink of daylight was streaming into our 17th floor room. Far below, in the city square, I could see hundreds of people exercising. Having seen the previous few days pass me by completely, I was eager to investigate. There was still a chill in the air as the spring sunshine sought to burn off the remnants of the night, but in their droves the older generations of Xi'an had congregated and were collectively warming themselves through beautifully choreographed Tai-Chi moves, fan dances and what looked like plain old aerobics.

The fresh air, the three day fast and some exercise (well, watching some exercise), had combined to kick my appetite back into gear and upon returning to the hotel my nostrils soon latched on to the unmistakable smell of bacon; not noodles or rice; it was definitely bacon. As if in a trance, my nose led me to the hotel restaurant and as I peered through the door, there it was; that most beautiful of sights; a self-service breakfast buffet. Due to the early hour, the large room was still empty. A member of staff welcomed me in. I probably should have waited for the rest of the group, or at least gone and got Cathy, but my stomach was telling me otherwise. I collected a plate and looked along the line of covered silver bowls in anticipation. Deep down I knew that a couple of slices of dry toast were the most sensible option, and so that's how it started; a couple of slices of dry toast on a plate. Then I saw the scrambled eggs; a helping of eggs surely wouldn't hurt? Next, there was the bacon that had lured me in the first place, and then the little sausages; half a dozen of those wouldn't go amiss, plus one for the journey back to the table. The bowl of chips (there wasn't enough room left on my initial plate) was admittedly excessive and not something I'd normally consider as part of my nutritionally balanced breakfast options, but I was in need of sustenance to aid my recovery and, by now, having completely dismissed the 'take it slowly and just eat toast' option, I was 'in for a penny, in for a pound'.

Food had never tasted so good. Two helpings later, I started to walk back towards my room feeling my energy levels rising with every step. As the lift opened in front of me, Cathy and the others all piled out.

"Good morning James! Are you feeling better?" asked Kris, looking relieved to see some colour back in my cheeks.

"Yes, I've been out watching the Tai-Chi in the square, and then I had a bit of breakfast. It's good to be back in the land of the living!"

"You need to take it easy, did you just have some toast?" asked Cathy, looking concerned.

"Yeah... I just had a bit of toast... but I feel fine, much better in fact."

I turned and went back with the others, fully intending to just show them where the breakfast room was, but once there, sitting watching everyone joyfully tucking into the feast, well, I just couldn't help myself.

"I think I'm going to have a little bit of something else... the toast went down really well" I explained, before heading back to the buffet.

I could see the waiter looking at me from the corner of his eye. He was trying to hide his surprise, but a raised eyebrow gave him away. Luckily everyone was so engrossed in their own breakfast that nobody questioned the overflowing plate I returned with. When the waiter came to clear the table, he must have secretly been impressed with the way I'd polished off three huge servings. Not for the first time, the fine line between 'just a little bit more' and 'overdoing it' had been crossed, so I was glad to hear that the mornings itinerary required a leisurely stroll through the centre of Xi'an and around its Ming Dynasty built city wall. A pair of giant 1,000-year-old Pagodas dominated the skyline, along with the equally impressive Drum and Bell Towers. The ancient city was beautiful, and the morning flew by as quickly as the thousands of cyclists that we dodged crossing every street. Just as I'd begun to walk off the triple breakfast, Alf pointed to a café ahead and gestured for us to go in.

"Lunch" he announced… "You'll like it in here" he continued, with a smile on his face.

After two weeks of eating little western food, we'd gorged ourselves at breakfast, only to find a lunchtime menu of pizza, pasta, burgers and chips. Xi'an was the home of the Terracotta Warriors; we were definitely back on the main tourist path, although we'd still yet to see other western faces since departing Hong Kong. Following a large pizza and more chips for good measure, I was again uncomfortably full. The pained expression on my face was obvious for all to see.

"I like a guy who clears his plate" laughed Kris.

"He never leaves a thing back home" said Cathy shaking her head.

"You're doing well… eating all that on top of breakfast after nothing for days" remarked Jane.

"I did have a lot of breakfast" I conceded, sheepishly.

"When we were at college, I worked in a pizza restaurant… and so did the other two girls I lived with…" began Cathy.

'Oh shit, please don't tell the story' I thought to myself.

"… James had been to the football and bought himself a Chinese takeaway on the way home. My shift finished at nine, so he'd finished it by the time I got home. I brought free pizza back and he ate the lot. Then Welsh Mary finished at ten… she brought pizza home too… he ate that. Then the other Mary, Sweary Mary, she closed up and got home just after midnight. She brought enough pizza to feed a family… and guess who ate most of that? Seriously, we had to help him upstairs to bed. He said he couldn't breathe!"

"Okay… okay! Thanks Cathy!" I interrupted before she could mention anything else about the night I thought I'd eaten myself to death. "She's exaggerating a bit" I tried to add, but Cathy wasn't having any of it.

"No I'm not! You couldn't even get your jeans off that night… me and the two Marys had to help you!" she added.

My humiliation was complete.

"Well, you might end up in that state again today mate" said Alf, gesturing to the huge cake that was being delivered to our table, before pointing at Kris and breaking into a rendition of 'Happy Birthday'.

"Ahhh! How did you know?" cursed Kris.

"I have your passport details... sorry!" giggled Alf.

"I might be able to squeeze in a little slither" I conceded... "It looks like chocolate... is it chocolate?"

As sure as night follows day, the familiar rumblings from the pit of my stomach started not long after we'd left the café, so I made my excuses and marched at a pace back to the hotel, leaving the others to continue on the exploration of ancient Xi'an. Thousands of years of history, the capital of the Ming, Zhou, Qin, Han, Sui and Tang dynasties; the starting point of the celebrated Silk Road that connected China, Tibet and India to Persia and Europe. It would all have to wait whilst I enjoyed the comfort of a modern hotel bathroom with its western style toilet. As I sat there, I consoled myself with the fact that I might be missing an afternoon of history and culture, but that the main draw to Xi'an was yet to come. If I could keep myself away from the breakfast buffet the following morning, I would be coming face to face with the Terracotta Warriors.

"Wake up sleepyhead, its nearly time to leave!" said Cathy, shaking me from my slumber. "Come on... you've slept straight through... we got back at 8 o'clock last night and you were already out for the count."

"Okay, you go to breakfast, I don't want to risk it this morning" I replied.

"You've missed breakfast! We've all been... we wanted to let you sleep for as long as possible, but we need to leave in ten minutes. I've packed your bag already... we just need to take them down to the lobby as we're checking out."

"We aren't staying here tonight?" I asked disappointedly.

"No, you've got another overnighter on a train I'm afraid... that's why we didn't wake you for breakfast."

"Yeah, fair enough... it's probably for the best. You go down... I'll be five minutes, I just want to say goodbye to my beautiful bathroom."

From behind the closed bathroom door, Cathy piped up again.

"Oh, I forgot to say, we found an internet place last night… Wycombe drew yesterday at home to Millwall, 0-0… but they lost on Saturday away to Walsall, 5-1. I'll see you in the lobby."

We lost 5-1 to Walsall? This didn't bode well for the Semi-Final. All I could do was hope that Lawrie Sanchez was resting our key players, just like I'd inadvertently rested myself yesterday afternoon in preparation for 'the big one' this morning.

We left the hotel at 8am and drove the ten miles out of Xi'an to the site of the famous Terracotta Army. We hadn't been assigned a State tour guide for the day, probably because there were already more than enough international package tours flocking to the site for them to bother about six scruffy backpackers. Luckily, we still had Alf to give us a crash course on ancient, and not so ancient, Chinese history.

What had been no more than a farmer's field until 1974 was now one of China's most famous attractions. When the farmers had tried to dig a well in the field, but found their route blocked by a layer of terracotta fragments, they couldn't in their wildest dreams have imagined they'd unwittingly stumbled across a vast army that had been guarding the first Emperor of China's tomb for over 2,000 years. Qin Shi Huang had unified the warring states into what is now the sprawling country of China. Upon finding his place as the first Emperor, Qin couldn't be accused of lacking ambition, setting about building an extensive national road network and unifying various State walls to create a single Great Wall of China. The Emperor also had a great fear of death and searched obsessively for the secret of immortality. I guess if you were the Emperor of China, you'd want the party to go on forever too. Throughout his reign, the Emperor oversaw the building of his own tomb (presumably hedging his bets against finding the elixir of life). Legend has it that 700,000 men were conscripted to complete the construction of his vast mausoleum and the terracotta army that was to protect it forever (or until some farm workers drilled a hole into their ranks two millennia later).

Alf's impromptu history lesson had only increased my anticipation, and I couldn't wait to see the iconic sight of the 6,000 warriors facing me, something I'd dreamed of since childhood. It felt strange that until I was two-years-old, nobody even knew that the army existed. As the minibus came to a halt in the car park, we looked around to find the place deserted.

"Is it closed?" whispered Cathy.

Alf laughed at the look of concern that was etched across our faces.

"Don't worry! This is why we had the early start... I wanted you to have the place to yourselves. Most of the coach parties will only just be settling down at their breakfast tables; they're getting a cooked breakfast, but you get the Eighth Wonder of the World."

We raced straight into Pit 1, the home of the majority of the discoveries, which was protected from the elements by a giant hangar. As we entered we were faced by line after line of the warriors, a never to be forgotten experience. For 2,200 years they'd been standing there, protecting their Emperor; I hoped they didn't mind me popping in to say hello. Nobody spoke; there were no words that could do the Warriors justice. I walked along inspecting the front row of soldiers, and then along the left flank, marvelling at the intricate detail which made each different from the next. When I got to the rear of the troop, I stopped to take pictures.

"Why are you taking pictures from here?" asked Cathy.

"Well, everyone's seen them from the front before... you never see pictures from the back, do you?"

After 45 minutes we were still the only visitors adding to the massed ranks of infantrymen, archers, generals and charioteers along with their horses and chariots. The others started to disappear through the doorway to explore the further exhibits, but I hung back enjoying the prospect of having the Terracotta Warriors all to myself. And, for the next ten minutes I did; with not even a security guard on hand to check that I hadn't dropped down into the pit to touch history. Admittedly, I thought about it; but visions of causing a domino effect as I accidently toppled the first infantryman whilst tying my Wanderers scarf around his neck stifled my ambitions. That would take a lot of explaining.

I may have been granted a private audience with the Terracotta Army but, as ever, my mind began to drift as I leant over the fence and stared down into the faces of the warriors who were, thankfully, just out of touching distance below.

'Line after line of soldiers... that's what Villa Park will look like soon... a modern day army filling the vast Holte End, row after row of Wycombe fans.'

The Roobarbs would be like the warriors over in the corner of the pit; the ones that had collapsed under the weight of the farmer's field. Yep, Buz would definitely be in a similar state if the pre-match drinking started too early. I was pretty sure the emotion of the day would weigh down upon my mates heavier than a Chinese farmer's field. I tried to imagine how plans for the big day were progressing back home. Kick-off was scheduled for 4pm, which meant a minimum of four hours in the pubs around Villa Park, even if they headed for the ground early for the first time in their lives. Add on the two hours travel; that's six hours drinking time. Plus it's the Semi-Final of the FA Cup; a very special occasion indeed. The only previous occasions that had been anywhere near as prestigious were our FA Trophy finals at Wembley, just before entering the Football League. Back then we'd arranged for 'breakfast' to be served at an ungodly hour in our local pub. Yep, all things considered, some of the Roobarb's were sure to end up crumpled in the corner, just like the fallen Terracotta Warriors.

Snapping back out of my daydreams, I found myself surrounded by dozens of excited tourists eagerly photographing the warriors. I took another glance into their ranks, thanked them for my private audience and stepped back from the crowd, who jostled for my prime spot on the railings.

The short journey back to Xi'an was subdued; a natural comedown following the high of seeing one of the most iconic exhibits on the planet. Anything that we would see in the future would need to be incredibly impressive to match the majesty of the first Emperor of China's Terracotta Army.

26 – Hitting the wall

'Nil by mouth' for 36 hours saw me come through the overnight train journey to Beijing unscathed. We had reached our final destination and it felt strange to know that Alf would soon be booking us into our final hotel, here in the capital city. But before that, he expertly commandeered two cabs to get us across town. The station was some distance from the city centre and the taxis were soon hurtling down the highway at great speed, taking advantage of the early morning commuter-free road, despite a huge convoy of military trucks crawling along beside the central reservation.

"What's going on there?" asked Cathy, as we all curiously watched the Chinese army positioning thousands of potted conifer trees between the two carriageways the entire way into the city.

"This is perfect timing" smiled Alf… "Guess who else is in Beijing this week? The Selection Committee for the 2008 Olympic Games… Beijing is a candidate city. China really wants the Olympics."

"But why the trees?" replied Cathy.

"It's just to make the city look nice… to break up the concrete sprawl a bit. This is one of the most densely industrialised areas in the word… but look out of the window… what do you see above you?" asked Alf.

"Nothing, I can't see anything" I replied.

"Yep, just blue sky right? I've been coming to Beijing for ten years; I've never seen the sky look like that… never."

"What do you mean?" challenged Cathy.

"All the factories in the city were shut down two weeks ago… normally all you see is a haze above… industrial smog. I can't believe what I'm seeing; seriously… this is amazing" explained Alf, shaking his head in astonishment.

"I'd love to see the Olympics in Britain" I sighed… "I can't see it ever happening though."

"Yeah, Sydney was a blast last year mate… I went home for it… what a fortnight that was, bloody hell!"

The Olympic makeover had been a great distraction, but as we got closer to the city it became evident that Alf might not need to book us into another hotel after all, as judging by the manic driving of the two cabs, a wager had been struck to see who could get to the hotel first. If anything, we were more likely to get admitted into a hospital than checked into a hotel. Alf and Cathy were firmly wedged into the back seat of the cab, protected by various pieces of luggage; I wasn't so sure I'd survive the journey sitting alongside the driver. When I saw the horrified look on Jane's face from the front seat of the other cab as it swerved precariously across our path, I could see that she was thinking the same thing. Behind Jane, Mick and Kris had already assumed the crash position. Our driver laughed hysterically at the audacious manoeuvre of the other taxi and was soon inches behind its bumper. He seemed to be giving us a running commentary, but not even Alf had a clue what he was saying. To add insult to imminent injury, I'd felt my legs being bitten constantly since entering the cab; I cursed that I'd worn my combat shorts.

"What the...!" I yelped in disbelief, as I saw the mad cabbie take his hand from the steering wheel to pluck another hair from my calf. I hadn't been getting bitten after all.

"What are you doing?" I screamed, pulling my knees to my chin to get as far from the driver as possible.

"What is it?" asked Cathy, sounding confused as to what could possibly have made the journey any more fraught.

"This nutter's pulling hairs from my leg! Alf, what's happening?" I pleaded, as ever assuming that Alf would have a logical answer.

"I told you before mate... they don't wear shorts here... and they don't really grow any body hair either. He thinks you're great!" laughed Alf.

"I think he's a frigging lunatic" I grumbled back, slapping away the next roving advance from my admirer.

Mercifully, the taxi skidded to a halt just a block later, but not before ignoring a red light in a final dash for the line, sending a dozen cyclists scattering for safety in the process. We quickly escaped into the sanctity of the hotel lobby, leaving the two cab drivers to settle their wager and also to deal with the furious cyclists.

"Welcome to Beijing" smiled Alf.

China had surprised us on a daily basis and our first 15 minutes in its capital had topped the lot.

"We're too early to check in, so just dump your bags here... use the loo quickly, and then we'll head back out for the morning... we've a minibus taking us to The Temple of Heaven."

"Can't we just walk?" asked Jane nervously. She was quickly backed up by ashen-faced nods from Mick, Kris, Cathy and me.

"We could" replied Alf, "... but believe me, on these streets it's safer to be inside a vehicle than out."

The Temple of Heaven lived up to its name, proving to be a secluded sanctuary of tranquillity from the madness of the city that surrounded it. Acres of beautifully tended gardens ushered us towards the 'Hall of Prayer for Good Harvests', a magnificent triple gabled circular building that rose from a base of three huge slabs of marble, soaring skywards in the middle of a vast stone square.

"Wow. These old emperors... they didn't mess about, did they!" I remarked, astounded at the scale and intricacy of the architecture.

"They had to keep the masses busy" replied Alf... "If you weren't in the army or tending the fields, then you pretty much built big things to help the Emperor outdo his predecessors."

"Thank god I bought this camera!" muttered Mick, who hadn't stopped snapping for three weeks.

"I wish I had too" groaned Jane, conceding that a digital camera would have saved her a fortune in rolls of film. "Beijing wins so far... the cost of a film in the tourist shop here is four times more than in Hong Kong!"

"Wait until you get to Tiananmen Square later; it'll be even more expensive there. And they say capitalism doesn't exist in China!" Alf laughed.

One 36-exposure film later, we left the great hall, following Alf back into the patchwork of ornate gardens.

"Hey Cathy... I never promised you a rose garden!" I quipped, feeling very pleased with myself.

"What?"

"A rose garden… I never promised you a rose garden."

"What?" Cathy looked increasingly annoyed.

"Look around… we're in a rose garden… don't you get it? 'I never promised you a rose garden'."

"Yes, it's lovely… now, do you promise to shut up?"

'Screw you… that was comedy gold' I thought to myself, before trudging off behind Alf. I guess three months of having to listen to my ramblings had started to wear a little thin.

Just ahead, Kris turned to Mick to point out a particular rose bush.

"Look at that… I'd love a rose that flowered to that shade of pink, it's adorable."

"Hey… listen lady… I never promised you a rose garden" responded Mick with his deadpan American drawl, drawing giggles and a playful smack of the arm from his wife.

I span around on the spot triumphantly.

"Cathy! Do you get it now… 'I never promised you a rose garden'… do you get it?"

"Yes, I get it. Ha-Ha… very funny. Mick's delivery was better. Are you going to shut up now?"

Mick and Kris were busy getting close-up shots of the rose that Kris had fallen in love with; Jane was again struggling to change her camera film; Cathy was just in a bad mood. I stepped up my pace to catch up with Alf, who was waiting at the foot of another giant set of three marble slabs in the middle of the gardens.

"This is the Circular Mound Altar. Back in the day, only the Emperor was allowed up there. He came once a year to pray for favourable weather to ensure a good harvest" said Alf. "Go on… climb to the top and stand on the slate in the middle… that's the 'Heart of Heaven'… I'll wait for the others to catch up."

"Will I get in trouble?" I whispered, looking around for security guards.

"Depends what you wish for I guess" shrugged Alf, looking confused at my concern.

I scanned around again then scampered up the first set of nine steps, before crouching like a ninja to avoid detection. Alf seemed to be giggling, but then gestured for me to get down; I flung myself to the floor, heart racing. Bloody hell, this could mean serious trouble. I'd managed to talk myself out of jumping down into the Terracotta Warrior pit, but here I was, about to get arrested on sacred ground for impersonating a Chinese Emperor. I couldn't imagine this going down well with the police, nor the British Embassy.

"James… it's okay… go!" Alf whispered.

"No, I'm coming down."

"There's nobody here… go on, go for it!"

With a burst of adrenaline I sprang to my feet and launched up the next nine steps to the second slab, and then on again up to the top; a marble plateau overlooking the gardens with the city beyond it; the perfect stage for communicating with the heavens. There was the Heart of Heaven, just a couple of steps ahead of me. I edged forward gently, half expecting an Indiana Jones style booby trap to strike me down. But, with one last tentative step, I was stood on the circular slate, standing in the footsteps of some of the most powerful men to have ever walked the planet. With feet planted firmly, I looked skywards, raising my arms to converse with the gods; this was a moment no mere mortal could be prepared for. I took a breath to compose myself. Suddenly I felt calm, all fear of getting caught disappeared; I didn't care, this was the most spiritual moment of my life; any punishment would be worth it. I gazed into the smog-free sky then closed my eyes.

"Hello. I am James; James from High Wycombe. I mean you no harm and I come in peace. I am not the Emperor, nor am I Chinese… but please… please hear my words today. Please deliver glory upon Wycombe Wanderers Football Club against Liverpool in the FA Cup Semi-Final. Please give Steven Gerrard a slight injury… nothing career threatening; maybe just a calf strain. I humbly ask only this of you, Your Mighty Buddha'ness … only this… and that you bring a wonderful harvest for China. Oh, and one more request if I may be so bold, Your Devine Greatness… please make my girlfriend cheer up a bit, for she has been a miserable cow all day. That's it, thank you."

"Who are you talking to?" asked Cathy, jolting me from my shaman-like state.

Along with Kris, Jane and Mick, she was now on the altar beside me; while a coachload of Chinese tourists were advancing up the steps. Beyond them, Alf wiped tears of laughter from his face as I cast him a withering glare. I comforted myself with the hope that someone up there had been listening anyway, especially as I'd asked nicely and been selfless with my requests.

"Nobody... I didn't say anything" I replied innocently.

"You said something about cows."

"Cows? Why would I be talking about cows?"

"Maybe because you're an idiot?" snapped Cathy, showing no signs of a mellowing mood. I could only hope that my wishes for the Wanderers and the Chinese harvest would fare better.

From the Temple Of Heaven we made our way across town to Tiananmen Square, a huge open space and the gateway into the Imperial and Forbidden Cities. Alf pointed out that, apart from the smattering of illegal postcard peddlers, the remainder of people milling about in the almost deserted square were likely to be undercover police. Looking around, it was impossible to think of anything but the iconic image of a lone protester standing firm in the path of a tank, as the army sought to crush the pro-democracy movement of 1989. The pictures shocked the world, and even a clueless teenager like me had struggled to believe what I was seeing. A couple of years later, in a vain attempt to impress a pretty politics student in the college refectory, I'd even bought a book on the subject. As ever, I hadn't got the girl, but the story that unfurled gripped me. Knowing that the dramas being described were all true only made the outcome increasingly unpalatable. So it was with some trepidation and mixed emotions that I stood there in the exact spot, excited to be experiencing yet another historical setting, but mindful that people of my age who had, just by fate, been born on the other side of the world, had died for peacefully protesting for democracy.

"Guys, take a quick look around if you like, but we'll be spending a whole day here later in the week. We've got a couple of hours to kill, so if you need me, I'll be over in that building on the corner checking in with HQ... it's one of the few internet cafés in town... you might not get onto all the sites you normally would... Big Brother is always watching around here" advised Alf.

The rest of us agreed to explore for a while. Cathy took great delight in seeing the giant portrait of Chairman Mao looking down upon the square from Tiananmen Gate, the gateway into the Forbidden City.

"Who's that?" she giggled.

"Chairman Mao... he was the top man... the founding father of Communist China... kind of a big deal in these parts" answered Mick.

"What's so funny?" I asked.

"He looks like he's wearing Mickey Mouse ears!" laughed Cathy, pointing out the thick tufts of black hair that appeared to have slid south with age, leaving a bald patch atop the revered leader's head.

"Stop it! You'll get us locked up!" I gasped, looking around for anyone who wasn't trying to sell us postcards.

"She's right though, he does have Mickey Mouse ears" conceded Jane, while lining up a picture of the iconic portrait.

"Mickey Mao!" added Mick, causing more giggles, this time from all of us.

"Maybe we should find Alf, before we get arrested" suggested Kris, ever the mother, keen to protect her brood.

I've no idea if the Chinese Secret Police were monitoring my internet usage, but I managed to get through to 'The Gasroom', the forum where fans could discuss all things Wycombe Wanderers related; my Hotmail, which seemed to be discussing nothing but Wycombe Wanderers; and finally the BBC website, which also had a fair share of Wanderers related stories. I'd the honour of receiving Smudger's maiden email, informing me that he'd seen my parents in the long queue at Adams Park getting Semi-Final tickets, which were now in danger of selling out. He took great pride in telling me that the club had asked the Football Association if more tickets could be made available. It looked like 20,000 people would be travelling to Villa Park to cheer The Blues on. Buz had written too, informing me that, as ever, my friends had failed to get organised in time to secure a block of seats together, but that they'd at least managed to secure fifteen seats on the same train up to Birmingham. Special trains were being laid on, departing every 15 minutes, but only 4,000 spaces would be available, so these were becoming almost as prized as match tickets themselves. The Roobarb advance party would be departing at 9.15am, providing ample time to explore the drinking establishments of Birmingham before kick-off. Dozens of other emails sat in my inbox, all excitedly talking about the game. Despite being on the most amazing adventure of my life, I couldn't help but wish to be back in High Wycombe, soaking in the atmosphere surrounding the build-up to the big game; a game bigger than I'd ever thought possible.

The 4th Round? Yes, I always believed we'd get there; next time.

The 5th Round? Possibly; if we could get a favourable draw I'd hoped to experience it one day.

The Quarter-Final? I conceded that this was highly unlikely.

The Semi-Final? Don't be bloody stupid, I'd had sleepless nights for a week before the FA Trophy Semi-Final back in Wycombe's semi-professional days, but this wasn't the FA Trophy, this was the FA Cup!

It had been three weeks since the Leicester game, but it still didn't sound possible. I whispered under my breath again and again.

"Wycombe Wanderers are in the Semi-Final of the FA Cup. Wycombe Wanderers are playing Liverpool... the biggest team in the world."

What was I doing? Why on earth was I sitting here in Beijing?

Leaning back in my seat, I casually scanned the room to check that nobody was looking at my screen, and then typed *'flights to London'* into the search field. My dad had told me about Scots who, in 1978, had told their wives that they were 'just popping out to buy a newspaper' but had failed to mention that the newspaper in question was in Argentina which, by pure coincidence, was where Scotland were heading to play in the World Cup Finals. I'd never really given much credence to such tales, but suddenly it made perfect sense. I quickly convinced myself that a few days apart from Cathy would do us both the world of good; over the past couple of days, it felt like she'd had enough of me anyway.

I started to look at the practicalities. We were visiting The Great Wall of China tomorrow, and I didn't want to miss that. Then the following day was the Forbidden City; anything that's 'forbidden' is generally pretty good, so I should stay for that too. I couldn't then leave Cathy to fly back to Hong Kong on her own, that wouldn't be fair. And leaving her there to travel to Australia a couple of days later seemed a tad selfish too. We were scheduled to arrive in Australia on the 4th April. I could get her there safely and then say 'I'm just going to get a paper'. Yep, that would work. I could fly home on the 5th, arrive on the 6th, see a proper English doctor on the 7th, go to the game on the 8th, fly back out on the 9th and be swimming on the Great Barrier Reef by the 10th.

I updated my search as *'Flights to London... from Cairns, Australia'*.

Everything made sense while waiting for the screen's hourglass sign to be replaced by a list of possible flights. But the moment the ticket prices flashed up, any thoughts of going home were dashed. The short notice meant one return flight to London from Australia would cost more than our entire round-the-world budget. My moment of madness was dashed as quickly as it had arisen.

"What are you looking at... flights to Wycombe?" chirped Cathy from across the desk.

"Oh nice... you think I'd leave you alone on the other side of the planet... just for a football match?"

I shook my head, looking suitably hurt at the insinuation.

Alf advised us to eat well at breakfast the next morning, as a long and arduous day awaited; a day that would see us hiking along The Great Wall Of China. We'd all seen pictures of smartly dressed global Heads of State enjoying a photo opportunity upon one of the world's greatest landmarks, so we weren't overly concerned about how gruelling the day could possibly be, but the noodles and fried rice on offer in the hotel's breakfast room were delicious, so we all obeyed orders. I finished my meal off with a precautionary helping of Imodium and then it was back into the minibus for the 100-mile journey northeast from Beijing to the Jinshanling section of The Wall. As we finally cleared the freshly tree-lined streets of the city, the commuter traffic ebbed away, leaving our small minibus in a convoy dwarfed by dozens of sparkling tourist coaches.

"I guess we're all heading to see the same thing" remarked Mick as we were overtaken by another coach.

"Kind of... we're all going to see The Wall, but they're headed for Badaling, they'll all disappear soon. Badaling caters for the masses; souvenir shops, toilets, chain restaurants" replied Alf.

"Sounds brilliant" I whispered to Jane, who nodded her agreement.

Alf went on… "We're heading further north, up to Jinshanling; it's remote and it's hilly, but I guarantee this… you'll never forget it."

"This all sounds a bit ominous" said Cathy.

Three hours after setting off, and an hour after leaving all the coaches behind, we pulled up on the side of a bumpy track. The further we had travelled out of Beijing the more the gently rolling hills had started to transform into steeper, more defined mountainous ridges. There was no sign of life, apart from a small wooden cubicle and a dilapidated, roofless shack.

"No McDonalds here then?" commented Cathy.

"Not yet" smiled Alf, "I'll get the tickets… feel free to use the facilities."

"I guess that shack is 'the facilities'" added Kris, just as a slight breeze wafted an unpalatable odour from its direction, leaving us in no doubt that this was indeed the toilet.

"Erm… probably a bit of a stupid question this… but where is it then?" I asked as Alf returned holding six raffle tickets.

"Where's what?" he replied.

"The Great Wall of China… you can see it from space, but not from the car park?" I continued.

"You'll see it in a minute… this little hill is in the way. Once we get over that, you'll be blown away" answered Alf confidently.

"That's not a little hill" I heard Cathy mutter to Kris.

True enough, after a quick scramble up the grassy knoll, a different world suddenly opened up. There, across the valley in front of us rose a steep ridgeway, and clinging to its back, snaking its way across the horizon for as far as the eye could see, sat The Great Wall of China.

"Bloody hell" I gasped.

"Holy shit" nodded Mick, bringing his camera into focus.

"Amazing, just amazing" mouthed Kris softly.

"It's incredible!" proclaimed Jane.

"And just how exactly are we supposed to get up there then?" asked Cathy, not sounding quite as enamoured as the rest of us.

"There are steps up... can you see that diagonal criss-cross over there? Just beyond those goats... we're going up there" said Alf, pointing to what looked like a vertical wall of rock half a mile away, before setting off in its direction.

"James..." said Cathy.

Generally, when Cathy started a sentence by using my name, it meant trouble; either trouble for me, or trouble for her. On this occasion, it sounded like I was in the clear, but my already out of breath girlfriend had decided that she was going back to the minibus, foregoing the opportunity to walk on The Great Wall.

"... I'll never make it up there" she gasped before we'd even reached the roughly cut steps in the hillside.

She sat on a rock and pulled out her asthma inhaler and a packet of Thai cigarettes. The stage was set for me to give a rousing motivational speech along the lines of those given by Martin O'Neill during the Wanderers glory years, or now Lawrie Sanchez, spurring his team on to ever greater heights through the FA Cup run. What she needed to hear was... "Come on love, take a breather and then we'll go up together slowly... you can do it"... It just didn't come out that way.

"You're having a laugh aren't you? We're stood a five minute walk away from the bloody Great Wall of China and... and... and you'd rather spend the day sitting in a crappy van smoking fags? That's fucking ridiculous!"

Whether it was my 'tough love' or the sight of our minibus disappearing into a haze of dust, driving off to our rendezvous point further along the wall, I'm not sure; but either way, Cathy hauled herself up and started trudging up the steps. Feeling a little guilty, I at least had the decency to carry her backpack.

Upon finally scaling the wall, the views were so spectacular that the others hadn't noticed our spat or the fact that it had taken us thirty minutes to cover the distance that they'd managed in no more than ten.

"This is amazing. I'm really sorry... I promise I'll give up... just as soon as I've smoked the rest of my Thailand stash" said Cathy, looking suitably embarrassed at nearly passing up this once in a lifetime opportunity.

"I'm sorry too. I didn't mean to be so harsh... I just worry about you" I replied.

We'd been at each other's throats after months without time apart, but we couldn't let petty arguments fester on a day like this. I pinched myself to check it was really happening. I was stood on The Great Wall of China and Wycombe Wanderers were preparing for an FA Cup Semi-Final against Liverpool; something had definitely knocked the world off its normal axis. The Wall was majestic, but showing signs of its age. The pictures I'd seen of famous people posing on the wall had all been taken in Badaling, which had been fully restored to its original state for the tourism trade. As ever, Alf was determined to give us an alternative view. He'd managed to deliver us to the Terracotta Warriors for a magical moment without the masses who trailed an hour behind, and now here we were on The Wall; and there appeared to be nobody around for miles.

"Hello, postcard?" piped up a voice from nowhere, before a beaming smile came into view up the steps.

"Oh not again!" laughed Kris.

"Hello, postcard? Cola? Candy?" Before we knew it, our party of six had become a party of twelve, as local women carrying an impressive selection of goods joined us on the trail.

"Don't worry, they'll keep out of the way when we get going" Alf assured us, "they'll even help you get across some of the tricky bits."

"Hello, book?" asked the girl who had assigned herself to me.

"Book?" I replied, just as the woman thrust a large hardback 'Great Wall Souvenir Brochure' under my nose.

"English, French, German... all language... you see?" she added, whipping out two more versions of the book from beneath her shawl.

Alf informed us that we would be traversing ten miles; a fair distance to walk across any terrain, let alone the mountainous path that The Wall followed. The first section we were to tackle required a steep climb, far tougher than the access steps that had almost scuppered Cathy's day, although the lookout tower at its peak offered even better views of the undulating tasks ahead, as well as the spectacular feat of engineering which The Wall's constructors had achieved in building a defence upon what appeared to be already impregnable land.

"It's a bit excessive isn't it?" I muttered to Alf, while looking out across the many climbs and descents that lay ahead of us. "Who on earth would try to attack China through here?"

"The Mongols... they loved a good scrap" he replied. "All of the land to the north... that was part of Mongolia and all of this to the south... China."

"It's all China now though?"

"Yes, for as far as the eye can see."

"There is literally no sign of life in any direction, apart from The Wall and the 'hello, postcard' girls... it's a bit unnerving isn't it?" I declared.

"What is?"

"...the sound of silence."

"Yeah, that's a rare commodity in this day and age" agreed Alf. "Legend has it that it's so quiet up here that if you shout, the sound will carry all the way across the plains to Mongolia."

"Come on you Wycombe boys!" I roared out across to Mongolia, with my arm's triumphantly aloft, before patting the club crest on my Wanderers shirt, which I'd worn especially as it was such a big day on our trip. "What do you think?" I turned and asked, prompting a round of applause from the 'hello, postcard' brigade.

"I think Genghis Khan himself probably heard that!" said Mick.

"Yep, the Ulaanbaatar branch of the Wycombe Wanderers Supporters Club will be very proud mate!" added Alf.

"I have to put up with this shit every day... every single day" Cathy sighed, looking towards Kris, Jane and the Chinese girls for sympathy.

The ten miles felt more like twenty, and by the time our minibus came into view just below the setting sun, we were all thoroughly exhausted. Despite the physical demands of the numerous climbs, our awe inspiring surroundings (and the constant supply of refreshments from our postcard wielding companions) could have spurred us to walk on through the night until dawn. Even Cathy, despite her stuttering start to the day, didn't complain about anything other than my attempts to start some Wycombe

Wanderers terrace chants to help us on our way. As we got closer to the end of our walk, our pace slowed.

"Come on guys, we're nearly there... there are cold beers waiting back in Beijing with our names on... keep going!" encouraged Alf.

"Alf, it's not that we're too tired" said Jane, "...we just don't want this day to be over."

We all nodded our agreement.

"Cool... then take as long as you want" he said with a smile.

And after buying the remainder of the girls' chocolate bars and soft drinks (and Mick generously purchasing one of the battered books), we did take as long as we wanted; sitting with our legs dangling over the turreted defences of The Great Wall of China, watching the sun going down on a very memorable day.

Back at the hotel, the ice-cold beers that Alf had promised helped to conclude proceedings perfectly, leaving just one more day of Chinese adventures.

Following the Great Wall was a hard act to follow, but The Forbidden City, the Summer Palace, and an evening watching the Beijing Acrobats all did their best. My lasting impression of the day, though, will be Cathy's unhealthy obsession with the previously unbeknown comedy side of Chairman Mao, which almost got us arrested following another unprovoked and incredibly ill-timed fit of the giggles; this time while filing past the man himself, in his mausoleum within Tiananmen Square. She couldn't find anything remotely funny about my 'I never promised you a rose garden' skit in the Temple Of Heaven's rose garden, but looking down on the long-preserved body of the founding father of Communist China, as people silently wept all around? That, apparently, was hilarious. Thankfully, the secret service agents who were then, no doubt, assigned to my warped girlfriend only had another 18 hours to monitor her movements, before reporting that she had left the country.

Just three weeks before we'd met as strangers, but having squeezed so many shared experiences into our whirlwind tour around China, we sadly bade our farewells to Alf, Jane, Mick and Kris as friends. Would our paths ever cross again? Who could tell? Whatever the future held, our time together in China would live with us all forever; and from various locations on the globe, there would be four more people cheering on the Chairboys against Liverpool in a weeks' time.

The following morning dawned with the realisation that Alf was no longer there to arrange our lives. Our brains would need to be re-engaged to get us from Beijing back down to Hong Kong, before venturing still further from home.

27 – Heading south

"So, you're travelling together, correct?"

With his dog sniffing furiously around our legs, I felt as guilty as hell under the Customs Officer's suspicious gaze, despite knowing I hadn't committed any crime. I focused solely on not cracking a joke about 'Australians all being convicts, so what's the fuss?'

"Yes, she's my girlfriend."

"And where have you flown from today?"

"Hong Kong."

"...Hong Kong? Interesting... and before that?"

"China, we've been travelling around China."

"China? Interesting... how long were you in China?"

"Three weeks."

"Three weeks? Interesting... and what were you both doing in China?"

"Just seeing the sights."

"The sights? Interesting... and before China... England?"

"No, we were in Thailand."

"Thailand? Interesting... and what did you get up to in Thailand then?"

'We smuggled copious amounts of heroin, made an absolute fortune and then blew the lot funding a militia to overthrow the government'... I said in my head, but again, decided now wasn't the moment to add humour to proceedings.

"We sat on the beach in Phuket for a couple of months. We didn't really do much of any interest."

"... Not much of interest? Interesting... and you were there for two months you say?"

"Yes, two months, and before that we were at home in England."

"Ah, England… interesting. And before you left England, did you have any intimate interaction with any farm animals?"

"What?"

"Farm animals sir, did you have any close interaction with any farm animals?"

"Erm, no… I've never really had any interaction with farm animals… not ever."

"… No interaction, interesting. And you Miss? Farm animals?"

"No, I've never been into farm animals either" replied Cathy, prompting an involuntary yelp of nervous laughter from me.

"You find something amusing, sir?" continued the custom's guy, showing not the slightest hint of emotion.

"No, I'm sorry… your dog tickled my leg" was all I could think to say. "You know, they don't wear shorts in China… it's good to be in a country where I'm not the only guy wearing shorts" I added, trying to find some common ground with the customs robot, who was wearing the traditional Queenslander uniform of a short-sleeved shirt and knee-length shorts.

"Really… the Chinese don't wear shorts… how very interesting" he replied sarcastically. "Okay, move along."

"What was that all about?" whispered Cathy as we hastily looked for the airport exit.

"I have no idea… and then when I did say something interesting, the cheeky bastard mocked me! Let's get out of here quick, before he calls us back."

Our taxi ride into Cairns was a bit different from our Beijing experiences. The driver couldn't have been more chilled out and barely bothered to shift out of first gear. There was no need for protection from hair plucking leg fetishists either. If anything, I was slightly concerned that beneath his beach-ruffled locks and baggy vest, the cabbie might not be wearing any shorts at all; if he was, they wouldn't have looked out of place on Kevin Keegan at the 1982 World Cup Finals in Spain, when shorts really were short.

"China? Dudes, that's real cool" nodded the driver agreeably. "Better than being back at home at the minute I guess… man, my sister's been living over in London for a year and she says it's gone crazy… she can't leave the city."

"Why's that?" Cathy leaned forward from the back seat and asked, while blatantly checking to see if surf-cabbie was wearing shorts.

"All the 'Foot and Mouth' restrictions… yep, she's staying put in Shepherd's Bush mate. She reckons they've closed the countryside down… it's like Marshal Law… some really heavy shit."

"I guess that explains the Customs' guy then!" I said to Cathy.

"No… I just think he's a weirdo" she replied.

"Dudes… I'm going to drop you here… hostel's just across the street on the left, loads of pubs down there on the right… and the oceans straight ahead. I'll see you around, okay?"

"Yeah, see you around" swooned Cathy, her cheeks blushing beneath her suntan.

"Oh, I nearly forgot… here, try this place for some food later. I generally eat there" he continued, handing Cathy a couple of vouchers.

"Yeah, see you around, okay?" I mocked sarcastically as we headed to the hostel's reception.

An Antipodean vision of beauty appeared from the back office.

"G'day, can I help you?"

"Erm, hi…hello, yes, g'day… a room… yes, we'd like a room please… hi" I replied, stumbling over each word as I tried to reel my tongue back into my mouth.

"Okay, that's you all set… enjoy your stay!" said the blonde bombshell, taking copies of our passports and a fistful of Aussie dollars, "Here's a welcome-pack for you… there's a street-map in there, day-trip leaflets and some discount vouchers for meals… the food's really good."

We hadn't even made it to our room before Cathy struck back; her impersonation echoing along the corridor... "Oh, hey... hello, hi... g'day... yeah, a room please."

"Shut up, that sounds more like Cliff Richard than me!" I retaliated.

"Oh... this is..." said Cathy pushing past me to get a first glimpse of our room.

"... sparse?" I added, looking into the room with its two single beds and very little else. "Maybe the girl on reception assumed we weren't together?"

"In your dreams James" muttered Cathy, pushing the beds together.

"It's not en suite then?" I remarked.

"It's not 'en-anything' is it!" sighed Cathy. "It's clean though."

"I'll find the bogs" I said, disappearing back into the corridor, thankfully discovering that we were nicely positioned for the communal toilet-block. If there was one thing that train travel in China had taught me, it was to always locate your nearest emergency toilet.

"I think this is what it must be like in an open-prison" declared Cathy upon my return.

"I think they get television... and a loo in the corner of the room" I replied. "Come on, let's go outside."

After Bangkok, Hong Kong, Kunming, Chengdu, Xi'an and Beijing, stepping out into downtown Cairns felt like entering an alternate universe. It was as though someone had turned the volume down and put the world into slow motion. We were even able to cross the roads without fearing for our lives.

"Well, this is nice" giggled Cathy, as we both realised that we'd barely paused for breath for a month. It took approximately five minutes to revert back fully into the idle slackers that had been so spectacularly unproductive in Thailand. After a couple of hours lazily flicking through Cathy's guidebook in the afternoon sun, I decided to call a 'business' meeting.

"I reckon a week here in Cairns, then down to Airlie Beach, a few days in Noosa, a week in Brisbane and then to Sydney... I think six weeks might drag a bit" I declared, not completely sure if the other half of our meeting was awake behind her sunglasses, or dreaming about her taxi driver. Either way, she didn't appear to be paying me any attention.

"It's funny, when we were in London booking the tickets, do you remember the massive map of the world that covered all the walls and the ceiling?" There was still no response from Cathy, but I continued anyway… "I thought Australia looked massive then, but now we're here… I don't know… it just doesn't seem so vast, I reckon we could have done this leg in a fortnight."

Cathy heaved herself up onto her elbows and took the book from me.

"You see this?" she said, pointing to a map of the east coast of Australia.

"Yes" I replied, intrigued to have at last garnered some interest.

"Right up here at the top… that's us in Cairns. And you see this bit, about halfway down?"

"Yes."

"Well, that's Brisbane. And you see across the water, up there… just above us? That's Papua New Guinea."

"Is it?"

"Yes. That's about 500 miles north of Cairns. Brisbane is about 1,000 miles south, and Sydney… that's another 500 miles below Brisbane."

Cathy raised her sunglasses onto her hair and stared intensely into my eyes.

"Right… sorry… your point is what?" I replied after a pause.

"The point is this… Australia is fucking massive… so no, we probably couldn't 'have done it in a fortnight'… not when you've decided we are travelling everywhere by bus… you twat" she calmly concluded, before returning to her prone position and sliding her glasses back down over her face.

With our business meeting concluded, somewhat abruptly, I returned to the map, before walking down to the shoreline to see if I could catch a glimpse of Papua New Guinea on the horizon. Unsurprisingly, I couldn't.

A short while later, Cathy followed me down to the water and offered an olive branch of sorts.

"Dinner? I've got these vouchers."

"Why don't we use these vouchers?" I replied, pulling out the card I'd taken from the girl at the hostel.

"What... the ones from your girlfriend on reception?" Cathy snapped back, withdrawing the proverbial olive branch and smashing it over my head.

"She lives here! She'll know where's best to go!" I protested.

"... and my taxi driver is a stranger in town is he?"

"Oh, it's 'your' taxi driver now is it?" I retaliated, seizing the opportunity with glee. "Yes, let's go there... I'll be your wingman, and then when lover-boy show's up, I'll just piss-off shall I?"

I grabbed the vouchers from Cathy's hand.

"That's a great idea, why don't you do that?" muttered Cathy under her breath.

"What was that?" I asked, getting ready for proceedings to escalate, before losing the wind from my sails, "Oh... hold on, these vouchers are all for the same place... I guess that decides it then."

Before long, we were in a long queue of fellow backpackers all deliberating over the big dilemma of the day; choosing either rice or jacket potato to complement the chilli-con-carne.

"I'm going rice" I declared.

"Potato for me" replied Cathy, as the queue split into two, towards a mound of potatoes on the right, or to a steaming cauldron of rice on the left.

"How's it going mate... are you settling in?" emerged a voice from behind the steam.

"Oh... hello again. Yes, everything's good thanks" I replied politely to the cabbie-turned-food-server, before turning to see Cathy smiling sweetly as she got handed a plateful of food from the hostel receptionist.

"Truce?" I suggested as Cathy made her way back across the packed room towards me.

"Truce" she agreed. "Well... this is nice" she added sarcastically as we scanned the room, unsuccessfully, for somewhere to sit.

"It's like a bad night in the Student Union bar, isn't it?" I remarked.

"Yeah, I actually feel old" agreed Cathy.

"You are a bit old."

"Screw you! I'm 26!" Cathy scoffed, expertly balancing her plate with all the skill of an ex-waitress while also digging her elbow into my ribs.

"Well I feel about 85 in here. This music's shite too" I continued, bemoaning the cheesy 80's pop 'classics' that were being played far louder than they deserved. "Did we get on the wrong plane in Hong Kong and end up in Magaluf?"

"My taxi-boy didn't look quite so cool leading a 'Men At Work' sing-a-long did he?" conceded Cathy, as we fought our way across the dance floor and out into the balmy Queensland night.

"Yeah, and hostel-girl can stroll on too... playing all that Kylie rubbish!" I sniffed.

"Back to doing our own thing, tomorrow?" suggested Cathy.

"You mean your thing?" I replied.

"Yep, that's exactly what I mean."

Alf would have been proud of us the following morning, as we bundled into the back of a truck at the crack of dawn for a day exploring in the rainforest, further up the coast around Cape Tribulation. After the man-made wonders of China, Cape Tribulation let nature do the work. As we ventured deeper into the dense rainforest it felt as if we were entering a different world; the jungle canopy shielded us from the scorching sun, leaving a cool, dimly lit subterranean world beneath, with weird and wonderful animal noises echoing through the trees.

Our guide, possibly Crocodile Dundee's dad, was determined to get us as close to nature as possible and, by early afternoon, decided upon a spot beside a stream for lunch. I was mightily relieved to see cool-bags being unloaded from the truck full of sandwiches, salads and pasta as, following his many stories about living off of the land, I'd become increasingly concerned that we would be hunting for our lunch. Instead, 'Croc' was settling for brewing 'billy-tea' the traditional way, using water straight from the stream.

"I'm not drinking that tea" I whispered to Cathy, pointing out the pack of Coke cans that had also been brought down from the truck and placed in the stream to cool.

"Coke... the healthy option?" remarked Cathy, raising an eyebrow.

"This is the purest water in the world!" proclaimed Croc, who was by now showboating, swinging his battered kettle up and over his head in a fast windmill action. "I'm 75 and I've never been ill... and you know why? It's all down to this water!"

"He can make it, but I'm not drinking it" I continued, before seeing my resolve crumble as soon as Croc started to proudly hand out steaming hot mugs to his dozen clients. Cathy looked at me and shook her head with a giggle.

"It's actually okay, isn't it?" I said, relaxing after downing my cup, before swapping mugs with Cathy, who had just been holding her mug politely after taking a token sip. Cathy didn't like hot drinks, as I'd found out not long after we'd started seeing each other. I'd met her in the Student Union bar at 9am for 'a coffee'. I couldn't abide coffee, but at least had the decency to order a cup of tea; she, instead, had a pint of cider!

"You like it mate?" smiled Croc, having seen me finish off Cathy's mugful too, "here... you can finish the pot with me... this is the best bit of the brew!" he continued.

Cathy smiled and left me to listen to another Croc survival story as she followed the rest of the group, who had been lured towards the bright glow that pierced the dullness of the forest like the exit from a tunnel, leading out onto a deserted pristine beach to rival any we had lazed upon in Thailand. After helping Croc to clear up the picnic remnants, I headed into the trees to discretely answer the call-of-nature that had been triggered by three swift mugs of billy-tea and a can of Coke. Luckily, being in a jungle offers a wide range of trees to hide behind, but I still walked away from the lunch spot for a couple of minutes just to be on the safe side. As I trudged further into the wilds I noticed the birds and insects fall silent as I took position behind my chosen tree. I was sure there were plenty of curious eyes watching me from the vegetation, but was equally certain that they were quietening down because they were scared of me. As I started to relieve my bladder I had a Doctor Doolittle moment and told the gathered inhabitants of the jungle that I came in peace. With about two mugfuls of billy-tea still to go, I heard footsteps.

"Croc, is that you? I'm just behind this tree mate… I won't be a minute" I warned, but the footsteps continued to rustle towards me. Unfortunately, when you're 'in full flow' there isn't really anything you can do to speed up or abort the process. What you can do though, especially when confronted with a dragon that waddles out of the bushes in front of you, is scream and run whilst still urinating. It's not something I recommend, especially if there are other human beings nearby, but on certain occasions it might save your life. I didn't run at first; initially I jumped back, only to nearly knock myself senseless on another tree behind me. Then I waved a warning spray in the direction of the dragon. Regrettably, after an inquisitive lick of his dragon-lips with his dragon-tongue, the taste of my billy-tea laced urine only made the dragon more inquisitive. It was at this stage that I felt prompted to run, mid-urination, as fast as I could.

Thankfully, I had the presence of mind to zip myself up before breaking out into the bright sunshine of the sandy beach, where I proceeded to keep running, beyond everyone, only slowing to deposit my money and passport onto the beach before flinging myself fully clothed into the ocean, to cheers and applause from the rest of the group who, at most, were paddling ankle-deep.

"What on earth was that all about?" asked a bemused Cathy after my impromptu dip.

"I pissed all over my clothes… a dragon attacked me… a massive bloody dragon thing. Just keep walking."

I spoke like a bad ventriloquist through a fixed smile, taking high-fives from the others who'd loved my 'crazy' antics.

"What? What do you mean a dragon?"

"I pissed on my shorts… I pissed on my trainers… I even pissed on my t-shirt. I was taking a leak behind a tree and a fucking dinosaur just walked out from the bushes towards me… mid-piss."

"Do you mean a gecko, like the ones in Thailand?" giggled Cathy.

"Yes... exactly like that. I pissed all over myself when a 2-inch lizard jumped out of the bush." I spat sarcastically. "It was massive... as tall as a dog, but 6-foot-long, maybe longer... it was a frickin' monster! I'm not joking... stop laughing!"

"Did it breathe fire?" continued Cathy, again trying not to laugh.

"You can fuck right off! I knew I should have gone home for the football instead of coming here!"

I stropped off along the beach, hoping that the sun would dry my clothes before the long journey back to Cairns. I also hoped that the dragon would show itself back at the other end of the beach, hopefully causing someone an injury; preferably my less than sympathetic girlfriend. When I eventually started to calm down and turned back to dry the front of my clothes, my thoughts turned more to hoping that someone had had the presence of mind to save my passport from the incoming tide and the honesty not to steal my money.

With wallet and passport safely returned my spirits lifted slightly as I sat, rather damply, at the back of Croc's truck. After questioning from Cathy, he confirmed that, although he hadn't ever seen anything as big as described, there were some 'big buggers' lurking in the jungle. When he alarmingly asked if I'd confused a young crocodile for the dragon, I simply said "no, it wasn't a crocodile."

I knew full well that if I'd seen a crocodile making its way towards me, I'd have done more than just urinate.

28 – Match fit

A night huddled on the floor of a toilet cubicle wouldn't normally be considered an enjoyable experience, but steeled from my months of practice and with 'that' ill-fated night on the train in China still painfully fresh in my memory, even in my billy-tea-induced state I managed to find a few positives. Firstly, there wasn't a train conductor hitting me with a broom; secondly, I didn't have an audience (and any unfortunate soul who did venture into the hostel's communal bathrooms that night did whatever they had to do and got out as quickly as possible); and thirdly, the novelty of being sick into a proper western toilet bowl was strangely comforting. Despite these crumbs of comfort, Croc and Cape Tribulation's 'purest water in the world' were cursed every time I regurgitated another mouthful of his 'stream of eternal good health' back into the Cairns drainage system. My stomach finally started to give up the fight as the sun began to rise, by which time Cathy's patience had finally snapped and I was marched to the nearest medical centre.

"You refused to see a doctor in Thailand… you wouldn't see one in China. Well, this is Australia… get yourself sorted out!" she ranted, while impatiently waiting for me to catch her up at the entrance to the hospital.

"Alright, alright… give it a break will you? I've been up all night!" I pleaded. "I didn't want to have some dodgy foreign doctor sticking cocktail-sticks in me, did I?"

"You mean acupuncture? I really don't think they give you that for chucking-up and the shits!" Cathy replied despairingly.

Twenty minutes later I found myself on a bed in an examination room, waiting and staring at the ceiling.

'This is probably what all Wycombe's injured forwards will be doing right now too' I thought to myself, thinking about Andy Rammell, Jermaine McSporran, Sean Devine and Andy Baird, who would surely be doing anything possible to be fit for the Liverpool game.

"Are you okay?" asked Cathy, who was sitting on a stool in the corner of the room.

"Yeah… my tummy's a bit tender, but I don't feel sick anymore" I replied.

"No, I mean why are you rubbing your knee, have you hurt that too?"

"Erm, no... its fine... just a bit stiff from my night kneeling over the toilet I guess" I replied, quickly thinking of an excuse and remembering that I wasn't shaking off a knee injury, and I wouldn't be leading the line for the Wanderers on Sunday afternoon at Villa Park.

"Hi, you must be James... I'm Doctor Wong" said the young woman entering the room. "So, you've had an unsettled stomach for some time, right?" she added, before starting to prod aggressively at my belly.

"He's been ill for three months. Since the day we left England he's either been running for the toilet or being sick" informed Cathy.

"Wow, that's a long time. What medicine have you been prescribed so far?" asked the doctor, still stabbing at me with more force than her slight demeanour would suggest.

"He hasn't had anything, except for Imodium on long journeys... he wouldn't see any doctors in Thailand or China" continued Cathy, who seemed to be confused about who the doctor was addressing.

"China? Where did you go in China? I'm from Chengdu" Doctor Wong said proudly.

"We went there! We saw the pandas, didn't we James!" replied Cathy excitedly, but before I'd had a chance to answer, she'd moved on, giving the doctor a detailed account of our movements through her homeland.

"Most of the travellers I see here haven't visited China... I'm glad you liked it" she smiled warmly to Cathy, before turning to me and swapping her smile for a frown. "You... why have you not seen a doctor if you've been so ill?"

"Good question... I've been asking him that too" piped up Cathy again, smiling from behind the doctor's shoulder and eagerly awaiting my response.

"Oh, you know... I didn't want to trouble anybody... I don't like to make a fuss when I'm ill. With hindsight, I should have gone to see someone in China... it was silly of me, because I know the medical profession there is world-renowned... I would have got really good treatment in China, I'm sure."

I tried to keep my focus on Doctor Wong, but from the corner of my eye I could see Cathy shaking her head in disbelief.

"Well, I'm glad you came to see me today. Your stomach is still very unsettled. I'm going to give you some strong drugs which should kill the bacteria. When are you leaving town?"

"… In three or four days" answered Cathy, deciding to take over the conversation again. "Are there any potential side-effects? Should he avoid alcohol?" she continued, sounding disturbingly more hopeful than concerned.

"Not really" replied Doctor Wong, "… don't drink too much, but as for side-effects… I don't think you'll experience anything as bad as you've been enduring already. If your symptoms persist… promise me you'll seek medical attention, okay?"

"He will. He promises" replied Cathy, looking at me like the mother of a five-year-old.

By the time we left the hospital with my antibiotics, the early morning sunshine had given way to ominous grey clouds, adding, no doubt, to the previous night's hangovers in keeping the hundreds of other backpackers in town from surfacing.

"What are you going to do now… go back and sleep?" asked Cathy as I ripped open the first strip of tablets.

"No, I saw enough of the hostel walls last night… let's go for a wander about." I felt better already for having seen the doctor, despite the fact that the tablets had yet to reach my stomach. "I could do with getting cleaned up though. Actually, I'm going to get my head shaved too" I added, ruffling the inch of hair that had grown since leaving Thailand.

It was by now 10am, yet the streets of Cairns were still deserted. Back home, the High Street would have been buzzing by now on a Saturday, with people perusing the market stalls; and if the Blues were playing at home, Buz and the rest of the rabble would have been skulking about, waiting for the pubs to open. Not on this Saturday though. I was sure that everyone would be taking it easy ahead of 'Semi-Final Sunday', when at 4pm Wycombe Wanderers would be taking centre stage on prime time television, the game being beamed across the world to millions. The global audience would be familiar with Liverpool's international superstars;

Michael Owen, Robbie Fowler, Steven Gerrard, Sami Hyppia, Christian Ziege, Emile Heskey, Jamie Carragher and Marcus Babbel. But what on earth would they make of Cousins, Carroll, Ryan, Taylor, Brownie and Macca?

"This is ridiculous, how can Cairns have no barber shops?" I moaned having trudged up and down the town centre to no avail.

"I don't know, but it's starting to rain. Let's go back to the hair-salon on the corner. I'm sure they will do it… it was empty" suggested Cathy, looking up at the rainclouds with disdain.

"Welcome to Sheena's Hair and Nails… I'm Sheena… how can I help you today?"

"It's not for me actually… my boyfriend wants a trim, would that be okay?" replied Cathy.

"Sure… I think I could manage that. Up you come sir, make yourself comfortable. Now, would you like a coffee?" asked Sheena.

"Could I have a tea please?" I said, sounding surprised, having never been offered a drink in the barber shops of High Wycombe before.

"Sure Sweetie, I'll be back in a jiffy" answered Sheena, who'd dashed from sight before finishing her sentence.

"This is alright, isn't it?" I whispered, as Cathy became engrossed in a showbiz gossip magazine. She had read three more from cover to cover by the time Sheena declared "that's you my darling… gorgeous… doesn't he look gorgeous?"

"Gorgeous" agreed Cathy, with what I sensed was a hint of insincerity.

"Are you sure you wouldn't like a little something done? I have a free slot" said Sheena, looking back to Cathy, who was now looking beyond me, at her own reflection in the mirror.

"Go for it if you want Cathy, I feel better for the trim… it looks good doesn't it?" I said, as we conversed via the mirror.

She didn't need asking twice, jumping into the chair without hesitation. Within seconds it was as if I was no longer in the room. For the next five minutes not a word spoken made any sense to me until, with the consultation finally over, Sheena turned and said "I'd better get you another cup of tea Sweetie."

The fact that Sheena had taken over 30 minutes with me to achieve what an Outback sheep-shearer could have done in 30 seconds should have given me enough warning, but by my third cup of tea I knew we were here for the long-haul. Cathy's hair was washed, dried, painted and then covered in some elaborate foil head-dress before Sheena suggested I go for lunch. Having read my fill of showbiz magazines, I left the girls to it and ventured back to the hostel for a shower.

"Nice haircut, soldier!" smiled Blondie from reception with a salute as I arrived back.

"Thanks" I smiled, trying not to blush outwardly.

"Will I be seeing you for dinner across the road again tonight?" she continued.

"Maybe" I replied, once again falling under her spell, despite the fact that I'd vowed not to go back, on account of both the cheesy music and average food.

"Maybe? Are you playing hard to get with me?" she teased. "It's 'Grease' night tonight… I expect to see you on the dance floor… you hear me?"

She may have been gorgeous, and I may have been a sucker for her flirtation, but with one word she'd managed to let me slip from her seductive clutches. I'd lost count of the number of girls I'd fallen in love with across a dance floor, only for my illusions to be shattered by the DJ putting on a Take That song, or 'Sisters Are Doing It For Themselves' or, even worse, a Grease medley; in the process giving the object of my desire the opportunity to throw all credibility out of the window. I guess somebody with my distinct lack of pulling-power shouldn't have been such a music snob, but how a girl could transform in seconds from grooving coolly to The Charlatans or The Stone Roses into a wailing, hysterical wreck of a woman always extinguished my flames of passion. I guess that was just one of the many reasons that had invariably seen me skulking off home on my own at the end of a night.

"Yeah… maybe. I'll see what my girlfriend wants to do" I smiled, before heading for the showers.

An hour later, armed with a freshly purchased UK football newspaper, I returned to find Sheena and Cathy still deep in conversation, and Cathy's head still resembling a Christmas decoration. At least when my fourth cup of tea appeared, it was my turn to become lost in print.

Liverpool had beaten table-topping Manchester United at the weekend in the Premier League, with Steven Gerrard scoring a spectacular long range effort to send David Beckham, Ryan Giggs and their European Cup winning teammates home empty-handed.

'So much for my Stevie G injury prayers getting answered then' I cursed.

My concerns soon deepened as I scanned down the results page to see that Wycombe had been beaten again, this time by Wigan. Achievements in the FA Cup, and the herculean efforts required, had taken their toll on the Wanderers league form. With only one victory since the stunning performance against Leicester, the Chairboys had dropped into the lower-reaches of the table and were now looking nervously over their shoulders towards the relegation zone. Liverpool and Wycombe may have been heading in opposite directions in the league tables, but after their respective weekend games they'd both travelled to Spain. Lawrie Sanchez took his players away for a brief training camp in the sunshine, paid for by the unexpected additional revenues of the cup run; his Liverpool counterpart, Gerard Houllier took his team to do battle with the Catalan giants, Barcelona, in the first leg of the UEFA Cup Semi-Final.

"Bloody hell, Liverpool drew 0-0 with Barcelona" I gasped, reading the match report.

"What's that Sweetie? More tea?" asked Sheena.

"No, I'm fine thanks... just saying Liverpool got a draw over in Barcelona."

Sheena looked back as if I'd been speaking in Chinese. "That's nice" she smiled, before returning to her conversation with Cathy, who's freshly-coloured red hair was beginning to reappear from under the foils.

I started to feel sick again, but it wasn't due to any bug or Croc's billy-tea; it was the dawning realisation that the next day, my beloved Wycombe Wanderers would be exposed to the world against the most successful football club in England. Liverpool had already won the League Cup and were now favourites to progress to the UEFA Cup Final at Barcelona's expense, with the return leg providing home advantage at Anfield, a couple of days after facing Wycombe. In truth, barring a few small town dreamers from South Buckinghamshire, the entire footballing world expected them to humiliate the Chairboys, just as they had embarrassed Wycombe's fellow third tier side, Stoke City, en route to winning the League Cup. Despite Stoke playing at home, Liverpool had shown no mercy and thrashed their hosts 8-0. The thought of that happening to my heroes didn't bear thinking about. I took the second dose of my tablets just in case the sudden onset of pre-match nerves pushed my delicate stomach over the edge.

"Right my lovelies, that's you both ready to razzle-dazzle!"

Sheena, looking very pleased with her work, unveiled a stunning looking Cathy.

"What do you think?" asked Cathy, appearing equally delighted with her new look.

"Yeah, you look alright" I replied, trying to look cool, although my pounding heart sent a tell-tale flush to my cheeks.

My amorous urges subsided as abruptly as they'd arisen, though, when Sheena said "Right my Sweetie... that will be 155 dollars please... 30 for you and 125 for the pretty little lady."

"I'm really sorry" pleaded Cathy, as we waved back to Sheena through the window from the street. "I had no idea it would be so expensive."

"It's okay... you seriously look great" I replied, before continuing with a more agitated outburst as we turned the corner... "Oh, for fuck's sake!"

"What? You just said it was okay... literally two seconds ago!"

"Look. Look at that!" I replied, pointing down the street. We had entered what was obviously 'The Barbers Quarter' of Cairns; every second building was adorned by a red and white barber's pole, with signs offering 'cuts from five bucks'.

Cathy just laughed and sheepishly apologised again.

"That settles it... we can't spend any more money today... back to the room to mess your hair up instead!" I declared hopefully, remembering that Cathy 'never' stayed on the dance floor when the Grease mega-mixes came on to ruin a night.

A lazy afternoon followed in preparation for what promised to be a day to remember; a visit to the Great Barrier Reef followed by the FA Cup Semi-Final. With the sun heading out of sight in Australia and up towards the northern hemisphere, our siestas drifted into a deeper slumber, and after the previous sleepless night's date with the toilet bowl, I was soon dreaming of Liverpool losing to Wycombe Wanderers. Back home, the town was waking up to a weekend of FA Cup fever. Saturday was football day in Wycombe; we escaped the constant rescheduling to Sunday afternoons and Monday evenings that the Liverpool fans had to endure to suit the television networks. The traditional time of 3pm on a Saturday was what our body-clocks were geared towards and, with this in mind, I'd been foolish in assuming the Roobarbs would be taking it easy in preparation for Sunday's clash. As per every 'home game Saturday', Buz, accompanied by Roger, stood at the pub's door, peering in, impatiently awaiting the sound of the locks unlatching.

"You know they ain't playing today don't you?" grumbled Barry, the most miserable landlord in the world.

"I know... but it feels like Christmas Eve... and what do we do on Christmas Eve?" replied Buz, rubbing his hands with excitement as he spoke.

"You come in here and make idiots of yourselves. You boys having the usual?" answered Barry.

"Oi Oi! Get me one in too Buz!" cheered Smudge while slapping Buz heartily on the back. "Have you been down the High Street today? It's mental... geezers selling all sorts of shit for the match... one guy's even flogging 'High Wycombe Wanderers' scarves!"

Within half an hour, Barry was on the phone calling for reinforcements as a couple of taxis pulled up outside, carrying Teddy, Little-Wanker, Flipper, Adam, John and Jimbo.

"Greetings landlord... we have travelled long and far from the beautiful villages of the west... three ciders, two Guinness and a lager-top, please" said Jimbo.

"You live in Lane End; it's a shit-hole" grunted Barry.

"Cheer up Barry... it's like Christmas Eve! Think of all the money you're making!" reasoned Flipper, still failing to raise a smile.

"Oi Teddy, if this is Christmas Eve let's hope Santa brings you a belt tomorrow for those trousers" teased Jimbo.

"What do you mean? I don't need a belt, these Farrah's fit me like a glove" protested Teddy, whilst sucking his beer-belly in to take an admiring glance down towards his faithful slacks.

"Get a belt man! The world doesn't need a repeat performance of you standing there in your Y-fronts on telly!" added Jimbo.

By noon Tony, Beany, Nicko, Ian, Bob, Lee and Oggy had all appeared to join the festivities, thankfully at the same time as help arrived for the beleaguered landlord, who soon raised his first smile of the day when Mike arrived, proudly showing off the souvenir scarves he'd bought for his kids, Claire, Jake and Ben.

"What's so funny?" asked a confused Mike, unnerved at seeing Barry smile.

"How much did you pay for them then?" sniggered Barry.

"Three for six quid... that's a bargain, the kids will be well chuffed" replied Mike.

"Yeah, that is a bargain... they've even thrown in the 'High' in front of 'Wycombe Wanderers' for free!" pointed out Barry, gleefully roaring with laughter at Mike's misfortune.

"Ah, sod it... Jake's always asking why we aren't called High Wycombe Wanderers anyway... I think they look pretty cool!" retorted Mike after a closer inspection, before waving the scarves above his head and dancing happily to the jukebox. This show of defiance was enough to wipe the brief smile from Barry's face.

"Semi-Final disco!" proclaimed Jason with his arms raised, bouncing into the pub and immediately joining Mike on the impromptu dance floor as The Stone Roses 'This Is The One' boomed around our little L-shaped pub.

"Where's the other one then... the student?" sniffed Barry upon serving Jason.

"He's still away Baz... Australia. He's here in spirit though, ain't he boys?" replied Jason, raising his glass in salute to his absent pal, who had not only committed the ultimate crime of ditching his best friend for a girl, but had then had the audacity to bugger off around the world with her for six months; during the football season too.

"Bloody student tosser. How did he afford that then?" moaned Barry.

As Les, Sharon and Jackie arrived to more cheers from the increasingly jovial crowd, Barry shook his head before disappearing to the shops to procure the cheapest bread and sandwich fillings he could find, eager to make more money from his beloved clientele.

"Buz... me and you are going to Villa Park tomorrow, to see the Wanderers play Liverpool in the FA Cup Semi-Final" said Roger matter-of-factly, smiling at the absurdity of his words.

Both Pisser and Billy Connolly pondered this statement for a moment before raising their glasses as Buz replied... "Come on the High Wycombe Wanderers! Cheers!"

Away from the hysteria that was beginning to overflow in High Wycombe, Laurie Sanchez and his team were cocooned in a hotel on the outskirts of Birmingham, preparing for one final night's rest before taking on their biggest test yet. The players could repeatedly quote the mantra to the world's press that this was 'just another game', but it wasn't just another game. Wycombe Wanderers couldn't afford overnight stays in plush hotels for a game just 100 miles from home. On 'just another' Saturday, half of the team normally got picked up at a motorway service station en route to the match, to save them the expense of petrol money. A 'normal' match in the Midlands against Walsall, Kettering Town, Kidderminster Harriers or Bromsgrove Rovers had never been preceded by a four day break to Spain either. Also, a 'normal' game didn't see the opposition's centre-forward earning more money in just one season than the entire Wycombe Wanderers team could realistically hope to earn in their collective footballing careers. No; this was not 'just another game'.

As the Roobarbs staggered home having increased their alcohol levels, and the Wanderers attempted to sleep as their adrenalin levels rose, the sporting world prepared to watch the football match that wasn't ever supposed to happen. Millions around the world would be discovering that the English FA Cup wasn't a competition that consisted of just a dozen or so Premier League teams, the teams that flooded into their living rooms each week.

'... Wycombe who?'

'... They play in which division?'

'... So Wycombe have played nine games to get this far... but Liverpool only four?'

Wycombe Wanderers weren't supposed to still be here but, in ignoring the script, the global media now had a new story; a story about the hundreds of football teams the length and breadth of England who were somehow surviving in the deep, dark footballing ocean, far below the colourful reef and crystal clear waters that played host to the other Semi-Finalists; Liverpool, Arsenal and Tottenham Hotspur; the teams whose instantly recognisable shirts were the emblems of global brands, worn by millions of football fans across the planet. Tomorrow, the Chairboys, who normally just represented a little furniture making town in Buckinghamshire, were representing the hopes and dreams of all the teams from all the small towns and villages who'd set out on the FA Cup adventure, months before Liverpool had joined the tournament at its ninth stage. The morning would herald the thirteenth and penultimate round in the world's oldest knock-out tournament; and Wycombe Wanderers would be there.

29 – Christmas Eve, in April

In my 25 years of daydreaming about football, I'd never thought I'd see the day that Wycombe Wanderers were playing in the FA Cup Semi-Final. And in my 15 years of daydreaming about lazing on the deck of a speedboat as it zipped across the ocean, surrounded by bikini-clad women; well, I hadn't held out much hope of that becoming a reality either. And so began one of the most memorable days of my life.

"How exciting is this!" squealed Cathy, as our boat picked up speed upon leaving the sun drenched marina in Cairns, destined for the Great Barrier Reef.

"It's pretty exciting" I conceded.

"Have you ever imagined anything like this?"

As she spoke, the boat bounced off the first of many waves, causing numerous wardrobe malfunctions across the deck.

"I have imagined this exact scene on many occasions" I nodded agreeably, admiring the view, along with every other male on board.

"I dived a bit in Thailand the first time I went there, but I've always wanted to see the Barrier Reef... I'm so excited!" continued Cathy, rubbing her hands together; just as Buz did when stood outside a pub at opening time.

"It's amazing... it's really amazing! I mean, it's going to be really amazing" I agreed, regretting that I didn't have sunglasses to hide behind.

"Do you think you'll be okay with the snorkelling?"

"Yeah, how hard can it be? There were little kids doing it back in Kata" I replied. "Cathy, can I borrow your sunglasses?"

The boat continued to bounce for another two hours; everything bounced for another two hours; providing a very enjoyable distraction from my pre-match nerves. Eventually, more boats came into view on the horizon, signalling that we were nearing our destination. I'm sure it was just an oversight on the tour operator's part, but the disclaimer 'against injury or death' forms didn't get distributed until our outward journey to the reef was complete. Nobody, apart from me, seemed to be bothering to read what the form said.

"Do you need a pen?" asked a bikini-clad girl, leaning across the table towards me and causing all thoughts of the small print to disappear from my mind.

"I wasn't looking at anything" I replied guiltily.

"What?" she said, looking confused.

"What? Nothing... I didn't say anything" I stammered.

"Do you need a pen... for the form?" she asked again.

"Oh... a pen! Yes, thank you" I blushed.

"Are you okay?" asked Cathy, who was already busy completing her form, "you look a bit flushed."

"I'm fine... I've got us a pen."

"Erm, well done" she added sarcastically. "Fill it in then... it's just name and home address, and tick the box... nothing too difficult."

In three months, I'd barely put pen to paper; now, with form-filling distractions leaning over all around me, I was struggling to remember how to write. Thankfully, a guy came and sat opposite, bringing me to my senses.

"Are you from High Wycombe?" he asked.

Wow, how did he know that? I hadn't even written my name yet, let alone my address. I didn't recognise him from home and my Wanderers shirt was drying back at the hostel in preparation for the big match. How did he know I was from Wycombe?

"Yes, well, I just live there... my boyfriend is a local though" replied Cathy.

"I saw your address on the form... we live in Wycombe too!" he replied, introducing his girlfriend to Cathy, and then to me. Thankfully, the girl had a t-shirt on, as by now I'd completely lost control of where my eyes gazed.

"Are you gutted about missing the game?" I immediately blurted.

"The game?" he replied, looking confused.

"The game… the Liverpool game is tonight" I continued.

"Oh, that… no, to be honest, I'm not interested in football. We were glad to get away from all the fuss, weren't we?" His girlfriend nodded her agreement. "It's all the town's been talking about. Should all be over by the time we get home though… thank god!"

"So! How long are you two here for? Are you just on holiday, or on a longer trip?" butted in Cathy, not giving me an opportunity to challenge this ridiculous statement, before ushering me away to get kitted out with flippers and a snorkel.

"Have you done this before mate?" asked the guy distributing equipment.

"No, first time" I replied grumpily, still annoyed at the Wycombe halfwit's attitude.

"Right… it's pretty easy. Stick this in your gob. Breathe in through your mouth, out through your nose. If you get some water in your mouth, blow back out of the tube, hard… okay?"

"Yep, in through the mouth, out through the nose" I mumbled, having already fitted the snorkel, but distracted as I tried to understand how anyone from Wycombe could possibly be looking forward to the FA Cup run being over. 'It'll be over in a month's time when we win the bloody Final… you prick' I thought to myself.

"Spot on… you've got it, mate!"

'Got what?' I wondered, as I smiled back at snorkel-man.

The gently chopping waves, that had provided so much entertainment on the journey out to the reef, suddenly didn't look quite so small now that I was standing on the diving platform between the boat and the ocean. All around me people were excitedly jumping into the sea and setting off, seemingly effortlessly, to explore the natural beauty on show just below the surface. I followed suit, but before my head had joined my feet in the water I came to the awful realisation that I didn't actually have a clue what I was doing. Unfortunately, that didn't give me much time to work it out, and so I instinctively took a gulp of air before disappearing through a cloud of bubbles, down into the underwater wonderland. I stayed submerged for at least two seconds before propelling back to the surface, frantically grabbing for the nearest part of the boat, which I then clung to for dear life as I pondered my next panic-stricken move. Ten minutes later I still couldn't work out what that next move was going to be. Each time I tried to push away from the boat's hull, I was repelled back, having been 'battered' by the next wave that gently lapped up against the boat's side.

"What are you doing back here?" asked Cathy, returning from her first successful foray into the reef. "It's amazing down there."

"I can't move... seriously... I'm exhausted... every time I try to swim out, the waves push me back against the boat."

"What waves?" asked Cathy, not making me feel any better about my predicament. "Come on, hold my hand" she added, saying possibly the only sentence less embarrassing than 'there, there... don't cry'.

Within three kicks of my flippers, I was again coughing up mouthfuls of salty water which burnt my throat and nose. I flapped around desperately, doing anything I could to keep my face above the surface.

"What on earth are you doing?"

"I'm drowning! The snorkel must be broken, the waves keep coming down the tube" I moaned, gripping Cathy's shoulders tightly.

"Ouch... get off!" she shouted, whilst giving me an instinctive knee between my legs to stop me dragging her down with me. This instantly succeeded in loosening my grip, but also sent me spiralling back under the water for another bellyful of the ocean.

"Are you okay mate?" asked snorkel-man, as he pulled me up to the surface. Cathy looked on, effortlessly treading water.

The panic in my eyes and the snot dripping from my nose spoke a thousand words; he didn't wait for my reply before darting back to the platform like a dolphin, returning moments later with a rubber ring.

"Dude, hold onto this and forget about everything except the 'in through the mouth, out through the nose', okay?"

I didn't reply, instead using all my energy to stop myself from crying.

"Keep your face down and then the snorkel will point up... you keep looking up and breathing, so the pipe tips back into the water behind you... you're using the tube as a giant straw... if you swallow much more, the bloody boat will get beached on the reef!" he laughed, trying to lighten my mood. It didn't help, and neither did Cathy's giggling.

Thankfully, with no more than breathing to concentrate on, I eventually managed to see the beautiful coral reef and its array of inhabitants, with snorkel-man diving below and pulling me along for a personal guided tour.

"Thank you so much, that was amazing" said Cathy, as the sickeningly muscular snorkel-man helped me back onto the boat. "He's been really sick... and he's not eaten for three days... it's left him feeling really weak" she continued, offering both excuses and apologies for my failings as an underwater explorer and general all round Adonis.

"No worries, swimming isn't everyone's thing... get up on deck for some food and a beer mate... that will get you back on track!" he replied, slapping me on the back and nearly sending my exhausted frame tumbling back into the sea.

I nodded my appreciation, before turning to Cathy and whispering... "Seriously... could you flirt any harder?"

"Oh, excuse me Mister Lets-Spend-The-Morning-Staring-Down-Bikini-Tops! I should have left you out there to drown, you cheeky sod!"

"What bikini tops? You're crazy... I was thinking about the football all morning, actually" I protested, rather feebly.

"Yeah, right" replied Cathy, shaking her head witheringly. "Are you coming to get some food and a beer then?"

"No, I'm too knackered. I'll wait until we get back onto dry land I think" I replied forlornly. "Actually, bring me back a beer, just in case... and maybe a slice of pizza or two?"

I was relieved to see the Australian coastline coming back into view later that afternoon and, recalling my 'shark, possibly rope' attack back in Thailand, consoled myself with the fact that I was born and bred in High Wycombe; just about as far from the sea as it was possible to get in England. I concluded that I just wasn't designed for sea survival; it wasn't my natural habitat.

At around the same time back in that natural habitat, groggy, hungover heads were starting to stir and, before long, the Roobarbs were commencing their various journeys to Villa Park. Normally, a couple of dozen travelling Wanderers supporters would be recognisable by the tell-tale clinking of beer cans hidden in carrier bags but, as Buz and the others started to congregate in the greasy-spoon café across the street from the railway station, thousands of excited Wycombians were already being marshalled into orderly queues around the station car park and back down the hill into town.

"God, I feel like shit" moaned Tony, his head resting on the table beneath his lucky FA Cup hat.

"Me too… I think we overdid it last night" agreed Buz.

"Last night? I think the damage was done at lunchtime!" laughed Flipper, before elbowing Tony off the table as the age old full-English breakfast hangover remedy was delivered from the kitchen.

"Tuck in boys, it's the diet of champions… soon to be FA Cup champions!" cheered Jason optimistically, as the Roobarbs started the recovery process in style by sneakily opening two bottles of champagne under the table; the perfect accompaniment to sausage, bacon, eggs, mushrooms, hash brown, chips, beans, black pudding, fried tomato and a tower of buttered toast.

On the other side of the valley, over a hundred coaches were labouring their way up the hill from Adams Park towards the motorway, transporting another 6,000 expectant supporters to Birmingham. The M40 was a noisy sea of blue as scarves and flags flew from car windows and horns tooted the entire way. Laura and Abby lost count of the number of coaches they waved to as their Dad raced up the motorway to meet the train travelling Roobarbs. My mum wasn't faring much better than Bob's kids on the coach-count, sitting in the back of Big Bri's Land Rover which, back in the chill of winter, had set me on my way to distant lands, or at least as far as Heathrow Airport. In all, the exodus from High Wycombe by coach, car and train neared 20,000. Thousands more, who had failed to get tickets, were left to while away the hours in the eerily deserted town until, along with football fans from around the globe, it was time to settle down in front of their televisions to see if Wycombe Wanderers could do the impossible and cause the biggest upset in footballing history.

In Cairns, I was grateful to set foot back on firm ground; the weather had taken a turn for the worse on the return journey, meaning that our stomachs were getting severely tested, and even more distressingly, all bikinis had been covered by extra layers for warmth. Equally grateful to set foot on firm ground were the hungover Roobarbs at Birmingham New Street station, who'd been crammed into a carriage more reminiscent of a midweek rush hour train heading into London, rather than a Sunday morning Express heading away from the capital.

"Come on Cathy... let's head back to the hostel. Quick showers, then something to eat... by then it'll be time for Spurs v Arsenal" I suggested. Decision making was coming more naturally now I was back on terra firma and focussing on football, as opposed to when floundering in the Coral Sea.

"Right, let's find a pub in the city centre for the Spurs v Arsenal game... get in there early, get a table, and make a base. That way, folk can nip out for food if they want, and the others who are driving up will know where to aim for" signalled Buz in Birmingham, who was also finding his decision making senses sharpened by the fact that it was very nearly pub opening time.

"Look, this one's showing the football" said Cathy, pointing to the chalk board outside an impressive old colonial style building on the corner of the street, with a veranda on the first floor looking down onto the increasingly deserted Cairns evening as darkness descended.

'FOOTBALL AT THE FIRKIN... SPURS v ARSENAL... 10.30pm KICK OFF'

"The pub's called the Firkin, like the one in Wycombe!" I smiled. "That's a good omen, surely?"

We walked into the vast, yet empty, bar to be greeted by a barman. "Evening, how's it going? Everyone's upstairs ready for the footy... I'll get your drinks down here though, as its getting pretty crowded up there. What will it be? I've got dozens of English Ales on tap."

"A pint of cider please" responded Cathy eagerly.

"I'll have a pint of Fosters mate" I added.

"Fosters? We've gone to the hassle of getting all this British stuff in and you want a Fosters?" laughed the barman.

"Yeah, that's pretty much what I drink most of the time back home... much to the distain of my 'real ale' buddies!"

"No worries mate! Enjoy the game" he replied, before returning to cleaning the bar top and stacking stools onto tables.

"I hope it's a bit livelier up there" Cathy whispered as we made our way to the staircase.

Her hopes were realised as we appeared into view at the top of the stairs, to be greeted with a roar that wouldn't have sounded out of place on the terraces. At least 100 folk were gathered, most sporting Arsenal and Tottenham shirts, but with a few Liverpool colours thrown in; all were facing us and cheering my Wycombe Wanderers top. Our new found novelty soon wore off, though, as all eyes returned to the screen on the wall as a real terrace roar announced the arrival of North London's bitter rivals, Arsenal and Tottenham Hotspur, onto the Old Trafford pitch in Manchester.

"Are these seats free?" inquired Cathy, who was highly skilled at finding somewhere to sit in even the busiest of bars.

"Sure Jenny-love, help yourself" replied a rather dishevelled looking man who was sipping slowly on his beer and casually leaning back against the wall, watching the excitement building in the room. "You pommies love yer football, don't ya?" he smiled, revealing a missing tooth or three.

"Yeah, it's a big night tonight... the London derby for this lot..." I said gesturing towards the lilywhite shirts of the Spurs fans and the red and white Arsenal tops, which had started to disperse to separate tables as instinctive tribalism set in with kick-off imminent. "... and then it's the big one; Liverpool against my team, Wycombe Wanderers."

"It's gonna be a late night for you then, Jenny. Do you like the football too? I'm Terry by the way... nice to make your acquaintance."

"I'm Cathy, this is my boyfriend James."

"Good to know ya, James... take a seat brother" said Terry, shaking my hand and revealing an array of crude and occasionally misspelt tattoos.

"Watch my beer please Jenny-love, I need to powder my nose" announced Terry, slowly rising from his chair and staggering off in the direction of the toilets, but not before stopping to make conversation with seemingly everyone that he passed en route.

"He seems friendly" said Cathy.

"He seems like a complete fruit-loop! Did you see his tattoo? 'Born a Losser'... what's a bloody 'losser'? There's a certain irony in a tattoo like that" I replied. "And what's with all this 'Jenny' stuff?"

"Oh he's fine... he's probably just had a few too many in the sun. Besides, these were the only seats in the house. He'll probably go in a minute... he's nearly finished his drink, look."

"Yeah, I'm sure he's great company... it was just a coincidence that these were the only spare seats was it?" I asked.

"Shush, he's coming back" hissed Cathy.

"Here you go... a pint of cider for Jenny... I do love a girl who drinks pints... and a lager for James the Wanderer. Cheers... to new friends from the other side of the world" toasted Terry.

"Cheers!" replied Cathy.

"Cheers Terry, but her names Cathy, not Jenny" I politely tried to point out.

"Did I call you Jenny? I'm sorry. My mother's name was Jenny" he replied, holding out his right fist to display the letters 'J-E-N-N' etched into his knuckles, before twisting his hand over to display a 'Y' on his thumb.

"Ah, that's nice" replied Cathy.

"Then my first wife, god rest her soul..." he continued, raising his left fist.

"She was called Jenny too?" I asked, reading the duplicate tribute on his other hand. Terry just nodded.

"Well, here's to them both" I added, raising my glass.

"Thanks James, I appreciate that" nodded Terry. "My second wife was called Jenny too, but she wasn't a nice woman" he continued, looking increasingly emotional.

Cathy and I exchanged a 'quick, think of an exit strategy' glance just before a roar broke the awkward silence. The white-shirted half of the room was on its feet punching the air, while the reds sat back dejectedly.

"Spurs have scored!" I stated, grasping the opportunity to change the subject.

"I really loved Jenny" mumbled Terry into his pint, oblivious to the excitement unfolding around him.

"Which one?" I mouthed silently to Cathy, who concealed a nervous giggle behind a forced cough.

Arsenal equalised before half-time, leaving honours even as everyone headed to the bar to sooth their throats in preparation for the second half onslaught. Cathy headed for the ladies and then out onto the veranda for a smoke, before joining the queue at the bar, leaving me to make polite conversation with our new pal Terry.

"So, are you from Cairns then, Terry?"

"No, I'm just passing through. I follow the sun... I'll head south in a few weeks when it gets warmer down there, then back inland."

"What do you do for a living?"

"This and that... seasonal work in the Outback mainly."

"What's it like in the Outback? We don't have time to explore the rest of the country; we're just sticking to the east coast."

"It's a harsh, hard place. It's not a place for people. Bad things happen out there" he muttered. All the while, Terry stared into his glass, no doubt thinking about one Jenny or another as I struggled to make conversation.

"Hi boys, having a nice chat?" smiled Cathy returning with another round of drinks.

"You're some girl Jenny, you really are" said Terry, looking up appreciatively and clutching Cathy's hand. "James... you look after Jenny, she's one in a million, y'hear me?"

"I hear you Terry, I will" I replied. "Listen, it's been great talking to you, but we're going to move a bit closer to the screen for the second half, okay?" I added, before extending my hand for Terry to shake, mainly in a bid to get him to unclasp his grip on Cathy.

"Spurs table or Arsenal table?" asked Cathy as we made a break for it.

"Spurs... they're the underdogs" I replied.

Attention was returning to television screens across the globe.

"Arsenal completely bossed that half, but Spurs are still in it... I reckon we could take Spurs in the final, but Thierry Henry? We'd struggle to contain him if it's Arsenal who go through" considered Smudger, having watched the first half, along with the rest of the Roobarbs in a relatively subdued mood in The Walkabout, an Australian themed bar in Birmingham city centre. 'The morning after the night before' had indeed taken the full morning to shake off, and Jason's ill-judged champagne breakfast idea hadn't helped to ease the hangovers, making for an uncomfortable journey north. Now, midway through the first Semi-Final, and with more of our friends finding Buz's basecamp, the atmosphere was steadily becoming more upbeat as excitement set in and the beers began to flow more freely.

"Oi, Buz! Get me another one of those Victoria Bitters... I bet that's what Jamesy will be on right now over there" shouted Jason, as Buz began to curse his plan to get everybody together in one pub. The round of drinks he'd been sent up to get a good ten minutes earlier had already doubled, as the group grew larger by the minute.

"He won't be on the VB!" boomed Roger. "He only drinks pissy lager. Fosters; he'll be on the Fosters."

"That's if he isn't still being sick!" chimed in Pat.

"He wouldn't have been the only one being sick this morning though would he?" remarked Flipper, prompting guilty raised hands from Oggy, Tony and Adam.

"Just pre-match nerves boys, wasn't it?" laughed Nicko.

"I'll tell you what though..." began Ian.

"No, don't tell me... being ill will have got him loads of shagging?" interrupted Lee.

"Well, yeah... I remember this one time when I was really sick in Morocco, there were these two Swedish girls who looked after me, and..."

"Hi Bob! Hi girls!" shouted Sharon, interrupting Ian again, as Jackie nudged him... "Shut it Ian, the kids are here now!"

"Ian, what happened with the Swedish girls?" whispered Smudger, before Pat and Roger joined them in a clandestine huddle to hear the rest of Ian's latest travel anecdote.

"It's the FA Cup Semi-Final... why are we in an Aussie fun-pub?" asked Bob, looking around at the surf boards, boomerangs and cricket paraphernalia hanging from the ceiling.

Back in our English themed pub in Cairns, we were welcomed into the Tottenham fold with open arms, and the second half was enjoyed in the safety of numbers, although I glanced back a few times and noticed Terry had disappeared. He'd been fine, if a little intense, but I was pretty sure I'd be seeing his mug shot on a 'Wanted' poster somewhere along the coast during the next 2,000 miles of our journey. As the referee drew the first Semi-Final to a conclusion, it was the Arsenal fans who celebrated reaching the final, having scored a late winner to take the game 2-1. In fairness, Arsenal had hammered Spurs, so there were few complaints from around the table, although everyone cursed the early loss of Tottenham's captain, Sol Campbell, after only half an hour. The Arsenal fans pointed out that he was useless anyway, and that his absence had probably only made Spurs stronger. Their general consensus was that he wouldn't make the reserve team if he ever played for Arsenal, although this was purely hypothetical, as they wouldn't want him anyway.

Anyone who hadn't been watching the football had by now disappeared and, after emptying their glasses, quite a few of the Spurs and Arsenal fans left too, but not before wishing my team luck for the second game. Everyone loves an underdog, and anybody watching the game around the world who didn't support Liverpool would be cheering on Wycombe this afternoon, or this morning, as it now was in Cairns; 1 o'clock on Monday morning to be precise.

"No wonder the town seems quiet" remarked Cathy returning from another smoking break, "it doesn't feel like one in the morning though does it... not with the game coming up."

"Here you go, look!" cried the remaining dozen or so football fans, as the screen moved from Manchester down to Birmingham; there was Villa Park, and there were Wycombe Wanderers warming up!

"That's time at the bar please gentlemen... time at the bar!" yelled the barman, causing consternation with all and sending a dagger through my heart.

"What! The games about to start!" screamed Cathy, switching instantly into full fighting mode after four pints of cider.

"You can't turn his game off... he's from Wycombe!" protested the Spurs and Arsenal fans.

As everyone remonstrated around me I sat silently, in a bubble, with eyes glued to the screen. Thousands of supporters were taking to their seats and, out on the pitch, there were the players going through their warm up routines. The camera was trained on the Wycombe players, just 30 minutes away from the biggest game of their lives. There was Steve Brown, kicking a ball with his son Maxwell in his arms and, further along the pitch, Lawrie Sanchez, resplendent in his club blazer, was casually passing a ball on the Villa Park turf with his son, Jack. In the background there was a blur of red which soon came sharply into focus as the camera zoomed in on Robbie Fowler and Michael Owen, the most fearsome strike-partnership in England, going through their stretching routines each with a personal trainer by their side. This was really about to happen.

"Listen you lot, its bloody 1 o'clock in the morning! You can have one more drink, while I clean up, but then that's it. There's a sports bar just down the street... that'll still be open."

"Did you hear that mate? We've got you a stay of execution. One of the Arsenal boys is going down to check out this sports bar place to see if the guy's telling the truth" said one of the Spurs fans, looking almost as angry as Cathy.

"Don't you worry yourself Jenny-love, I'll sort this out" came a voice from the veranda. Terry was back.

"Oh, hello Terry, we thought you'd left" said Cathy.

"I just had some business to attend to" replied Terry; causing raised eyebrows from the rest of us, who were thankfully facing away from him, towards the screen.

"Isn't your girlfriend called Cathy?" whispered an Arsenal fan.

At Villa Park, Smudger wasn't happy either. "This is ridiculous, why can't we all sit together?" he moaned.

"Because you weren't organised enough to arrange tickets together" answered Abby sweetly.

"Our mummy says you lot couldn't organise a drink-up in a brewery" added Laura.

"A drink-up? Is that what she called it?" laughed Smudger.

"We told her that you could organise it though Smudger, because you always ring the taxi to get us from the pub to Adams Park" said Abby.

"… And because you are really good at drinking, and drink comes from a brewery… did you know that, Smudger?" asked Laura.

"I did know that. Thanks for your support though girls!" said Smudger blushing. "Did your mum say anything else?" he added, grinning across the little girls' heads to Bob.

"Yes… that we weren't allowed to repeat any words that you say during the match" said Abby.

"She said you wouldn't be able to stop yourself from saying some bad words" explained Abby. "Come on Smudger, get your card ready. It's nearly time!"

"What are we supposed to do with these then?"

"Smudger! How many times do we have to tell you? Just hold it up when the Wycombe boys come out!" chorused both girls.

Inside the ground, the anticipation was reaching fever pitch. Buz gulped as the Liverpool anthem 'You'll Never Walk Alone' began to echo from the red half of the stadium. Giant banners paying homage to idols of Liverpool's past swept across the terraces, while others, commemorating the four times that Liverpool had been crowned Champions of Europe and their 18 English titles just emphasised the task in hand.

"We should have knocked one up showing our 24 Berks and Bucks Cup wins" suggested Tony, nervously, as Wycombe banners too began to unfurl.

"Look at that one, '*DAVEY CARROLL IS NOT THE MESSIAH - HE'S A VERY NAUGHTY BOY*'… brilliant!" giggled Buz.

In the guise of Robbie Fowler, Liverpool might have 'God' in their line up, but at least Wycombe had his son in the form of Davey 'Jesus' Carroll, primed and ready to spring a miracle from the substitutes bench if required, like his goal against Wimbledon in the 5th Round replay. Despite appearing almost 600 times for the Blues, Davey had never witnessed anything like this.

"That's the best one… '*WYCOMBE TIL I DIE 1884*'… 117 years… and to think that after all that time, this is our biggest game ever" said Tony.

"Look down there, James' mum has made one!" pointed out Jason, "'*JAMES AND CATHY IN OZ – WATCHING BLUES FOR YOU*'… I wonder if he's seen it on the telly?"

"Have you seen your mum and dad yet?" asked Cathy, pulling up a seat next to me. "James… earth to James… James, are you receiving me?"

"Sorry, I was engrossed" I replied, and evidently looking pained to be so far from the action unfolding on the screen.

"Listen, this trip was a once in a lifetime opportunity. No job, no mortgage, no kids… remember? If you ever get another redundancy when you're a bit older, you probably will have responsibilities… they'll get another shot at the FA Cup next year, and the year after that. No regrets… yeah?"

"Yeah, no regrets" I smiled, choking back tears. I wasn't sure if my eyes were welling up because I wasn't there, or just because my beloved Wycombe Wanderers were there; standing shoulder to shoulder in the tunnel next to one of the most successful football teams in the world.

"I've had a little chat with the barman and there's no rush to leave… and these are on the house" announced Terry, casually placing a tray holding a dozen pints on the table for the remaining late-night football fans. "That one on the end is your cider Jenny-love."

30 – Liverpool

Mick and Kris sorting holiday photos back home in Wisconsin; Hayley and the NYU women's soccer squad eating brunch in New York; Alf, Forest, Betty and Elsa drinking beer in China; the beach boys, the owner of the indie bar and Cathy's girlfriends in the football pub in Thailand; Scouse John eating a Pot Noodle on a bunk bed in a construction site dormitory beside the M25; and Sally, on her sofa with Vonnie and their triplet sons in a very quiet High Wycombe, all stared at their televisions as the teams entered the arena to a cacophony of noise and colour.

Whereas Liverpool were embarking on their twenty-first FA Cup Semi-Final, the Wanderers were venturing yet further into unchartered territory; an adventure that had now captured the imagination of the sporting world. As the Blues approached the enormous Holte End, the entire terrace held aloft cards, transforming the sea of 13,000 faces that rose towards the rainclouds hovering above into a giant quartered Wanderers shirt. If ever a twelfth man was required, it was today, with Liverpool's squad of international superstars having been assembled for £50,000,000 and their home-grown talent of Robbie Fowler, Michael Owen, Steven Gerrard, Danny Murphy and Jamie Carragher being worth as much again, only confirming the challenge ahead for Sanchez's Wycombe, who by contrast had cost a mere £200,000.

"For the value of the Liverpool squad, you could buy 500 Wycombe teams" whispered John uneasily to his sons, whilst perusing the matchday programme.

"So what!" replied Adam defiantly, full of adrenalin, "It's just eleven men against eleven men. Anything is possible."

"Have you had a bet on Wycombe then?" asked his brother Flipper.

"Have I bollocks!" conceded Adam… "That's bloody Liverpool out there in red today, not Harrow Borough!"

The roar that reverberated around the ground as the referee, Paul Durkin, whistled the game into life was like no other ever heard by a Wanderer, be they player or supporter from any generation of the club's history. But it was the Liverpudlians who were immediately back out of their seats and raising the volume further still, as England's World Cup star Michael Owen bore down upon the Wanderers goal within seconds of kick-off. The Holte End gasped with relief at the sight of the ball flashing across the goalmouth to safety from Owen's flicked effort, but the respite didn't last long. Martin Taylor was called into action moments later, sliding out across the rain drenched turf to intercept a Robbie Fowler cross that seemed destined to meet the on-rushing Owen's right boot. Most in the ground expected to see the familiar sight of Owen wheeling away in triumph having put Liverpool ahead, but instead he was left flailing his arms in frustration as a blur of green flashed past him in the form of Taylor, diverting the ball away as he prepared to pounce. Millwall, Grimsby, Wolves, Wimbledon and Leicester had all set out to put their supposedly inferior opposition to the sword from the outset, but none had succeeded. None, however, had Michael Owen and Robbie Fowler leading the onslaught, aided up by a world-class supporting cast.

"Shit... this could be a disaster!" gulped Buz, panicked by the ominous start and the thought of Wycombe being mercilessly torn apart before a worldwide audience of millions.

Scattered around the packed Holte End, the Roobarbs were exchanging concerned glances. As the rain drove down with increasing ferocity, it washed away any illusions of Liverpool not taking the Wanderers threat seriously, or hopes that they'd start lethargically following their exploits just days before in Barcelona. I was looking around anxiously too, but thankfully our Australian barman was still nowhere to be seen and, for now, I was safe to keep watching from afar.

Back on the pitch, though, there was no lack of self-belief and the Chairboys looked unshaken by Liverpool's flying start, with Michael Simpson and Steve Brown relishing the battle in the middle of the park against the German internationals, Dieter Hamman and Christian Ziege. If anything, Simpson was too assured and was dispossessed by Ziege, but before his countryman, Hamman, was able to set another Liverpool attack in motion, Brown leapt into action, harrying Hamman out of contention, allowing Simpson to regain control. Simmo didn't dwell a second time, swiftly pushing the ball forward into Liverpool territory towards his captain, Keith Ryan, who was again playing as a makeshift centre-forward alongside Andy Rammell, who had been fighting to regain fitness since limping from the mud plains of Selhurst Park during the replay against Wimbledon a month before. Ryan and Rammell were there primarily to provide the first line of defence, using their height and strength to give Liverpool's defence an uncomfortable afternoon, but Ryan turned sharply on the ball and with his first contribution nonchalantly chipped the ball 45 yards towards the backpedalling Liverpool goalkeeper, Sander Westerveld. The audacious effort just cleared the crossbar before falling tantalisingly behind the net of the relieved Dutchman Westerveld. Ryan's daring immediately lifted the spirits of the Wanderers faithful. Owen had let Wycombe know that he was hungry for goals, and now Keith Ryan had thrown down a marker of his own. From all four sides of the stadium, the noise of the crowd echoed. Names and reputations were being forgotten; this was the Semi-Final of the FA Cup and both teams were here to win.

Soon, Owen was again cutting his way into the Wycombe penalty area, weaving first past McCarthy and then Vinnicombe, before seeing his cross smothered by Taylor. Liverpool, despite all their skill and guile, weren't averse to playing a more direct style though, and minutes later a free-kick was lofted high into the Wanderers box from the halfway line. Taylor leapt to punch clear, but under pressure from Ziege, he failed to get a clean contact on the ball, seeing it drop into the path of the ever alert Owen. As the striker tried to bring the ball under control, Vinnicombe and McCarthy again closed in to try and dispossess him. In a melee of bodies Owen tumbled to the ground, prompting screams of 'Penalty!' from the red half of the stadium. Paul Durkin was in the perfect position to see that the forward hadn't been touched and waved play on as Macca dispatched the ball safely into the banks of spectators. The only screaming Owen could hear was that of an irate Jason Cousins, who, with head firmly pressed against Owen's, voiced his displeasure at the superstar's theatrical fall; he might have got away with that in the rarefied atmosphere of the Premier League or on the World Cup stage, but not when Jason Cousins was in town. Owen looked like he'd just had his dinner-money stolen by the big boys at school, but the anger in Cousins' eyes warded off any would-be protectors coming to the centre-forward's aid.

"Go on Jase... do the little Scouse twat!" screamed Cathy, prompting a startled reaction from the Spurs and Arsenal fans who'd temporarily moved their allegiances 25 miles west from their respective North London clubs, along the M40 to the little team from High Wycombe.

"Jenny... what a wonderful woman you are!" marvelled Terry from the table behind.

Back in Villa Park Durkin did soon whistle for a foul, but at the other end of the pitch. Andy Rammell had won a free-kick just outside the Liverpool box, having been bundled over by Markus Babbel. With the Wanderers just looking for him to hold the ball up to provide a brief respite for his defensive teammates, Babbel's misdemeanour was an added bonus. Against Liverpool's technical superiority, such a set piece situation was likely to provide Wycombe's best chance of snatching a goal and their supporters roared with anticipation as Bates, Cousins and McCarthy advanced to take up their well-rehearsed positions around the Liverpool goalmouth. Brown shaped to cross the ball, before leaving it at the last second for his partner in crime, Simpson, to whip a pass into the throng of bodies between himself and Westerveld, who was stood poised on the goal-line. The unmistakable shaven head of Keith Ryan rose highest and flicked the ball goalwards. A fraction more purchase on the ball would have seen it fly past the helpless Westerveld and into the net but, agonisingly, it fell gratefully into the Dutchman's arms. The noise intensified again as the Holte End screamed with increased belief, while the Liverpool fans roared their disapproval with the realisation that, with the game now 30 minutes old, Wycombe Wanderers were growing increasingly confident and looked a legitimate threat to Liverpool's seemingly invincible march towards a silverware treble.

Liverpool heeded the warning from their supporters, and also the call for urgency from their increasingly animated management team; the Frenchman, Gerard Houllier and their ex-captain, Phil Thompson, who knew what it took to win, having held aloft the European Cup and countless League titles in his own stellar playing career. Ryan's header had been as clear a chance as any of Owen's forays into Taylor's penalty area and, as the first half wore on with no sign of the underdogs weakening, they realised that their opponents were going to provide just as tough a challenge as their midweek adversaries Barcelona. Wycombe continued to be dogged in the tackle and although they created no further clear-cut opportunities, neither did their esteemed opponents.

"I think Owen's had enough!" chirped Nicko, as Cousins again towered above the diminutive striker to repel the ball back to the halfway line with a powerful header.

"His shirt must weigh more than he does by now!" added Pat, as the rain soaked Owen watched the ball fall back into the midfield battleground, before spinning and exploding forward as Nicky Barmby advanced along the right flank. Barmby sent an inch-perfect pass sliding into the path of Owen who, with just one touch of the ball, found himself only six yards out with the goal at his mercy. Taylor sprung from his line and heroically threw himself at the striker's feet, taking the full force of Owen's shot on his chest at point-blank range, before scrambling across the sodden turf to fall on the ball before Owen could slam home the rebound. Once again, the Wanderers supporters roared their appreciation for the goalkeeper's never-ending string of seemingly impossible saves. Owen jogged back onto the pitch shaking his head, wondering what he had to do to beat the inspired Wycombe glovesman.

"I think you two had best keep your gobs shut, don't you?" suggested Tony, placing the blame for Owen's latest near-miss firmly at the door of Nicko and Pat.

As half-time drew closer and the rain grew even heavier, Buz's mind became increasingly torn between heading for a much needed toilet break before the near 20,000 other Blues fans got ahead of him in the queue, and risking missing a goal. He'd gladly sacrifice missing the Blues score, in fact he'd take the plaudits for it, but could he live with the burden of sending Wycombe into the break a goal down after such a valiant first half effort? He decided that he couldn't and so, as Liverpool looked to send one final free-kick towards the Wycombe goal, he crossed his legs and prayed for the referee's half-time whistle. Dieter Hamman sent the free-kick hurtling high into the Wycombe box and found the head of the imperious Finn, Sami Hyppia. Hyppia headed the ball back across goal towards the centre spot in a carbon-copy of the move that had set up Roy Essandoh's killer goal for the Wanderers, right at the death against Leicester. The ball sailed slightly behind Christian Ziege though, rather than into his path, but with a moment of acrobatic brilliance he threw his legs up over his body and executed a perfect overhead kick, sending the ball flying towards the Wycombe net as Taylor looked on helplessly. The ball grazed the foot of the goalpost and crashed into the advertising hoardings beside the pitch; the Wycombe faithful still flinching in anticipation of the ball nestling into the corner of the net.

'Thank god I never went for that piss!' thought Buz, letting out a huge sigh of relief before deciding Wycombe would have to fend for themselves in the final few seconds as he couldn't wait a moment longer. As he dropped out of sight of the pitch into the underbelly of the stadium, he heard the shrill of Durkin's whistle signal the end of the half, followed by the loudest cheer of the afternoon yet. Midway through their sternest ever test, the Wanderers FA Cup dream was still alive.

"Oi, 'Wycombe'... the barman was telling the truth. There is a sports bar round the corner, it's got a giant cinema screen and everything!" gasped the Arsenal fan who had been dispatched on a reconnaissance mission just prior to kick-off. "It's literally a minute down the road."

"Why did it take you so long to come back then?" quizzed one of his mates.

"I pulled!" 'Arsenal' proudly replied.

"But you still came back though?" queried his pal suspiciously.

"Well... I pulled, but it didn't really work out."

"Wow, that must have been a tough break-up... after such a long time" teased Cathy.

"Oh yeah, I'm heartbroken. Anyway... what's happened to the barman? Why is he shouting down there?"

A puzzled silence followed.

"He's in the cupboard halfway down the stairs... didn't you hear him? He's going mental!"

We all looked towards the staircase and, sure enough, there was the muffled, but unmistakable sound of a very angry Australian.

"Oh no! The football's been blaring out... we didn't hear anything... we'd better see what's wrong" said Cathy.

"Leave it fellas... he's fine" said Terry calmly, walking back in from the veranda. "...although you lot should probably go. I'll catch you up in the other pub in a bit, okay?"

"Erm, okay Terry" replied Cathy. The rest of us just nodded nervously.

Based on the continued rantings that were emanating from the cleaning cupboard, we concluded that Terry had locked the barman in there soon after he'd told us to start drinking up. My initial reaction was to unlock the cupboard door, but having to explain our innocence to the irate barman would surely mean missing the start of the second half, so along with the remainder of our party, I scurried down the stairs past the barricaded cupboard and out into the night air, walking as quickly as possible without breaking into a suspicion-raising jog. Thankfully, we managed to slip past the doorman of the sports bar under the guise of English backpackers without being exposed as a gang of dangerous hostage-takers.

The sports bar turned out to be more of a nightclub and, although it had possibly the largest television screen in Australia, music was blaring from the ceiling-high speakers, rendering the football commentary inaudible. Just as the players trotted back onto the pitch, a foam party was exploding into life behind us. Soon the 50 or so people who had been standing staring at the screen disappeared into the bubbles on the dance floor, leaving just a dozen Liverpool fans alongside Cathy and me to watch the game. As Liverpool pushed forward and the bass boomed around the club, I felt a tap on my shoulder. I assumed it would be one of the Arsenal or Spurs boys bringing refreshments, so was alarmed to find the huge frame of the bouncer beckoning me towards the door. I looked at Cathy with horror.

'Shit... I'm getting arrested... I'm getting arrested in Australia... I'm getting arrested during the semi-bloody-final!'

Thoughts raced through my brain as I looked back behind me. Cathy was following me, but gesturing back to the Spurs and Arsenal lads to stay submerged in their frothy hiding place. As I got to the door, the bouncer leaned towards my ear.

"We've got a little telly out here on the veranda if you want to hear the game" he shouted, struggling to make himself heard above the music.

With a huge sigh of relief I smiled at Cathy, who turned, issuing a thumbs-up signal to the sets of cowering eyes peering back out from the mass of foam.

"We saw your shirt... we thought you'd want to watch the game in peace, mate... your boys are doing alright so far!" said the second doorman as we left the din of the club behind us and stepped back out into the serenity of the entrance hall.

"Here you go, take a pew" said the first bouncer, placing a couple of chairs in front of the tiny television perched up in the corner. "It's supposed to be for the CCTV, but we always stick the big games on when the night's dying down."

"That's brilliant, thanks!" I replied, settling into the chair without taking my eyes from the screen, once again immediately transporting myself from the heat of the Australian night to the rainy English afternoon.

As the ball went out of play for a throw-in, I heard a voice.

"Are you from Wycombe mate?"

I looked round to notice that we were sitting directly beside a couple of guys, equally transfixed on the game.

"Oh, hiya… sorry, I hadn't noticed you there. Yes, I'm from Wycombe" I replied, proudly holding up the badge of my Wanderers shirt.

"Do you know a bloke called Buz?" he continued.

I paused for moment.

"It depends… does this Buz chap owe you money?"

"Ha-ha! He does actually! I work with him. He's Wycombe mad. I thought you might know him… small world, eh?"

It was indeed a small world, but now wasn't the time for idle chit-chat, so after the briefest of introductions we all turned our focus back to the task at hand; knocking Liverpool out of the FA Cup.

"Substitution" mouthed Buz's workmate, again not taking his eyes from the screen.

"Barmby's going off… good… he was playing well" said his friend. "Who's coming on?"

"Shit…. It's Steven Gerrard" I answered, as the recently crowned Young Footballer of the Year eagerly waited for the injured Barmby to make his way across to the touchline. 'I guess I didn't pray hard enough in Beijing' I thought to myself, cursing.

Moments later all concerns of Steven Gerrard were forgotten, with everyone's attention drawn out into the darkness which was suddenly being illuminated by the flashing lights of four police cars just down the road.

"Something's kicking off!" The bouncers eagerly went to investigate, but before they'd crossed the street the convoy of police cars drove past and there, in the back of the second vehicle, was Terry. He nodded as he caught sight of our faces, mouthing something that looked like 'be good Jenny'.

"Houllier's making another change… he's getting worried!" cheered Buz's colleague, drawing all attention back to the game.

"Heskey's on for Zeige... another forward for a midfielder. He doesn't fancy extra time, does he?" replied his friend, chuckling at the sight of the mighty Liverpool changing their tactics in an attempt to break the Wanderers resilience.

"This could work in our favour" I added, happy to get distracted from thoughts of Terry. "They're going for all-out attack... that's got to leave gaps at the back for Wycombe to exploit."

"Here comes that new guy!" announced Cathy, as Sanchez, too, used the hour mark to make his first change, relieving the tiring Rammell of his duties and providing the 'Ceefax Kid', Roy Essandoh, with his reward for heading the blues into the Semi-Final; 30 minutes to show the world what he could do.

"Come on Roy... another last minute winner lad!" I yelled at the television, willing the unwitting star of the tournament to repeat his party piece that had sent me spinning into a daze for a month as I wandered around China.

My vocal encouragement was taking its time to reach England though, as following good work from Steven Gerrard and Jamie Carragher, it was Heskey who was next to power a header goalwards, rather than Essandoh. Once again, Taylor was there to thwart the danger, this time with a full length dive to pluck the goal-bound ball from the air. Following his duel with Michael Owen in the first half, Martin Taylor had been little more than a spectator since the re-start, but Heskey's header proved to be just a precursor as the game pushed towards its final ten minutes. The Liverpool midfield soon regained possession as Brown and Simpson, aided by the young legs of Danny Bulman and Ben Townsend, chased every pass down, forcing Gerrard to drop deeper and deeper to find time and space. Pressed back to the halfway line Gerrard flicked the ball up, before dissecting the Wanderers defence with a raking long-range pass that zipped across the greasy surface and into the path of Michael Owen, who again sprang to life with the goal at his mercy. Reminiscent to his first half heroics, Taylor raced from his line and threw his body to the ground, meeting Owen and the ball at the same time with a crash. The ball spat from the heart of the collision, spinning to safety behind the goal, but the Wanderers goalkeeper was left spiralling with even greater velocity. Taylor grabbed his right arm and grimaced with pain as he rose to his feet and instinctively made his way back to the goal-line to prepare to defend the resulting corner, but referee Durkin could see that the keeper was hurt, and signalled to the Wycombe physio to come onto the pitch to ensure Taylor was fit to continue. Gary

McAllister waited to take the corner in front of the Liverpool fans, who, after seeing Heskey and Owen both come close to finally breaking the deadlock, had once again found their collective voice after spending the majority of the second half with very little to cheer about, in contrast to the Wycombe supporters who had been steadily getting louder as every minute passed. Having done all he could to keep Taylor's arm moving freely following its violent meeting with Owen's right boot, Wycombe's physio departed and McAllister immediately sought to test the goalkeeper by sending over a high cross into the goalmouth. Taylor leapt and punched the ball back towards McAllister with his left fist; his injury rendering him unable to raise his other arm to attempt a catch. McAllister knocked the ball to Steven Gerrard, who immediately whipped a powerful cross back into the penalty box before the Wanderers defence had time to reorganise. The ball found Emile Heskey leaping unchallenged just six yards out and he thundered his header into the top corner of the Wanderers net past the maimed Taylor. The stadium shook as the Liverpool supporters and players alike erupted into wild celebration. They may have been playing against a tiny team who had misread the script, but that fact had long been forgotten due to the performance Wycombe had produced for almost 80 minutes; the Liverpool players' unbridled celebrations paid testament to that.

As a cheer rang out from inside the Cairns sports bar, silence reigned out on the veranda. The bouncers went in to supervise the celebrating Liverpool fans, leaving the four Wycombians slumped back into our seats, as if we'd been poleaxed alongside Martin Taylor in the collision with Michael Owen.

"That's not fair!" protested Cathy, "They wouldn't have scored if Owen hadn't crocked Taylor."

I don't know if the others replied, but my head was spinning. The disappointment and emotions running through me were too much to bear. I knew that beating Liverpool was close to impossible, but I'd allowed myself to believe. Wycombe Wanderers had made me believe. Gerrard Houllier's tactical changes had made me believe. The assured coolness of Laurie Sanchez had made me believe. Martin Taylor's brilliance had made me believe. The madness in Jason Cousins' eyes had made me believe. The frustration in Michael Owen's eyes had made me believe. A lifetime of dreams had made me believe.

By the time the Wanderers restarted the game I, like most of the supporters in the stadium, had managed to grasp back some semblance of reality and, once again, the Holte End roared down onto the pitch, proudly doing whatever it could to raise the players. Sanchez had immediately made his final changes; the warrior, Steve Brown, along with the tiring Ben Townsend left the pitch, replaced by the latest 'rent-a-striker' to come through the revolving door of Adams Park, journeyman Guy Whittingham and, fittingly, a true Wycombe legend in the form of Davey 'Jesus' Carroll who, when he'd joined Wycombe 13 years before and first encountered the sloping pitch of Loakes Park, could only have dreamed that one day he would be representing the then non-league club in an FA Cup Semi-Final. Both men pushed up to join Ryan and Essandoh in attack. Chris Vinnicombe advanced into midfield, leaving just Bates, Cousins and McCarthy to defend, and even they had a licence to attack when opportunity knocked. Sanchez knew that this was a high risk strategy, but with just ten minutes remaining Wycombe had to score. If they didn't, the dream would be over.

The noise in the ground was deafening. The Liverpool fans sensed victory and a place in the FA Cup final, whilst the Chairboys supporters rallied behind Sanchez's last throw of the dice, willing their brave team to summon yet another miracle. The frenetic pace of the game became even more hurried with Wycombe pushing forward and the Liverpool defence looking to bypass the now redundant midfield area as both teams either attacked or defended with equal desperation. As another Wycombe effort was snuffed out by the impressive Liverpool back line, Emile Heskey chased a long clearance towards the Wycombe penalty area, jostling for the ball with Bates as McCarthy and Cousins flanked him. The tiring Bates attempted to hook the ball away from the charging Heskey, but only managed to pull the powerful forward to the ground, leaving Durkin an easy decision to award a free-kick in an invitingly central position. The entire Wanderers team trooped back to form a wall between Taylor and the swarm of Liverpool players eagerly looking to argue their case to take the free-kick. Robbie Fowler duly won the discussion and quickly lifted the ball with his left foot just above the strained jumps of the Wycombe wall, before watching in delight as his world-class effort sailed into the top corner past Taylor's despairing dive. The Liverpudlians roared their acclaim again, although this second goal was celebrated more with a sense of relief than the outright delight of the first, just minutes before. With only seven minutes to go the game was surely won and at last, the feisty upstarts who had repeatedly refused to accept their place were being taught a cruel lesson.

The rain, which had become increasingly heavy throughout the afternoon, was now joined by tears on thousands of faces, as the hopes of the Blues faithful appeared dashed. The Wanderers had been the equal of the mighty

Liverpool for 78 minutes, but now, just five minutes later, all of the work of the past six months had started to unravel. Soon, Danny Murphy was unleashing another shot as Liverpool began to slice through the Wanderers at will. Martin Taylor fell on the ball, took a moment to catch his breath and then turned and roared defiantly at his team to keep going, before sending the ball hurtling back towards the Liverpool end of the pitch, where now all but Bates and Cousins were permanently encamped. Again, there was no way through the Liverpool rear-guard, and the ball was despatched back to Wycombe's defensive duo. Bates was chased down by Liverpool's reinvigorated forwards, leaving no option but to frustratingly send the ball all the way back to his goalkeeper. Taylor again sent the ball deep behind enemy lines. The ball reached the mass of players on the edge of the Liverpool box, where Whittingham and McCarthy launched themselves with Hyppia to meet it. This time Macca managed to get the first touch and flicked the ball on towards goal, where it bounced awkwardly above waist height between Keith Ryan and Jamie Carragher. Both leapt towards the ball like martial arts experts, but Ryan reacted quickest, lofting it above and beyond the advancing Westerveld, who could only watch as the ball dropped behind him into the Liverpool net.

Wycombe Wanderers had scored.

As Ryan saluted the delirious supporters in the Holte End, Chris Vinnicombe, in an opponent's penalty box for possibly the first time in his career, retrieved the ball from the net and charged back to the centre-spot in an attempt to save valuable seconds. With five minutes remaining, the Blues were back in the game, just a goal away from forcing extra time. The dream was resurrected and suddenly it was the Liverpool players who were now on the back foot. The Wanderers fans screamed manically rather than singing in unison, but only their voices could be heard as the Liverpool faithful looked on in stunned silence. They'd seen Wycombe perform miracles against Wimbledon and Leicester; surely they weren't about to witness another?

Clearing the next Wycombe attack, Liverpool pushed the ball forward to McAllister, who was caught in an obvious off-side position. He saw the linesman flag for the offence and paused momentarily, before continuing for a couple more yards and suspiciously delivering the worst pass of his life to an empty space in the farthest corner of the pitch. He immediately turned to the referee and apologetically signalled that he hadn't heard the whistle; I'd heard it all the way in Australia. Liverpool were now hanging on, using any method necessary to kill the games momentum; whether legal or not. Taylor raced to retrieve the ball and Wycombe attacked again, but Hyppia managed to win the next aerial contest, calmly heading the ball back towards Westerveld, who fell theatrically onto the ball, remaining prone until Paul Durkin roared none too politely at him to stop time-wasting. Westerveld then proceeded to hammer the ball into the stand along the halfway line, much to the chagrin of the thousands of Wycombians stood behind him. On the touchline, Sanchez gesticulated for the crowd to keep up the crescendo, while yards away, Houllier urged his players to keep their concentration.

The Liverpool supporters began to bellow 'You'll Never Walk Alone', signalling that the game was truly in its dying embers. Wycombe continued to fire the ball into the Liverpool box, and Carragher, Hyppia and Henchoz continued to do whatever necessary to repel it. Bates headed the ball in again and found his partner McCarthy on the edge of the Liverpool box, Macca knocked the ball down into the path of the goalscorer, Ryan, who was being closely marshalled by Henchoz. Ryan lurked behind the Swiss international, ready to pounce if he slipped, but Henchoz stood firm and hammered the ball as far from goal as possible, just as the Wycombe fans thought Rhino was about to equalise. The ball fell to Jason Cousins on the halfway line but as he tried to prolong the relentless pressure, he was dispossessed by Robbie Fowler, who eagerly looked to expose the glaring gaps in the, by now, almost non-existent Wanderers defence. Thankfully, the referee adjudged Fowler to have obstructed Cousins and awarded Wycombe a free-kick; a final lifeline as the seconds ebbed away. Sanchez looked ready to run onto the pitch himself as the entire bench of substitutes and coaches stood to watch the final act. The Liverpool fans fell silent as the players jostled for position around Westerveld's goalmouth. Jason Cousins placed the ball on the halfway line and then sent it on its way into the Liverpool box, but Hyppia again leapt highest and knocked the ball away from goal. It fell to Gerrard, who desperately hooked the ball further upfield, where Robbie Fowler met it and rolled it into the path of the fresh-legged substitute Danny Murphy, who sprinted past the weary Wanderers. As he advanced, Murphy saw his fellow substitute Gerrard charging towards the Wycombe penalty area. Murphy slipped the ball into his path behind the Blues retreating defenders. Gerrard now looked to secure victory and he flicked the ball past Taylor's dive, only to see his shot bounce tamely wide of the post when he had looked certain to score. The crowd gasped for breath as the match's finale became increasingly frenetic. Gerrard covered his anguished face with his shirt in disbelief at his spurned opportunity to kill off the Wanderers comeback, whilst Taylor ran to retrieve the ball, quickly knocking it back into play. But Paul Durkin already had his whistle pursed between his lips ready to signal full-time. Seconds later, the roar of the Liverpool supporters behind Taylor's goal confirmed that the game was over. Liverpool were going to the FA Cup Final, and Wycombe Wanderers were going home; after ten glorious football matches, Wycombe's flirtation with the FA Cup was over and consigned to the history books.

A moment of silence fell across the Wanderers half of Villa Park at the realisation that the rollercoaster ride had abruptly ground to a screeching conclusion; then a roar of pride grew as the players disconsolately went through the motions of congratulating the jubilant Liverpool players and exchanging shirts. After the Liverpool players took the acclaim of their adoring supporters for a final time, they retreated to the sanctity of the changing room and their millionaire lifestyles, far removed from those of their vanquished opponents who had, for one wonderful day, competed with them as equals. Sanchez gathered his shattered team in the middle of pitch, determined to ram home the point that they may have lost the football match, but they had won so much more; the respect of the entire footballing world. If their manager's words needed any endorsement, it was provided when all four sides of the ground stood and applauded as, eventually, the Wanderers reluctantly left the pitch and their FA Cup adventure behind.

The majority of fans began to head for the exits as the players disappeared from view, but not those who had witnessed the start of the journey against Harrow Borough in November; and not those who had skipped Christmas shopping duties for a trip to Millwall in December; and not those who had returned victorious in the small hours from Grimsby in January; and not those who had answered the early morning call to clear Adams Park of snow prior to the visit of Wolverhampton Wanderers; and not those who had sacrificed all hope of getting home from London in order to witness Wycombe defy all odds against Wimbledon in February; and not those who had dared to dream that Premier League opposition could be conquered away to Leicester City in March. Now, on a rainy afternoon in April, those who had dreamed of such days since childhood remained; fully aware that when they left Villa Park they would be leaving behind those dreams that for six magical months had danced hand in hand with reality. The team they loved unconditionally had come so close to reaching the FA Cup final, matching Liverpool for 78 minutes, and then given them a final almighty scare with Keith Ryan's late goal. But as the Villa Park cleaning team began to sweep through the now almost deserted terraces, only the memories remained.

Old men, who thought they'd seen it all before; the drunken Roobarbs and youngsters like Laura and Abby just starting out on their own love affair with their hometown team, stubbornly remained clinging to their dreams for just a few moments longer as the cavernous stadium emptied. They had enjoyed Wycombe's 90 minutes of global fame, and were just as proud of the Wanderers as anyone but, like the players, all they could feel right now was the bitter disappointment of losing a Semi-Final. It didn't matter that it was the mighty Liverpool who had knocked them out; it wouldn't have hurt any less if they'd been playing Harrow Borough again. Soon the tears would cease and the pain would go, to be replaced by a pride that would last a lifetime and be passed on through future generations but, for now, the acute disappointment left those remaining in the pouring rain utterly bereft.

At 4am in Australia there was no rain to hide the tracks of my tears.

"Come on... you didn't really think you could win did you?" asked Cathy, as we shuffled through the Cairns darkness.

"Don't... please. Just don't" I pleaded.

Cathy could see the pain in my eyes and didn't say another word. The only sound to be heard as we walked through the deserted streets was the snuffling of a heartbroken man whose childhood hopes and dreams had just been crushed having briefly, and unexpectedly, flourished so spectacularly.

31 – Better than Barcelona

'Win or lose, support the Blues… win or lose, get on the booze' was the Roobarb motto and, in all honesty, it had to be; if you support a small town team like Wycombe Wanderers, you're going to go thirsty if you only celebrate the victories. Normally, by the time we'd reached the bar we would be over a defeat and looking forward to the next game but, having just played against Liverpool in an FA Cup Semi-Final, the thought of travelling to fellow relegation-threatened Swansea in a couple of nights time didn't sound too appealing to Buz as he stood waiting to get served back in The Walkabout, surrounded by celebrating Liverpudlians.

"You'll stay up pal… play like that for the rest of the season and you'll have no problems. Who have you got next?" asked the Scouser stood beside him.

"Swansea… away. What about you?" Buz replied.

"Barcelona… back at Anfield."

"A bit different then!" laughed Buz, getting a further reminder of just how mismatched and unlikely the day's events had been.

"I went to the Nou Camp last week… you lot were better than Barcelona… we'll turn them over at our place, no problem" the Reds fan replied confidently.

'Better than Barcelona?' Buz smiled at the notion and wished his fellow football fan all the best, then returned to the Roobarb fold to inform them that Wycombe were better than the giants of Spanish football, "so Tuesday night in Swansea should be an absolute doddle lads!"

By the time the Roobarbs staggered out of High Wycombe train station several hours later, not only were they convinced that the Wanderers would avoid relegation, but next season would likely bring promotion and more FA Cup glory too.

As the Roobarbs were passing out back home, I awoke in Australia to find Cathy staring at me from across the pillow.

"You were actually crying in your sleep just now" she said pitifully.

As I gathered my senses, recollections of the past 24 hours flashed through my mind; the Barrier reef, the bouncing bikinis, nearly drowning, the pub, mad Terry, the barman, the bouncers, the foam party, the police, the football; oh yes, the football.

"I was thinking… shall we move on today?" she added. "If there's room on tonight's bus, that is."

"Yeah, if you want" I mumbled, although in my head I wasn't moving on; I was still thinking about the game.

"Well, we don't have to… it's up to you Mr Moneyman. Hey, what do you think happened to Terry last night?"

"God knows. He didn't have that panicked look of someone being arrested for the first time though, did he?" I remarked. "You know what… I think leaving town is probably a good idea. Let's go to the bus station and book up… I'll need to get some money out first though."

Venturing out, the streets were a lot busier in the midday sunshine compared to eight hours earlier.

"Are you ever going to take that off?" asked Cathy, alluding to the Wycombe Wanderers top that I was wearing again, today more proudly than ever.

"The world supports Wycombe Wanderers now… I've no intention of taking it off" I declared as we turned onto the main street, where lots of people were already enjoying al fresco lunches before we'd had a chance to even consider breakfast.

"Ha-ha! Loser!" shouted someone from a large group, drinking outside a bar.

"2-1, to the mighty Reds… 2-1, to the mighty Reds!" he continued, bursting into song.

"Wycombe are shit mate… you want to start supporting a proper team."

I hadn't realised the first jibe was being directed at me, and the second was just mildly annoying; the third stopped me in my tracks.

"Leave it James, he's not worth it!" muttered Cathy, automatically slipping into protective girlfriend damage-limitation mode. Before I had a chance to identify who I was about to punch in the face, another member of the loudmouth's party stood up and started taking him to task.

"Where are you from then soft lad… London?" he asked with a thick Liverpudlian accent.

"No mate, Cheltenham" replied the boor.

"Oh aye, you're from Cheltenham and you support Liverpool do yer? And you think you look clever slagging a Wycombe fan off?" my Scouse defender continued, before turning towards me. "Sorry about 'superfan' over there mate, your team were superb last night… I was bricking it until Heskey scored. Even at the end there, when you got one back, I was dead worried you'd get another."

"Cheers. I'm gutted… but proud. They played really well" I replied.

"You were better than Barcelona on Wednesday, I'll tell you that much!" he replied. "Anyway, I'm really sorry about 'him'… he doesn't even like football that much… he's a bloody rugby player."

"No problem, I wasn't bothered anyway" I lied, whilst realising that the gobby rugby-playing-Liverpool-fan-from-Cheltenham was actually about seven feet tall and with a face that looked like it had been punched by people a lot stronger than me.

"I would have battered that cheeky bastard if the Scouse lad hadn't stepped in" I whispered to Cathy as we headed off to find the bus station.

"Oh, there's no doubt babe. And it would have been really embarrassing for him… a massive muscle-bound rugby player like that… getting knocked out by a skinny guy like you" Cathy replied, giggling. "He was a complete knob though… shall I get Mad Terry to sort him out?"

After numerous comments throughout the day prompted by my Wanderers shirt, our bus pulled out of Cairns at dusk for the first of several overnight journeys that would eventually lead us to Sydney. A couple of miles out of town, the bus slowed to a halt at a junction, ready to turn onto the main ocean route south. There, sat on a fence in the middle of nowhere beside the road was a man, just watching the world go by, flanked by a horse on one side and a donkey on the other.

"He looks familiar… where do we know him from?" I said.

367

"I don't believe it. That's the creepy Customs guy from the airport!" gasped Cathy.

"... Out with his friends the farm animals" I added.

"I told you he was a weirdo!" replied Cathy, as the first person we'd set eyes upon in Cairns also became the last.

While Wycombe were doing their survival hopes no favours at all by losing 3-1 at Swansea, and then scraping a draw back at Adams Park against Wrexham, my life was slowly getting back to normal; with a week spent in Airlie Beach doing absolutely nothing. Another 16 hour overnight bus trip then brought us to the small beach town of Noosa Bay.

"So... you've arrived at a great time... with the Easter holidays being upon us we're fully booked. The campus is buzzing! You guys got the last double bed" said the enthusiastic receptionist at Noosa's most recommended hostel.

"Double room" replied Cathy.

"What's that?" smiled the receptionist.

"You said we had the last 'double bed', but I booked a 'double room'... that's the same thing, right?" continued Cathy, sensing trouble.

"Erm, well... it's actually a double bed in a dorm. As I said, we are completely full all week. The dorm is great though, and it's all girls... well, apart from your partner obviously!" laughed the girl.

"Sounds okay to me" I replied, before turning to Cathy... "I'm sure it'll be fine." Looking back at me, the daggers in her eyes suggested that it wasn't fine at all.

Things started out quite well, with the girls in the room being oblivious to my male presence; everyone being far too busy preparing for a big night out. I'm sure that if this had been Ian Roobarb's trip, then the evening would have panned out completely differently. But for me the night spent sharing with a dozen party girls mainly consisted of listening to the loudest snorer on the planet, being disturbed by the room being showered in light from the hallway every 20 minutes as someone else sneaked in or out and, above all, two very drunken girls from Bristol amicably discussing the shared love of a boy they'd just met, then less amicably completely falling out over him. Mercifully, the argument eventually resulted in a frosty silence; at 3am any form of silence was appreciated. Unfortunately, the peace didn't last for too long as by 3.30am the girl on the top bunk was back down with the girl from the bottom bunk, holding her hair in an emergency ponytail as she spewed up her evening's alcohol into a carrier bag, with neither looking quite as glamorous as they had several hours before. At any other point in my life, this would have been a rock bottom moment, but I was just glad that for once it wasn't me being ill. Even so, at the crack of dawn we had packed and I was struggling to keep pace with Cathy as she marched to the local Tourist Information Centre.

The woman in the office took pity on us; firstly, because we must have looked a pathetic sight, huddled on the doorstep waiting for her to arrive, and secondly, because Cathy was ranting about the hostel which turned out to be the lady's pet hate.

"Oh you poor dears... that place is a den of iniquity, it must have been awful for you" she sympathised, whilst flicking rapidly through her accommodation folder. "There really isn't much I'm afraid... because of Easter. Let me just make a call."

"We'll just have to go to Brisbane on the next bus if we can't get somewhere else to stay... we can't go back now after storming off" said Cathy as the woman turned to the phone.

"I can go back... I didn't tell the receptionist to 'stick her hostel up her arse'... did I?" I replied with a smug smile that wasn't fully appreciated by Cathy, who punched me in the ribs.

"Shush" she whispered, as the woman started to speak on the phone.

"Hi... Trevor? Yes, it's Judith from the Travel Centre here. I'm hoping you can help me out. I have a lovely couple in the office. They've had a terrible time up at that hell-hole hostel, and I was wondering if you'd be willing to do a short-term rental on the house? I know you don't take backpackers, but I think they would be fine, they're absolute sweethearts... what do you think?"

We adopted our best 'sweetheart' expressions as Judith turned around and looked at us with her fingers crossed.

"Yes? Oh Trevor you're a darling! Just hold the line please my love."

"You have something?" asked Cathy hopefully.

"I've got Trevor on the line, he's a dear friend and he has a property that's vacant. It's not normally available for short-term stays, but he's willing to give you the apartment on a daily basis for a very reasonable rate."

"What do you think?" asked Cathy. "Noosa's supposed to be really nice… it would be a shame to have to move on without having seen it."

"Okay, but if you want any more shampoo and conditioner, you'll be sent out shoplifting for it… this is double the cost of the bloody hostel… we'll need to find somewhere cheaper tomorrow" I whispered, before turning to Judith with a thumbs-up to signal for Trevor to drive down with the keys.

"Oh, I'm so happy that we've been able to help. Now, can I be frank with you?" said Judith, suddenly looking very serious. "My bastard ex-husband owns that fucking shit-hole of a hostel… anything I can do to take money from his philandering pocket is fine by me. Now my dears… please don't let me down, no wrecking Trevor's apartment, okay?"

Regardless of Judith's true intentions, she'd hit the jackpot in finding us somewhere to rest our heads. Bunk beds and four walls would have sufficed, but a detached bungalow with its own swimming pool at the end of a residential cul-de-sac was also perfectly acceptable. By lunchtime, we were suddenly living like Scott and Charlene from Neighbours.

"It's got a proper kitchen!" screeched Cathy as we explored. "A washing machine… it's got a washing machine too! I've died and gone to heaven! Come on… let's go to the supermarket and buy fabric conditioner!" Cathy was transforming into a domestic goddess before my very eyes.

"Why don't we go to the beach first, then to the shops later?" I suggested, remembering that we were actually in Australia, rather than crashing out after a tough week at work in Cathy's bed-sit down the road from Adams Park.

After our basic dwellings in Thailand and the constant living out of a backpack ever since, our 'one night' stay in the bungalow soon turned into a fortnight. We ended up taking a proper holiday from our travels. Each day was spent at the beach, pretending that we were proper surfers while clinging for dear life to body-boards that skimmed atop the crest of the waves as they crashed back towards the sandy shore. The rush that came from catching the surf 'just right', maybe once an hour, more than made up for the many misjudgements that invariably saw my ribs getting pummelled by the board, or my crumpled body crashing face first into the sand beneath the churning waves. Despite being barely able to breathe each night as I nursed ever more bruises, I was addicted to the body-boarding; possibly because the pain emanating from my ribs helped to fill the gap left by the hurt of Wycombe's FA Cup demise slowly diminishing. As I moaned and groaned on the sofa, as any hardcore surfer would, Cathy reintroduced herself to the world of television, and a new social experiment on Australian television called 'Big Brother'. I couldn't be bothered with it and instead kept up to date with the latest football stories with the plethora of football magazines on the Aussie market. The latest edition showed a jubilant Liverpool team on the front cover under the headline *'TREBLE CHASERS... Wycombe and Barcelona defeated as Finals beckon'*. I showed the cover to Cathy, but she was far too interested in seeing what a dozen Australians were having for their dinner on television to care.

'At least we scored a goal... that 'is' better than Barcelona' I thought to myself contentedly.

"Watching this is making me hungry... can you make dinner tonight?" asked Cathy.

"Sure... what do you want?"

"Surprise me" she replied.

A real surprise would have been anything without toast; all I'd mastered as our fortnight of domesticity wore on was beans on toast, cheese on toast, beans and cheese on toast together, spaghetti hoops on toast, tinned macaroni on toast, and my greatest achievement yet; scrambled eggs on toast. My ribs were in far too much pain to be messing about with making anything as tricky as scrambled eggs tonight though, so tinned macaroni cheese on toast it was, with the chef's added special, ham slices chopped and mixed in for good measure. This level of opulence couldn't be sustained forever though, and after one more day of surfing for me and a final evening of beans on toast while watching Big Brother for Cathy, we reluctantly handed back the keys to our landlord Trevor and headed back out on the road, this time to Brisbane. After ten hours on the bus to Airlie and then 16 more to Noosa Bay, the two hour jaunt into Brisbane felt like cheating, but a few days later, we more than made up for it with the 18 hour trek to our final port of call in Australia; Sydney.

After overnighters through Thailand and China, the Australian bus journeys had held little fear for me, especially after finally seeing a doctor and easing my dodgy stomach issues. This final bus trip started out without any concern too, with the bus packed full of backpackers from around the globe, except for an elderly Australian couple who were sitting directly opposite us. The bus had barely left Brisbane before the old woman started to unpack a bundle of sandwiches. There was nothing out of the ordinary about that, but within minutes it became obvious to all aboard that both were hard of hearing and spoke very loudly. Soon after that, it also became apparent that they hated each other.

"What's in this?" asked the old man.

"Cheese and piccalilli" replied his wife.

"What's that?"

"I said cheese and piccalilli!" she yelled.

"Strewth Pearl! I can't eat cheese and bloody piccalilli on the bus... Jesus Christ... you know what cheese and piccalilli does to my guts... why didn't you do ham and mustard like I said?"

"You asked for cheese and piccalilli... I've got ham and mustard. You could've had ham and mustard too, but you asked for cheese and piccalilli, you stupid old goat!"

"That was for lunch, you silly cow! I wanted cheese and piccalilli for lunch... so I could have a good turn-out before the journey. Cheese and piccalilli for lunch... ham and mustard for the journey. You had one job to do Pearl, one bloody job! I should have left you years ago!"

"I wish you bloody had Albert... you're nothing but a miserable, good for nothing, lazy old bastard!"

An awkward silence fell across the bus, only broken by the rustling in dozens of bags for earphones and a Walkman by those lucky enough to possess them.

"Just another 18 hours and 15 minutes to go" I whispered to Cathy.

"Yep, good luck with that" smiled Cathy, placing earphones over her head. Her smile soon disappeared though with the realisation that her only batteries were flat. Before I'd had a chance to gloat over her misfortune, Cathy received a tap on the shoulder from across the aisle.

"Excuse me my dear… do you know when the bus is scheduled to stop for the first break? I'll need to get my husband something to eat you see" said the old woman, in a far more pleasant manner than she'd used when dealing with her 'miserable, good for nothing, lazy old bastard' of a husband.

"I'm sorry, I'm not sure… it won't be for quite a while I suspect" replied Cathy.

"Oh you're English, that's lovely. I love the Royal Family. I'm Pearl dear, nice to meet you" the old woman continued, before raising her voice upon noticing the Japanese couple in the row in front of me and Cathy. "Pearl… the name's Pearl, as in Pearl Harbour."

"What's that Pearl?" grunted Albert.

"He's on these tablets you see" continued Pearl, before Cathy could hide behind her book. "For his heart… he's had five heart attacks already… big ones. He needs to eat with the tablets four times a day."

"Pearl… just give me the cheese and piccalilli, will yer. I need to take my tablets… if my arse goes, I'll just have to deal with the consequences."

"Albert, this is Cathy. Cathy is from England."

"And this is James" said Cathy, turning around to find me fast asleep with my face pressed against the window. "Oh… he seems to have fallen asleep… all of a sudden. He was wide awake a minute ago."

"Ah, that's nice, I wish we could sleep on the bus, but we can't… can we Albert?"

"What's that Pearl?"

"I said we can't sleep on the bus!" Pearl shouted, before turning her attention back to Cathy, who again had failed to raise her book in time. "It's the pain you see. I've had both hips done, but they didn't do them right" she continued, before leaning across to Cathy and whispering excruciatingly loudly whilst gesturing towards the Japanese passengers, "Foreign doctors… coming over here… they don't know what they're doing. I don't mean 'foreign' like you Cathy-love… you know… 'proper' foreign."

"You'll have to talk to James about that when he wakes up… he doesn't like foreign doctors either" replied Cathy, before quickly opening her book as Pearl retrieved Albert's cheese and piccalilli sandwich.

"Thanks for that James… you're a miserable, good for nothing, lazy old bastard too!" hissed Cathy from behind her book, as I struggled to contain my silent laughter from exploding.

"This is going to be a very long journey!" I sighed, as Pearl and Albert started to bicker again.

After the longest six hours in the lives of everyone on the bus, the sun set and darkness was soon upon us. Mercifully, Pearl and Albert had been quiet for almost ten minutes and all along the bus, passengers were discreetly glancing across, willing the pair to drift off to sleep. One of the two Dutch girls sitting directly in front of them twisted around on her knees and peeped through the gap between the seats, becoming the most popular girl on the bus when delivering a triumphal 'at last… they're asleep' thumbs-up to the relief of all.

"So much for 'we can't sleep on the buses' then!" whispered Cathy.

Then Albert started to snore. A collective groan swept the bus. Albert asleep was louder than Albert awake. It wasn't long before Pearl chimed in, still asleep, but groaning and muttering about her hips. Albert's snoring ensured that the rest of the bus stayed awake late into the night and then, suddenly, after a deep wheeze, he stopped. Apart from the whirring of the engine, there was total silence.

"Do you think he's okay?" whispered Cathy.

The same thought crossed the minds of everyone.

"Is his chest moving?" I replied.

"It's too dark, I can't see."

As Cathy replied, the Dutch girl swivelled around in her seat to check on Albert again. As she did so, everyone around us shuffled to the edge of their seats as we strained to see the girl's assessment through the darkness. She slowly leaned right over her seat until she was just inches from Albert's face, then drew back and looked up with a non-committal shrug. She knelt back down on her seat and had a whispered discussion with her friend, before popping back up into view and leaning forward towards Albert again. She slowly raised her hand to see if she could feel his breath. Suddenly, Albert jolted up and spluttered out a cough before returning to his snoring, prompting everyone to jump with fright and several to scream; not least the poor Dutch girl, who smacked her head on the overhead luggage rack before coming to rest in an undignified heap on the floor. She was wedged between seats with her legs stuck up in the air beside her ears, much to the delight of her friend who had to contain her tears of laughter before freeing her companion from her tangle.

"What's all the fuss Pearl? What's going on?" mumbled Albert, as the girl scrambled back into her seat, muttering something angrily in Dutch; no doubt along the lines of "someone else can check on the noisy bugger next time, I quit."

At 5.30 in the morning, the bus pulled into Newcastle bus station for a final toilet stop, but very few people could muster the energy to move after the sleepless night listening to Albert and Pearl. Then, like a messenger sent from heaven, the driver walked up the aisle and crouched beside Pearl.

"This is Newcastle love... can I help you down the steps?"

"Albert... Albert... wake up Albert! We're here!" yelled Pearl. "Goodbye dear" she said turning to Cathy, patting her on the arm. "I'll be glad to get home... we've not slept a wink."

A spontaneous round of applause rippled through the bus as the driver closed the doors behind them, declaring "next stop, Sydney."

Within minutes, everyone was asleep, freed from the concerns of witnessing Albert's last breath on this mortal coil. Two hours later, I awoke to find myself crossing Sydney Harbour Bridge, looking down upon the iconic Opera House.

32 – Sydney, turning for home

Sydney lived up to expectation. I'd been glued to my television seven months earlier as the city enchanted the world when playing host to the Olympic Games. And now, here I was, standing amongst the vibrant bars and cafés, looking out onto the busy waterways that ferried commuters and beach bums alike into Darling Harbour, which nestled between the Harbour Bridge and Opera House. I could just about make out figures climbing along the frame of the imposing bridge and recalled seeing Billy Connolly (the real one, as opposed to Roger Roobarb) standing on its top in a television documentary. It was one of the things I'd frequently daydreamed of doing on my imaginary journeys, while staring out into space from classrooms and my list of failed jobs.

"I'm going to sign up for that" I informed Cathy, inspired by my surroundings.

"I'm not" was her less than inspiring reply.

"Come on ... I want to do it now... before I bottle it" I continued. "Where do you think I have to go?"

"Erm... probably to the foot of the bridge?" replied Cathy sarcastically. "Can we at least find the hostel first and dump the bags?"

Three hours later, I was standing on the top of the bridge looking out across the whole of Sydney. My plans of unzipping my standard-issue climbing suit to display the Wanderers quarters across Australia didn't materialise though; the bridge was a lot higher than I'd envisioned, rendering me unable to do anything but hold on to the safety rails in sheer terror, paralysed.

"Bloody hell... Billy Connolly made it look like a stroll in the park... I thought I was going to pass-out up there" I confessed, as Cathy and I celebrated my epic ascent with a beer back down at ground level.

Our next touristy outing was to explore the Olympic Park, admittedly seven months after the event, but still exciting all the same with the heroics of Cathy Freeman, Ian Thorpe and Steve Redgrave still fresh in the memory. Four years earlier in Atlanta, Juan Antonio Samaranch had called upon 'the youth of the world to assemble four years from now in Sydney, to celebrate the Games of the 27th Olympiad'… and that they did; from nearly 200 nations, over 10,000 athletes assembled, competed and partied together. The Sydney Olympics had been a celebration of athletic endeavour and excellence that rose above political and cultural differences. For a glorious fortnight, the youth of the planet set a shining example of how to behave. Unfortunately, as I stood proudly upon the podium in the Olympic Stadium, my idea of transforming the Australian national flag into the Union Jack by neatly folding it into quarters seemed to cause offence; not to the Australian tour guide (who just ribbed me about not having seen many of those flying during the actual Olympics), but to a crowd of Italian tourists who booed and then tried to force me from my gold medal position. The nations of the world had managed to find common ground under the Olympic banner for two whole weeks; I'd caused a diplomatic incident within two minutes.

After a panic attack on top of the Sydney Harbour Bridge on our first day, followed by a fight on top of the Olympic podium on our second, we decided to give up on any more organised tourist activities; instead exploring the city and its nearby beaches by day, and then by night, living like children on their first residential school trip away from home. This was made all the easier by our room consisting of just bunk beds and a portable black and white television, the size of a microwave oven. To our credit, we upheld a certain standard of decency and invested in a party pack of paper plates and plastic cutlery, before stocking up on the essentials needed to survive; chocolate, crisps, doughnuts and beer.

It was with mixed emotions that we settled down on the top bunk to watch the grainy images of the FA Cup Final being contested between Arsenal and Wycombe's conquerors, Liverpool. All the heartache that had slowly ebbed away over the past month came flooding back as the pre-game show revisited the story of the FA Cup so far; a review that featured the Wanderers throughout.

"Imagine what it would be like if you'd beaten Liverpool!" remarked Cathy

I did imagine it. I imagined it every day. I imagined it whilst gazing at the amazing night skies, devoid of light pollution, as we drove hundreds of miles down the sparsely populated eastern seaboard. I imagined it while treading water in the ocean when waiting to catch the perfect wave. I even imagined it as I saluted the non-existent crowds whilst the Italians charged at me in the Olympic Stadium. Oh yes, I'd imagined it. What if Martin Taylor hadn't been crocked by Michael Owen and had been able to claim

McAllister's corner? What if Keith Ryan's flicked header had been directed just a few inches beyond Sander Westerveld and given the Blues a first half lead? It didn't matter anymore, but regardless, it was impossible to rid my head of such thoughts.

After the stress of the Semi-Final, the match came and went without too much hysteria, although I was happy to see Michael Owen score two late goals to snatch victory for Liverpool from Arsenal's grasp. At least this meant that the history books would record that Wycombe Wanderers had only been defeated at the last hurdle by the eventual champions.

With the FA Cup settled, Bondi Beach beckoned, and Coogee too, both playing host to lazy days away from the city centre, although it was always easy to escape the hustle and bustle of Sydney by wandering into the parks and gardens that hugged the harbour. With our departure from Australia rapidly approaching, we strolled the familiar route from our hostel through the Botanical Gardens, pausing at Mrs Macquarie's Point to take in the picture-postcard view of the harbour and to watch the small penguins diving for fish from the rocks before taking a ferry out to the seaside one final time. Our destination was Manley, but the sunshine that had brought both Bondi and Coogee to life was conspicuous by its absence as we disembarked from the boat.

"No wonder it's deserted... it's bloody freezing" moaned Cathy, cuddling up against me as we sat on the beach, although more out of a need for warmth than through an act of affection.

"Oh yeah... and that ice cream is helping to warm you up is it?" I replied.

"I'm at the seaside; therefore, I'm eating an ice cream... that's the law. You'll be buying me some chips too, just as soon as that café over the road opens."

"It's a bit dead here, isn't it? Shall we try somewhere else?" I commented, understating the fact that apart from the hardened handful of surfers who were keeping us entertained, we were the only people on Manley's famous beach.

"It's still early... and it's a work day remember" pointed out Cathy.

I smiled and leant back into the sand. We may have been away now for five months, but the novelty of not having to work still hadn't worn off. It was cold, our money was rapidly running out, Wycombe Wanderers were out of the FA Cup and had yet to guarantee safety from relegation, but I still had a wonderful thought to cling to; I was on a beach, and everyone I knew back home was at work.

My attention was momentarily drawn away from my surfing brethren by the sound of a vehicle pulling up on the road. A couple of middle-aged guys dressed in green tracksuits jumped out of the van and proceeded to throw three big sacks out onto the sand, not far behind us.

"What do you think that is?" asked Cathy.

"God knows... are they just dumping garbage?" I replied.

"G'day... how's it going?" greeted one of the men as he followed the bags onto the sand.

"Obviously not dumping their rubbish then" pointed out Cathy, as a net was pulled from the first sack.

"Maybe fishermen, like my Thailand pals?" I offered.

"No... it looks like they're going to play volleyball... I wondered what these big posts in the ground were for" Cathy added.

"Taking it pretty seriously aren't they?" I whispered as we switched our attention away from the surf towards the two gents who were now meticulously marking out a court with tape. Once the playing area was completed, they picked up one of the remaining sacks each and took them to opposite ends of the court, before proceeding to empty a dozen volleyballs at each baseline.

"How many balls do two guys need?" replied Cathy, but before I had time to crack any smutty jokes, a second minibus pulled up behind the first. The driver waved across and then she joined the advance party along with another woman, both of a similar age to the men and dressed in matching attire.

"They must be playing mixed doubles... we might get asked if we want a game" I suggested.

"I hated volleyball at school... it killed my wrists" moaned Cathy.

"We're much younger than them though... I reckon we could give them a game" I countered.

379

"Oh, that's just perfect!" cursed Cathy.

"What? I was only joking... you don't have to play" I replied, confused by Cathy's sudden outburst.

All soon became clear, though, as I followed Cathy's gaze up towards the road and the second minibus; the minibus that had 'Volleyball Australia' and the logo for the Sydney Olympics emblazoned across its side. Eight tall young women were striding down to the beach who, like their elders, were all clad in green tracksuits. A Great White shark could have ridden a surf board towards the beach singing 'Waltzing Matilda' at this point and I wouldn't have noticed, as the girls were put through a series of stretches and warm-up runs along the beach by their coaching team, before stripping down to their match kit, which really wasn't much kit at all.

"Do you still want to 'try going somewhere else' then?" snapped Cathy.

"No... I'm fine" I replied, hypnotised by the view.

"Come on... the chip shop's open, let's get some lunch" she continued.

"No thanks... I'm not hungry."

"James! Come on, we're going for chips... now!"

I felt around in my pocket for cash, before handing it to Cathy without casting my eyes from the training drill. "Here... I'll have a can of Coke please."

Two hours later, the Team Australia women's beach volleyball squad packed up and departed. It was another 20 minutes before I was able to look away from the scene and a further ten before I realised that Cathy still hadn't returned. Watching the volleyball had been thirsty work and so I headed across the street to buy a drink before realising I'd given Cathy all of my money. Luckily, Manley wasn't the biggest of places and I soon found her leaving a shop.

"Been busy?" I remarked, looking down at the assortment of bags Cathy was carrying.

"Yep... you?" came her terse reply. Cathy was not happy.

"What?"

"You know what!" she hissed.

"No I don't actually… it wasn't my fault that you chose to sit where we did on the beach, and it wasn't my fault that the volleyball girls turned up either! Anyway, how often do you get to watch Olympians going through their paces at such close quarters? I think we were incredibly lucky."

"Oh you were lucky alright… I'll give you that much. 'Olympians'? They were no more than common bloody whores!" Cathy yelled, almost giving an old lady who was walking past a heart attack. The look of disgust that Cathy received was priceless; the pair of us could do nothing but giggle sheepishly.

"Friends?" I asked.

"Friends" conceded Cathy, before adding "… which means you can't be cross, okay?"

"About what?"

"About this…" she replied, holding up her right arm to display several bags, "…and this" she continued, raising her left. "I was really mad. I didn't want to spend my last day in Australia ogling at volleyball girls… so I, erm, spent it spending your money instead."

"I suppose we won't be needing Aussie dollars again after today" I conceded, not wanting to create any more conflict, especially not on what had turned into such a spectacularly memorable morning!

Back on the ferry across to the city we marvelled at the beauty of our surroundings, trying to soak in as much as we could. Australia had, initially, just been a stopping off point for me, a means of getting from China to Easter Island, but our six weeks here had been amazing, even if Wycombe Wanderers hadn't made it to the FA Cup Final.

"I think we should go on a date tonight" I suggested as the ferry dropped anchor.

"A date?" recoiled Cathy, "We never go on dates."

"To celebrate our final night in Australia… every journey from here on in takes us closer to home" I explained.

"I think that tomorrow, when we land in New Zealand, that's technically further away from home than Sydney" replied Cathy.

"Oh, is it?"

"But you're right… we should still go out… we can't have a 'turning for home' date at Auckland Airport, can we!" Cathy hastily added, seizing on the opportunity to avoid another night of eating cold food from paper plates.

That evening I put on my best trainers and Cathy wore a new outfit that I'd unknowingly bought her in Manley, and we ventured out on a proper date; or at least to a proper restaurant, for a proper meal, with proper cutlery.

"Would it be bad to come all the way to Sydney and then just order a roast dinner?" asked Cathy.

"But they sell Kangaroo, Emu and Crocodile… don't you fancy any of that?" I said, reciting from the menu.

"Nope… not in the slightest… I want roast beef, roast potatoes and Yorkshire puddings" replied Cathy determinedly.

"Hi there" said the waitress, who had caught the end of our conversation as she approached our table. "I can definitely recommend the Yorkshire puddings. They aren't quite as good as my Grandad's back home, but that would be impossible. Now, what can I get you to drink?"

Remaining true to our classy tastes, Cathy scanned the drinks menu and opted for a pint of cider, and I joined her with a lager; the perfect accompaniments to any meal, regardless of how fancy the setting.

Ruth, the waitress, was spending a year in Australia following university. She was from York and, therefore, a genuine connoisseur of the Yorkshire pudding. True to her advice, Cathy was extremely happy with the Yorkshire pudding that dominated her plate, rising like one of the waves that had crashed onto Manley's beach earlier in the day. Surprisingly, neither girl seemed overly interested in hearing recollections of my first trip to York, when Wycombe had been robbed 2-0 after having three goals disallowed in the FA Cup. Ruth did redeem herself slightly by saying that all the staff had watched the Wycombe versus Liverpool game after closing the restaurant for the night, and although the chef and half the kitchen staff were Scousers, she'd supported Wycombe.

"So you're leaving Oz tomorrow?" Ruth said as we settled our bill, "I've got a few months left to explore after I finish up here, and then it's back to the real world for me too."

"What are you going to do when you get home?" I asked.

"No idea... what about you?"

"No idea either! Oh well, good luck... see you at the Job Centre!"

Quickly putting thoughts of working for a living behind us, we headed back to the hostel for a night of packing.

33 – Easter Island, yesterday today

Despite the early wake up call, I was in a jubilant mood as we boarded the Auckland-bound plane at 10am on Tuesday morning. In preparation for the three connecting flights that would lead us to Easter Island in the middle of the Pacific Ocean, I'd just bought the latest football newspaper at the airport.

"They've done it!" I cheered, having quickly flicked to the 'results and standings' page. Wycombe had managed to garner enough points from the congested final weeks of the season to ward off the threat of relegation. Fresh from the money-spinning FA Cup run, next season would surely be one to look forward to.

After three hours spent studying the league table, we landed in New Zealand; another country I could now say I'd visited. Admittedly, 30 minutes gazing through the transit lounge window could hardly be called an extensive exploration, but on our tight budget, New Zealand had always been scheduled to be the briefest of visits. As we queued to re-board the plane, it dawned on me that I wasn't even sure what country our next destination was in.

"Cathy, this Papeete place... where is it?"

I spoke in a hushed tone, conscious that, even by my standards, this sounded a bit stupid.

"It's in the middle of the Pacific" replied a preoccupied Cathy, more interested in people watching than talking to me.

"What country is Papeete in?"

This time I spoke more forcibly to get her attention, unfortunately, exposing my cluelessness to all those around me.

"The Windward Isles."

"French Polynesia."

"Tahiti."

Cathy didn't answer, but three complete strangers did, and they didn't agree. An uncomfortable silence followed as the queue shrunk back into its shell.

"Awkward" mouthed Cathy to me silently, now paying full attention to the social drama unfolding.

Five hours later, as the plane homed in on the tiny speck of light that flickered from the darkness of the Pacific Ocean below, I still wasn't sure what country was next to be added to my list. It was almost midnight when we touched down, and maybe even the pilot wasn't sure of Papeete's true dominion, as he announced only "Welcome to Papeete, we've crossed the International Date Line and the local time is approaching 12 o'clock, so that's midnight 'last' night, and the weather is... as always, nice and warm!" Waiting on the tarmac to greet us stood four muscle-bound men playing tiny guitars and wearing even tinier grass skirts. Beside them were six similarly clad young women, swaying rhythmically to the music and placing flower garlands around the neck of each passenger as they descended from the plane. If this wasn't a tourist board sponsored welcoming committee, it was the most exotic Customs team I'd ever seen.

"This is definitely Tahiti!" I smiled to Cathy, whilst joining in with the dancing and accepting a garland from one of the girls. "It's just like in the Elvis film."

"Which Elvis film was based in Tahiti then?" challenged Cathy as she shepherded me away from the dancing girls.

"You know... the one where he does the hula-hula dancing on the beach and wears a Hawaiian shirt."

"So the one that's set in Hawaii and nothing to do with Tahiti at all then?" she sighed.

"You know what I mean... Hawaii... Tahiti... they both have a certain ring about them, don't they? Not like the Windward Isles or French Polynesia. No, this is definitely Tahiti" I concluded.

No sooner had we sorted out which country's soil we were on, than we were watching it disappear beneath us. Cathy soon had her latest travel guide out as we jetted up towards the stars, on the third and final leg of our journey to Rapa Nui, which, according to Cathy, translated to 'The Navel of the Earth'. The facts and figures kept coming. Easter Island (as it had been christened by the first European sailors to stumble across it, on Easter Sunday in 1722), had the honour of being the most remote inhabited island on the planet; 1,300 miles from its handful of 'neighbours' who lived on the Pitcairn Islands, and over 2,000 miles west of Chile.

Following my crash course in all things Rapa Nui, there was little to do but sit back and watch as our plane chased the early morning dawn across the South Pacific for the next five hours. Easter Island's remoteness was being brought into context; below us, there was nothing but ocean to be seen. The Dutch explorers who Cathy had referred to would only have set eyes on the island after months at sea, but thanks to NASA requiring an emergency landing strip in the Pacific for its Space Shuttle programme, Easter Island was now accessible to halfwits like me, although only the twice weekly flight from Auckland to Santiago took advantage of NASA's mile of concrete that traversed a corner of the tiny island.

Land finally came into view, much to everyone's relief, about two seconds before we touched down on the remotest runway in the world. After 13 hours in the air and a couple more spent briefly in New Zealand and Tahiti, we had finally arrived on the mysterious Easter Island at 9.45am on Tuesday; 15 minutes earlier than we'd set off from Sydney.

Walking across the runway towards the small airport terminal, it became apparent that the 6,000 miles travelled into the heart of the Pacific had effectively brought us to a different world. Ours was the only plane in the airport and, until a small truck eventually ambled past to collect our luggage, the overriding sound was that of silence. Easter Island promised to be like no other place on earth.

Immigration was little more than a stamp on our passports and a smile, before we headed out to collect our bags and to find somewhere to stay. Our travel book had advised that most people who visited stayed with the locals, who generally kept a couple of spare rooms to host visitors. Max, one of the islanders, approached with a beaming smile and assured us that his rooms were 'the best on the island'. With no reason to doubt him, and due to the fact that he'd started carrying our bags towards his car, we decided to stay with Max.

"I have one more room… wait here and I'll be back with another in a minute!" laughed Max, and, true to his word, within 60 seconds he was returning with another bag, hastily being followed by its owner, an Australian chap who'd been sitting opposite us for the duration of the journey. The Aussie smiled an acknowledgement towards us before jumping into the front seat alongside Max. A couple of minutes later, having manoeuvered the dirt track that led back into the island's only village, Hanga Roa, we were settling into our latest temporary home.

The crazy journey had left Cathy exhausted and she was asleep within minutes, but the rush of adrenalin from finally being on the island I'd dreamed of visiting since childhood meant that I wouldn't be joining her anytime soon. I gently closed the door behind me and walked the short distance down to the ocean. The strong tropical sunshine combined with a cool sea breeze to form a perfect cocktail as I strode along the coastline, looking to encounter my first Moai - the giant carved stone figures that littered the island and the main attraction to visitors. The distances to the closest neighbours that Cathy had quoted on the journey soon made perfect sense as I gazed out across the curvature of the planet on the horizon; there was literally nothing out there. My moment of peaceful contemplation was soon rudely interrupted by the roar of jet engines catapulting our aeroplane back into the sky and onto its final destination in Chile. I watched it quickly disappear, leaving nothing but a faint echo trailing off far above. I suddenly felt very exposed; the Pacific Ocean looked incredibly powerful compared to the inconsequential lump of rock upon which I stood.

'One giant wave could wipe this island out' I pondered.

All thoughts of impending tidal waves and Moai hunting were forgotten by the unexpected discovery of goalposts, nets and the white lines of a football field, although the small herd of wild horses grazing in the centre circle added a distinct Easter Island feel. As I looked out across the pitch, which even had a small set of floodlights, the Rapa Nui vibe became even stronger; there on the halfway line stood a lone spectator watching over the pitch from the water's edge; my first Moai. He wasn't slumped abandoned on a hillside as in the images I'd seen in books, but upright and proudly placed upon an equally large stone plinth. Along with the Terracotta Warriors in China, this was the type of moment I'd long dreamed of, as opposed to getting beaten by Chinese train conductors or spending endless nights squatting and praying for the Imodium to kick into effect. I wasn't sure if it was acceptable to touch a Moai, but as there wasn't anyone around and, unlike the Warriors in Xi'an, the big fellow didn't look likely to topple over at the faintest touch, I tentatively extended by arm to pat the statues belly.

"Basta! Basta!" came a yell from across the pitch, making me jump out of my skin and retreat from the Moai.

I turned to see a portly old fellow waving a stick in the air and marching across the pitch. "Shit, touching Moai is a no-no then" I muttered, but luckily, the target of the stick waver's ire appeared to be the horses, who waited until he was within striking distance before casually trotting off along the coastline. As the herd disappeared behind a cloud of dust, the man caught sight of me standing on the side-line. He waved across with a smile, and then continued towards me at a more leisurely pace.

"Hello, I'm English" I said; using the universally understood phrase to explain that you cannot converse in any language other than English.

"Ah, English? Gazza... Bobby Charlton... good!" he replied.

"Yes!" I replied, quite enjoying our in-depth conversation. "I like your football pitch!"

"Horses..." he replied, before raising a clenched fist in their direction and laughing.

"Yes... it saves you cutting the grass... free manure too!" I said, completely confusing the old guy and taking the conversation too far.

"This team..." he said, raising his stick towards my Wycombe Wanderers shirt. "...FA Cup ... play with Liverpool? The little team?"

"Yes! Wycombe Wanderers! FA Cup Semi-Final with Liverpool... we were the little team!" I exploded into excitement, grabbing the emblem of my shirt.

"You lose" he added matter-of-factly.

"Yes... 2-1" I replied, less excitedly.

"Here..." he said, tapping his stick on the ground, "... Rapa Nui play Chile" before turning and walking off in the direction of the changing rooms.

"Really! When?" My excitement was regained. "Excuse me... when is that game?"

I shouted after him, but stick-man was again preoccupied by the returning horses. I walked back to find Cathy still fast asleep, and decided I'd rest my eyes for five minutes, too, before getting dinner. I woke up the next morning.

"Come on...wake up, I've got Max to book us on a trip" said Cathy, shaking me from my slumber.

"There's a football pitch with floodlights... and they know about Wycombe Wanderers" I garbled, before rolling over and drifting off again.

"Seriously, get up. We're getting picked up in 20 minutes."

"You go... I'm too tired" I suggested, still thrown by jet lag and time travel.

"Come and get some breakfast... they've got Frosties and Rice Crispies!"

"Did you say Frosties?"

I may have been exhausted, but a bowl of sugar coated cornflakes was a treat at any age, and one not to be ignored. Just as I polished off a second bowl, the beeping horn of a minibus signalled our departure and also a near-miss for Max's dog, which appeared to be a permanently sleeping fixture on the driveway. It wasn't just the dog who had a laid back lifestyle; the whole island appeared to be operating at a slower pace than the rest of the world, with the main form of transport being by horseback to anywhere outside of Hanga Roa, and by foot for anywhere within it. As we bumped along the dirt track out of town, I started to wonder if we had now travelled in the only two vehicles on the island.

Our guide, Peggy, gave us a whistle-stop tour of the island's main attractions and we were soon admiring examples of the magnificent Moai sculptures by the dozen. She explained how they had been lovingly carved to represent the Rapa Nui tribal ancestors, and that most were now toppled due to wars, earthquakes and tidal waves.

"Don't worry... the islanders are all very friendly now... we don't have wars anymore!" she joked.

"Did you hear that?" I whispered to Cathy.

"Yes... this isn't a war zone."

"It's not the war bit I'm worried about. What about the earthquakes and the tidal waves? She didn't mention them, did she? What does it say about them in your book?"

"I suggest you don't think about them... there's no way off the island until the next plane in a few days anyway, so what's the point?" figured Cathy, hardly calming my concerns.

The sheer magnificence that met us upon arrival at the extinct volcano, Rano Raraku, soon distracted me. The volcano was used as a quarry to carve each Moai from the rock face, before it was somehow moved across the island to watch over a settlement. Hundreds of Moai in various states of completion littered the volcano and its surrounding slopes, staring out towards the Pacific Ocean from the spot where they had all suddenly been deserted over 500 years before.

"Peggy... what happened? Why did they all get abandoned?" I asked.

"Nobody knows for sure ... maybe an earthquake or tsunami killed most of the people, or maybe it was just a war or famine."

"Oh. Okay... thanks" I replied, looking down nervously from our vantage point high on the volcano's rim, back towards the sea level Hanga Roa.

The following morning, over more bowls of Frosties, we eventually introduced ourselves to Andrew from Australia, who had sat silently across the aisle from us for the whole journey from Sydney and was now also Max's guest for the duration of our stay. My lack of interpersonal skills on the flight proved to be my loss, as Andrew turned out to be a great guy and a mine of information. He was a geologist stopping off en route to an assignment in the Atacama Desert; a drummer in a band; a glassmaker; a sports fan and a keen off-roader. It's amazing how much you can learn about somebody over a bowl of cereal. He knew that Reni was the drummer in The Stone Roses and Jon Brookes with The Charlatans. He also knew that Wycombe Wanderers had been a sensation in the FA Cup this year. By the time we had moved on to toast and marmalade, Andrew was my new best friend. His glassmaking hobby didn't really come up much in conversation, but the fact that he'd hired a four-wheel-drive vehicle and knew more than a thing or two about volcanoes meant that we were in for a day of adventure when he invited us to join him in exploring the island.

"So you guys did the official tour yesterday then?" said Andrew as we jumped into the hire-car, which meant that there were at least three vehicles on the island. "That's good... you can point me in the right direction and I'll steer. I slept for 24 hours solid and missed the bloody trip... those flights absolutely floored me!"

As Andrew blasted his way across the grassy hilltops towards our first destination, Cathy and I couldn't contain our excitement as we were bounced around inside the truck.

"You've seriously never been off-roading before?" repeated Andrew in disbelief, following a comment I'd made at breakfast about not knowing what 'off-roading' was.

"Well, we went to a music festival a couple of years back... Ian Brown from The Roses was playing, and The Charlatans... I had to park our Vauxhall Corsa in a field, does that count?"

Andrew's driving around Rapa Nui somewhat outdid my parallel parking manoeuvre in a muddy English field. Before long, he had managed to get us within scrambling distance of the island's highest point, a perfectly rounded volcanic crater sitting over 500 metres above sea level, offering wonderful unbroken views of the island in all directions and then the thousands of miles of ocean beyond.

"The guide book says 'Terevaka can only be reached by horseback or by a four hour trek'... I would never have made it up here!" declared Cathy. "It's stunning... thanks Andrew."

Once we'd all marvelled at the view out across the island, we turned our attention to Terevaka's crater, which reassuringly seemed to be full of nothing but long grass.

"Do you think it's safe to go down into it?" I asked our resident geologist.

"Not if you're allergic to long wavy grass mate!" he replied mockingly.

"Right then, here goes!"

Throwing caution to the wind and courageously ignoring the fact I suffered from hay fever, I jumped from the crater's rim, launching into an uncontrolled charge down into its belly some 50 strides below. I wasn't sure what I was doing, but I knew that I'd never had such an opportunity before and might not get one again, so down I descended at speed until I reached the grassy base, whereupon I discovered that the long grass was not growing out of firm soil as assumed, but rather a one foot deep layer of volcanic ash. I proceeded to stumble into it, causing an abrupt halt to my progress. I fell flat onto my face, sending a plume of soot wafting into the air and, no doubt, sparking mild hysteria in the village far below. Wild applause greeted me from above as I stood up dejectedly, covered from head to toe in the volcanic ash that had been hidden from view.

"It's in my mouth and everything" I spluttered as I clambered back out of the crater, looking like a baddie from an episode of Scooby-Doo, who'd convinced the local townsfolk that he was a volcanic monster, only to be foiled at the last minute by those pesky kids.

"To be fair, what good did you think would come from running into a volcano... extinct or not?" pointed out Cathy.

"No, it's not extinct..." advised Andrew, "it's just dormant... she'll blow her lid again one day."

"Oh... right, shall we head down then and visit the Moai quarry?" I hastily suggested, while dusting myself down.

For the rest of the day we retraced our steps around the tourist route Peggy had introduced us to, but this time with the added attraction of being the only people there, as the guided tours had passed through earlier in the day. Under no time pressure, we spent hours wandering around the giant monoliths until the sun began to drop.

Later, after I'd had a much needed shower to wash away the ash, the three of us walked down to a house that doubled as a restaurant overlooking the sea and the football pitch. Just as we were finishing off a post-dinner beer and watching the setting sun teeter on the horizon before disappearing completely, a familiar sound caught my attention.

"What is it?" asked Cathy, seeing a huge smile spread across my face as I swung around in my seat.

"That's the floodlights firing into action!" I replied, hearing the familiar fizzing sound shooting up the pylons and engaging the bulbs above; a sound I hadn't heard since Wycombe Wanderers had left their old Loakes Park ground a decade before.

Sure enough, 30 seconds later, the floodlight bulbs gently started to flicker into life, before exploding with light. The sudden illuminations, along with my old friend and his trusty stick, soon saw the grazing horses canter away into the hills. The floodlights also signalled the villagers to start making their way down to the pitch. Before long, it felt as if the island's entire 3,000 inhabitants were surrounding the field, which sat within a glowing bubble as darkness encroached from all around.

"This should be good... who's playing, Hanga Roa United versus Hanga Roa Wanderers?" mocked Cathy, "I'm surprised they can muster two full teams!"

"The old fella over there told me it was Rapa Nui against Chile... so an international match!" I replied.

"Chile?" queried Andrew.

"That's what he said... there's a fair chance something was lost in translation though!"

The teams came out onto the pitch to a rapturous ovation. Well, Rapa Nui did; the opposition, who turned out to be from the visiting Chilean Navy supply ship, received a more muted yet polite round of applause. The match was keenly contested and, much to the delight of the supporters, the key difference between the teams was the Chilean goalkeeper. He was, quite possibly, the shortest member of the entire Chilean Armed Forces, a weakness that the Rapa Nui forwards exploited on five occasions by simply lobbing the ball over his head at every opportunity.

"That was brilliant! I never thought I'd be watching a football match on Easter Island!" I exclaimed. "Wow... this has got to rank up there with Wycombe beating Leicester! Little Rapa Nui... 5, the might of Chile... 0."

After two days of exploring every inch of the island, the next morning started in a more mundane fashion with an hour long wait in the queue to withdraw some cash from Easter Island's bank. Our visit had, unfortunately, coincided with the only cash machine between Tahiti and South America (some 5,000 miles) being broken. Having finally managed to get some Chilean pesos, we set about spending them in the local craft market, which sold all things Rapa Nui; 'all things' being stone Moai figures of all sizes or mugs, mats, hats, t-shirts and pictures of the Moai. Up to this point, we'd held back from doing much souvenir buying, but as we were nearing the end of our trip Cathy was given a free rein to shop. With Santiago and New York still to go, we wisely settled for several sets of one inch-high Moai, but couldn't help but wonder who would be buying the eight feet high version, and how much it would cost them in postage. On the way back to our room we continued the spending frenzy, having been lured by the smell of freshly baked bread.

"See you at the airfield tomorrow... James and Catherine, right?" asked the baker as I tore into the loaf whilst he counted out our change.

"How did you know our names?" replied a startled Cathy.

I would have asked exactly the same question, but had a mouthful of blisteringly hot dough burning the roof of my mouth.

"Ah, Rapa Nui is a very quiet place. I try to remember the names when I stamp passports when you arrive; then if the visitors come to my bakery, I surprise you!"

"You're the immigration man at the airport! I remember now!" laughed Cathy. "I can't believe you remember everyone's names from the plane, that's incredible."

"Okay, I joke with you... I do try to remember the names on the passport, but I never get it right. But you stay with Max... I am Martin, brother of Max ... he told me your names!"

A final afternoon spent strolling along the coastline under the scorching hot sun was followed by several beers with Andrew; purely for medicinal purposes, as I sought to sooth my scalded mouth. After a dinner spent watching another day sinking into the ocean, it was time to pack our bags again.

After breakfast we made our way to the airport to await our flight to Chile. Max loaded our bags into his car for the short drive, stopping off in the village on the way to pick up his brother who was locking up his bakery in order to take on his customs duties; but not until he'd baked bread rolls for me, Cathy and Andrew for our onward journey. When we arrived at the deserted terminal, Martin unlocked the entrance door before quickly closing it behind him, leaving the rest of us out on the street. As Martin switched on the lights and prepared the Easter Island International Airport for business, we were joined by the increasingly familiar faces of the fellow visitors with whom we'd shared small talk and check-in queues at Sydney, Auckland and Papeete airports and then tours and restaurants on Rapa Nui. There were Bob and Pru from Melbourne; six-times married Jeff from Texas; the German guy who always said 'hellooo'; and the pretty Ecuadorian girl, who didn't know that Jeff had designs on her becoming his seventh wife. The airport didn't need an arrivals board or a PA system; instead everyone just looked to the sky, waiting for the inbound plane from Tahiti to come into view. After a couple of false alarms played out by seagulls, a tiny speck that looked like a plane eventually came into view, growing in size until the roar of its engines confirmed that our flight was moments from arriving. Martin, transformed by a clean shirt and clip-on tie, unlocked the doors and welcomed passengers for the outbound flight to Santiago. He'd received us onto his island with a passport stamp and a smile; now he processed us ready for departure with a passport stamp and a hug, during which I couldn't help but notice his flour covered shorts and flip-flops. I wondered if he'd been wearing the same attire when we'd arrived, and also if any of the new arrivals would notice as they stumbled off of the plane, their minds mashed by jet lag.

As we bypassed the next set of visitors about to be captivated by the charms of Easter Island, it was time for us to say our farewells. Walking across the tarmac to board the plane, I paused for a moment at the foot of the steps, taking in one last breath of fresh Pacific air and stealing a final memory from the Navel of the Earth.

34 – From remote to remote control

Flanked by the Chilean Coastal Range to the west and the mighty Andes to the east, north and south, Santiago can boast the grandest city wall in the world. The mountains that surround its five million inhabitants also prevent the city's pollution from escaping. As our plane descended through the smog towards the Santiago rush hour, the world we had left behind on Easter Island suddenly felt like a wonderful dream; the four hour ride that followed across the gridlocked city was no less than a nightmare.

"Thank god we got the free hotel bus... a taxi fare would have cleaned us out" I said, struggling to find a positive angle on the evening's excruciatingly slow proceedings.

"How long are we staying here?" asked Cathy as we eventually turned into the street of our pre-booked hotel.

"Just a few days" I replied.

"Can we change the flights? I hate it already. I want to go back to Easter Island."

"I'm with you on that one" I agreed.

After just four days in our Pacific paradise, the years of growing up on the outskirts of England's own sprawling metropolis, London, appeared to have been completely wiped from my memory; Santiago was noisy, dirty and too big. We wanted the silence of Rapa Nui back, and we wanted it now.

"Oh, this looks nice" cooed Cathy, her tone softening as the bus pulled up outside our destination, a plush 5-star hotel. "Can we afford it?"

"I pre-paid it before we left home... you must get a bloody good deal if you pay six months in advance, because I wasn't expecting this!"

I discretely double checked that I'd given the right address. Much to my relief, and Cathy's delight, we had arrived at the correct hotel. It wasn't long before the tranquillity and serene remoteness of Easter Island were happily traded for Chilean room service and a television remote control.

After rotating through the hundred television channels on offer and finally conceding that none were showing the Australian Big Brother programme,

Cathy relinquished custody of the remote control. I skipped to the sports channels, discovering that while we'd been watching Rapa Nui knock five goals past the Chilean Navy, Liverpool had also been scoring five of their own, leading to a thrilling 5-4 victory over the French side Alaves in the UEFA Cup final. They had now won the League Cup, the FA Cup and the UEFA Cup in the same season; a historic treble. It felt good to know that only such an unstoppable force had been able to halt the Wanderers' own extraordinary cup run; perhaps if we'd drawn Arsenal or Tottenham Hotspur in the Semi-Final things would have turned out differently. Then again, if Wycombe had progressed to the final, I would probably have missed out on ever visiting Easter Island, and Cathy would definitely have been hatching a plan to kill me for abandoning her in Sydney, as I flew home to watch the football.

A day of sightseeing around the city, and then another taking us up above the smog to the snow-capped Andean peaks, managed to soften our initial impressions of Santiago. Following our brief dalliance with the thin air at high altitude, we crashed out in our hotel room on our final night in the southern hemisphere, in preparation for a flight northeast across the American continents to our final port of call before home, New York City.

"Right… the flight leaves Santiago at 10 o'clock tomorrow night" I announced.

"Three hour check-in again?" asked Cathy, engrossed in a South American soap opera on the television.

"Yep… but we've got that horrendous journey across town again… it took four hours from the airport remember" I cautioned. "We need to be there for 7pm… which means travelling through rush hour again."

"What do you think… leave the hotel at 5 o'clock?" mumbled Cathy.

"No way! 3 o'clock at the latest."

"Whatever. Tell reception to book a taxi then" responded Cathy, eager to return her full attention to the adulterous couple on the television who were about to get caught.

In the middle of the night we awoke with a start.

"Hello sir, your taxi is waiting."

"What?"

"The taxi you ordered... its downstairs, sir."

"What taxi?"

"...Your taxi, sir."

"No, you've dialled the wrong room."

"Yes sir, room 118."

"No... I ordered a taxi for tomorrow... to take me to the airport."

"Yes... your taxi for the airport is here, sir."

"I ordered a taxi for three o'clock... tomorrow."

"It is three o'clock now, sir."

"Three o'clock in the afternoon... not now!"

"In the afternoon? Oh."

"Goodnight."

"Goodnight sir."

"Did you screw the taxi up?" mumbled Cathy from under the duvet.

"No I bloody didn't... the twat on reception screwed it up!" I protested, whilst the night porter, no doubt, called me considerably worse while explaining to the taxi driver that he'd had a wasted journey.

Twelve hours later, we did get into a taxi to take us on the tortuous journey through the congested city to the airport. Less than 30 minutes later we arrived at the airport, nearly seven hours before our scheduled departure time.

"Shit... sorry" I sheepishly said to Cathy, as we found the airline's check-in desks completely deserted. Her mood didn't improve when we were informed that we couldn't check our luggage in for another three hours either.

Cathy's replies could often be terse, but when there was no reply at all it generally meant I'd really annoyed her. As we sat in the deserted departure lounge, the silence emanating from my girlfriend was akin only to that experienced from the solitude of Rapa Nui.

I fully blame my Dad for the wall of silence that divided me and Cathy for the next few hours. Growing up, I'd always assumed that you had to be at London's Kings Cross train station three hours before the train up to Aberdeen departed, as that's what he ensured we did every summer.

It wasn't just when travelling that my dad liked to be early. Memories of my first visit to watch Wycombe Wanderers weren't of walking up the alleyway between the two giant gas holders to the sound of the Gasworks End singing; no, when I first set foot inside Loakes Park there wasn't a soul to be seen. I watched my dad gently prise apart the giant iron 'Loakes' entry gate from its 'Park' counterpart and squeeze through the gap, before beckoning me to follow him through. Even at the age of four-and-a-half I was slightly dubious about doing this. The stadium was completely empty, but immediately I knew that I liked it. The football pitch looked like a good place to play, but not half as interesting as the sweeping terrace beside it, and even that paled into insignificance once I'd caught sight of the giant horse-chestnut trees that towered above, fully loaded with ripe conkers that were falling with every gust of the autumn breeze that swept through the valley.

He'd told me that the reason for visiting Wycombe Wanderers while on our regular Saturday morning trip 'down town', was to collect his winnings from a lucky scratch card. I had no concept of what either Wycombe Wanderers or a scratch card were, but with my pockets full of conkers and my 'Starsky and Hutch' t-shirt stretched out of all proportion to make an improvised pouch for carrying many more, I triumphantly made my way back to my dad who was sitting behind the grandstand on the grass bank, waiting for the 'Blues Club' bar to open. Not unlike my friend Buz on numerous occasions some 15 years later, my dad helped to inform the barman that opening time was upon us, by knocking repeatedly on the door. With more conkers than I could carry, I sat in the corner of the bar with a bottle of Coca-Cola and a packet of crisps. Yes, whatever this 'Wycombe Wanderers' thing was, I liked it; with a fistful of cash, my dad seemed to like it too.

Several cokes and crisp packets later, the bar, which by this stage was full of people and a haze of smoke, suddenly emptied and my dad grabbed my hand. I assumed it was time to go home, but instead he took me back to the terrace and lifted me onto the fence beside the pitch. I couldn't understand why so many grown-ups would want to stare at a sloping field, but then all was revealed as a roar went up around the ground and eleven men dressed in light blue shirts and dark blue shorts ran out onto the pitch.

"That's the Wycombe Wanderers, that's our team" my dad advised.

And so it began.

I guess the apple doesn't fall far from the tree but, even by my dad's standards, here in a South American airport I'd excelled myself this time.

"Oh look at that... they're closing the gate on a direct flight to New York" commented Cathy sarcastically after two hours of complete silence.

"It's the wrong airline though. I asked if we could change, but it would've cost a fortune" I replied apologetically. I could still sense her anger, but was relieved that at least Cathy was speaking again.

"...And what's that further down the departure board? Oh yes, a second direct flight to New York... and that one leaves three hours before we do!" Cathy continued, showing no signs of appeasement.

"That's not our airline either. Besides, our flight means we get to see Miami and stretch our legs" I added cheerfully.

At this point Cathy deigned to look at me, giving hope that relations were thawing.

"No James... we don't get to see Miami. We get to see the transit lounge of Miami Airport. We also get to delay our arrival in New York by another three bloody hours! It doesn't take this long to fly to the fucking Moon!" she snapped, before turning her back on me.

It turned out that relations weren't thawing after all.

"Do you want me to buy you some cigarettes from Duty Free?" I responded after a pause, throwing my last roll of the dice in a desperate attempt to avoid spending the next five hours accompanied by nothing but a very stony silence. One giant bar of Toblerone and 400 Marlboro Lights later, diplomatic relations were tentatively restored, but it wasn't until the following morning when the Empire State Building and World Trade Centre book-ended Manhattan's skyline on our descent into New York, that I saw a genuine smile on Cathy's face again.

35 – New York, one last hurrah

"No volcanoes today then" I observed, as we stood awestruck and in danger of getting trampled in the middle of Times Square, having ventured from our hotel for the first time.

Five days before, I'd stood on the remotest inhabited island on the planet; today I found myself in a different world. Rapa Nui's 63 square miles of rock was home to 3,000 people, giving a population of just 47 per mile. Manhattan was only a third of the size, but housed over 72,000 folk per mile. Add in the two million commuters who arrived each morning and Manhattan squeezed 170,000 people into each of its 23 square miles of very expensive real estate. It was no wonder the locals could be a little abrupt.

"It's just like in the movies!" squealed Cathy, soaking in the sights, smells and sounds of the city. "Look... there really is steam rising from the street! I thought they just used that for effect in films! Quick, take my picture walking through it before the traffic light changes."

The steam was indeed rising; along with the volume of the police car, fire engine and ambulance sirens that echoed incessantly between the buildings that literally did scrape the sky. On first impression, everything about New York was proving to be very real. The cyclist who jumped the red light and nearly crashed into Cathy whilst she strode through the steam was very real too, as was his 'apology' in the form of an aggressively delivered "Fuck you!" as he rode past.

"Fuck you too... you wanker!" Cathy shouted back, just as I pulled her from the path of the next on-rushing batch of yellow cabs to come hurtling up the multi-lane 7th Avenue. "I love this place!" she giggled.

Any thought of retaining the pretence of hardened travellers was blown out of the water. We quickly became seduced by the iconic sights that appeared around every street corner, posing for photo opportunities at each, much to the annoyance of the locals busily scuttling about their business.

"I think it's quite a long walk from here; we should take the subway" I remarked, stepping away from the madding crowd for a moment into a side street.

"No, I want to walk… there is so much to see! Plus we've got all day" replied Cathy, determined to walk all the way to the southern tip of the island, where we planned to take a ferry across to the Statue of Liberty.

"Okay, can we just cut across a couple of avenues then?" I replied.

"What's wrong with Broadway?" she replied. "Broadway's famous… I want to walk on Broadway."

"We can cut back onto Broadway further down. I just want to get a quick picture between 10th and 11th."

"10th Avenue? Why? It's hardly Broadway is it?" asked Cathy, sounding confused.

"I want a picture 'Between 10th and 11th'… do you get it?" I replied cryptically.

"No… I haven't the faintest idea what you're on about."

"The Charlatans album… my favourite Charlatans album" I prompted.

"Oh… 'Between 10th and 11th'…yes, I get it! Good idea. Let's take a right on the next block."

One detour and Tim Burgess-esque pout later, we were again on the march south.

"I can't believe we haven't seen anyone famous yet" remarked Cathy as we made our way through Greenwich Village. "There are so many people about though… we've probably passed loads of celebrities already and just not noticed… I need to pay more attention, instead of listening to your shite."

"I would have noticed" I stated, "I've got a good eye for spotting famous people… and what shite?"

"When have you ever spotted anyone famous?" challenged Cathy.

"Liam and Noel from Oasis… I recognised them down at Adams Park."

"How does that count? They were in the bar after the Man City game signing autographs!"

"I recognised them though... they were famous. How does that not count?" I answered.

"Buz told me that you'd been talking about the game for five minutes before you even noticed they were sat at the same table! As soon as you realised, you clammed up like a star-struck teenager!"

"That's not true... I'd shouted so much during the game I was losing my voice... and I was just giving them some space. I'm not the sort to get all excited just because someone famous is in the room. Anyway, we'd just beaten Manchester City, so I thought they'd be a bit pissed off."

"Well, from what I remember, when you got home that night your voice was fine. You couldn't stop talking about how you were now mates with Oasis and how you'd tried to get Noel to invest in Wycombe Wanderers."

For someone who spent long periods trying to ignore my ramblings, Cathy had an annoying knack of remembering a lot of them.

"I... I... I was only excited because you liked Oasis and I knew you'd be chuffed when I told you about it. I love you, so I was just happy to make you happy."

Shamelessly, I'd played the 'love' card; the desperate last line of any man who knows that he is losing an argument. Worryingly, Cathy didn't respond at all. Shit, had I used that line to gain an undeserved draw once too often? Maybe she'd finally had enough. I'd just said 'I love you'... the unwritten rules of the world stated that she should say the same back to me. Oh god, now she was looking at me in a funny way too. Was this a 'James, we need to talk... it's not you, it's me' type of look? Brilliant, I was days away from going home, having blown my redundancy money and having missed the Wanderers cup run, and now, to add insult to injury, I might also be going home dumped.

For five blocks I struggled to match Cathy's pace as she marched, taking her lead from the locals on when to stop and when to risk getting mown down crossing streets. All the while, she refused to speak, instead giving me an array of strange facial expressions; I wasn't sure if she was breaking-up with me or having a stroke.

"What's wrong? Just tell me!" I pleaded as we came to an abrupt halt at the next 'Don't Walk' sign, but before she had a chance to respond, our attention was drawn to a man risking life and limb to join us from across the street.

"Mike! Hey, Mike! Mike, it's me… Jerry! Joe's friend Jerry… we met at Joe's opening. It's really great to see you again Mike. This is crazy… I'd been hoping to bump into you again Mike, I've got some great ideas! Coffee… we should do coffee! You're good for coffee one morning Mike? Yeah? Shall we do that? Great… let me get your number and we'll set something up for coffee" rattled the overly excited guy. Whoever he was, he looked like the last person on the planet in need of more coffee.

"Jerry… hi" the Mike chap replied calmly. "I'm just in the middle of a conversation here, but I'll get your number from Joe, okay?"

"That's great Mike. Okay… call me. Great seeing you Mike… coffee… soon… you and me buddy!" continued Jerry, bounding backwards across the avenue, oblivious to the traffic he was bringing to a halt and the furious honking of horns being directed at him.

"I think he wants to buy you a coffee Mike" I remarked, as we both watched Jerry somehow make it across to the safety of the sidewalk. Mike smiled back and the traffic sign turned, prompting the marching to resume. Cathy continued to glare at me, and my thoughts returned to which of us would be sleeping on the floor of the hotel room tonight; I guessed it would be me.

Two blocks further, Mike disappeared into a coffee shop. I saw this as my opportunity to try and get Cathy talking again.

"Poor Jerry, Mike was already going for coffee look!" I joked, hiding a world of worry behind my smile. In return, Cathy punched me in the stomach.

"Did you see who that was?"

I tried to catch my breath. If she was going to dump me, she could at least be a bit more sympathetic about it.

"Who 'who' was? Why did you hit me?"

"That was Mike Myers from the movies! I've been trying to tell you for the past ten minutes!" replied Cathy excitedly.

"Austin Powers?"

"Yes!"

"Wayne's World?"

"Yes! Get in there and buy a coffee... quick, before he goes!" said Cathy, pushing me towards the coffee shop doorway.

"What do I ask for?" I whispered as we stood in the queue behind Cathy's first celebrity sighting of the day.

"What do you mean?"

"I don't drink coffee; I hate the taste of coffee... I can't even eat a bag of Revels... the coffee and the orange ones look exactly the same."

"Shush... he's ordering!" replied my girlfriend-turned-stalker. This should have been disturbing, but I was just relieved that I wasn't getting jilted.

"What can I get you sir?" asked the woman behind the counter.

"Erm, do you do tea? A cup of milky tea please" I replied, never having felt more English, as everyone in the small café paused from they're conversations to see who was ordering a cup of milky tea.

I'd even gotten the attention of Austin Powers.

"Jerry's not with you is he?" Mr Myers said with mock concern, before collecting his mocha-choca-something-or-other and heading back out onto the street and his celebrity lifestyle. I walked back out onto the street with a cup of tea in one hand and my girlfriends hand in the other.

"Mike Myers spoke to you!" she shrieked excitedly.

It was hard to compare with walking on the Great Wall of China, volcano diving on Rapa Nui or even watching Wycombe playing against Liverpool, but if it got me back into Cathy's good books, I was happy.

The novelty of our surroundings and 'doing coffee' with movie stars had started to wane by the time we eventually finished our five mile hike down to Battery Park. Cathy's remaining excitement was all but extinguished by the hour long queue that culminated with us being informed that we were now too late to visit both Liberty Island and Ellis Island. Ellis Island's Customs House had been the starting point for millions of immigrants from the 'old world' as they ventured into the 'new'; we were going in the opposite direction and New York marked the end of our adventure. But after six months on the road, we'd had bigger setbacks, so bought our tickets for the next day and started the long walk back uptown.

The early summer sunshine radiating between the imposing buildings created a stifling heat; a cooling Pacific breeze from Easter Island wouldn't have gone amiss. Without nature's air-conditioning, I turned instead to one of the many news stands on the street for a cold drink.

"I don't believe it, this country in amazing!" I declared upon taking the first sip from my Coke can.

"What is it?" asked Cathy.

"Take a sip…"

"What?" she repeated, still mystified after taking a swig.

"They've put ice inside the can! I know the advertising always says 'serve ice-cold', but they've actually found a way of putting ice in the can before its sealed… that's amazing!"

"You're kidding, right?" responded Cathy, looking decidedly unimpressed.

"No, I'm not… didn't you notice it? Have another sip… there is actually ice in the can! I wish they would start making it like that in England."

Cathy gave me 'that' withering look.

"Yeah, maybe they're just trialling it in America first. You should write to Coca-Cola when we get home."

"That's a good idea… I could e-mail them" I replied, missing the mockery in her tone. I started composing my letter as we walked.

The pity in Cathy's eyes soon turned to anticipation as she caught sight of Canal Street and its market stalls full of clothes, handbags, shoes and watches.

"We should get you a watch… you'll need one when you start working again" she suggested, before proceeding to browse at one of the stalls.

"Hmm, work…" I replied glumly, having given little thought to our return to the real world. "Are these fake? They seem really cheap" I continued, not realising that the stall holder was hovering behind me.

"Not fake... just replica. Same standard as real Rolex, just a bit cheaper" he cheerfully declared.

"How much is this one?" I asked, holding up a hefty silver model.

"Eight dollars... all the watches are eight dollars" he replied.

"Wow... that's really cheap, even for a fake."

"Replica... not fake" corrected the trader.

"Get it... you'll really look the part in your new job with that hanging from your wrist" encouraged Cathy.

"Eight dollars? I'll take it. Don't wrap it... I'll wear it now" I said, putting the watch on before fumbling into my pocket to find some cash. "Here you go... one, two, three, four, five... oh, hold on... it's stopped!"

"No, it's fine, give it to me" snapped the market man, ripping the watch from my wrist. He proceeded to hold it up to the sun then shook it fiercely and finally held it to his ear. "Yes, that's better... it just needed some movement. Put it back on, it's working perfectly!" he urged, looking to seal the deal as quickly as possible.

"Let me see it" said Cathy, taking the watch for closer inspection.

I returned to counting out my dollars, albeit slower than before. I hadn't got to my fourth dollar-bill before Cathy laughed and said "It's stopped again!"

"I think I'll leave it for today thanks" I informed the deflated seller.

"Six dollars! For you any watch... six dollars!" he called after us, but the deal was lost and I'd returned to my Coke.

"Oh, that's weird... the ice has gone."

Even without a replica Rolex, we made it to the Statue of Liberty the next morning in good time, and having pounded the streets the day before, Cathy was more than happy to let the subway get us to the ferry terminal at Battery Park before the crowds started to arrive. Catching the practically deserted first ferry out into New York Harbour meant plenty of room to line up classy tourist-free photos of the city's skyline and the iconic statue of the Roman goddess Libertas, majestically holding her torch aloft to enlighten the world. It also meant we were in no rush when taking the less classy, but obligatory, snap of Cathy lighting her cigarette from Miss Liberty's torch.

On our return to Lower Manhattan in the afternoon, we wandered around the labyrinth of streets that had been established long before the city planners had the vision in 1811 to map out the remainder of the island in its familiar grid layout. Walking through the financial district into Wall Street, and seeing all the people dashing around in business suits, just provided another reminder that the world of work was beckoning again and that we had to make the most of our final few days.

It was almost impossible to get lost in Manhattan with its numbered avenues and streets providing a reference further up the island, and even here in the older warren of downtown streets, wherever we ventured, we only had to look skyward to get our bearings, with the twin towers of the World Trade Centre watching over us at all times.

"I'm not sure about this" said Cathy nervously as we stood at the entrance to the South Tower.

"Come on, we'll regret it if we don't go up" I coaxed.

"I feel sick just looking up from here, and we haven't even gone in yet."

"Well I'm going in... it's not like the Sydney Harbour Bridge... it's all enclosed."

"Is it? You don't have to go outside?" Cathy sounded slightly less reluctant.

"No. Not if you don't want too. There's a viewing observatory indoors on the 107th floor, and an outdoor viewing deck on the top floor, just above... let's try the indoor one and see what happens. Besides, we can't afford the helicopter tour, so this and the Empire State Building will have to do. What's the worst that could happen...? King Kong climbs up and steals your cigarette?" I reasoned.

An hour later, back down at sea level, Cathy was euphoric. "That was amazing. I can't believe how cool the view was from up there! The people... the cars... they looked like ants. What an unbelievable experience!"

"Glad you enjoyed it" I replied, taking a seat on a railing outside the towers entrance, my head bowed between my legs.

"Are you feeling any better?" asked Cathy softly.

"Nope."

"It's a shame... you were the one who really wanted to go up there too."

"Yep."

"Do you think you're going to be sick again?"

"Maybe."

"Excuse me, sir... you can't sit here. I'm going to have to ask you to move along" a security guard politely requested.

"Sorry, just give us a moment... he's feeling a bit poorly after being up on the top floor" explained Cathy.

"Oh shit! Is this the dude who just puked on 107? Oh man, that's funny!" roared the doorman, before subduing his laughter. "Sir, I'm real sorry... but you really can't loiter here... it's for security reasons, y'understand?" he continued apologetically.

"Sure" I managed to mutter as embarrassment superseded nausea.

"Sir... man is not supposed to be 1,300 feet up in the sky... that's why I work on the ground floor... you wouldn't catch me going up there! You take it easy and enjoy the rest of your stay now, y'hear me?" the doorman shouted after us, before breaking into another roar of laughter as I shuffled away.

"Ah, that was kind of him to say that, wasn't it..." remarked Cathy. "...because you really did make a twat of yourself up there."

Our plans to visit the Empire State Building the next day were discreetly swept under the carpet and instead we embraced another aspect of American culture; eating. Nobody goes to New York without visiting a diner for brunch, but after the many miles already walked and the fact that my stomach was empty following the World Trade Centre incident, we didn't let brunch stand in the way of enjoying breakfast and a late lunch too. By mid-afternoon, we were good for little more than a quiet stroll around Central Park, as in six hours I'd consumed more calories than I had during two months in Thailand.

Even for a couple who'd spent the past six months living in each other's pockets, enduring bouts of sunstroke, diarrhoea, sickness bugs and more than the occasional sulk, it was impossible not to feel romantic when walking hand in hand through Central Park. With the noise of the city buffered by the trees lining the park and the soft grass underfoot, we didn't need to say anything to each other; we just smiled a knowing smile and walked. We'd travelled around the world together and despite my Mike Myers-induced 'she's about to dump me' panic, our relationship was stronger now than ever; nothing could ruin this special moment.

"Oh my god! James? Is that you? Check out the skinny sun-tan boy!" squealed a girl in full football kit, trotting across the path in front of us to retrieve a ball.

"Hayley? Wow... hello, fancy seeing you here!"

An icy sensation replaced the warmth in Cathy's increasingly firm grip on my hand.

"Look Cathy, its Hayley... Hayley from the hostel in Koh San Road... remember? She's here... here in Central Park."

"Wow, you two stuck it out, huh? That's cool" smiled Hayley.

Cathy smiled back; the smile of an assassin.

"I think your friends are waiting for you" Cathy eventually replied diplomatically.

"Oh yeah, it's soccer try-outs for next semester" Hayley replied while impressively knocking the ball back to her teammates. "How long are you guys in town?"

"A few more ..." I started to say, before being interrupted.

"Not long... it's time for us to go home" Cathy concluded.

"Okay. Well, great to see you again. Maybe see you in London next time!" smiled Hayley, before jogging back towards the training drill that was carrying on without her. "Hey... James, I saw your team in the FA Cup play-off game... the Wycombe Wonders... I thought you said they were no good?" she shouted back up the hill, before blowing a kiss and returning to her game.

"The cheek of that bitch!" hissed Cathy. "Wow, you two stuck it out, huh? That's cool" she continued, mimicking Hayley's American accent. "I'll rip her fucking eyes out."

"Come on, I'll buy you a hotdog... we haven't eaten for almost an hour. I want to try one of those giant pretzel things too" I replied, trying to change the subject, but secretly chuffed that my girlfriend was acting so jealously, and that Hayley was now a Wycombe 'Wonders' fan.

Another long day of exploring by foot followed as we looked to cram in as much as possible on our final full day in New York. The bustle of Broadway gradually eased into the farmers' markets on Union Square, followed by the bohemian charms of Bleecker Street and Soho that led us into Little Italy. This soon gave way to Chinatown, which could have been mistaken for the streets of Kunming, Chengdu or Beijing, before the East River finally stopped our progress temporarily until we reached the Brooklyn Bridge. We collapsed onto a bench on the Brooklyn Heights boardwalk to admire the view back across the river to Manhattan, which sat spectacularly beyond the bridge we had just crossed; the twin towers as ever looming in the foreground. Then, five miles uptown, and still towering imperiously from afar, the Empire State Building that we had walked past some three hours earlier.

"I'm exhausted, I need one of those American Cokes" I gasped.

"You mean the 'special' ones with the ice in?" smirked Cathy.

"Yeah, what's so funny?"

"Nothing... I'll see if that hotdog stand's got some" she smiled before heading off to source refreshments.

It turned out that the iced Cokes were, again, in limited supply; I'd received lots of blank expressions when asking for them all across the city.

"Are you coming up there with me later?" asked Cathy, pointing towards the Empire State Building on her return with hotdogs and cold, but not limited edition, cans.

"I'm not sure... not after what happened at the World Trade Centre... security has probably got a picture of me on the front desk for a start... 'Have you seen this man? Wanted for vomiting from the top of the twin towers'."

"Oh come on... I should give you the pep talk you gave me. What are the chances of us coming back here anytime soon? This is New York... it's the Empire State Building... it's our last day. Come on! Come up with me!" pleaded Cathy.

"We'll see" I begrudgingly conceded.

"Come on then... we'd better start heading back if we want to get there for sunset... we'll see if we can find the guy who sells the magic Coke cans on the way too" said Cathy, hauling me back to my feet.

Thankfully, when we made it to the top of the Empire State Building, the fresh air and cooling breeze that couldn't penetrate the city below eased my fears of any vertigo related repeat performance. The view was stunning and, being outside, exposed to the elements, made the whole experience even more special. We'd timed our visit perfectly to see the city in full daylight, before watching the sun drop rapidly beyond New Jersey on its journey west. As the dying embers of the day spat out glorious shades of orange and red across the horizon, the city fought hard to retain our attention, putting on a dazzling light show of its own at dusk; its towers began to illuminate all across the city, creating a fluorescent wall of light which appeared to hover between the darkening sky and the never-ending streams of white and red car lights that flowed against each other through the streets below.

"That was our last sunset" I pointed out as we took one final lap around the observation deck under the stars.

"We've seen some pretty spectacular ones, haven't we?" Cathy replied. "Are you glad we did it?"

"Yeah. I wouldn't have missed it for anything."

"...even the FA Cup?" tested Cathy.

"Hmm, that's a difficult one! I've kind of lived my own FA cup adventure, though, I guess. I'll never forget the Leicester game in Hong Kong, or even reading the internet report of the Wimbledon replay from Thailand... bloody hell!"

"... or Mad Terry saving the day against Liverpool!" reminded Cathy. "I wonder if the police have let him out yet?"

"Who knows... he certainly liked you though!"

"Yep, I'd make a lovely third wife for Terry … although I'd have to change my name to Jenny."

"If you do that, I might stay in New York and look up Hayley!"

"Don't you bloody dare… that's not remotely funny!"

36 – Home

After checking out of our final hotel room, we had an afternoon to kill before heading to JFK airport. A quick browse through emails at the 800-terminal internet café on Times Square (which was somewhat bigger than the Fantastic Hill café back in Thailand, despite its hastily constructed extension) confirmed that our flight was on schedule and that Buz, Smudger, Jason, Tony and the rest of the Roobarbs were expecting my presence, and presents, in the pub the following evening. Our final slice of Americana was played out back in Central Park where, despite having never sported such a tan before, Cathy was insistent on catching some final rays before travelling home. All too quickly, we said farewell to the park and the city, looking back through the rear window of a yellow cab as the Manhattan skyline began to shrink into the distance.

Everything felt different as we boarded the London-bound plane. Gone was the cocktail of excitement and trepidation driven by venturing into the unknown, replaced by an equally confusing mix of sadness that the adventure was over and a yearning to get home to see our friends and family; to tell them about all the wonderful things we had seen, and to hear about everything that we'd missed. In the morning, I wouldn't have to do a quick conversion every time I spent money to work out if I was being ripped-off, I wouldn't have to double check which direction to look in when crossing a street, and I wouldn't need to have a street map in my pocket at all times.

As the lights of New York disappeared beneath the clouds and the cabin lights dimmed, my mind began to race. What on earth had I done? Why had I squandered my entire redundancy? I could have been six months into a new job by now, and we could have been settled into our first real home together. I would have been preparing to spend the summer in the sun, revelling in the glorious memory of the Wanderers cup exploits too. But here we were, about to head home with no jobs, no money, nowhere to live, and I'd missed out on the Wanderers once in a lifetime journey through the FA Cup. I'd have to cling to my friends' every word as they retold the stories for decades to come. When we graduated to being the miserable old gits who sat at the front of the supporters coach, I'd be the one who people always pointed at; 'That's him... he's the bloke who missed the cup run!' ... 'That's Jamesy... he's 80-years-old and he's never seen Wycombe play in the 4th Round of the FA Cup!'

Indeed, what on earth had I done?

As the rest of the passengers slept, I remained restless and wide awake, troubled by my thoughts. I manoeuvred past Cathy who was sprawled over the spare seat between us as well as her own, and headed to the back of the plane, where the stewardesses sat talking quietly.

"Excuse me... can I get a drink please?" I asked.

"Sure, what can I get you?"

"A Coke please."

"Ice?"

'Ice'; I smiled, remembering my excitement upon discovering that in America the manufacturing process had advanced to such a level that ice could be placed inside a can.

"Yes please, ice would be great, thank you."

We weren't even halfway across the Atlantic yet, but the stewardess's mention of ice had already prompted a happy memory of my travels. My mind raced once more; there were so many things that I wouldn't forget; so many things I'd grown up dreaming about; dreams that had become tinged with sadness as I grew older, tainted by the realisation that they were indeed just childish aspirations. I'd never really live beside a beach in Thailand for two months, not on four weeks annual leave. I'd never see the giant pandas in China; I'd just have to buy my children a cuddly version if I was ever lucky enough to be a dad. I'd never see the Terracotta Warriors or walk on The Great Wall; that was the stuff of television documentaries. Australia was half a world away; and that's as close as I'd ever get to it. How could I ever afford to travel to the other side of the planet when I struggled to fund a trip to see Wycombe play away in Carlisle? Would I ever find myself walking down the hillside of a volcano, meandering around the ancient Moai of Rapa Nui? I was just a kid from a council estate in High Wycombe; people like me didn't go to places like Easter Island; the closest I'd ever get was the Easter sales in River Island.

The feeling of panic in the pit of my stomach began to subside, replaced with a euphoric sense of relief. I'd done it; as an adult I'd realised my childhood dreams.

In an age of innocence, before money and practicality had begun to limit the ambitions of my mind, these were the things I'd planned to do. This hadn't been a wasted six months; no, this had been the best six months of my life. I'd spent over 20 years dreaming of seeing these places, now I could spend the rest of my life enjoying the memory of having visited them. Exam rooms and boring month-end deadlines might be approaching almost as quickly as the sunrise over the Atlantic, but surely they would be more bearable now that I could just close my eyes and take myself back to the crest of a wave in Noosa, getting drunk in Yangshou, or falling head first into a dormant volcano. Maybe I couldn't share the wondrous sight of seeing Hayley jumping naked from the shower in Thailand with my grandchildren someday, but there would be plenty of stories I could tell. Perhaps I would have been wiser investing my redundancy in bricks and mortar, but I'd invested it in something all the same; a lifetime of memories that would make every day, from this one onwards, that little bit more enjoyable. My late night Coke with ice had inadvertently made my journey home all the more comfortable; soon, I drifted into a contented sleep. I was looking forward to the morning now, rather than fearing it.

No sooner had I closed my eyes than they were flickering open again, brought to life by the lights of the cabin being raised and the shards of sunlight piercing through the merest of gaps in the window shutters signalling that morning had arrived. As my eyes became accustomed to the brightness, land came into view.

"It's Ireland! We're nearly home!" proclaimed Cathy, who was now taking up most of my seat along with her own two as we competed to get a view from the tiny cabin window.

Before long, we began to cross South Wales and my mind clicked into gear; there was Swansea, they'd been relegated so Wycombe wouldn't be playing them next season. Cardiff was sighted soon after; we would be playing them, as they'd been promoted; one Welsh team replacing another, just with an hour less travel time from High Wycombe, so a good trade. On we flew across the Severn Estuary, for our first glimpse of England.

"It really is a green and pleasant land, isn't it" I remarked.

"I'd never realised how lucky we are... everywhere we've been was amazing, but just seeing it like this... so lush... it's nice to be home isn't it?" replied Cathy.

The sprawling city of Bristol sat across the water from Cardiff, but I wouldn't be going to Bristol Rovers either as, like Swansea, they'd been relegated. As the plane slowly descended, it held its path straight towards London, next passing above Swindon who had beaten Rovers by one point to stave off relegation, meaning a nice short trip for the Wanderers to Swindon's County Ground. Moments later, we flew over Oxford United's Manor Ground, sitting derelict, having been vacated a month before. United were looking to the future, and had built a modern stadium to see them into the new century, just as the Wanderers had done a decade before when leaving Loakes Park. I wouldn't be visiting Oxford's new stadium imminently though, as our nearest footballing neighbours had also been relegated to the league below.

"Look down there!" I said, smiling.

"Is that Wycombe?" Cathy replied.

"Yes. Just above the motorway look, there's Fernie Fields... I can see my mum and dad's house on the edge of it! Then beyond the woods, there's Adams Park!"

"I can't believe it's all over" Cathy sighed tearfully. "Ever since we saw land, all I can think about is what jobs are we going to get and where are we going to live... are you thinking the same?"

"Erm, yeah... mainly that. I've been thinking a little bit about next season too. I really hope the Wanderers make it back to the FA Cup 4th Round... I'm sure they will."

THE END

Liverpool added to their cup treble of the League Cup, FA Cup and UEFA Cup in August 2001, winning the Charity Shield against the English title winners, Manchester United, and the UEFA Super Cup against the champions of Europe, Bayern Munich.

Wycombe Wanderers returned to their own world.

Fifteen years later, James was still waiting to see his team make a second visit to the FA Cup 4th Round.

17106441R00249

Printed in Great Britain
by Amazon